Before, Between, and Beyond

Three Decades of Dance Writing

SALLY BANES

Edited and with an introduction by
ANDREA HARRIS
Forewords by
JOAN ACOCELLA
LYNN GARAFOLA

THE UNIVERSITY OF WISCONSIN PRESS

THIS BOOK WAS PUBLISHED WITH THE SUPPORT

OF THE ANONYMOUS FUND FOR THE HUMANITIES

OF THE UNIVERSITY OF WISCONSIN—MADISON.

The University of Wisconsin Press
1930 Monroe Street
Madison, Wisconsin 53711

www.wisc.edu/wisconsinpress/

3 Henrietta Street
London WC2E 8LU, England

1   3   5   4   2

Printed in the United States of America

Library of Congress Cataloging-in-Publication Data
Banes, Sally.
Before, between, and beyond: three decades
of dance writing / Sally Banes;
edited and with an introduction by Andrea Harris;
forewords by Joan Acocella and Lynn Garafola.
p.   cm.
Includes bibliographical references and index.
ISBN 0-299-22150-4 (cloth: alk. paper)
ISBN 0-299-22154-7 (pbk.: alk. paper)
1. Dance—Reviews.
I. Harris, Andrea.   II. Acocella, Joan Ross.
III. Garafola, Lynn.   IV. Title.
GV1599.B36   2006
792.8—dc22   2006031770

Contents

1. Dance before Midnight:
Dance Journalism, 1974–87

2. Between the Arts:
Interdisciplinary Writings on the Arts in Culture

3. Beyond the Millennium:
Recent Dance Writings

Voice of the Zeitgeist

Sally Banes and Her Times

LYNN GARAFOLA

Some writers belong wholly to their age. They speak in its voice and accent, and in their work one hears its many tonalities—the broad sweeping themes, the minor chords and dissonances, the countless, almost imperceptible variations that enrich the historical moment and complicate its analysis. Although she was only ten years old when the decade began, Sally Banes was a child of the 1960s. She believed in its liberatory promise and the idea that everything was possible, above all for artists who stood at the vanguard of both social and artistic change.

From the first, Banes was a polymath. She graduated from the University of Chicago in 1972 with an interdisciplinary degree in criticism, art, and theater. During her college years she worked as a lighting assistant and a wardrobe mistress, and in 1970 she joined a group of actors called The Collective that met several times a week and staged collectively written workshop and public performances. She spread her wings even further after she graduated. In 1973 she became the dance editor of the *Chicago Reader,* a position she held until 1976. The following year she founded Community Discount Players, a loosely organized group of actors, dancers, filmmakers, and visual artists who collaborated on performances, and created her first performance work, *A Day in the Life of the Mind: Part 2,* which was given in Hyde Park. That year, too, at Oberlin College, she appeared in *Paris/Chacon,* a dance-theater piece by Meredith Monk and Ping Chong, and coauthored her first book, *Sweet Home Chicago: The Real City Guide.*

In 1976 Banes headed for New York. The city had declared bank-
ruptcy only a year before, and crime was high. But for artists and opti-
mists, it was an international mecca, a hive of creative activity. Banes
threw herself into life in New York. She took classes at the Martha Graham and Merce Cunningham studios, raised $70,000 for an alternative
multicultural bicentennial celebration, and began writing criticism for
the *SoHo Weekly News* and the *Village Voice*. Over the years she had attended workshops with members of the Judson group and appeared in
pieces by Simone Forti and Kenneth King as well as Monk. Now, as the
1970s waned, she transformed this physical passion into a critical project. She made friends with former Judson artists like Yvonne Rainer
(whose *Trio A* she later filmed) and wrote about their performances. It
was the high tide of minimalism, or "analytic post-modern dance," as
she later called it, and she brought it all to vibrant life in *Terpsichore in
Sneakers: Post-Modern Dance*, her 1980 classic. The same year she earned
a Ph.D. from New York University's Department of Graduate Drama
with a dissertation on the Judson group, later published as *Democracy's
Body: Judson Dance Theater, 1962–1964* (1983). With this unparalleled record of achievement, she put Judson on the dance map, analyzing its experimentalism, identifying its key figures, and offering a convincing rationale for understanding them.

Banes hadn't finished with the 1960s, however. In *Greenwich Village
1963: Avant-Garde Performance and the Effervescent Body*, published in 1993,
she broadened the focus to include experimentalists in all media who
were "forging," as she wrote in the introduction, "new notions of art in
their lives and in their works, and—through their art—new notions of
community, of democracy, of work and play, of the body, of women's
roles, of nature and technology, of the outsider, and of the absolute."[1]
Greenwich Village 1963 addressed issues such as race, patronage, and politics that her earlier books had largely ignored and sought to embed
artistic production in contexts that gave it political, social, and cultural
meaning—1963 was the year that President John F. Kennedy was assas-
sinated and when hundreds of thousands of people, led by Martin Lu-
ther King Jr., marched on Washington for civil rights. At the same time,
it offered a degree of theoretical sophistication absent from Banes's earlier books. Her idea of "the effervescent, grotesque body" by means of
which "unofficial culture has poked holes in the decorum and hege-
mony of official culture"[2] revealed a debt to the Russian literary critic
Mikhail Bakhtin, so popular among leftists influenced by the antiestablishment politics of the 1960s.

In the years that followed, Banes grew increasingly interested in ballet. By 1998, when she published *Dancing Women: Female Bodies on Stage*, she had abandoned her earlier focus on the avant-garde in favor of a treatment that embraced mainstream as well as experimental practices. Tracing the representation of women in Western theatrical dance since the Romantic era of the 1830s, the book was the first to analyze the subject in a compelling and intellectually sophisticated way. Fusing feminist and other theoretical perspectives with the sensibility (and eye) of a critic and an admirable breadth of historical knowledge, she took on the master narrative of Western dance history and showed how it could be subverted. She wrote with clarity, moving easily between movement description and historical analysis, and she brought a welcome skepticism to long-cherished ideas. Unlike most feminists, she empowered her subjects, viewing the ballerina, for instance, as a powerful agent in her own right, rather than someone solely identified by her roles and the ideology of victimization they frequently represented. The book made unusual connections, juxtaposing successions—modern dance, postmodern dance, ballet, African American concert dance—typically viewed in isolation. *Dancing Women* established Sally Banes as this country's preeminent dance scholar.

Over the years Banes has revisited Judson and the avant-garde of the 1960s, examining it from different perspectives. In subsequent editions of *Terpsichore in Sneakers*, for instance, she has recontextualized her initial account by viewing Judson and the Minimalists as part of a longer historical narrative in which all those things proscribed by Yvonne Rainer in her celebrated "NO" manifesto gradually returned to experimental dance. Quoting her husband, soulmate, and sometime collaborator, Noël Carroll, she described the phenomenon as "the return of the repressed."[3] But she also gave a political twist to the return of content, glamour, virtuosity, and spectacle in the 1980s, linking them to the emphasis on personal spending and market-driven competition that followed the election of President Ronald Reagan. She noted as well the emergence in the 1970s and 1980s of an important group of African American postmodern choreographers.

She has added to the Judson story in other significant ways. In several essays she has moved back in time, exploring earlier avant-gardes, in a search both for antecedents and for explanations of the avant-garde's propensity to annihilate the past in order to reinvent itself. She was particularly fascinated by the Soviet avant-garde of the 1920s, with its red, hot jazzmakers and hugely original talents, such as choreographer

Kasian Goleizovsky and film director Sergei Eisenstein—all silenced in the decade that followed. She studied Russian dance intensively in the early 1980s and was instrumental in getting published both Elizabeth Souritz's pathbreaking *Soviet Choreographers in the 1920s* (1990) and Si-Lan Chen Leyda's *Footnote to History* (1984), the memoir of a Chinese dancer who worked with Goleizovsky and settled in New York in the 1930s.

In *Reinventing Dance in the 1960s,* an edited volume subtitled "Everything Was Possible" (2003), she expanded the horizons of the 1960s avant-garde far beyond Judson. The result was a fascinating compendium of artists and movements either marginalized or ignored in *Terpsichore in Sneakers* and *Democracy's Body* because of the focus on Judson. *Reinventing Dance* ranged broadly, with articles about early postmodern work in Britain and the West Coast experimentalist Anna Halprin. It embraced secondary figures such as Gus Solomons jr (an African American postmodern who danced with Merce Cunningham), Wendy Perron (a one-time ballet student who performed with Trisha Brown), and James Waring (a Judson guru who choreographed ballets with a postmodern sensibility). Even more surprising, it included an interview with dance critic Arlene Croce, that indefatigable champion of Balanchine who founded *Ballet Review* in 1965 and two years later devoted an entire issue of the magazine to Judson. Pressing the revisionist theme even further, Banes added statements by Judson choreographers who reconstructed some of their Judson dances for Mikhail Baryshnikov's PAST*Forward* project, performed by his White Oak Dance Project in 2000.

A powerful revisionist impulse can be discerned in a number of Banes's later essays. In "Sibling Rivalry: The New York City Ballet and Modern Dance" (1999) she contended that ballet and modern dance had "regular intercourse" throughout the 1930s, 1940s, and 1950s, despite "a cherished dance world myth" to the contrary.[4] Even more controversially she argued that as a result of this encounter modern dance was "taken over, usurped, and weakened by ballet," while ballet, "rather than defeating the alien form in a Darwinian struggle for survival, adapted to and absorbed it, taking it in its stride."[5] In "Institutionalizing Avant-Garde Performance: A Hidden History of University Patronage in the United States," an essay published in 2000, she challenged the notion of avant-garde performance as an exclusively anti-institutional practice. To the contrary, since World War II, she insisted, colleges and universities "have played a central role in the development of avant-garde performance, serving as research and development centers,

venues, catalysts, and patrons."[6] This relationship was only strengthened by huge cuts in government funding, astronomical increases in the
cost of living and making art, and a growing cultural conformism that
looked askance at art perceived as "iconoclastic, deviant, or alternative."
If the university, as she argued, had become "a protected haven . . .
for experiments in performance," such experiments added "dissident
voices" to the university's larger intellectual conversation that were "crucial politically as well as culturally."[7] Today those dissident voices are
more necessary than ever.

Here, as in other recent essays, Banes has ventured into the public sphere, linking artistic practice to larger political, intellectual, and
economic issues. In the 1960s it was easy to think of artmaking as an activity independent of the everyday, workaday world, even if pedestrian
gestures and found objects had become the stuff of art. By the 1990s
attacks were coming from all sides, from mounting real estate costs—of
huge import in dance, an art of space no less than time—to slashed arts
budgets, AIDS, and gay-bashing by a growing and increasingly fanati-
cal evangelical movement. In this climate she has continued to uphold
certain core values whose origins lie in the 1960s. Among these is the
notion of community, which institutions like The Kitchen continue to
espouse, despite rapid gentrification that prices artists out of neighborhoods they initially made hospitable for the upper middle class. Her
analysis of the consequences of the Copyright Act of 1976, the first to
offer protection for choreography in its own right, also emphasizes dance
community values. She notes, for instance, the reluctance of choreographers to sue for infringement of copyright, as well as the feeling among
many artists of the 1980s and 1990s that appropriation and pastiche are
valid compositional methods. "Some postmodern choreographers," she
writes, "view choreography entirely as recycling; rejecting the very concept of originality, they blatantly appropriate movements, phrases, and
dance styles, . . . radically challenging notions of plagiarism and intellectual property and raising the question of how one marks quotations or
allusions in a dance or other performing art."[8]

Over the years Banes has written extensively about African American popular dance. In fact, along with the avant-garde, this has been
a favorite subject, especially in essays and reviews. From the start she
has stressed both the continuity and hybridity of the African American
dance tradition, its ability to generate new dances by absorbing a host of
outside influences, while "build[ing]," as she explained in connection

with break dancing, "on the solid foundations of the Afro-American . . . repertory."[9] As in her writings on the avant-garde, her interest in break dancing marked the beginning of a broad-ranging investigation of the impact of African American vernacular dance forms on both elite and mainstream social dance practices. In a 1995 essay written with anthropologist John F. Szwed, she shows how dance instruction songs like "Ballin' the Jack" and "The Jerk," which literally told would-be dancers how to move, "served crucial aesthetic, social, and political functions." "The dance instruction song . . . has played an important part in the democratization of social dancing, . . . spread African American dance forms and styles throughout Euro-American culture, . . . and . . . helped create a mass market for the work of black artists. In short, [it] has contributed to the formation of a syncretic dance culture . . . in multicultural America."[10]

Her influential essay "Balanchine and Black Dance," published in 1993, was among the first to explore how African American movement and rhythms had seeped into such canonical neoclassical masterpieces as *The Four Temperaments, Apollo,* and *Concert Barocco.*[11] In a 2001 essay, "Our Hybrid Tradition," she expanded upon the idea, arguing that "theatrical dancing in Europe and America has long been a hybrid tradition, borrowing freely from non-European (that is, Asian and African) ritual, folk, and classical theatre forms."[12] She delights in the eccentric and the absurd. An assignment to investigate a 1942 "ballet" by Balanchine for fifty Ringling Brothers and Barnum and Bailey elephants elicited a fascinating meditation on "boundary-crossing between cultural strata and representations of female bodies," as well as a history lesson in John Ringling North's efforts to modernize the "most popular" of our "live popular entertainments."[13] No wonder she named the chair she occupied at the University of Wisconsin–Madison after the pioneering historian of American popular dance, Marian Hannah Winter.

The journey from artist/critic to scholar/intellectual is not unique to Banes. Rather it is a mirror of the field of dance writing as it has developed since the 1970s, when she began writing. It was a time when everything seemed possible, when writers who were willing to write for fame and free tickets could find newspapers and magazines to publish their work. Like the dance they covered, many were alternative publications, allied with countercultural practices and leftist political ideas. These included the *Chicago Reader,* and in New York both the *Village Voice* and the *SoHo Weekly News*, for which she served in the late 1970s as both dance and performance art editor. However, as the dance boom drew to a close and the dance field contracted, opportunities for dance writers began to dry up. *Dance Scope* folded in 1981, followed in short order by the *SoHo Weekly News* in 1982, *Dance News* in 1983, and *Ballet News* in 1986, while *Dance Magazine* shrank to almost half its size.

At the same time a growing number of writers began to move into academe. Here, again, Banes was a leader, landing her first assistant professor job at Florida State University in 1980. From 1981 to 1986 she taught at SUNY Purchase (since renamed Purchase College). Jobs followed at Wesleyan University (1986–1988), Cornell University (1988–1991), and the University of Wisconsin–Madison (1991–2003), where she was promoted to full professor in dance and theater history in 1993. She was the academic star of the dance field. Others imitated her exemplary path, taking jobs across the country and climbing up the academic ladder. Although they continued to write, their writing belonged to a new, increasingly academic conversation, one rooted in ideas generated by the academy as opposed to performance. Critics became theorists and historians, opening a rift between journalists and academics that continues to widen.

This split is evident in Banes's own writing. By the 1990s the hip, young critic of the mid-1970s had become a hip, mature academic, at home in the theoretical debates that have transformed the methodologies of numerous disciplines. Yet, even if the questions she asks—about artistic syncretism, hybridity, cultural inclusiveness, and the representation of female bodies—reflect latter-day concerns within the academy, she continues to write in plain English. Her sentences move across the page with energy, and for all her interest in ideas, she still wants the reader in his or her mind's eye to see the movement and experience it imaginatively. At the same time, she has remained loyal to the political convictions of her youth—ideas of democracy, community, personal liberation, and the perfectibility of the individual. Finally, there is a generosity of spirit that infuses all her writing. As a critic she is rarely judgmental; she prefers to interpret what she sees and to set it in historical context, to make the unique phenomenon come alive and enter the reader's imagination. She writes from within, as a member of the dance community, rather than as an alien from without. More than any other critic or scholar of dance, she belongs to her time, writing with the voice of the Zeitgeist.

NOTES

1. Sally Banes, *Greenwich Village 1963: Avant-Garde Performance and the Effervescent Body* (Durham, N.C.: Duke University Press, 1993), 2.

2. Ibid., 192.

3. Sally Banes, *Terpsichore in Sneakers*, 2nd ed. (Middletown, Conn.: Wesleyan University Press, 1987), xxviii.

4. Sally Banes, "Sibling Rivalry: The New York City Ballet and Modern Dance," in *Dance for a City: Fifty Years of the New York City Ballet*, ed. Lynn Garafola, with Eric Foner (New York: Columbia University Press, 1999), 73, 97.

5. Ibid., 98.

6. Sally Banes, "Institutionalizing Avant-Garde Performance: A Hidden History of University Patronage in the United States," in *Contours of the Theatrical Avant-Garde: Performance and Textuality*, ed. James Martin Harding (Ann Arbor: University of Michigan Press, 2000), 217.

7. Ibid., 235.

8. Sally Banes, "Homage, Plagiarism, Allusion, Comment, Quotation: Negotiating Choreographic Appropriation," 10.

9. Sally Banes, "Breakdancing: A Reporter's Story," in *Writing Dancing in the Age of Postmodernism* (Hanover, N.H.: Wesleyan University Press, 1994), 126. This essay was originally published in 1986 in *Folklife Annual.*

10. Sally Banes and John F. Szwed, "From 'Messin' Around' to 'Funky Western Civilization': The Rise and Fall of Dance Instruction Songs," *New Formations* 27 (winter 1995–96): 60.

11. Sally Banes, "Balanchine and Black Dance," in *Writing Dancing*, 53–69. This essay was originally published in 1993 in *Choreography and Dance.*

12. Sally Banes, "Our Hybrid Tradition," in *Danse: langage propre et métissage culturel / Dance: Distinct Language and Cross-Cultural Influences*, ed. Chantal Pontbriand (Montreal: Parachute, 2001), 21.

13. Sally Banes, "Elephants in Tutus," 1, 2.

Electrification

JOAN ACOCELLA

This collection of writings by Sally Banes covers thirty-odd years, taking us from her young, here-I-am beginnings in a small alternative paper in Chicago to the long, sober, Bakhtin-citing essays she wrote as the highly honored Marian Hannah Winter Professor of Theater History and Dance Studies at the University of Wisconsin–Madison. Even her beginnings are not shy, however. "An interesting sequence of events happened last week that's been on my mind ever since," she says at the opening of the first essay, written when she was twenty-three. "I haven't figured them out yet." The sequence of events was a concert by Pilobolus, and by the end of the essay she has figured it out: this must be what college boys think of as dance—innocent, physical. In a review of a concert later that same year, she tells us that she got to be part of the dance: "I take off my glasses and then a sock and start to crack my toes." The tone is empirical, confiding, assured.

When Banes started out, the new imperative in dance criticism was description: sentence-by-sentence accounts of what actually happened on the stage ("she ran upstage, she raised her arms"). This was part of a new seriousness in dance criticism, an effort to cleanse it of impressionism and fan-club effusions. It was also a response to the transience of the art. If these dances were going to disappear, as so often they did, the critic should at least leave a record of what happened—a task that seemed all the more pressing in the case of the new work being done in downtown New York, at Judson Church and other venues, in the 1960s and 1970s. Those dances were often one-night-only affairs, and they were widely ignored by the mainstream press. So for a thinking critic, describing the events—and, if possible, interviewing the choreographers and documenting their intentions—came to seem almost a moral duty.

The classic example of that critical enterprise is Banes's 1980 book *Terpsichore in Sneakers*, a record of the dances done by Yvonne Rainer, Simone Forti, David Gordon, Trisha Brown, Lucinda Childs, and others at Judson in the 1960s, plus the artists' explanations, exhortations, charts, and other supplementary materials. But there are good specimens of the method in the present book as well, for example, "Douglas Dunn Talking Dancing" (1979) and "Trisha Brown and Fujiko Nayaka Play Misty" (1980), for the *SoHo Weekly News* and the *Village Voice*, respectively. (Those two journals, together with *Dance Magazine*, were Banes's two main reviewing outlets in the late 1970s and early 1980s.) The thing to notice in these essays is that unlike much of the other descriptive criticism of the period, they are not boring. To start with, Banes had a preference for the more outrageous sort of work, in which the artists grilled hamburgers or did monster moves or took off their clothes. With such events, even the most factual account was not without a certain piquancy. But Banes's descriptions, even of more demure work, were not strictly factual. She did "thick description"; she tucked in judgments, nuances. Furthermore, as seriously as she took description, it was only part of what she did. She is a natural and brilliant generalizer. She thinks she knows what the essence of a thing is, and she wants to tell us. So, while she may be reporting on a tap concert (in "Rhythm for the Eyes, Ears, and Soles"), she cannot help adding, in one excellent sentence, what seem to her the unique glories of tap: "a gestural capacity for a true comedy of the body, testing physical limitations and making satire; a format that unabashedly parades the skill, capabilities and intelligence of the human body; the abstract rhythmic qualities it shares with music and the ways in which it makes those abstractions uncannily visible; its fundamentally mundane origins in the act of walking, which makes its intricacies all the more marvelous." She also can't help speculating. In her essay on Meredith Monk's *Quarry*, for example, she respectfully describes the piece and lets Monk have her say about what it means. But is that *all* it means? For example, Monk didn't say much about *Quarry*'s use of radio—how radio was the medium through which many people got their information in the old days, and how information relates to power—so Banes tells us about this: "Content is only part of meaning. We don't understand the dictator's words, but we understand his tone and we are terrified." This is the best part of the essay, the most unsettling part.

Banes's main subject, throughout her career, has been avant-garde movement. The vanguard might be Russian, of the 1920s, or French, of the 1890s, but her primary subject was the birth and development of postmodern dance in New York in the 1960s and after. (This was the subject not just of *Terpsichore in Sneakers,* but also of five subsequent books of hers: *Democracy's Body* [1983; an expansion of her doctoral dissertation], *Greenwich Village 1963* [1993], *Writing Dancing in the Age of Postmodernism* [1994], *Subversive Expectations* [1998], and *Reinventing Dance in the 1960s* [2003].) Ironically, though it was her writings on Judson that made her famous, she did not witness that movement. She was a teenager at the time, growing up in a suburb of Washington, D.C. Once she got to New York in 1976, however, she caught up fast—looked at videos and photos, saw revivals, indeed arranged revivals, and filmed them when she could. (It is owing to Banes that we have a film of Yvonne Rainer's epochal *Trio A.* She persuaded Rainer to do the dance one more time, and put her in front of a cameraman.) And, she was present for Judson's later avatars, in the 1970s.

With this revolution under her belt, she seems to have felt, ever after, when she was writing about dance, that she was writing history, and she took on the responsibilities of an historian: to explain things, note trends, chart developments. In one essay, "A Walk on the Wild Side," she quickly lays down the principles of the 1960s version of postmodern dance and then says that now, in the late 1970s, the movement has branched off in two different directions: first, what she calls "dances of repose" (with "movements that are small and unprepossessing and strung into phrases that are creamy, slow, and clear"), and second, "the wild side," dancing that is full of "raw action." Journalism, they say, is the first draft of history, but there are many ways of writing that draft. You can do it timidly, by just recording, or you can try to make sense of what you see, even at the risk of being wrong. Banes always took the second route.

This historical sense is the backbone both of the reviews and of the longer essays gathered in the present volume. Banes never shows you anything without giving some historical context for it. To her, everything has a past. At the same time, she is not one of those who, having seen a revolution, feel that nothing coming later can ever be as pure and fine. Sometimes she does regret the passing of the old days. She was not a fan of disco dancing, the rage of the 1970s. In a 1977 essay she contrasts disco's regimentation with the free-form social dancing of the 1960s, in which, she says with frank nostalgia, "you shook and stepped, . . . waved your hair and flailed your arms, and sometimes stood still, in a stream-of-consciousness, ego-dissolving ecstasy." She notes acerbically how disco fits into the renewed concern with discipline, and the recession economy (DJs are cheaper than bands), that followed the Vietnam era. Also, after her examination of the 1960s there is not much that the dancers of the 1970s and 1980s can do to shock her. In the course of a day-long dance series at a downtown space, she writes, "I took a dinner break . . . and missed Pooh Kaye and Elaine Hartnett dancing bare-breasted in grass skirts and Peter Rose dancing on broken glass, among other things." She's sorry she missed them, she seems to say, but she's seen that kind of thing before. Nevertheless, she very much wants the experiments of the 1960s to go forward, bear new fruit, and she is generous to the newcomers: Johanna Boyce, Karole Armitage, Jim Self, and others.

These impulses of charity and inclusiveness also inform the more scholarly essays that occupy the latter half of the present volume. Again and again in the later articles we see her taking on matters that drew fire from the highly politicized, highly leftist academic writers of the 1980s and 1990s. Banes, too, is a committed leftist. (In a piece on the Bolshoi Ballet, she complains, basically, that the work of Yuri Grigorovich, the company's director and chief choreographer, is insufficiently Communist.) But always, she is correcting the too-simple position. Always, she is pouring oil on the waters, in the form of historical knowledge or just plain sophistication. Was it bad that The Kitchen, a downtown dance collective, abandoned its utopian, communal, dinner-sharing origins and started taking money from funders, building an administration, and putting on more audience-friendly work? Was it a crime against women that Madonna uncovered her belly button in her early dance videos? Was it likewise an insult to feminism that Karole Armitage used spike heels and S&M paraphernalia in her early shows? And is it really true that avant-garde dance, by virtue of its anti-institutional character, has shunned, and must shun, the support of universities? No. Banes is an enthusiastic revisionist, and witty and realistic. As she sees it, everything is done by negotiation, compromise—a gain here, a concession there. What we get from these essays is not just the pleasure of hearing a smart scholar answer less smart ones, but also the relief, and sheer truth, of seeing art function in the real world, a world where even a sexpot like Madonna may have a sense of humor, and where the universities and the avant-garde saw in each other a good opportunity.

One more thing to mention regarding Banes's work is the high level of curiosity. I was told once that when she participated in an intensive summer course in Russian at Middlebury College in 1980, the students were asked to choose Russian nicknames for themselves. She chose *elektrichestvo*, or "electricification." Everyone thought this was perfect, not just because she has a big head of curly hair that looks as though it might have had contact with a high-voltage mechanism, but also because of her crackling mind. Her alliance with avant-gardes never overpurified her, never discouraged her from writing about disco or MTV or hip-hop, or even ballet. At the end of this book she suddenly addresses the use of scent—actual smells—in theater works. In another essay she analyzes George Balanchine and Igor Stravinsky's 1942 ballet for the elephants of the Ringling Brothers Circus. Only she would have taken on these subjects, or taken them on seriously, giving us, for example, a long, carefully researched history of the use of scent in the theater and, as for *The Ballet of the Elephants,* explaining how this project was related to American cultural anxieties over European art in the 1940s, and how that matter was also implicated in the 1940 Disney movie *Fantasia,* and how *The Ballet of the Elephants* handled the business with greater ambition and flair. Underneath all this—smells, elephants, bare-breasted women—is an anarchic spirit, walking on the wild side. And joined to it is exactly what one needs with it: scholarship, moderation, wisdom.

Before, Between, and Beyond

Introduction

ANDREA HARRIS

Sally Banes became a dance writer because of a fear of close spaces.

After finishing her undergraduate degree (an interdisciplinary degree in arts criticism) at the University of Chicago, Banes was writing restaurant and theater reviews for Chicago's weekly newspaper *The Reader* and book reviews for the *Chicago Tribune* when a colleague asked her if she would be interested in taking over a project he was working on. He already had a publishing contract to write a book about modern dance, but, due to his severe claustrophobia, he couldn't sit through a single concert. Banes agreed to write the book and, as she states, decided the most efficient way to learn how to write about dance was "to do it in public." In 1974 she asked her editor at *The Reader* if she could start reviewing dance performances. The first dance review Banes ever wrote, "Substanceless Brutality," opens this collection.

It is ironic that Banes's career was jumpstarted by a phobia about space closing in, because her interests tend toward the centrifugal, the efferent. As a writer, and even in her early years as a practitioner, Banes's concept of dance does not draw inward but instead opens outward, traversing borders, exploring new spaces, and expanding the contexts of those that are already "known."

Banes was not a newcomer to dance when she approached her editor at *The Reader*. She had taken dance classes since childhood in Silver Spring, Maryland, a suburb of Washington, D.C. As a young dancer she performed in *The Nutcracker,* and, like thousands of young girls, she dreamed of quitting school and joining the ballet. Later, as a dancer living in Chicago and New York, she studied ballet with Ed Parish and Peter Saul and modern dance with Jim Self, Maggie Kast, and Shirley Mordine, as well as at the Martha Graham and Merce Cunningham studios.

Never content to focus merely on one art form, Banes worked with different cross-disciplinary performance companies in Chicago in the 1970s. One of these groups, The Collective, was comprised of actors who met each week to experiment with acting techniques, create workshops, and give public performances. In 1974 Banes founded the Community Discount Players. Later she and her associates opened the MoMing Performance Center, a collectively owned theater in Chicago. The members of MoMing—primarily actors and dancers—taught classes to each other daily, made collaborative works, and gave performances. At MoMing Banes danced in Kenneth King's work and created her own performance pieces.

With dancer Ellen Mazer, Banes created a series of works about a character named "Sophie," an imaginary woman in the nineteenth century, who, as Banes describes, was "sometimes a ballerina, sometimes a Communist." The contemporary infatuation with ordinary movement and episodic structure clearly influenced Banes's performances. In *Sophie Eats Shrimp,* for example, Banes and Mazer loaded cartons on and off a rental truck. Another "Sophie" piece included an old-fashioned washing machine and broken glass littered about the stage. Banes and Mazer also created *A Day in the Life of the Mind, Part II,* a day-long work that began in the lagoon at the Museum of Science and Industry in Hyde Park and ended at Jimmy's, a popular neighborhood bar. Along the way, the audience followed Banes and Mazer down 57th Street, had soybeans thrown at them, and heard the same Charlie Parker record played over and over. They were led into Banes's own apartment (she happened to live on 57th Street at the time), were greeted by her grandmother, and went out on her back porch. When dark fell, nightgown-clad dancers appeared in the large, lighted windows at the Regenstein library. The performance was intended to be a celebration of Hyde Park and also a blurring of the distinctions between everyday life and art.

Banes moved to New York City in 1976 and entered the Department of Graduate Drama at New York University. In the city Banes also took the opportunity to study dance with Simone Forti, Kenneth King, Meredith Monk, and the members of the Grand Union. She performed in Forti's dance *Planet* and brought Sophie back to life in a work-in-progress she called *Sophie Heightens the Contradictions*, which she presented at P.S. 122 in 1983.

Given Banes's background in avant-garde performance styles, it is not surprising that the claustrophobic colleague's book about modern dance would turn into one about a group of choreographers whose work rejected the expressive drama of modern dance and challenged the very definition of "dance" itself. In her master's thesis Banes had examined the experimental choreographers of the 1960s and 1970s. Her first book, *Terpsichore in Sneakers: Post-Modern Dance*, published in 1980, emerged from that thesis. The book gave critical and theoretical shape to postmodern dance and has impacted the discourses of dance history, theory, and criticism ever since.

By the time *Terpsichore in Sneakers* was published, Banes had already been writing about dance and performance in New York for several years: at the *SoHo Weekly News* from 1976 to 1980, the *Village Voice* from 1976 to 1986, and *Dance Magazine* from 1977 to 1986. As her first book was hitting the presses, Banes began her doctoral work at NYU. Her class reads like a "who's who" of late twentieth-century American dance scholarship, including Banes, Sally Sommer, Barbara Barker, Brenda Dixon-Gottschild, and Joan Acocella (who was not an NYU student, but sat in on classes). Banes's dissertation advisor was Michael Kirby, and she also studied with dance scholars Deborah Jowitt, John Mueller, Dale Harris, Gretchen Schneider, David Vaughan, and Selma Jeanne Cohen. As a doctoral student Banes felt she needed to extend her work on postmodern dance and ground it in a larger cultural context. Her Ph.D. dissertation turned into her second book, *Democracy's Body: Judson Dance Theater, 1962–1964*, published in 1983. Banes also became editor of *Dance Research Journal*, a position she held from 1982 to 1988.

Back in Chicago, at a performance of the Grand Union at MoMing, David Gordon introduced Banes to a fellow critic named Noël Carroll. Banes jokes, "He had a job I wanted" (Carroll was the dance and performance art critic for *Artforum* at the time), "so I thought I had to do away with him to get his job." However, she not only let him live, but she went on to write with him, teach with him, and marry him. Two of the articles Banes and Carroll cowrote as dance critics in New York City are included in this volume.

Banes recalls it was Carroll, "lying in bed, reading, and eating bon-bons," that drew her into academe (although he thinks he was more likely eating meatball subs). If being a professor was that easy, Banes thought, she wanted to do it. "I later realized he was reading student papers," she explains, laughing. Her sense of humor underplays an impressive and distinguished university career as a scholar and teacher. After her doctoral degree, Banes taught in the dance departments at Florida State University and the State University of New York at Purchase (from which she took a year's leave to accept the Andrew W. Mellon Postdoctoral Fellowship at Cornell University), and then the theater departments at Wesleyan and Cornell University.

In 1991 Banes became associate professor of dance and theater history at the University of Wisconsin–Madison, where she served as chair of the dance program from 1992 to 1996. In 1996 Banes was named the Marian Hannah Winter Professor of Theater History and Dance Studies. At Wisconsin, especially accomplished scholars are often allowed to choose the name of their chaired positions. Banes titled her position in honor of Dr. Winter, whose extensive research on dance outside of the mainstream echoed Banes's own passion as a dance historian: her dedication to seeking out dance that existed off the beaten path.

Banes's desire to discover as much as possible about all kinds of dance led her to the street corners and clubs of Brooklyn and the Bronx in the early 1980s. There, break dancing was the hottest new dance style but little known outside of the African American and Latino communities. Banes's article "To the Beat Y'All: Breaking is Hard to Do," which appeared in *Village Voice* on April 10, 1981, was the first to talk about the popular street dance form in a mainstream newspaper (the article is reprinted in Banes's book *Writing Dancing in the Age of Postmodernism*). It introduced break dancing to the mass media and then to a widespread audience, anticipating the break-dance craze that catapulted the form from urban streets into mass culture in the early 1980s, generating Hollywood movies, fashion trends, and worn cardboard squares laid on suburban sidewalks by young, aspiring B-Boys across the country.

The selections in this collection include reviews that Banes wrote as a dance critic, longer essays from her years as a scholar and academic, and talks she gave at national dance and theater conferences. These writings were chosen to represent the diverse scope of Banes's inquiry over three decades of her career as a dance writer. Whether she is trying to sort out the impact virtuosity has on an audience, exploring non-European influences on Western dance forms, reconstructing the only ballet ever created by Russian filmmaker Sergei Eisenstein, interrogating beauty in the ballet canon, or theorizing gender and popular culture in Balanchine's choreography for elephants, Banes always pushes the boundaries of how dance and the dancing body are understood in our culture.

The title of part 1, "Dance before Midnight," refers to Banes's deadline as a dance critic. In the late 1990s Banes proposed a book of her dance reviews, bearing this title, to the University of Wisconsin Press. At the same time, however, she was also completing her book *Dancing Women: Female Bodies On Stage* (which she calls her version of Lincoln Kirsten's *Movement and Metaphor*, "but from a feminist perspective"), participating on the research team of the Balanchine Foundation's *Popular Balanchine* project, and conducting her own research on scent in performance. Then, in 2001, she became Director of the Institute for Research in the Humanities at UW–Madison. Thus "Dance before Midnight" sat on the back burner, until now.

The reviews included in this volume have not been published since their original appearance in newspapers or magazines. Particularly striking in this collection of Banes's dance reviews is the historical scope they encompass. These writings record the earliest performances of Bill T. Jones/Arnie Zane and Pilobolus and recall for us that Elizabeth Streb once danced in Molissa Fenley's company and Eric Bogosian was dance curator at The Kitchen. Many of the emerging artists Banes reviewed are now luminaries of the historical canon, while others have drifted into the margins of dance history and are overlooked today. Like all collections of dance reviews, this one not only provides a valuable register of dances and dancers, it also points out the importance and responsibility of dance criticism as it engages with an art form whose history largely exists in movement, in a culture that privileges what can be written down. Banes contextualizes dance performance in a way that the back-of-the-house video camera cannot capture, leaving an eyewitness account of dance's three-dimensional, multivalent embodiment. These reviews are a model for not only how, but also why dance criticism should operate as a deliberate consideration of what takes place in the space between the dance and the viewer.

As a critic, Banes's writing engaged with artists on the level of chore-ography and meaning, instead of just performance, and she brought a courageous honesty to her reflections and analysis. Some of the things she wrote must have been unpopular, and she wasn't afraid to take aim at the prestigious bigwigs of the dance world. She compared what she called the "ballezz" in Alvin Ailey's work—the "incessant, legible, and pleasing movements"—to muzak, and underscored the "bland, ho-mogenous skeleton" of movement that lay at the core of Paul Taylor's accessibility. Banes did not limit her response to whether a dance was beautiful or exciting or well-conceived; she cared most about the way in which the dance made its meaning. Her craving in these reviews to look beneath the surface and understand how dances relate to the larger world around them forms the foundation for her later work.

"Between the Arts," part 2 of this book, showcases Banes's work in places where dance intersects other art forms or entities. Some of the es-says take an interdisciplinary approach, examining the dance instruc-tion song or the intersections between dance and film. Others inter-weave Banes's deeper concerns with how dance practice relates to the larger world and her immersion in the progressive politics of the 1970s. While writing about dance and performance in New York, Banes par-ticipated in various organizing efforts, playing an instrumental role in unionizing the *Village Voice* and leading a drive to organize the *SoHo Weekly News* (which unfortunately failed). Banes's interest in the legal and financial rights of dance workers, including performers, choreogra-phers, and writers, can be traced through her essays in this section on dance and copyright law and her investigation of the relationship between the avant-garde and the university.

While we were selecting the pieces for this section, Banes remarked, somewhat cryptically, "There's a lot of dance in the one about Ericka Beckman." While the essay, which explores the filmmaker's work, is not literally about dance, Beckman's use of movements inspired by child's play undoubtedly resonated for Banes with postmodern dance's atten-tion to everyday movement and game-like scores. The "delightful slip-periness of meaning" Banes focuses on in Beckman's films is what she values most about dance—its openness to alternative meanings and its potential for resignifications. While Banes was drawn initially to this at-tribute in postmodern dance, it is a perspective that also characterizes her approach to dance in her later scholarly work, embodied by her dedication to drawing concentric circles of historical, social, and artistic contexts ever outward from a dance. This approach to historiography (perhaps epitomized in *Dancing Women*) enlarges the picture of dance to encompass multiple, even contradictory levels of interpretation and theorizes dance as a complex cultural entity, intricately interwoven with its surrounding environment.

Part 3, "Beyond the Millennium," encompasses some of Banes's most recent scholarly dance writing, done since 2000, as the Marian Hannah Winter Professor at UW–Madison. The essays and lectures included in this section summarize some of the most salient features of Banes's career in dance: her investigation into dance that happens in and around the corners of the mainstream, her thoroughness as a historian, and her efforts to contextualize dance in larger cultural frames. In these essays we see Banes sharpening her inquiry to finely targeted points, teasing out details in order to broaden the picture even more. Banes convinces us that the details matter, plucking out the cross-cultural motifs in ballet and modern dance, the history of scent in dance, the complex facets of female balletic beauty, and the same-sex partnering of elephants. If the metaphor of expanding outward into new spaces characterizes Banes's earlier work, in these later pieces, she chisels in. Her purpose, however, remains the same: giving us a kaleidoscopic look at dance and drawing our attention to what might otherwise go ignored or overlooked.

In May 2002 Banes suffered a massive stroke. She spent the next three years undergoing extensive physical and cognitive rehabilitation, recuperating from the traumatic experience. In 2003 her book *Reinventing Dance in the 1960s: Everything Was Possible* was published by the University of Wisconsin Press. She remains professor emerita in the Department of Theatre and Drama at UW–Madison and presented a paper at the Society of Dance History Scholars' 2005 conference.

In 2003 the dance world showered Banes with honors. The Congress on Research in Dance and the Society of Dance History Scholars each presented her with lifetime achievement awards for service to the field. Banes was also awarded a Bessie, the prestigious New York dance and performance award, for her lifetime contribution to dance criticism. David White, the former executive director of Dance Theater Workshop, wrote the inscription to that award, which stated:

> For a sustained achievement as the master chronicler of postmodern dance-making, and then as the tour guide of its course and connection

to all the corners of this city and culture's brave new 21st century world; for uncovering a Terpsichore in all kinds of sneakers, from the lofts of Greenwich Village and SoHo to the streets and b-boy clubs of Brooklyn and the Bronx, thereby giving us an art form and its denizens in all their teeming variety; forever, our favorite far-flung correspondent reporting live from the frontlines of the dance wars.

The principle that guided Banes as a youthful creator and performer of dances—that the boundaries between art and life are indefinite—comes full circle in her writing. Banes sees dance as an integral part of culture and believes that it can affect how we experience and understand our environment. Perhaps this is what White means when he refers to the "dance wars"—dance's struggle to be recognized as an essential and vital part of our culture. If so, Banes has indeed spent her career on its frontlines, showing us why dance does make a difference in our world.

Dance before Midnight

Dance Journalism, 1974–87

Substanceless Brutality

An interesting sequence of events happened last week that's been on my mind ever since. I haven't figured them out yet, make of them what you will.

I went to see the Pilobolus dance concert at the University of Chicago. The concert promised to be new and revolutionary dancing, anyway that's how they were billed. Male dancing. Nice, I thought. It's so rare to see male dancers, rarer still to see a whole group of them. And what would make a dance particularly male, I wondered. Is there a difference between genderless, androgynous, feminine, masculine dancing? Hasn't most dancing until recently been masculine dancing, been about a masculine world, whether it was danced by men or women? Even Martha Graham with her goddesses, her arch-bitches.

OK, here we are in Mandel Hall, watching dances made collectively by a group of four young Dartmouth graduates and two women friends (one the dance teacher who inspired the troupe). *Ciona* is the first dance. Ciona (it says on the back of the program) is the name of "a

SOURCE: *The Reader*, February 15, 1974

light-sensitive marine creature that has the unique ability to turn it-self completely inside out." There is some very pretty dancing on stage, watery and mineralish, eddies and whorls of movement, and some eye-openers too: acrobatics, people throwing themselves—wham!—across someone else's torso and sticking there; people suspended from parts of other people's bodies, people upside down and such. Very snazzy light-ing, the resilient-bodied fresh-faced white-tighted dancers painted tur-quoise and pink as they circle round the stage. Geological forms. Sym-metrical poses. Strange inhuman organisms. The eeriness of all these people dancing about other systems of life. This fascination with forms could lead to some very beautiful dances.

And next is *Syzygy* ("the immovable union and partial concrescence of two joints of an arm of a crinoid to form a single segment. Also the segment so formed. Or, temporary union of certain protozoans, as greg-arines"). It's a small formal dance (with all the appearances of something quite informal), Lee Harris comes out on stage in silence, cigarette in hand, shaken with spasms that travel all over his body. Well yeah, OK.

After *Syzygy* my interest lagged considerably, so I won't describe the next six dances which were strangely alike even though unlike. They all had to do with virtuosity, achieving magnificent near-impossible posi-tions, standing on people's shoulders and heads, crouching with one leg completely straight, handstands, flips, girls picking up boys, a lot of im-pact between bodies. OK. On another level they looked like dances about this and that, viral organisms, a day in the park, cells dividing, greetings, gems, Victorian women, social relations.

But on some other level they weren't about much at all and that's why early on in the evening I felt saturated and remained unimpressed with all this impressiveness.

Don't get me wrong. It's not that I didn't admire the technical skill of these athletes, it's not that I didn't gasp and wish I were that strong, that focused, that daring. It's not that I didn't find them breezy and blooming. And it's not even that I ask that a dance have any kind of lit-eral meaning. But a little substance, is that asking too much? Pure pab-lum is such a drag, no matter how candied it is with stunts and feats.

It was especially disappointing since I'd read a lovely statement made for the collective by Robert Pendleton: "We were not concerned with technique as such but rather with the making of the dance. The choreog-raphy and the performance of these pieces were essential. In short, the choreography came first and we would spend months on developing our technique in order to execute and perform the dance . . . At times we work on stunts which by themselves are merely stunts. The excitement and of course the difficulty is providing a logical flow from one stunt to another, which moves through time and space and could be viewed as dance." So what happened? Good intentions are not the same thing as a good dance.

To get on with the story: a lot of people in the audience reacted as you might expect at a circus. Cheers, yells, a standing ovation. Well, yeah, uh-huh, OK. I for one was not thrilled but I could understand where that response was coming from.

Afterwards some friends lingered in Mandel corridor, trying to figure out this phenomenon. Why was a serious audience getting so turned on by showmanship? Another thing that is not the same as a good dance is good technique. This of course is true of all the arts but in dance it becomes a tangled issue to unravel.

The peculiarity of the medium complicates matters. It's happening in the human body. The human body is something a little more mysterious, unpredictable, complex, and variable than, say, film, a violin, paints, a script. Dancing is the most fleeting of all the performance arts because there is no decent way to notate it; so a dance really only exists at the moment it is experienced; in the dancer's body and in the dancemaker's head. When the dancemaker and the dancer are one and the same person (or collective) you can see how confusions begin to arise.

So was it the dancers themselves or the hard technical work that the audience was acclaiming? That's what we were standing around wondering . . .

Suddenly, a young clean-cut man who was standing nearby and had overheard the discussion kicked one of my friends. Hard. In the ass. The friend he kicked was not the burly over six-foot tall man who had engaged in this discussion but the much smaller woman. When she, hurt and horrified, asked why, the guy said, "How dare you criticize? Do you know how hard those people work? Who have *you* studied with?"

Now it just so happens that my friend is a dancer and knows exactly how hard the Piloboli have to work to do their stunts. And she appreciated it too. But that doesn't mean that she has to like the dances. This was the first time I ever saw someone assaulted for voicing an opinion about a performance and it was difficult to understand.

Still is difficult to understand. Was the guy simply psychotic? Maybe. Was he a friend of the troupe who felt personally insulted and couldn't find any other expression for his anger? Maybe. Someone who doesn't bother to sort out what kind of impact a dance has on him and what kind of impact it has on other people? Or was the incident perhaps a residue of the brutality underlying the apparently innocent male physicality of the whole evening?

I looked on the back of the program for a definition of Pilobolus. "A phototropic fungus notable for the forcible ejection of its ripe sporangium." It's derivation: from the Greek, throwing balls.

Bizarre Newborn Universe

Inside Jim Self's improvisation at MoMing: Friday evening, and people are gathering in the lounge of the four-story ex-church. Jim goes upstairs to turn on the tape and his two sets of instructions are passed out to the spectator/participants, half receive instructions No. 1, half get No. 2. They're dancers and students and neighborhood people, a grey-haired man, someone from the church up the street, someone's friends from out of town, a dog.

My instructions request that I try not to talk or comment during the session; they explain that "there are no impossible feats; most things we do every day. Nevertheless, you may find some things challenging and unfamiliar. Don't let this bother you, just try to do each step . . . watch out and be aware."

The first thing I have to do is go upstairs to the performance space, take a seat, and watch for fifteen minutes. "Red Sails in the Sunset," and then a Joplin rag . . . and meanwhile people (all silent now) file into the room. Some take seats, some start to walk around the edge of the huge

SOURCE: *The Reader*, November 22, 1974

17

dance floor in the middle of the auditorium. The grey-haired man is pacing back and forth across the little proscenium stage at the other end of the room. Some people have walked onto the dance floor, executing strange turns with one arm in the air, slowly or quickly, but all with the same quiet task-fulfilling concentration. Sets of instructions are folded and clutched in a mouth or hand; from time to time the papers are consulted and then replaced.

More people walk into the room, sitting down to watch or starting their course around the floor. Even the balconies do not escape this gradual ant-like activity: figures pace above purposively while an overalled, braided woman rushes, muttering, from side to side of the little stage. And now a whole muttering chorus crosses the stage in various tempi, but others are lining up facing the bleachers, humming and inching backwards randomly. The dog is doing this and that, investigating the floor, the movers, the sitters. It *is* all part of someone's master plan.

So, itching to move I decided fifteen minutes must be up, and (as instructed) I walk up to the edge of the floor, touch my toes, enter the space, and start crawling slowly among the people who are now boogying gently. Some rush away, and back, and away. The floor is getting rather swarmy, and presently I run into the eastern balcony, taking my place facing west against the railing, becoming one in a whole line of sentry-like figures. I'm humming and swaying, hearing faintly—above the music—a generalized low hum emanating from my neighbors, watching various quirky movements going on above and below. Check the directions: go to the stage and perform a repetitive action that you do not usually do in public. I take off my glasses and then a sock and start to crack my toes; someone else is walking around buttoning up his fly; someone else is beating his head against the wall; someone else is slowly traversing the stage with a rocking step; someone else is flicking her head around, flicking her arm around.

Focusing my eyes on one spot while moving "in an appropriate way to the music that is playing"—some dreamy romantic song—I can see everything else only peripherally. I know that weird things are happening to my body as I keep shifting directions while my head stays still, my eyes fastened to the radiator. I see equally weird things going on all around me, out of the corners of my eyes.

"You Are the Sunshine of My Life" . . . finally walking to the stage to sit as myself, but myself as the opposite sex. Looking at people quietly sitting down near me: everyone looking not so different, just some kind of heightened awareness, a certain tension wrapped curiously around each crossing of a leg, each lifting and placing of an arm. Across the huge room from us, most of those who were moving at first are now watching. On the floor, a woman is walking backwards slowly, slowly, her face to the ceiling, her long hair swinging behind her. Someone is turning with her arm in the air. Another woman rushes around and around the edges of the room. Spurts of activity, while most of us—in two groups facing each other at the ends of the room—watch and watch. Until there is only one figure standing still on stage; the music has ended; this bizarre newborn universe of taskmaking has evaporated; we put on our coats and go home.

About *Quarry,*
about Meredith Monk

Ladies & Gentlemen, Meredith Monk will attempt the death-defying feat of presenting history as both a circle and a line in the opera *Quarry*, a four-ring circus of the Holocaust, at Brooklyn Academy of Music, beginning December 15.

It's terrifying. It's hilarious. It's gigantic and it's tiny. It's a person; it's the world. It's a grotesque reflection and a prayer.

Like most Monk works, *Quarry* looks like a narrative but refuses to act like one. Events occur, but their meanings shift and are wiped away. Time and space become shattered and rearranged; in newly constructed frameworks, individual lives and objects become metaphors for larger systems, and theatrical relationships symbolize real situations.

Quarry begins with a child's complaint: "I don't feel well. I don't feel well. I don't feel well. It's my eyes. It's my eyes. It's my eyes. It's my hand, it's my hand, it's my hand. It's my skin, it's my skin, it's my skin." Little Meredith? A child's memory of World War II, hopelessly entangled with Biblical mythology and Freudian fears of parents? In the four corners

SOURCE: *SoHo Weekly News*, December 16, 1976

of the performing area, four households function simultaneously: ordinary people eat dinner, rehearse their lines, discuss their research. But among these twentieth-century people, whose world is permeated with radio broadcasts, lives an Old Testament couple. Later, people from all the different households will become dictators. Later still, they will become victims. And will the child survive?

Juxtaposed against the possibilities of individuals are the actions of the chorus of thirty. They appear three times: once to neutrally wash away the past, once to rally in support of the mesmerizing dictator, once to sing a requiem. The changing scale is reiterated in a film. Among what at first looks like a pile of tiny pebbles, even tinier people emerge, and we realize that the stones are enormous. History can change its scope as well as its shape. Will the child survive, will the nation survive, will the world survive?

Quarry

1. (from the Latin quadrus, a square) A flat, square or diamond-shaped piece of glass or tile.
2. (from the Medieval Latin quarreia, place where stones are squared) A place where stone is excavated for building purposes. To excavate.
3. (from the Middle English querre, parts of a slain animal placed on the hide and given to dogs) An animal, or anything, that is being hunted down.

Is it autobiographical? I ask Meredith. Her mother was a radio singer, as is one of the dictators; Meredith was born during the War; her great-grandfather was a cantor in Russia. Is she excavating the history of a people by digging into her own past?

Of course, the answer is yes and no. She says it's not, though there are a few details from her own life. In the Monk lexicon, anyway, personal references are only a jumping-off place. She hadn't even wanted to cast herself as the child, Monk explains. She had auditioned children for the part, but they didn't have the necessary vocal stamina; she'd auditioned other people but finally decided she'd have to do it herself. She'd originally wanted to play the dictator. Or the radio singer.

But actually, her role as a child in *Quarry* is a fitting inversion of her real-life role as director (dictator, mother). Everyone has it in them to become a dictator, she says. It's something she's struggled with for a long time as a director, and that's why it was much more interesting to see the material unearthed when six different people played dictators in the piece.

And now, writing this, I remember that during the performance at LaMama Annex last spring, I had wanted to be shown more clearly how a dictator comes to exercise power. What's the relationship between the comic, banal, and evil dictators and the chorus with its beautiful rituals? Are they dances of complicity? The leader and the led don't simply exist side by side; there is a political relationship that the dictator manipulates to his/her advantage.

It was frustrating to have so much going on at once in the four corners scenes, I complain. I never knew where to look. I was afraid I'd miss something.

Oh no, Meredith protests. All of that activity was timed and manipulated perfectly so that your eye would be drawn first to one place and then to another.

How often are we really choosing freely at circuses, sideshows, theaters, supermarkets, in elections and wars? For Monk, spectacle is a metaphor for freedom, its possibilities and its frustrations. Monk's use of sound, for instance, shows us how subtly we can be controlled. The radio is the central image in the opera: a means to power, a source of information, both true and distorted. So many people can be reached via radio; yet we see the radio announcer in the sound booth, lonely and insulated. Listening to songs and speeches without words, we realize that content is only part of meaning. We don't understand the dictator's words, but we understand his tone and we are terrified. We hear a weather report that has all the wrong words, but we know it must be a weather report because formally it resembles one.

Meredith Monk, benignly dictating our theatrical visions and aural imagery, warns us gently and mourns our pliancy. Look and listen to what we can become: victimizers or victims. Monk's vision, usually utopian, in *Quarry* turns dark.

Disco Dance
Boogie Down the Blues

"Artists from all over the world recorded 'Onda Nueva' music. It didn't catch on because it didn't have a dance," Tito Puente, the legendary Puerto Rican musician, claims.

"Shame on you if you can't dance to it," Shirley, the disco singer, scolds.

The country has been infected with dansomania on a scale unparalleled in nearly twenty years. A song's popularity is determined by its disco usage even before it hits the radio charts; there is a strong social imperative, as Shirley suggested in the early days of disco, to get on that floor and dance. Discos are opening on every corner—in former square dance barns, former bars, formerly sedate restaurants, former any-kind-of-space that can house a sound system, flashy lights, and a few square feet of dance floor.

The current choreomania has been dismissed as a faddish nostalgia for the 1930s, or even the 1950s. But though the style of dancing may share certain traits with the dancing popular in either of those decades,

SOURCE: *Moving On*, May 1977

the resemblance is more than superficial. Disco dancing of the 1970s is a cultural response to very real and current conditions, some of which recall the past.

Like 1930s dancing, disco dancing features close body contact, partnering, an emphasis on fancy technical feats performed with grace and style. The disco beat, like the Big Band jazz beat, is regularized and repetitive. The disco clubs are swank and often exclusive, providing the clientele with the setting for a variety of fantasies: here upwardly mobile aspirations can be played out, a temporary compensation for the drudgeries of everyday life created. In the 1930s people flocked to see Busby Berkeley's marathon dances, each a fantasy of instantaneous money and fame. In the 1970s we create our own, and live out the fantasy—even if only for an evening.

Like 1950s dancing, disco dancing is highly choreographed—the couple or crowd dances are designed to the point of monotony, repressive of individual expression. No one can get the steps exactly right, but at least there is a model of perfection to aim for. Despite occasional touches of Latin syncopation, the dancing is regimented and controlled.

Remember what dancing was like in the 1960s? For black kids, the Mashed Potato, the Philly Dog, the Funky Chicken, and Funky Broadway were just a few examples of structured, stylized dances that nevertheless provided room for self-exposition. White kids, with occasional forays into black forms, evolved an improvisatory style over the course of the decade which grew more and more individualized and anarchic as the drug culture, aspects of political liberation movements, and other factors created an atmosphere which valued "doing your own thing" and "letting it all hang out." You didn't touch your partner. You shook and stepped, twisted and jumped, waved your hair and flailed your arms, and sometimes stood still, in a stream-of-consciousness, ego-dissolving ecstasy.

It had to change, and dancing in the post-Vietnam United States reflects a subdued concern with order and structure. The new style co-opted elements of 1960s black dancing (the stylized movements and strict design) and of the gay bar culture (suppressed but clear sexual expression and the need for anonymity and exclusivity). Disco dancing transmuted these phenomena, originating in repressive social conditions, into an ideal: the dancing—disciplined, suave, stylish yet anonymous and uniform—demanded a certain kind of music, a certain kind of technology, and a specific social setting.

No more the unpredictable rock concerts and festivals of the 1960s, where you paid exorbitant prices and then the speakers broke down and the bands didn't show and the police used tear gas on the crowds of stoned kids to deter them from expressing any anger at the rip-off.

At latter-day discotheques, the sound equipment is peerlessly crafted to play records that have been flawlessly engineered. The only disco employee resembling a musician is the DJ, who is not a musician but another engineer. No risks. Even with steep disco admission prices, it's still cheaper to go out dancing than to a live concert. The music is polished, repetitive, with an insistent bass line. As one disco fan points out: "It removes any element of choice. You're forced, when the music comes on, to get up and pump your pelvis." The music is so loud that you can't talk or listen; dancing, touching, and looking are the only options here.

Recession Dancing

The reliance on technology makes the disco an important capital-intensive trend in the music and entertainment industries. Hiring a DJ for a night costs only a small fraction of what a live band costs; the investment in sound equipment is a one-time expense. For customer and owner alike, the disco scene caters to a recession economy.

Ironically, as the blue- and white-collar workers in the United States meet with more attacks on living and working standards, we turn for release to disco dancing, which physically replicates the rote motions performed all day on the job, in a crowded atmosphere that simulates the subway rides to and from those jobs. But unlike on the job, we go to discotheques to experience the physicality of the movements with others. Here the purpose of the individual is identical with that of the group; at our jobs, usually our individual purpose is to earn a living, while the overall purpose of the group is something quite different. And while we're dancing, we don't have to go on for eight hours at a stretch.

Dancing has always fulfilled certain social needs, and disco dancing is appealing for single people and couples (whether straight or gay) who don't have children and can spend more time and money on entertainment. Dancing provides physical release and contact within the boundaries of social conventions. The current group of dances especially—like the Bus Stop or the L.A. Hustle—builds a satisfying sensation of group cooperation and coordination, an excitement in fact which is neither a prelude to nor substitute for sex, but an event with its own sensuous, special nature. There are indications too—in the use of everyday movements and rhythms—of a determination to recycle the forms present in degrading situations (i.e. work) into means for gratification (i.e. dancing as play).

Yet whatever real pleasures and met needs we find in disco dancing are refused in the long run by the basic social structure it proposes. In fact, integration is not achieved; the division between work and play is maintained, and patterns of alienation reinforced. The subliminal message of most of the songs—sometimes the overt message (for example, the Hues Corporation's "Rock the Boat")—is to accept authority and the status quo; songs that seem too militant or political (like the Isley Brothers' "Fight the Power") are squelched. The dancers may determine the success of records to a degree unprecedented in the record industry, but their response can come only after the DJ filters out what he—and usually it is a man—doesn't like or approve of.

The excitement generated in the huge, unison group dances doesn't imply free collective action any more than does a military review, which can generate a similar response in both participants and onlookers. The ban on invention, the imperative to be cool, the monotony and boredom, all seem emblematic of a willingness by the working and middle classes to relinquish control and accept external structures of regimentation.

The Art of Ballezz

Alvin Ailey American Dance Theater
City Center 55th Street Theater
May 4–22

Unlike Rob Baker (see *Dance Magazine*, February 1977), I don't enjoy the Alvin Ailey American Dance Theater's ability to do everything— classical, modern, pop, vernacular, and show biz dancing. I do agree that the mixture of physical types, races, and nationalities on stage is exciting—in fact, it's uniquely democratic and expressive of our country's cultural mix. And there are aesthetic implications, as well as social ones, in the original way the company uses its multinational makeup; for instance, this season's *According to Eve* was performed with an all-Oriental cast, which provided (for a predominantly black and white American audience) a different reading of the Biblical story. What I don't like about the mix of choreographic types, abundantly evident May 4–22 at City Center, is that it makes watching an evening's dances come to resemble listening to Muzak.

Rather than switching clearly from one genre to another, the company coats various kinds of dances with the same stylistic veneer. In much the same way, you can hear Neil Diamond, Charlie Parker, and

SOURCE: *Dance Magazine*, September 1977

Mozart in rapid, indiscriminating succession while sitting in a dentist's waiting room—all sounding exactly alike, the work of the great ones diminished to the level of the mediocre ones. Muzak is to music as ballezz is to dance originally choreographed in ballet, jazz, Cunningham, Graham, Humphrey, Horton, tap, folk, or other idiom. And just as Muzak can devour Beethoven and the Beatles but also has its own composers—like Mantovani—some choreographers specialize in creating dances that are ballezz from the moment of conception.

There are slight technical accommodations to signal the original genre of the piece: hips swivel more in the bluesy pieces choreographed by Ailey, jumps are crisp and naïf in the scrubbed, devil-may-care ballezz by Falco or Muller; the dancers go up on pointe here, go barefoot there, wear jazz shoes there. Yet the *style* of the dancing remains remarkably fixed from dance to dance.

I don't think the dancing blurs through any fault of the dancers; they're dexterous and polished. Nor am I claiming that polish or technical brilliance creates the ballezz veneer. Ironically, I think that one reason ballet becomes ballezz for Ailey is that his generosity encourages an eclectic repertory filled with new works by young choreographers.

In fact, Ailey is on a kind of sabbatical, having choreographed no new works this season. (Of the new works, I missed Dianne McIntyre's *Ancestral Voices*.) The company's star dancer, Judith Jamison, too, is less visible, appearing only in *The Wait*, by Milton Myers. This dance seems to have been designed simply as a setting for Jamison's stunning body. To Vivaldi's "The Winter" from *The Four Seasons*, she first stands revealed, her back to us, her head bent. (Jamison can always make a powerfully dramatic statement just by standing there, just by being there with an averted head.) Then she walks back and forth along diagonal lines, breaking the walk occasionally to stand motionless again. Most of the dancing is in the arm movements, angular and crisp; but the gestures seem like excuses, frames for the long and special arms which can be thrown with such force. The abruptness of the arm movements, the interruptions of the walk, the downcast demeanor all give the first section an anguished tone. In the second part to "Concerto in A Minor for Violin" (also by Vivaldi), the tone changes to one of joy and resolution. The movements themselves are more assertive—Jamison manipulates her torso from side to side, for example—and kicks and turns augment the walk.

Throughout the piece, the movements mimic the music quite literally. But in a strange way the dance suffers because its actual structure is based on the mood, with its dramatic clichés, and the anatomy of the dancer—not at all on the musical changes. The dance follows the music mechanically, without logic or motivation; it ends by restricting Jamison rather than showing her off.

Anyone who has seen Louis Falco's *Caravan*, made last year for the Ailey company, wouldn't be surprised by Jennifer Muller's *Crossword*, new this season. Falco and Muller are among the foremost practitioners of pop ballezz, using constant, windblown, fashionable athletic streams of movement based on white go-go dancing from the 1960s. There is a lot of energy spent, and not much distance covered; vertical jumps, spinning runs with heads thrown back. People are impelled to move helplessly, flung by other people or by invisible forces; most of the action either faces squarely front or side. It all has a soulless, watered down cheerfulness and carefreeness that loses any visual interest or sensual appeal after the first minute; thus choreographers working in the genre are forced to look for production conceits to hang the next nineteen or so minutes on. In *Caravan* the diversion is the bright clothing and the high-heeled platform shoes. In *Crossword* the trick (which doesn't sustain interest through the rest of the dance) is to have a set that's a giant crossword puzzle—with moveable parts so that during the course of the performance the puzzle gets filled in—and wings that have the clues printed on them, and costumes for the dancers that turn them into letters of the alphabet. As the dancers group and regroup, various words are formed and transformed. "One quit," as a dancer leaves the stage. "It." "In." "On." Quick changes one at a time. "USA": a salute, just what you'd expect for an accompanying gesture. A group of dancers reclines: "supine." The words and phrases progress from simple words, similar in structure, to comments on the stage action, to statements unrelated to the dancing (like "A gnu is no pet.").

But because the changes in the pacing or the gestures can only be motivated by the word game, and not by choreographic invention, any pleasure for the audience has to be located in the curiosity and sense of order provoked by the word-making. The pleasure is not much; the device is a one-liner. And the matching of the words to gestures and actions is so unoriginal and obvious, the design of the movements is so bland, so affectedly naïf and modish, that the piece is all surface, no substance.

Oddly enough, though I don't usually like Rudy Perez's work, I think both his *Countdown* and *Coverage II* look terrific on Clive Thompson. In *Coverage II* we see Thompson in coveralls and a hard hat, holding a roll of tape. The lights go on, then off, then on. He lays down a line of tape. To bagpipe music, he takes some tiny turns and steps. He lays down another line of tape, then walks along it gingerly, using it like a tightrope. He lies down for a long time. Then, stripping himself of the coveralls, he is nearly naked, and his movements betray his vulnerability. He backs away, slides his torso from side to side, shields his crotch with his hands. As the tape collage shifts into Stevie Wonder singing "For Once in My Life," Thompson's actions belie the sanguine words: he backs up contorted, as if in pain. He mimes shooting a gun, then runs back and forth leaping, doing quick ports de bras, striking arabesques. To "God Bless America" the character puts the coveralls back on, pulls up all the tape from the floor matter-of-factly, and, in a gesture resembling standing at attention, slowly raises his hat to cover . . . his crotch.

In *Countdown* Thompson remains in one place during the entire piece. This time the music is uninterrupted—poignant soprano folksongs. The dancer sits on a stool, takes a drag of a cigarette, leans forward very slowly to put the cigarette out on the floor. In a single motion, he straightens up and is suddenly standing. His torso curves slightly to the side, then bends over and back. With a modicum of movement, his body seems to change planes and perspectives hundreds of times.

Both of these pieces are riveting and rather grand. They demand a close scrutiny of the body and of simple movements generated by the functional aspect of a single action. Perez uses the music and sound effects intelligently as a foil to his movements in two ways: either the contrast between them serves to heighten the attention to the movements (as when the sweetly melodic folksongs accompany the stark gestures of *Countdown*), or an apparently conventional use of the music is subverted at the last minute (as when a knee-jerk gesture of salute turns out to be somewhat obscenely irreverent in *Coverage II*). And the pieces are not turned into ballezz because Thompson is absolutely uncompromising in his respect for their intentions. The dances aren't ground up into instantly digestible material, but left intact, hard and pure. And that must be a cruel task when one senses (as I did) that the audience is uneasy watching these slow-moving, often difficult pieces. Ballezz trains us to want incessant, legible, and pleasing movements to look at. But by the end of each performance of the Perez pieces, the spectators had been clearly knocked out by the power of the composition. Perhaps because Perez isn't working in a categorizable genre his pieces resist the ballezz veneer.

Changing and Growing and Changing Colors

Remy Charlip is a kind of legend. It's been seven years since New Yorkers have seen a dance that he's choreographed here, through he *has* been leaking dances by correspondence into the city from South America and Europe by a method I'll explain in a minute. But he's not only recognized for his choreography: Charlip's relationship to the Muses is polygamous.

During the 1950s, he choreographed for and acted with the Living Theatre, started with their first production at the Cherry Lane in 1951, and co-founded the Paper Bag Players, the well-known children's theater group. From 1950 to 1961 he danced in Merce Cunningham's company, designing costumes for the company for eight of those years. And in 1959 Charlip began to write and illustrate children's books. During the 1960s, he choreographed, danced, directed, and designed productions at Judson Church, Caffe Cino, LaMama, Brooklyn Academy of Music, City Center, and The Osaka World Fair, among others.

SOURCE: *SoHo Weekly News*, September 29, 1977

For me, he first became a legend through photos and films of Cunningham's company and then through his own scores for the dances by mail, some of which were published in *eddy* (spring–summer 1976). "It came about one jet-lag evening in New York," Charlip wrote of *Instructions from Paris* (1972), for Nancy Lewis. "I awoke to a call from Nancy asking if I would do a dance for her. I said yes, and fell back to sleep. Weeks later I met Lucas Hoving in Rotterdam. He said, 'I hear you are doing a dance for Nancy's concert in two weeks.' Then I remembered the phone call. Immediately I mailed off a postcard of a woman lying on a couch with her legs and arms akimbo. I wrote, 'This is the first movement of the dance, if you want more call me in Paris and I'll send you the rest of the dance.' After Nancy's call I stayed up that night making drawings of figures in different positions from French postcards. Each position was followed by a turn, each turn followed by a conceptual gesture in sign language I had just learned while directing 'Biography' for the National Theatre of the Deaf." Last year he made a page full of tiny stick figures in all sorts of folded-up, stretched-out, and off-balance positions for Eva Karczag, one of the dancers in Charlip's evening of dance works which opens tonight, September 28, at American Theater Laboratory. The order and transitions, he instructed, were up to her; he added only a pentangle for a floorplan, and the suggestion that "if you want it longer hold the reverse side to the light and start again to the opposite side backwards."

The first time that Charlip worked directly on a score-generated performance, editing the solos that came out of the instructions into duets and groups, was last year in Sydney. Arriving in Australia without his yellow fever certificate, and with very little time to make a piece promised for The Dance Company, he chose to go into quarantine and send scores to the dancers for five days, rather than be forced to leave the country. The first time the choreographer saw his new dance, *The Woolloomooloo Cuddle,* was "when I got out of quarantine, on a television with a voice-over telephone interview—the 6:30 news on Friday. The first time I saw the company was on the following Monday. It was sort of like an open classroom: they were cutting out papers and holding them up to the light and doing them backwards and upside down, rearranging them on the walls and in the air and on the floor. It was fabulous." Two of the dancers from Sydney, Russell Dumas (who will be replaced by Albert Reid this week because of an injury) and David Hinckfuss, have been working on the current concert.

Glimpses from a rehearsal, last week at ATL: Remy stands in one spot, making detailed gestures mostly with his hands that look like symbols in a private language, meditative, but charged with a contained vigor. Touching points on his body that seem to correspond to Indian *chakras*, or perhaps Kabbalistic *sefirot*, he descends from the crown of the head, down the body, to the feet—pressing, mapping, absorbing, and shaking off impulses from the air around him. As the dance takes him from standing in the central spot to stations about the room, someone knocks on the locked door of the studio. Without any break or acknowledgement, Remy continues on his inexorable course, serenely ties off the strand of movements, and, ending up at the door, turns to admit the visitor.

Eva traces a diagonal path across the space, swift actions erupting, repeating, and submerging in the smooth surface of her constant path. She stops for them almost as if listening to a signal, waiting for a message, though the air is very still. She throws an arm behind her, over and over and over; she steadfastly snaps a shoulder downward, then fluidly courses onward.

David stands on a small rubber ball, making tiny adjustments with his entire body as the ball rocks him just slightly off-balance in various directions. Then the three dancers do something together, something that is so wonderfully seeded with details, tiny flickerings of a finger, a string of gestural sentences, or sudden cryptic large movements, that it seems like a wistful unfolding of some ancient hieroglyphic scroll.

In all there will be nine dances on this week's program, and guest artists Dan Wagoner, Sara Rudner, Nancy Lewis, Christopher Banner, Bertram Ross, and Valda Setterfield will join in on different nights.

M.C. Richards, poet and potter and a friend of Charlip's, has spoken of the dialogue between hand and clay that the potter transacts—part of the "centering" process that makes both pot and person. Remy Charlip's works and the way he talks about the works reflect a similar meditative sensitivity, even reverence for the materials. He speaks of using oneself well, of healing, of learning patience. And one sees in the dances, in the gentle drawings, in the sweet and skillful renderings of this strange world, a way of growing, changing, caring, paying attention.

Trained, of course, in ballet and modern dance since 1949, and as a visual artist even before that, he has also studied other physical techniques: for the past seven years the Alexander technique, and more recently *jin shin jiutsu*, a Chinese precursor of acupuncture using the hands rather than needles to find pulses at the body's meridians. "In Alexander training, you don't try to *do* something beforehand; although you might think of a direction to take your body, you wait for *it* to go. And then it goes. And then you figure out where you've gone. What is happening to me about these dances is that I'm discovering the structure after I do them. And it turns out to be very personal."

And, later, "Artists work in different ways. One is to have an image in your head, and to try to reproduce it on paper. Another way is to look at the piece of paper until the paper reveals an image to you." And, still later, "When I was little, someone at a settlement house threw down a piece of clay and said, 'Don't touch it for ten minutes, just look at it and see what is revealed in it.' I saw a dead horse in it, which I then dried or baked or painted, or cast in plaster—I don't remember which. That was one of the most important lessons I ever had."

It doesn't surprise me that Remy Charlip works so well with children. At times he seems to still see the world with a child's-eye view—a kind of innocence and wonder at the mysteries of scale, color, touch, and language. In his newest book of illustrations, an entire mountain is contained within a blind person's walking stick. He delights in the kind of poetic misunderstanding that turned the overheard phrase "melon-colored dress" into a song about a melancholy dress, written by Ruth Krauss for the play *A Beautiful Day*, for which Charlip, who directed it in 1965, won an OBIE. Working with others, he seems to generate a sense of play and mutual self-discovery that translates as tenderness. He taught a workshop called "Making Things Up" for several years at Sarah Lawrence, where students prepared to help children create theater by themselves making dances, songs, games, self-portraits. Two plays Charlip directed for National Theatre of the Deaf, from 1970 to 1971, involved helping the kids to present their own lives, dreams, and fantasies through sign language monologues and paintings of their own construction.

And, like a child, he wears his heart on his sleeve. A solo from 1966, *Meditation*, is part of this week's program. Danced to music by Massenet, it is alarming, winsome, distressing, passionate, ineffably delicate and precise. He passes through a rapid catalog of emotional transformations in it, his face shuddering with tension, or peaceably nodding as his mouth forms tiny kisses in the air. Later he tells me about the time, watching Cunningham perform a new solo, he turned to John Cage and said, "He's not going to perform that in front of an audience, is he?" "I had never seen anything like it—it was so bare, with all his emotions hanging out. It's that courage he has that I think is just extraordinary." *Meditation* is just such an extraordinary dance, the plaint of a captivating Pierrot.

As openly, he speaks of this performance, how happy he is to have a place and a situation to dance, how in the dancing and in life he feels a healing, growing process. "I've discovered that I'm retrieving my own body. By sitting down, working on books or choreographing for other people I've allowed a lot of confusion to happen in my own body. But I'm able to pinpoint the trouble spots, and to release those places, dissolve the tensions. I identify so closely with Harlequin, in the book I wrote with Burt [Supree]—his costume of little pieces, a patchwork of his friends. And now I think it's all getting integrated, somehow the edges are melting and it's changing, becoming other colors."

Stepping into Time
Charles Cook, Jane Goldberg, and Andrea Levine

WITH NOËL CARROLL

At the Village Vanguard

The late 1970s is a period of retrenchment in the arts. We are in a time of uncertainty. The accepted projects of the 1960s have all but exhausted themselves. The very nature of the crisis breeds a respect for the past as if we fear that we have taken the wrong route. In visual art there is a desperate lurch in the direction of realism, both in terms of photography and photo-realism. In dance as well, the radicalism of the 1960s has been confounded, yielding a special kind of lull in which a yearning for freedom from what are now the oppressive freedoms of post-Cunningham dance has insistently emerged. The spirit of the times calls out for discipline; this is true of dance as it is of many other fields. But not the sort of discipline that Arlene Croce barbarously calls "mercist." Ballet has a new respectability among young dancers, and young audiences. And, though a minority movement, so does tap.

SOURCE: *SoHo Weekly News*, April 6, 1978

But what is tap? It seems a commonplace thing. And yet it is so close to the roots of dance that it seems a natural target for our modernist sensibilities. Tap is a temporal art; tap, unlike ballet, is stylized walking. Both these attributes make it a likely subject for the artist committed to investigating the mysteries of the medium. That is, tap dancing affords a phenomenology of something quite ordinary—walking—while also interrogating the origins of an art.

Our sense of time originates in movement. Our bodies have learned how to measure time and space by walking even before we learn numbers. Time is biologically linked to the foot. Our gait and the cadence of that gait is our first inkling of time—we punctuate the world in terms of the number of steps it takes from here to there, and their rhythm. Tap celebrates the fact that our temporal sense grows out of our feet as it beats out wonderful contractions and expansions of the moment, making clocks of felt duration beyond the ken of the most profound Swiss craftsperson.

Tap dancing is a quintessentially American form of dance, our oldest theatrical dance style. A random alloy of the syncopated rhythms, sliding steps, and flexible body parts of African dance, and the off-on footwork and held torso of English and Irish step dancing, tap first became popular as entertainment in America's white culture by white minstrels "blacking up" to portray their vision of black culture. Black minstrels, in turn, imitated whites imitating blacks. Despite the racist origins of the form, its birth in a violent clash of cultures, since the mid-nineteenth-century tap dancing has often provided a situation where racial tensions could be temporarily ignored. Blacks could coach and teach whites, even though they performed in segregated entertainment circuits. From pre-Civil War saloons in New York City's Five Points district to pre-World War II Harlem clubs, black and white dancers contended informally and amicably, trading new steps, scrutinizing each other's styles, and "borrowing" routines for their own acts.

For various reasons hoofing flourished in black vaudeville, and black vaudeville lived on, long after jazz-ballet had edged tap out of white Broadway musicals. So today when our love for elegant discipline fuels a revival of tap among blacks and whites, many of the old black hoofers are still around, teaching and once again performing the almost-lost art.

Jane Goldberg, a young white modern dancer, has been seeking out the old masters over the past few years, learning some of their routines, helping to set up concerts and teaching situations. Last year she helped organize concerts in New Paltz by the Copasetics—a loosely organized group of musicians and dancers who got together in the 1940s in honor of Bill "Bojangles" Robinson, whose favorite expression was "Everything is copasetic!" Last month Goldberg collaborated on a loft concert with Andrea Levine and Charles Cook, a Copasetic and part of the old vaudeville team Cook & Brown. Now Cook, Goldberg, Levine, and various guest dancers had a weekend of performances to packed houses at the Village Vanguard.

Though we've seen several of the fifteen or so numbers they performed, the pleasure of watching the dancing was heightened in the compressed space and close-range view at the Vanguard. The format of the concert was more concise as well as more formal. Cook and Goldberg came out first in snazzy clothes, he in a shocking pink suit, she in top hat and tails, both carrying canes, to do a high-stepping routine called *Old Man Time*. They demonstrated clearly that the canes were purely decorative, since their feet were quite capable not only of carrying them but of carrying on. In *Buddies*, they beat out elaborate tattoos in a drill that was practically military.

At times the concert was almost like a history lesson in comparative styles: Goldberg showed the subtle differences in time steps by some of her teachers, and Cook contributed his own airy version, with his foot whipping out to the side before the emphatic downbeat. Together, they danced a breezy number by Pete Nugent, in which the casual manner belied the complicated virtuosity of the elaborations, including a smooth beat by one foot along the inside of the other, as both feet left the ground. As they performed Robinson's *Doing the New Lowdown*, buoyant with jumps and brushes and work done up on the toes, Cook warned Goldberg that Bojangles might reappear on earth to shoot her if she didn't do it just right.

In *My Hungry Days*, Cook recalled how poor hoofers would spend all night at the Hoofers Club, dozing in chairs and occasionally tapping away to show "I ain't asleep!" The chair dance exemplified the basic stance of the tap dancer: Cook sat as he tapped complex, abbreviated rhythms, his face, torso, and arms completely relaxed.

The night we saw the show, guest Ralph Brown appeared, reminiscing about Cotton Club days, and dancing in pink leather shoes to Duke Ellington's "Satin Doll"—mixing noiseless brushes, squeezed sides, fast splits, and tiny heel taps with a style so elegantly cool it almost stung. A professor of "Heel-ology," Brown somehow traveled backwards the entire length of the stage, tapping his heels together just above the floor, which he never quite seemed to touch.

There were new pieces, too, by the younger dancers. Andrea Levine mixed Latin rhythms with jazz standards, at times suggesting a Spanish dancer with her arms curving to enclose her body, her carriage stiff, her heels clicking rapidly like castanets, to a drum accompaniment by Chris Braun. Levine and Goldberg punctuated jitterbug turns and pattycake handslaps with constant markings and divisions of steps; Goldberg improvised with saxophonist Harvey Ray, circling close around him, and using torso, head, and shoulder movements to emphasize or counterpoise the rhythms of her feet.

The evening showed that the mysteries of balance and the pleasures of cadence the non-working foot creates are endless. Despite some problems with the music (Braun has a rock musician's touch on the drums, which sometimes clashed with the more subtle piano work by George Stubbs), and despite our feeling that Goldberg's physical enthusiasm jars her skillful footwork, the concert seemed to end much too soon. If the choreography of the younger dancers looks sparse compared to that of the older generation, well, they haven't been at it for fifty years. We hope Goldberg and Levine's technical competence and the daring that prompts them to invent and perform will not only strengthen their own voices, but spur more young dancers to tap.

David Gordon, or,
the Ambiguities

David Gordon's work over the past eighteen years has been concerned with finding structures for framing the individual, fleeting act. His focus on the differences between people's bodies—rather than design or the organization of space—has led him to single out everyday movement, its contexts and distortions, as a central motif.

In one sense, Gordon views choreography as self-defense: since the ideology of modern dance has always promoted tolerance for individual performance styles and body structures, it can be forced to make room for those dancers whose bodies and styles fit no one's vision but their own. They survive artistically by becoming the choreographers. But this kind of self-defensive thinking has also put Gordon on the offensive. Inventing new systems for ordering movement—changing the rules—means criticizing and discarding academic formulas. In the heyday of Judson Church, his incisive *Random Breakfast* (1963) parodied his peers' new methods of making dances. And his latest dance, *Not Necessarily*

SOURCE: *Village Voice*, May 1, 1978

41

Recognizable Objectives, which opens April 27 at 541 Broadway, comments ironically on its own content and construction.

Finding highly systematic constructions to frame the most elusive or undistinguished movements, concentrating on minute details of simple actions, and using repetition as a key device, Gordon has evolved a choreographic practice that works analytically. Like a Cubist painter, he organizes multiple views of a single phenomenon into one composition—a method that, despite apparent distortion, often reflects more accurately the complex processes of visual perception. As Cezanne and his followers made near and far objects equal in the picture plane, so Gordon erases hierarchies between classes of movement. Transitions between one kind of gesture or step and another become as important as the step itself. Or transitions disappear entirely. Habitual or functional gestures appear side by side with abstract movements. But an inclination of the head or the lifting of a chair may be given even more weight than a jump. The process of isolating and focusing on particular movements tends to stress their formal qualities, though the dances also bristle with humor and social comment.

In the debate on theatricality among post-Cunningham choreographers, Gordon stands in favor of spectacle. But he uses spectacular moments and glamorous touches cunningly, often intensifying them until a gap between the movement relationships and their extravagant theatrical overlay throws the movement into high relief.

Gordon was born in Manhattan and grew up here, getting a BFA from Brooklyn College and performing with the school dance club. In 1956 he began dancing in James Waring's company. From Waring he learned to value style and wit, to honor any material as something that might be included in a dance, to look at the work of Merce Cunningham, Merle Marsicano, Katherine Litz, and others who were outside of what was then mainstream modern dance. He studied composition with Waring and choreographed his first duet for himself and Valda Setterfield (*Mama Goes Where Papa Goes,* 1960) for a program of work by Waring's students given at the Living Theatre. Studying with Cunningham one summer at Connecticut College, Gordon decided to take the Graham technique and Louis Horst composition classes as well. But he found it impossible to accommodate his own ideas and values to those of the modern dance academy.

Continuing to study sporadically with Cunningham, and by now married to Setterfield, Gordon discovered that refining technique interested him far less than making dances. He took composition with Cunningham, and then the class taught by Judith and Robert Dunn, which later exploded into the Judson Dance Theater. But having learned chance techniques already from Waring, Gordon found himself as uncomfortable with what he perceived as a rigid approach to chance in the Dunn class as he had been with Horst's preclassic forms. He continued to look for ways to beat the system. When the Dunns gave an option to use Satie music in various ways, Gordon chose to ignore the music entirely. He made *Mannequin Dance* and *Helen's Dance* partly, he claims, to irritate the teachers.

Gordon's fascination with show biz reached an apotheosis in *Random Breakfast,* in which all sorts of performance styles and conventions were presented and pulled apart, from Spanish dancing to Milton Berle's imitations of Carmen Miranda, from striptease to happenings to "Judson Church Dance Factory Gold Rush" to Judy Garland. In several dances since then, he has used flamboyant costumes, stagy demeanor, lavish music, or Hollywood cliché imagery. But Gordon's use of glamorous signals is paradoxical. Glamour excites a whole set of romantic cultural connotations: luxury, power, mystery, instant success, sexual display and desirability, vanity, artifice, and nostalgia. Partly, those signals function as sincere tributes to movies, performers, and music Gordon admires. But also, embedded in the context of a Gordon dance, the glamorous qualities clash violently with other elements: casual activity, everyday or sloppy clothing, repetition approaching tedium, the acknowledgment that dancing is work, and especially the presentation of individuals as unique beings with highly idiosyncratic bodies. The notion of glamour proposes a standardized ideal of physical beauty, one that provides a key to total transformation of one's future life. But Gordon's dances ultimately emphasize the differences between bodies and celebrate awkwardness and confusion as well as grace, elegance, and authority.

In 1966 Gordon gave up on choreography after his solo *Walks and Digressions* was badly received. But in 1971 he began to make dances again, partly fortified by his work with Yvonne Rainer, and partly impelled by a teaching situation in which he could work at leisure with a large group of dancers and nondancers. The piece that emerged from the classes was *Sleepwalking*.

The theme of *Sleepwalking* is acceleration. The dance is a cluster of identical solos—a sequence that moves from strolling to walking to running to racing, between two walls. Finally, the performers lean against one of the walls as if asleep, leave to put on hats and coats, return to the wall and fall, writhing violently, as if shot. The differences between the various styles of walking in the group are clear long before the movement changes. But as the walking metamorphoses into running and then racing, we notice how effort and muscular deployment change as speed alters the action. Since each performer chooses randomly when to change pace, at times the dance is a rich field of walking, running, turning, and bolting. The shoot-out imagery at the end provides an overlay of meaning, a possible motivation for the speedup. And the accompanying sounds—sexual moans, sighs and shrieks that intensify as the movement quickens—provide another possible, conflicting significance for the heightening activity.

The Matter (1972), another large group work, uses an opposite operation for clarifying movement details. Throughout the piece, the performers suddenly freeze, or take positions and revise them. Setterfield's nude solo in *The Matter*, a series of held poses taken from Eadweard Muybridge's *The Human Figure in Motion*, exemplifies Gordon's shared concern with the photographer: to capture the mercurial attitudes of the body by arresting it constantly in motion. The comparisons between nude and clothed bodies, and between people in underwear, night clothes, and street clothes, magnify the different readings of a single pose.

In *Chair, Alternatives 1 through 5* (1974), Gordon uses persistent repetition to point out two types of distinctions. It begins with an empty stage and a sixteen-piano recording of "The Stars and Stripes Forever"; next, two conflicting, taped fictional accounts "explain" how the piece was made. Then Gordon and Setterfield repeat four times an eight-minute sequence of evenly flowing action with a folding chair—sitting on it, kneeling on it, lying on it, falling off it, folding it, pulling it over the body, leaning in it, stepping over or through it, etc. But each repetition of the double solo is a slight variation. First, the sequence is stated by the two simultaneously. The second time, each performer stops the flow at various points to repeat a fragment of the movement over and over. The third time, Setterfield reverses directions, so that instead of a double image of the same dance, we see one image and its symmetrically inverted reflection. And the fourth time, the two sing the Sousa march while executing the actions.

During the first statement of the chair material, you notice how Gordon's solid muscular male body and Setterfield's thin, angular yet sinuous female body accommodate the physical facts of the chair and, reciprocally, are emphasized by it (dragging the chair over the body traces a profile, for instance). Differences rather than similarities are stressed since the movements are rarely synchronized and tend to slip into rhythmic canon. And the internal repetition and the music evoke images that lend contrasting meanings to the abstract movements in two of the alternatives, making any interpretation ambiguous.

The duet *Wordsworth and the Motor + Times Four* (1977) carries this ambiguity further. A series of arm and leg gestures, again performed several times in overlapping rhythmic canon, reads differently when the performers (a) describe what they are doing ("turn, jump, straight arm, walk, walk, walk"); (b) assign functional meaning to the gestures ("hi, put it there, where did I put it? who's he?"); and (c) give soliloquies from Shakespeare while moving. Spectators' visual screens are wiped clean with an interlude, *Times Four* (1975), a chain of semaphoric actions performed in precise unison, with each gesture or step repeated in four opposite directions. Then the *Wordsworth* sequence is done again, accompanied by the sound of a motor, as a wall is built between the two dancers that blocks each one from the view of half the audience.

In order to understand how Gordon's repetitions function, you have to visualize his movement style. He says of himself that he is not a technically trained dancer, and that he is lazy. Yet movement looks easy and authoritative on him. Whether working with dancers or nondancers (in *Not Necessarily Recognizable Objectives* there are three dancers—James McConnell, Martha Roth, and Stephanie Woodard—besides himself and Setterfield), he uses movement that looks more like *behavior* than choreography. The sorts of movements people make routinely, unconsciously, and therefore decisively. Legs rarely go straight in the air; even a high kick is done with a bent knee. Torsos yield, arms relax. Only occasionally do gestures reach out beyond the area close to the body. In every Gordon dance I've seen, the movements are specific and deliberate, yet performed with a casual demeanor that nearly belies their careful design.

If all behavior is performance, as sociologist Erving Goffman argues, how can we distinguish between performances that are spontaneous/rehearsed, scripted/improvised, accurate/flawed, controlled/out of control, fact/fiction? *NNRO* rubs the possibilities together. In this dance/play, where occurrences at rehearsals were incorporated into the script, almost every action possesses an ambivalent meaning. The dancers trip and fall, but when they trip in unison you realize it's planned. They stop to have an argument—is it real? They express confusion verbally as well as in movement, but provide clues that the confusion is scrupulously choreographed. They scratch their arms, smooth their hair, rest their hands on their hips, stop to complain, hold their noses, mutter to themselves, ask to go back to the beginning, consult with each other. And all this behavior forms a movement combination that is repeated many times. They run, but in slow motion. They look in one direction and move the opposite way. Clear positions crystallize momentarily during transit. It is a dance of crossed signals first one way, then another.

The three women squish together gently to lie down and get up in unison, turning their action around constantly so that now we see knees descending, now we see buttocks rising in the air. They pile slowly on top of one another, then cradle like spoons across the floor. Nothing remains fixed, even for a moment.

At one point, four of the dancers stand in a cluster, becoming a corps de ballet that functions now as dance critics, now as groupies. They comment on Gordon's solo, an erratic distribution of seemingly arbitrary offhand gestures, preparation, repetitions, transitions, and stillnesses. They misunderstand each other. They note his character and depth ("Oh, I didn't know his work was like that," one exclaims), and they worry that his appearance of indecision will be misread ("What if someone thinks he doesn't know what he's doing?"). A taped voice has earlier explained that these comments are supposed to undercut the vanity inherent in the solo; but "Don't be fooled for a minute," the voice warns. And yet, the solo as egocentric manipulation by the choreographer *is* undercut when the group replicates it exactly, and in its slowest, most concentrated version it is transferred to Setterfield as a grand finale.

Gordon's dances, persistently changing meaning, raise questions about the theory that movement constitutes a language. Yet the most appropriate description of his stratagem is a literary one. He is a supreme ironist, subverting impressions as fast as he projects them.

Merce Cunningham 101
An Introductory Course

If you haven't seen dances by Merce Cunningham, the best thing to keep in mind when you go to see them at City Center next week is a word Cunningham himself often uses. Flexibility. It applies to so many aspects of the dancing itself: his elastic use of space and time, of the feet and spine, of the shape and order of the dance phrases.

The pieces we'll see at City Center during the two-week season—among them, *Summerspace* (1958); the newly revived *Rune* (1959) and *RainForest* (1968); and *Inlets* (1978), not yet seen in New York—are full-length repertory works, complete with the originally commissioned music, décor, costumes, and lighting. Usually in New York we see "Events"—reassembled fragments of dances. But in the context of Cunningham's work, even a repertory season is unconventional.

Often the different components in an evening have appeared together for the first time on opening night—the music, for example, surprising the dancers as much as the audience. This is both for lack of time and for aesthetic purposes. For Cunningham, the different sensory

SOURCE: *SoHo Weekly News*, September 28, 1978

channels are autonomous, a situation that reflects the arbitrary corre-
lation of sensory events in life. It also frees the dancing from slavishly
following or contrasting with the music. Yet without corresponding
directly in rhythm, tone, color, or shape, the expressive elements that
coexist simultaneously in the dancing, music, and design do create an
overall effect. Cunningham isn't interested in making sure the audience
"gets" a particular message from a dance, but rather in presenting a
variety of experiences—aural, visual, kinetic—which the spectator is
free to interpret or simply absorb. Cunningham's collaborators have included composers John Cage, David Tudor, David Behrman, Christian
Wolff, and La Monte Young, and visual artists Robert Rauschenberg,
Jasper Johns, and Andy Warhol.

So much of modern life requires that we live by our wits rather than
by rules. Things rarely turn out as we've planned them, and to live at
any given moment means to change plans at the last minute, to hear
one thing and see another, to try to make some kind of personal order
out of the bewildering chaos of sensory and mental experience. Cunningham's dances celebrate the states of uncertainty and simultaneity
that characterize modern life and art. They decentralize space, telescope
or stretch time, and allow for sudden unison activity, repetition, and
rich variety and dispersal. They do away with the familiar comfort and
predictability of dance movement that follows either a musical structure, a story, a psychological makeup, or the demands of a proscenium
stage-frame.

Yet by staying within a dance-technical system while relinquishing
certain kinds of control, Cunningham reserves physical logic and continuity in the works. He may use chance methods like tossing coins or
dice or picking cards to determine the order of movements in a phrase,
sequence of phrases in a dance, places on stage to put the dancers, number of dancers to use in a section, or parts of the body to be activated.
Chance subverts habits and allows for new combinations. It also undermines literal meanings attached to sequences of movements or combinations of body parts. But Cunningham's program does not allow for
improvisation by the dancers or spontaneous determination of phrases,
since the speed and complexity of his movements would make certain
situations physically dangerous. Once determined, the paths and positions of the dancers must be exact.

Cunningham's radical innovations in dance (beginning with the
dances he made in the early 1940s, while still a dancer in Martha

Graham's company) parallel those of John Cage, his long-time friend and associate, in music. Essentially, they make the following claims: 1) any movement can be material for dance; 2) any procedure can be a valid compositional method; 3) any part or parts of the body can be used (subject to nature's limitations); 4) music, costume, décor, lighting, and dancing have their own separate logics and identities; 5) any dancer in the company might be a soloist; 6) any space might be danced in; and 7) dancing can be about anything, but is fundamentally and primarily about the human body and its movements, beginning with walking.

For Cunningham, the basis of expression in human movement comes from the fact that everyone walks differently. You don't need externally expressive features to create significance in a dance when movement already *is* significant, "in its bones." Though a Cunningham dance is made out of movements by technically skilled dancers doing complicated steps, it is as inherently expressive and distinctive as the action you might see on a city street. And each dance has its own qualities and features, just as you'd never mistake Times Square for Piazza San Marco.

But, unlike some postmodern choreographers who, inspired by Cunningham's revolutionary ideas, carried them even further, Cunningham remains entrenched in a dance-technical idiom. It is an idiom that he invented, combining the elegant carriage and brilliant footwork of ballet with the flexibility of the spine and arms practiced by Graham and her contemporaries. Added to the synthesis were Cunningham's own contributions of clarity, serenity, and sensitivity to a wide range of speeds and sustainment in deploying steps and gestures. And, as well, the qualities of isolation derived from chance combinations. The technical inventions and freedom of choreographic design create a style of dancing that seems to embody flexibility, freedom, change, and—especially in Cunningham's own solos—pleasure in the idiosyncratic drama of individuality.

> perpetual proof that the world
> is energy, that to land
> in a certain space at a certain time
> is being alive.
>
> Lisel Mueller (from the poem
> "Merce Cunningham and the Birds")

Douglas Dunn
Talking Dancing

WITH NOËL CARROLL

In Douglas Dunn's *101*, a dance he made in 1974, he lay motionless for four hours a day, dressed in white overalls with blue and red makeup on his face, on top of a large maze he had constructed in his SoHo loft.

The piece questioned a number of expectations about dance. It seemed to say, first, that dance might not only be about motion— it might consist only of stillness, the negation of motion. Expectations about the relationship between dancer or choreographer and spectator were also turned upside down. In *101* Dunn seemed to say that the choices in a dance could rest almost entirely in the audience's hands. Dunn remained passive while the spectators chose how long to make the dance last for themselves, how close to get to Dunn, what to notice about their own movements through the maze.

Yet Dunn, one of New York's major postmodern choreographers for the last ten years, is certainly interested in motion. His *Gestures in Red* (1975), a long solo, was virtually the opposite of *101*. Here the dance was a catalog of an astounding range of movement possibilities. It began

SOURCE: *SoHo Weekly News*, September 20, 1979

50

with Dunn standing, setting different parts of his body in motion one at a time; then he systematically expanded the dance to cover the whole performance space, with his entire body moving rapidly.

In *Nevada* (1973), performed in a program at the New School where choreographers comment on their work, Dunn juxtaposed pure movement invention against pure word play, incorporating the critique section of the evening into the format of his short dance. But his next work, *Time Out* (1973), was a drastic contrast: a static work using various props and costumes but no words at all, to create a series of theatrical tableaux peppered with small movement episodes. The ten or so dances that Dunn has made over the past six years all share highly symmetrical structures, rigorous in their concentration on particular themes and their negations.

Born in California in 1942, Dunn was a latecomer to dance. He has always been athletic, but didn't start dancing until he was in college, at Princeton. Eventually he came to New York to study dance, and he began performing with Yvonne Rainer in 1968. The following year he joined Merce Cunningham's company, where he remained until 1973. When Rainer's *Continuous Project—Altered Daily* eventually gave rise to the improvisatory Grand Union in 1970, Dunn also danced with that group until it disbanded in 1976.

Dunn has collaborated on choreography with other dancers (including Sara Rudner, David Gordon, Pat Catterson, Sheela Raj) and with filmmakers (Charles Atlas, Amy Greenfield). He has also published poetry, often under the name Fanny Logos.

Many of Dunn's works have been solo dances, but *Lazy Madge* (1976–79) was a long, changing, ongoing work for a stable group of dancers who could exercise many independent choices in performance. *Octopus* (1974), again on a New School program, gently involved the audience by enticing them to sing and to throw balls at the dancers. With *Celeste* (1977), Dunn used a cast of forty.

His newest work, *Foot Rules*, an hour-or-so duet in three acts for himself and Deborah Riley, has been gestating for a year; it was filmed for a program on German television during the summer. *Foot Rules*, which will open the fall season at American Theater Laboratory on Thursday night, is a dance about partnering. For the first two acts, Dunn and

Riley both are on stage continuously, but don't always dance together: during the final act, when Dunn sometimes leaves the dancing space, the aloneness of the solo dancer becomes striking. Throughout the piece there are fleeting images of prayer, of fights and games, of eroticism. Yet the dance never settles into a single literal meaning. Several elements give *Foot Rules* a quality of openness as well as density—the variety of its choreographic material; the complex ways the movements are put together and varied; the extreme contrasts between very fast and very slow movements, as well as the contrasts between pausings and movements; the length of the duet; the gradual stripping down of the costumes (designed by Mimi Gross Grooms) between acts; and the music (by John Driscoll) that is independent of the dancing.

Unlike many postmodern choreographers who drastically simplify dance in order to make movements and bodies easier to see, Dunn complexifies dance in *Foot Rules*, teasing the memory with inversions, expansions, reversals, and symmetries.

SOHO WEEKLY NEWS: In some of your dances, like *Gestures in Red* and *Octopus*, a discernible structure seemed to be the most important theme of the work. But in *Foot Rules* we found it difficult to keep track of all the structural manipulations. If you don't consider the structure as the foreground of your present pieces, what qualities do you consider as the foreground?

DUNN: I don't. I want everything to be middle ground. I don't want foreground and background; I'm interested in a visible dance, which means that I and the dancing and the imagery and the structure all must have equal value, so that what emerges in the foreground is a *dance*. Ultimately this neutralizes hierarchy, not so that there's nothing there, but so that there is something there that is not closed off. It doesn't say, "If you don't see my structure, then you don't get it." The audience can make its own inventions, using it as a source.

SWN: That sounds like the way Merce Cunningham talks about how people can look at his dances.

DUNN: I see a dividing line between two kinds of work. One kind assumes that one is an illustrator of something or that one is trying to do something to an audience. My impression from being with Merce is that he doesn't do that, and my impression of the way I work is I don't do that. Merce is trying to understand movement for himself. It's the attitude of an experimenter. One of the things in the back of your mind is that you're going to present this to an audience, but it isn't in the foreground.

The reason Merce is so shocking is that he's really into his material. And that can be objectionable for an audience that doesn't feel it was top priority when the stuff got made. That's kind of scary. It turns them back on their own resources as individuals, which is an odd place to be when you're in a public space, sitting with a lot of other people, watching the same thing.

SWN: Are you talking about openness just in terms of composition, or are other factors relevant?

DUNN: Yes, for example not focusing the attention more one place than another, or not considering one part of the space—like the middle—to be more special or to have more meaning than another. I've always thought of Merce as dedicated to clarity and I feel I share that interest of his. Clarity for me has to do with the movement as movement, the body as an instrument, able to articulate itself. What the audience does have a chance to see, and what can be shared, is what happened, physically.

SWN: What are your differences from Cunningham?

DUNN: Merce's adoption of a parallel upright position as a tonic is noble. It's more classical than Martha [Graham]'s work. My work seems to tend toward a slightly goofier tonic note.

SWN: It seems to be intentionally awkward at times.

DUNN: There is a potency about feeling identified with the material that makes it a real pleasure to perform. You try to do the steps and you don't worry about what they might mean. I can't work with a dancer who has to know what something means as I make it. I need someone who's interested in moving around, learning new coordinations—who wants to dance.

I tend to prefer to watch people behave in public rather than most dancing. Because in comparison most dancing seems self-conscious. To me, working has something to do with trying to connect all my experience, of seeing anything, with the experience of working on dancing. In most dancing, a lot of the rest of the world is made to seem very unimportant and I feel like I'm being asked to participate in a fantasy when I watch it.

swn: There's a real ambiguity about the notion of material. People are often tempted to compare dance movement with movement on the street. Yvonne Rainer's *Room Service,* in which people carried mattresses, might be called "real" movement. And her *Trio A* has another kind of "real" movement, but in a different register. One is ordinary and real; the other is more abstractly designed, but "it is what is." Yet even these examples are not like movement on the street. It's like comparing apples and oranges.

DUNN: I went through Yvonne's late work with her. And her terminology—her ideology—was that the movement was "natural." We had to get away from stylization. But I never believed it for a minute. It seemed to me all equally stylized. Once you'd thought about it, and made it, the movement was no longer un-self-conscious. Pedestrian seemed more appropriate a term than natural or real. The energy level of *Trio A,* the attack—those are the important things. She was making those materials available, saying, "This too is stage potential."

swn: Often in the Grand Union you seemed belligerently "dancey." Once at Barnard, perhaps in '73, everyone else was doing tasks like laying down mats and you chose to dance around the space like Jerome Robbins' *On The Town.*

DUNN: When there was a scene going on, if there was going to be a gadfly, I was it. The movement part of whatever scene was evolving in Grand Union was always my main interest. As a result, I often felt I had to take a peripheral role to do it.

swn: How do you deal with the movements you choose as material in your own work?

DUNN: In *Gestures in Red* I made the dance out of my head, without any paperwork or anything telling me what to do. One of the things I had in the front of my mind was the space: how I got around it, whether I filled it or not. And the next thing I made was *Lazy Madge.* I wanted to do something else, but I didn't feel I knew how. So I came up with a structure that was outside myself: I made the material and then let the dancers all go out and do it, without considering the relationships beforehand. And in fact, immediately I saw exactly what I wanted to see: a fragmented broken-up, unclassical space. And I was overjoyed.

When I went to make *Rille* (1978), I was ready to face my symmetries again. When I made *Coquina* (1978), I did another avoidance—I manipulated it through paperwork, I made the parts piecemeal. I didn't make overall spatial decisions.

Recently I have wanted to be vigorous again, to be involved with speed. *Lazy Madge* had a slow tempo because of the safety problems in moving a lot of people. Now I'm interested in speed, to the extent that it prevents me from getting involved in open-ended structures. I want the dancing to be fast and big and vigorous. I want it to be visible from a long way off; it has to be simpler and clearer.

SWN: What were other motivations in making *Foot Rules?*

DUNN: I thought it was about time I made a duet. There's been so much couple work in all my pieces, and this is a concentration on that aspect. In *Lazy Madge* there's lots and lots of partnering—pairs of men, pairs of women, and men and women. Partnering has always interested me. And yet it's strange that in this piece there's not a lot of partnering.

SWN: When it happens, one's attention is drawn to it exactly because you both spend so much time dancing simultaneously without actually partnering.

DUNN: In the third act, someone actually goes away.

SWN: It almost seems that when you come together, that will dictate that you'll break apart and suddenly move around the whole space at a faster speed. Things get narrow and then they spring open.

DUNN: Yes. I was definitely concerned with how to make a dance with only two people in which the space isn't ignored. You don't have to go all over a space to register it and make it visible. But that's one way to do it.

SWN: Are there specific rules in *Foot Rules?*

DUNN: Yes. We've given the feet rules. There are specific steps; they're not choices. The dance is quite set and repeatable. There are a number of structural elements that came out through a kind of logic. There's a section where we do side steps all around the space. One person does a certain floor pattern and the step, which is made for it, repeats over and over on six counts. After one person does the first round, the second round has the other person doing the same pattern, but with the front turned 180 and with four counts added to the original phrase so it becomes a little different. Some steps get turned backwards and other switches occur; this is an extension by manipulation and reversal.

I made Debbie [Riley]'s long phrase at the end on video. I put various phrases on the tape, numbered them, and then I did some chance operations that told me how to use them: how many times, which part, and in what direction it would face.

But if I looked at it and didn't like it, I could change it. And the space wasn't indicated by the instructions. That left me a chance to clarify the material, through making choices about where it went.

SWN: You have Riley kneeling during the lifts. Kneeling is a sculptural, static position but the lifts are dynamic.

DUNN: I'm making movement from positions, rather than the other way around. I started with positions, and then I made the space, and then I began to develop the rhythm. That's a linear order for things I usually make all at once.

SWN: There's a specific vocabulary of images we saw in the piece, including prayers, suggested by the kneeling and clasped hands. It also includes a lot of references to fighting. Riley pushes you, trips you, twists your arm. We wonder if that sense of violence comes from a sex-role reversal. We're not used to seeing women manipulate men's bodies during partnering.

DUNN: The imagery is stronger than simply that reversal. But aggressive is too strong a word. It's pushy. The woman is pushing the man around. It's not a joke or a takeoff on male-female partnering. That doesn't interest me. Here is a situation with two people, and I'm interested in the possibilities. One of the things I wanted to happen was that the woman would take a very active role and I would be passive.

SWN: You make certain movements that have hand gestures as central elements. There's one that resembles a shuffling gorilla, and when that's done with your back to the audience, it's odd.

DUNN: In *Coquina* I got involved in gestural work: specific arm positions in terms of rotation and finger, hand, and wrist relationships. Often the hands are used around the body in places I'm not accustomed to using them, like close to the face. To include these kinds of careful and unfamiliar positionings is hard to learn. They're not those bold, simple, and extended arm positions I learned with Merce and in ballet. They come out of imagery that doesn't have to do with dancing, but with sitting or standing or posing. When you get in motion and try to do those things, it's very contradictory. The gestures come from relaxed postures, whereas leaping takes a tremendous amount of energy. It doesn't look right. And I'm particularly interested in that tension between contrary energies in my work now.

Patterns

Molissa Fenley and Dancers
The Kitchen
59 Wooster Street
September 13–16

"If Lucinda Childs and Laura Dean got married," a friend mused after we'd seen Molissa Fenley's *Mix*, "their child would be just like Molissa Fenley."

Fenley, a young choreographer who has given four works in New York City over the past year, belongs to a generation that has a rich heritage from various modes of postmodern dance. Both Childs and Dean often work with geometric floor patterns and repetitive phrasing. Yet there are enormous differences between their styles, and Fenley has obviously learned from both.

Childs's group dances have been rather short—averaging about ten minutes—and consist of precise phrases that are varied minutely so that the final work is the concise set of variations on a single shape and rhythm. The excitement in watching the dance comes from the way the pattern shifts slightly, almost imperceptibly, challenging the eyes and ears as well as the intellect; the dancers are distanced from the audience, becoming like fine instruments tracing out a baroque design.

SOURCE: *SoHo Weekly News*, September 27, 1979

Dean, on the other hand, often uses movement systems that are quite simple, in unchanging, hypnotic, long stretches of dancing. What we finally pay attention to in these works is not the rigorous intricacy of the choreography, but rather the personal style of each dancer, playing his or her role in the homeostatic dance.

Fenley combines aspects of both kinds of pattern choreography. Her arrangements are complex, often asymmetric, and ever-changing; one looks for a strict structure in the floorplan—the kind of shape one immediately sees in Dean, or finally grasps in Childs—because the eight-count rhythmic phrases provide such a strong, regular beat. But no single spatial design remains for long. The elusiveness of the structure entices one to keep track of repetitions and contrasts. But the individuality of the dancers' styles and bodies also become salient as they make idiosyncratic gestures, dance one against three or two against two, smile animatedly at each other. Each dancer (John Bernd, Fenley, Kate McLaughlin, Elizabeth Streb) wears a shiny outfit in a different color, adding to the emphasis on singularity.

There's a lot about the movement that is fresh and energetic. During the first, longest section, when the only accompaniment to the movement is the clapping and stamping of the dancers (the floor is miked and an Echoplex delays the sounds, so that we hear them twice), the dancing at first has a regular, straightforward shape. The dancers move around a circle counterclockwise, mixing stamping and shuffling modes of locomotion, taking turns moving in and out of the center. Sometimes they bunch up so that two are in the middle and two are in one corner, but they always return to their positions on the circle, like square dancers with a definite, if mysterious, set of protocols. Each claps a different pattern on the eight-count standard, so there is always a base line of rhythm, which each dancer joins and leaves. They scoot back from the center with heads down, hips wiggling, arms stretched forward, an eccentric scurry that becomes emblematic.

Suddenly the clapping stops and the dancers break into individual activities—galloping, whirling, hopping. The circle breaks up and then resumes; the clapping starts again but is interrupted frequently whenever the four gather at the center of the space to lay a hand gently on each neighbor's shoulder. There is a kind of intimacy communicable to the audience that contrasts pleasantly with the precision of the clapping. There is also a cheerful sloppiness that is both endearing and refreshing.

After about half an hour the dancers pick up sandblocks and start a new movement motif; their hands and arms are no longer free. They step closer to each other, casting glances and smiling coyly at each other as they rub the blocks together in syncopated rhythms. Certain sections from the first part are repeated, and then, about ten minutes later, the dancers trade sandblocks for maracas and, having systematically heightened the noise level, they stop.

When *Mix* had gone on for around ten minutes I thought it was the most wonderful new dancing I'd seen for a long time. Ten minutes more and it simply seemed dull. Perhaps if the three sections had been equal in length the variety of movements and sounds would have constantly renewed itself. But the first section seemed both too hypnotic and too long. By the time the changes came, with the sandblock and maracas, my senses had been numbed. Yet I look forward to more dances by Fenley and group; even if her sense of timing taxes my patience, her movement invention can charm and the social interactions she presents on stage are terrifically appealing.

A Walk on
the Wild Side

Boyce Dances
The Kitchen's Dance Now Series
Collective for Living Cinema
52 White Street
Wednesdays through October 31

Choreographers during the 1960s performed a number of radical operations on modern dance, raising questions about the nature of dance
movement as well as the ways it could be put together. Several key tac-
tics that people like Yvonne Rainer, Deborah Hay, Steve Paxton, Simone Forti, and others used were game structures, casual demeanor,
everyday movements, large groups, nondancers dancing. The effect of
these strategies was to make the spectator see dance as movement by
isolating movements not ordinarily looked at for their esthetic value, or
by comparing the look of movements done on untrained versus trained
bodies.

A lot of postmodern dance in the late 1970s has refined 1960s
casualness—along with the uninflected phrasing valorized by Rainer's
Trio A or Trisha Brown's Accumulation Pieces, and an everyday
vocabulary—into a new dance style, what I call dances of repose. Made
of movements that are small and unprepossessing and strung into
phrases that are creamy, slow, and clear, these dances are natural ex-

SOURCE: *SoHo Weekly News,* October 25, 1979

tensions of several aspects of postmodern dance. Mary Overlie, Wendy Perron, Susan Rethorst, and collaborators Diane Frank and Deborah Riley are exemplary choreographers of the 1970s generation in this mode, a style that at its best can be elegantly breathtaking, at its worst dryly dull.

The choreographers of repose often use high-energy moments in their dances, but the impression that remains has to do with stillness, serenity and control. Lately I have been seeing works that are totally opposite, dances that use wild, raw action—but still have their roots in another aspect of the 1960s: its pedestrian vigor.

Johanna Boyce is one of the wild ones. She is doing wacky, peculiar things with groups of nonprofessional dancers. Though Boyce's works are reminiscent of some 1960s dances, they are neither nostalgic nor pretentiously derivative. Boyce's program on the Kitchen series includes six dances and a film that compares nudes, pedestrians, and dancers. The dances themselves are quite varied, revealing a fecund choreographic imagination.

In *Styles* four women dance simple phrases in four dance styles—modern, jazz, ballet, and "gymnastic" or natural—while reciting curricula vitae. Eventually they break up these phrases, performing fragments from each style in unison. It is terrific to see, among other things, Mary Galpin, the "nondancer" whose résumé begins, "I started walking when I was twelve months old," shaking her head and shoulders in an awkwardly jazzy fashion.

It's How You Play the Game breaks the music to which the dance has been choreographed into randomly ordered phrases. Three women (Boyce, Fern Schwartzbard, Robin Wilson), wearing loose flowered blouses over leotards and tights, keep lining up in the middle of the space and then, when they recognize the phrase, either take running jumps against a wall, or lie down and slither across and through each other's bodies, or stride, or leap up in the air in a bent-up pose, and so on. They do this in varying groups—one against two, all in unison, or all separately—so that though the musical phrases repeat (they are composed and performed by Boyce and others, based on the Velvet Underground's "Murder Mystery"), the dance phrases never repeat exactly.

The longest piece is a complex work for nine dancers titled *Pass,* with three subtitles: Interchanging, Changing, Exchanging. I meant to keep track of what I thought would be three separate sections of the work, but one engaging thing kept leading to the next, and getting more and more complicated, until all attempts at cool observation vanished. The dancers, dressed in blue shorts and print t-shirts, sit cross-legged on the floor. They count, recite words, sing words, walk around, rearrange some of those words into sentence fragments, meanwhile running very fast, a few at a time, around the stationary performers. Later, the words recombine into Frost's poem "Meeting and Passing." Later still, the lights go out and the dancers reappear with thick layers of t-shirts on. They group as they shed t-shirts, hooking up in varying small groups, color-coded according to the variegated shirts that appear. They jump, twitch, roll around. They do a relay race and hook their t-shirts around their necks and bared chests. Much later, everyone is naked and holding identical fancy, gold-rimmed waterglasses, casually chatting in small groups, as at a cocktail party. At some point they're rolling around with delightful uninhibitedness on the floor, and then forming a series of bridges that others roll over backwards, one at a time. Finally, the piece closes with a rerun of a relay game, this one based on drinking all the water from the glasses.

Ghost Dance (set to part of Patti Smith's song of the same name), in contrast to the multifarious operations of *Pass*, sets up a constant beat within which the dancers, in jeans and colored t-shirts, step-hop in interweaving, changing files.

Especially in *Pass*, but in all of Boyce's fierce, precise, concentrated dances, the energy of the dancing, the intelligent faces and bodies of the dancers, and the compelling originality of the designs effect work that is fresh and startling.

Bolshoi Bravura

The Bolshoi Ballet
New York State Theater, New York City
August 1–26

The latest tour of the United States by the Bolshoi Ballet was surrounded by controversy at both ends of the New York leg. Rumors pre-
ceded their arrival that the Moscow troupe was plagued by infighting,
with one faction led by Yuri Grigorovich, the main choreographer and
director of the company, and the other by Maya Plisetskaya, the internationally acclaimed ballerina. The enormous Bolshoi company apparently operates more like several dance troupes, and it was the subgroup
led by Grigorovich that we saw here.

Thus we were shown only ballets choreographed by the director and
not, for instance, Plisetskaya's *Anna Karenina* (co-choreographed with Natalia Ryzhenko and Victor Smirnov), ballets with modern Soviet themes
like *The Geologists* (by Natalia Kasatkina and Vladimir Vasiliev) or *Asel*,
about a woman who loves a truck driver (by Oleg Vinogradov). One
would have wished, as well, for older Soviet ballets like *The Path of
Thunder*, on race relations in Africa. To compare American and Soviet

SOURCE: *Dance Magazine*, November 1979

incorporation of African dance material into European dance traditions would have been intriguing.

The other frustration the factionalism of the company created was the absence of several leading dancers: Marius Liepa, Vladimir Vasiliev, Ekaterina Maximova, and Plisetskaya herself. Then Ludmila Semenyaka was injured and did not dance in New York until the end of the first week.

At the end of the New York appearance, of course, was the much-publicized defection of Aleksandr Godunov and the dramatic return to Moscow of his wife, Ludmila Vlasova, a soloist in the company. American authorities detained Vlasova's plane for three days, questioning the ballerina to see if she wanted to stay in this country, too.

The five ballets that were given here form the basis of the Bolshoi's repertory and give the American viewer a thorough understanding of Grigorovich's choreographic method, as well as evidence to understand various debates in Soviet ballet history. From his *The Stone Flower* of 1957 to the *Romeo and Juliet* he completed just last season, Grigorovich follows certain predictable formulae for popular appeal in his evening-length ballets. The use of the corps is lavish, the steps are simple and bold (read heroic), the sense of spectacle everywhere, and often overblown. Every three-act ballet (and they are stretched to a full three acts, even those that seem finished by the end of the second) begins with themes and characterizations that are iterated and reiterated, rather than developed or elaborated, until the spectator can predict from the first five minutes precisely what the rest of the ballet will look like.

Yet there is a certain grandness in the conceptions of the stagings. Grigorovich loves to trace out the expanses of the stage to stress the sense of enormous scale, and there seems to be an unwritten law in his ballets that no one may take more than three flying leaps to cross the space, preferably on the diagonal. Occasionally the men do turning leaps straight toward the audience from the back of the stage, creating the startling effect of a head-on attack. These ballets are precisely calculated to wrench certain emotional effects from the audience; they are huge, plodding machines that churn out inspirational, monumental dramas— melodramas with an individualistic, very un-Marxist message, tinged with martyrdom.

Of the five, I most enjoyed *The Stone Flower*—perhaps partly because it was the first work given here and the peculiarities of Grigorovich's choreography, although immediately evident, were not yet tiresome. The ballet, based on tales by Pavel Bazhev, which in turn are based on folktales from the Ural mountains, tells the story of Danila, a stonecutter, and his adventures with the Mistress of the Copper Mountain who spirits him away and teaches him the secrets of carving malachite, and of Danila's bride-to-be, Katerina, who must fight off the advances of the evil bailiff, and whose search for her lover at the village fair provides the pretext for an entire act of Russian and gypsy folk dancing. In the end, the Mistress of the Copper Mountain—who can change from a lizard to a Russian beauty, and who is a kind of people's fairy godmother, nurturing Danila's art and protecting Katerina's virtue by making the bailiff fall into the bowels of the earth, but who nevertheless shows human weakness by falling in love with Danila—finally reunites the lovers in domestic bliss.

The choreography shows traces of the experiments of Lopukhov, Goleizovsky, and others in the 1920s: the many acrobatic pas de deux, in which the hero's body is totally engulfed by the twisting arms and legs of his partner, or in which he lifts the contorted woman straight above his head like a strongman pressing a medium-weight dumbbell (in one scene, the ecstatic Katerina does a handstand on her betrothed's shoulders); the music-hall antics of the anthropomorphic semiprecious stones, decked out in lavender, turquoise, and spangles, who are turned in cartwheels in the air and paraded and manipulated into more labyrinthine poses; the expressionistic, grotesque gesticulations of the bailiff, who stomps with turned-in knees and toes, splays his hands, and surveys the scene with smoldering eyes; the angularities and asymmetries of the Mistress, whose bent arms and legs flare across the stage each time she crosses it, her head thrown back, her eyes flashing enticingly.

Yet this ballet, choreographed when Grigorovich was a young dancer at the Kirov in 1957 and first performed by the Bolshoi in 1959 (they danced it on their first visit to New York, twenty years ago), follows the prescription for the correct Soviet ballet developed during the 1930s and 1940s: the right combination of authentic folk dances, perhaps doctored up a bit for theatrical effectiveness, and classical dancing in resolute postures that blatantly signal the strength and determination of the new Soviet hero and heroine—in this case, the artist-worker and the pure Russian girl who loves him.

Grigorovich is considered a reformer because the Moscow style of ballet drama had become so riddled with pantomime and so bogged down in acting out the story that his nonstop dancing seemed clean and fluent in the early 1960s. He is also credited with creating strong and active dance roles for men. And his designer, Simon Virsaladze, has turned away from the detailed, epic scenery of the realists in the preceding generation in favor of abstract settings with shifting parts. Yet to the Western eye, Grigorovich's avoidance of complicated step patterns only makes the constant movement look simple-mindedly turgid, rather than stark. One wishes for a moment that the dancers, who are technically quite admirable, would either stand still or at least stay in one spot long enough to do more than one thing. Instead, they leap to signal joy or military skill, stretch their arms out while running (longing), cuddle and skip (domesticity), flicker hither and thither (temptation), and so on. The scenery still looks complex to us. It is the nineteenth-century theatricality, rather than any modernism I discerned in the choreography, that impressed me here: the magical effects created with lighting, scrims, and trapdoors; the character dancing, so skillfully done by this troupe and so little seen in American ballets; the use of huge crowds.

As Katerina, Irina Prokofieva showed a quiet, noble determination. Yuri Vetrov played the bailiff as a sinister, stalking giant, reminiscent of Death in Kurt Jooss' *The Green Table,* while Anatoli Simachev was a smaller, more finicky villain. I was especially impressed by the precision of the mild, stony-faced corps.

Spartacus showed the flaws in the Grigorovich-Virsaladze collaboration most clearly. It often seemed as though half the choreography, especially the redundant monologues each character danced, had been designed only to mask the scene changes. In *The Stone Flower,* the scrim turned opaque while the background behind it changed unobtrusively; in *Spartacus* that scrim became a tyrannical presence, interrupting the action and upstaging the dancers. The mediocre score by Aram Khachaturian made all the action even more unbearable.

The ballet began, as most of Grigorovich's seem to, with a single figure spotlighted in a massive setting. In this case Crassus, the cruel Roman commander, is surrounded by shields and spears; behind him is a wall of huge stones. He is returning from a war in Thrace, and among his prisoners are Spartacus and his wife Phrygia, who mourn their separation as they are sold as slaves.

Eventually Spartacus leads the other slaves to rebellion and brings Phrygia with him; meanwhile Aegina, the ambitious mistress of Crassus, succeeds in splitting the slave army into factions by seducing them, hastening their defeat.

The ballet is a cinematic montage of the climaxes of action in the story. Lines of soldiers cross the stage, pirouetting with parallel legs, or goose-stepping, or leaping, all in unison. The slaves, by contrast, have a stooped posture that gradually changes to proud, upright defiance. The lines and designs made by the soldiers in the first act are echoed by the stately prancing of the courtiers in the second and third acts, and by the final battles; Spartacus's heroic solo in chains is echoed by a later solo with a blanket. And there is the predictable episode of folk dancing in the scene when the shepherds decide to join the slaves.

In each act, too, there is a contrast between the spiky, stabbing movements of the imperious Aegina (Tatiana Bessmertnova, in the cast I saw) and the tender yet strong dancing of Phrygia (Nadezhda Pavlova). Every act ends with a colossal tableau that seems like a quotation from a famous painting—a scene from David, perhaps, or some other neoclassical, epic painter? The first act ends with the slaves posing dauntlessly, with Spartacus at their center; the second, Spartacus's capture of Crassus. In the third act, Grigorovich actually manages two majestically frozen finales: the first, Spartacus's death, his corpse surrounded by spears and raised arm high (one can't help but think of crucifixion); and the mourning by Phrygia as the slave-soldiers carry the body.

The legend of Spartacus leading the slaves to revolt is a favorite of Marxists, and not only in the arts; countless political parties have been named after this hero. In a sense, it is in the Socialist Realist tradition of Soviet art to use the historical lessons of the past, recast into art, to draw inspiration for a new, revolutionary future. Still, the shape of this *Spartacus* makes one wonder what kind of lesson could be drawn. Despite the constant use of the corps, the ballet seems more like a glorified love story, telling of individual heroism and villainy in the course of the tragic separation of a couple by death. Generally, the corps acts only as an amplification of the actions of the principals. One never has the sense, for instance, that either Spartacus or Aegina goes through any political process of winning the slaves over to their sides; they each simply dance in front of the men and immediately are followed. Surely symbolic dance terms could be found to express the dawning and solidification of class consciousness. Instead we see a combination love story and religious iconography. The pas de deux become central climaxes because they are more intricate and riveting than the more broadly sketched mass scenes, whose power is diffuse. And without a live, apparent connection to his fellows, Spartacus (danced crisply and spiritedly by Vyacheslav Gordeyev) as a leader becomes a martyred saint.

In much the same way, *Romeo and Juliet* emphasizes the romantic, individualistic aspects of the tragedy over the class analysis one might expect from a Soviet artist. The story can be seen as a lesson in the cruelty and human toll of the rise of capitalism in Renaissance Italy, personified in the struggle between two noble houses, exemplars of a crumbling class. Certainly the Lavrovsky version of this ballet is more generalized, ending with the two families, agonizing over the loss of their children, swearing friendship. Grigorovich's ballet sets the stage for an acutely personal rendering right from the start: In a vision, Romeo has a flash-forward of the events to come.

The many small scenes and the scrim that must be walked around while moving from upstage to downstage, the swirling groups populating the stage, the highly elliptical action (I found myself constantly consulting the program), all lend *Romeo and Juliet* a cinematic rather than dancerly appearance. In many ways the Capulets' ball is the height of the ballet; its choreography in terms of the interweaving of individual character within the group into a flow of movement is masterful. Though *Romeo and Juliet* has fewer contortions than *The Stone Flower* or *The Legend of Love*, a contrast is drawn between the pure classicism of Romeo (danced by Gordeyev and Alexander Bogatyrev) and the character steps of Tybalt (Leonid Koslov, in a violently sultry interpretation) and Mercutio (Mikhail Tsivin), whose verbal pyrotechnics are translated into frisky capers, often ending on the floor in a split. A contrast is similarly drawn between the more classical style of Juliet (ironically, more little-girlish as danced by Natalia Bessmertnova than by the younger Pavlova, who plays the role with delicate ripeness), and the bawdy dancing of the nurse (Agnessa Balieva).

Juliet's situation as an object of competition is symbolized by several pas de trois, in which she is partnered by two men; at the ball, her partnering by Paris displays her confidently, but when Romeo dances with her, his lifts are tentative.

Other movement themes are repeated to drive home specific meanings: Juliet's ecstatic backbends when dancing with Romeo presage the final pose they take in death; the mourning gestures the Capulets make in the histrionic scene after Tybalt's death are reiterated ominously when Juliet accepts Paris's marriage proposal.

The depth of the stage is especially emphasized in this ballet. The scenes in Friar Laurence's cell take place on a tilted platform that gives them violent perspective reminiscent of high Renaissance paintings. At the ball the seemingly infinite layers of dancing are impressive, with the young people and jesters in the back forming a light tapestry of motion as the older couples, in heavy costumes, dip and lunge with a mannerist elegance.

Two elements in the ballet are especially dissonant. There is a group of women in peach-colored chiffon, a kind of chorus who seem all too much like Wilis; and in the third act there is a divertissement (ostensibly, Paris's wedding preparations) of Syrians, Moors, and Clowns. It is certainly well within the Petipa tradition to conclude a ballet with a whole act of dances that don't pertain to the plot, yet in the context of this dramatic ballet the scene only serves as meaningless filler, as if the act would have been too short without it.

Prokofiev's searing score has been overorchestrated, but that has been its history ever since the ballet was first written. And again, the choreography for the individual dancers is too simple. Nothing profound can be said with the dancing, no complex emotions expressed. These excellent dancers are only limited by it. The ballet has a surface grandeur that is all too shallow.

Stylistically and thematically *The Legend of Love* resembles *The Stone Flower* closely. Choreographed by Grigorovich in Leningrad in 1962 (it was his second ballet), it was first given at the Bolshoi in 1965. The music is by the Azerbaijan composer Arif Melikov, and the libretto by the Turkish poet Nazym Khikmet.

The story is of a Persian queen who sacrifices her beauty so that her sister may recover from a deadly illness. Both women fall in love with an artisan, Ferkhad. (In Natalia Roslavleva's *Era of the Russian Ballet* he is called a stonecutter; in the program notes here he is a painter; it doesn't really matter, since we never see him working in the ballet anyway.)

Ferkhad loves the younger sister, Shirin, and in a terrible fit of vengeance, abetted by her Vizir, the Queen captures the two lovers as they flee the palace, and demands that Ferkhad cut a canal through a mountain to bring water to the drought-ridden kingdom. In the final scene the Queen remorsefully decides that the couple may be reunited, but Ferkhad refuses to abandon the needs of the people.

The ballet makes use of all sorts of anthropomorphisms and eccentric dancing that sometimes look downright silly. In the first act, when the Stranger appears to cure the sister, the Queen offers him gold—in the form of a corps of dancing girls with tambourines and coin jewelry, who skip and march like drum majorettes and sit cross-legged like Hollywood Indians. The Stranger himself, dressed in a grey dervish's turban and robe, has a lovely, eerie dance that reminds me of Mary Wigman's *Witch Dance*, lunging and leaning rhythmically sideways, arms bent and hands scrabbling in the air. In a vision Ferkhad has in the third act, a crowd of women with white scarves—water—appears, among them Shirin, his inspiration. The Queen has a vision, too, in which Ferkhad makes love to her; a corps of dancers in bright red accompanies this vision, like some strange abstraction of passion.

In *The Legend of Love* there are scenes where the common people dance their despair and thus Ferkhad's role as their champion has more credence than Danila's in *The Stone Flower*. The final tableau in the ballet has Ferkhad striking a pose that clearly reads "popular hero," even though one only knows through the program notes what complex emotional transformations are transpiring in the final scene.

Yet the heart of the ballet is the doomed triangle, the love story, and this aspect is embodied in the pas de trois for the Queen, Shirin, and Ferkhad that is central to each act. The three dance separately, in pools of light, to recorded music that is meant to sound like it comes from a great distance.

I must admit that in the solos and trios, which are supposed to reveal the innermost feelings and motivations of the characters, I am unable to read anything but the most generalized and stereotypical emotions. It is, to be sure, very difficult to express remorse through dancing, and even more difficult to show the complicated thought processes that bring one to that state of mind. However, the pas de deux for Shirin and Ferkhad are rather touching and beautiful in their power and variety; in the first encounter he literally chases her and, never touching, they strike poses quoted from Persian miniatures in a demurely erotic flirtation. In the second duet he partners her tenderly and they leap away from the palace like two young gazelles. Both Natalia Bessmertnova (who created the role of Shirin at the Bolshoi in 1965) and Nadezhda Pavlova were fetching sloe-eyed heroines, and Gordeyev was especially striking as the adventurous Ferkhad. Yuri Vetrov was a suitable mysterious Stranger.

The Bolshoi has two *Swan Lake*s in its repertoire. According to Alexander Demidov *(The Russian Ballet: Past & Present)*, the leadership of the troupe decided that Gorsky's version, which was a classic, should continue, but that since it was also archaic, a new version should be made. We saw here Grigorovich's reworking of several earlier editions of the ballet, including some of Gorsky's innovations, like the role of jester. In a jarring way, it was interesting to see the more conventional enchaînements threaded together with Grigorovich's symptomatic diagonal bounds. The role of Siegfried seemed almost that of a schizophrenic, switching dance styles between frustratingly reductive combinations and the more traditional, virtuosically complex pas. Again, the result of what once must have looked like a welcome abstraction, a paring down of realistic detail, simply became a fragmented attenuation.

I rather liked the fairytale look of Siegfried's mother, young and pretty with burgundy hair, and the musty castle décor. Mikhail Gabovich (son of the elder Gabovich, long a mainstay of the Bolshoi company) was a demonic Rothbart and, in the cast I saw, Ludmila Semenyaka was simply wonderful as Odette-Odile. I saw the company's final performance of *Swan Lake*, in which Godunov had been slated to dance Siegfried. Perhaps the company's dismay at his defection earlier in the week, or the fact that the matinee itself began late (it was announced that the curtain would be held until Grigorovich returned from the airport, where Vlasova's plane was still grounded) accounted for a certain nervousness in the performance. Leonid Koslov, substituting for Godunov, was a starry-eyed Prince, and if he occasionally wobbled while supporting Semenyaka, in what was apparently his first appearance as Siegfried, he was fine. The most alarming thing about Grigorovich's *Swan Lake* is its happy ending; in this version the Prince remembers Odette at the last minute and refuses to swear an oath to Odile. He rushes back to the lake where he and Odette hug each other and watch the sun rise on their happiness.

The season left me aching to see more of these dancers in more varied and exciting roles. When Diaghilev brought Russian ballet to the West, he instituted the one-act ballet. Perhaps our attention spans have been permanently shortened. But a program of shorter ballets and selected acts from these epics might be a more suitable program for the Bolshoi's next U.S. tour.

Notes on Some Dances

Dance Day
The Kitchen
January 20

Dance curator Eric Bogosian organized Dance Day, a benefit for the dance program at The Kitchen. Bogosian has presented a lot of fine dancing there since he took over the dance program a couple of years ago, and his taste and sense of organization were everywhere obvious in this eight-hour concert. Actually, the day began with an open-movement session and then four two-hour dance concerts followed. But they were so tightly scheduled that one experienced them as a single, eight-hour event with twenty-eight chorographers showing twenty-minute pieces. I took a dinner break at some point and missed Pooh Kaye and Elaine Hartnett dancing bare-breasted in grass skirts and Peter Rose dancing on broken glass, among other things.

Mary Overlie and Wendell Beavers did a wonderful dance (by Overlie) called *Paper Waltz*. Two exact repetitions of a few discrete actions. They do some warm-up movements, shrugging and shaking out hands, picking at clothing, the kind of thing you dismiss as incidental

SOURCE: *SoHo Weekly News,* January 31, 1980

movement. They face each other, walk around in circular paths to face us. Beavers silently mouths a monologue. They circle again, smile wide. They circle and sit down cross-legged with a zigzag motion. Overlie has to tug at her straight red skirt to sit properly. They take wide, stiff strides and walk away in a mechanized stagger. Then repeat the whole thing, no variations, like a paper-doll cutout series, hard-edged, flat, and charming.

Simone Forti slides three long, curving sticks through her sleeves and holds one in her mouth, so she looks like a sea lion or some kind of regal, ceremonial, mythic Chinese beast. Peter Van Riper puts two saxophones in his mouth. She crawls while he plays a double tune. Her legs flop and tangle behind her. His melodies change, sounding distant or steady, while she advances in a low, balancing walk, a warrior with outstretched, vulnerable hands. The music shakes and the dancer shakes, pelvis thrusting, stamping, lying down to shudder uncontrollably in a kind of ecstatic fit. And then both music and dancer tone down, winding to a calm close. Forti's dancing gets clearer, more complex, and more absorbing for me over the years. After paring movements down to basic actions like crawling, falling, circling, she lets a certain wildness creep in now that is like a gift.

Ann Hammel and Alice Eve Cohen performed their *Separation in Four Parts*. Part one: a domestic drama in which Hammel is a nervous, twitchy overbearing mother/wife figure who flutters about making breakfast, burning toast, shaking orange juice. Cohen peels a grapefruit and sulks. Part two: Hammel sits at a writing desk while Cohen slowly approaches her, playing an oboe, I think. Part three: they do a little puppet play in which Hammel, as a giant, stands on a ladder. Draped in a cape, she forms a curtain through which a tiny puppet pops; the puppet has been rejected, in the letter, by the giant and tries to win her back. Part four: there is a dance Hammel does to Cohen's percussion—a kind of meditative, gathering, shaping dance that suggests Oriental rituals with its flexed wrists. I wasn't sure what Cohen and Hammel were up to with this patchwork performance. Some of it was nice, some of it silly, and its sketchiness made me lose interest.

Karole Armitage made *A One Time Objectstacle for the Kitchen*. It had a setting composed of a turquoise-painted window frame hanging in space, a smashed, turquoise ironing board, a space heater, a table full of groceries. Armitage stands behind the window frame, becoming less visible because the glass isn't entirely clear, and crouches and springs, moving her leg outward fitfully. She runs around doing things like pouring a clear liquid and then milk into a bottle, to the brim, moving the ironing board to behind the window frame, unplugging the heater. She walks quickly around two pillars flanking her space, setting a repetitive, rhythmic route, and tossing off some quirky gesture or other each time she rounds the pole. She sets her long legs bouncing and plays hands and arms in counterpoint to the regular one-two swing of hips. She walks over to The Kitchen's actual window and walks its edge. She heads back to the groceries and puts something in the bottle that makes the white liquid froth over the brim. Armitage has danced with Merce Cunningham's company for several years and the movements she makes for herself are entirely different from the ones he makes for her, but just as perfect for the lissome body she has.

Charlie Moulton did an amazing dance/game with two women, handling small rubber balls in intricate weaving patterns of handcrossings as they stood shoulder to shoulder. An accompanist played organ chords that cued changing patterns, and one of the pleasures of the piece was the casual way in which Moulton would "call the shots" when the team made a mistake and had to start over. At one point he looked at the audience and said, "Just a second, we've got to work this out first, OK?" The whole game looked fun for the players, and the eye-hand coordination made the audience go wild.

Christina Svane is a one-woman group, projecting dance phrases onto imaginary characters and then sitting back to comment on their continuing actions, then getting the spectators in on the fantasies and belting out a song and dance to "Tell It Like It Is." . . . David Woodberry and Sara Vogeler do *Leverage,* tenderly lifting, flipping, rolling, carrying, jumping onto and with each other . . . three films are shown, including Robyn Brentano and Andrew Horn's film of Andy deGroat's *Cloud Dance,* kneeling and moving through a fiber sculpture, and Yoshiko Chuma's film *August 27, 1979 — The Girl Can't Help It* (cinematography: Jacob Burckhardt), wonderful, lively images of Chuma moving through water, fields, woods and falling, running, moving possessed. . . . Cesc Gelabert woos and kneels hieratically, then smiles wryly, disowning everything that he's just done, slides, whirls, falls several times, does two separate things with the two sides of his body. . . .

Johanna Boyce's untitled work in progress is yet another marvel from this bright, young choreographer. Her sense of design is incredible. Seventeen people in crazy clashing polyester clothes come out and sing a round, of which the words are their names. They stand posing like a family portrait but then take off their shoes and make whooshing sounds, running, sliding. Five women stripped down to white undershirts and underpants yell, shriek, jump, and groan as the rest freeze. Then everyone takes off their socks and throws them, making kiddie machine-gun sounds, takes off clothes, ties them around the posts to sag there like a candy-colored sculpture. There are lots of other things that happen, like people shinnying up poles and waiting there, two per pole, like koala bears; and a kind of caterpillar formation with all the dancers scurrying in and out of line; and the five lead women counting loudly while performing variations on an athletic dance phrase. And finally, people chanting vowels while running and falling, so that "o" turns into "ohhhh!" and "e" into "eeeeeee-eh!" because of the physical effort. The vowels, amazingly, turn into a pattern and melody that constitutes the same (but consonantless) round composed of names.

One of the best things about Molissa Fenley's *Boca Raton* was that there was loud calypso music and an empty space before and after the dancing for a duration about as long as the dancing. Not that I didn't like the duet, Fenley and Elizabeth Streb in striped T-shirts and pants, moving incessantly, dancing to each other, hands on each other's shoulders, shifting hips from one direction to another, feet always flying, breaking apart to leap and run, making circles with the hands. I always think of Fenley as a pattern-dancemaker, but that image is too tidy for her. The dances are repetitive and rhythmic but within that structure things always seem just off center and about to veer away from regularity.

Kenneth King danced *Space City*, a dance with a taped message from King about how dancers are going to have to colonize space because there's no room to dance in New York City. Moving from puns to facts to technological fantasies, King moved in the space in his inimitable swift, energetic, gesture/symbol-making way.

The other choreographers on The Kitchen concert were: Ellen Webb, Dana Reitz, Satoru Shimazaki, Nancy Topf, Deborah Gladstein, Grethe Holby, Charles Dennis, Nancy Lewis, Joan Strasbaugh, and a film by Gabrielle Lansner.

Rhythm for the Eyes, Ears, and Soles

Paul Draper
Harkness House
December 27

Steps in Time: A Tap Dance Festival
Opera House, Brooklyn Academy of Music
December 29 and 30

"Geriatric dancing," Honi Coles called the program at BAM in a mock self-deprecating tone, and everyone in the audience roared with laughter. We knew full well that there's very little dancing today that's livelier, sexier, more smashing or breathtaking than that of the sexa- and septuagenarians gathered on the stage for only two performances in Brooklyn.

The recent interest in tap must partly be connected with the thirst for history that obsesses our generation, makes us search for familial and cultural roots, trace the bloodline of every artwork, and create whole institutions devoted to revivals. But this newfound love for our oldest indigenous dance form comes from more than that. Tap has an appeal of its own: a gestural capacity for a true comedy of the body, testing physical limitations and making satire; a format that unabashedly parades the skills, capabilities, and intelligence of the human body; the abstract rhythmic qualities it shares with music and the ways in which it makes

SOURCE: *SoHo Weekly News*, January 10, 1980

77

those abstractions uncannily visible; its fundamentally mundane origins in the act of walking, which makes its intricacies all the more marvelous.

—⁓—

One of the institutions of the 1970s that is devoted to keeping American popular dancing alive is The American Dance Machine, founded and directed by Lee Theodore. (By popular dancing I mean dancing in popular entertainment, not social dancing.) The American Dance Machine preserves dance numbers from American musicals, and recently the group spent six weeks with guest teacher Paul Draper, the white tapper who "elevated" (according to the tap history books) the art by adding ballet movements and setting his dances to classical music.

Draper, at seventy, has been a solo dancer and choreographer since the 1930s, but as part of his residency at Harkness House he showed his virgin effort at group choreography. Only eight minutes long, *Tap in Three Movements* was danced by ten members of The American Dance Machine. The program had to be padded with something else, so Draper led the dancers through an abbreviated warm-up while keeping up a running patter that glistened with fifty years of show-biz gloss. He also performed his satire on a stumping politician, making promises, kissing babies, and slamming the competition with a few gestures and onomatopoeic footwork.

He warned us, before the group work was performed, that he learned just how difficult group choreography is while making this piece. You can't have people doing unison movements that are also complicated tap steps, he explained, because the appeal of a complex step dissipates if the multiple sounds aren't clear. That is, a step with six taps performed by ten people involves so many sounds that the chances of achieving absolute precision are vastly reduced. Yet in each of the dance's movements—"Steady Beat," with unison movements done in lines crisscrossing the space; "Swing 3," with Fred-and-Ginger partnering; and "Go!" a kind of fireworks conclusion—seemed to me to suffer from their deliberate simplicity and the emphasis on synchrony. The beauty and rightness of Draper's style looks more like jazz with the life drained from it on these younger dancers who don't yet have his panache.

—⁓—

The nearly four-hour event at BAM has been equaled in recent years probably only by the Newport Jazz Festival of 1963, when Marshall Stearns brought together some of the then-forgotten black hoofers, and by the Tap Happening of 1969, both of which did a lot to spawn the current tap revival. My only complaint about this program is that it tried to do too much. The first hour, music by Dizzy Gillespie and scat singing by Joe Carroll, made the program too long and intense instead of stimulating the appetite.

The Copasetics—who have been seen regularly in the New York area over the past few years—were in fine shape, doing old favorites as well as new numbers. They began with *Tapology*, a facetious lecture-demonstration of how tap grows out of walking that ends with their personal variations on the time step. My favorite version this time was Honi Coles's *The Exterminator*, in which the accents are marked by feet flying out to unpredictable spots to stomp out "those little fellows" with vehement finality. The continuing gag with tiny, white-haired Ernest "Brownie" Brown, long the partner of Charles "Cookie" Cook—the whole group takes turns grabbing Brown by the collar and throwing him on the ground, banishing him from the stage until he repeatedly sneaks out to take someone else's bow—is laced with a certain cruelty that, like the antiwoman and antigay humor, gives one occasional pause amid the chuckles.

A surprise guest was Chuck Green, of the famous team Chuck and Chuckles. Looking something like a cubist undertaker, his huge lanky frame in black evening clothes constantly threatening to turn into an assemblage of oblique planes, his large, assertive feet angling out from his ankles, Green tapped with a beautiful liquidity in a gentle reverie, his stream of movement unperturbed even as he bent to pick up a flower that dropped from his lapel. His shoulders shrugged with that same serenity, making a coda to his dance, and then, urged to do his specialty, he took a series of steps across the stage that set him sliding slowly on one large foot while the other hitched up to knee level.

The styles ran a gamut: Green's halcyon grace; Coles's "class act" lightness and elegance that make his feet seem to kiss the ground; Leon Collins's utter cool; the clipped accents of Sandman Sims, whose body always seems near a bursting point with a kind of generalized lusty power; Bubba Gaines's genial lasciviousness; the knockabout antics of Cook and Brown. Partnered by Marion Coles (Honi's wife) and Jane Goldberg (the young white tapper who has produced and danced in a number of concerts), Cook danced a tribute to Dizzy Gillespie and another to Fats Waller. Leon Collins brought in a group of young women from his Boston class to do a group dance that let each take her turn with a contrasting solo style. Amazing how a single genre can generate so many styles, rhythms, compositions. Amazing, too, how a single small gesture or expressive nuance can transform an abstract dance into a highly articulate message, making the body "talk." And then the moment of literalness disappears into the flow of pure motion.

One of the greatest "flash act" teams of all time closed the show. Flash acts combine jazz and tap with improvised acrobatic stunts, creating a mood of "desperate sophistication, a calculated impulse of *carpe diem*" that perfectly expressed its Depression origins, according to Marshall and Jean Stearns in the classic book *Jazz Dance*. The Nicholas Brothers, Fayard and Harold, began dancing as children and opened at the Cotton Club at ages fourteen and eight. We saw them at BAM first in film clips from *Sun Valley Serenade* ("The Chattanooga Choo-Choo") and *Stormy Weather*, doing spectacular stunts like leapfrogging down a giant staircase and ending always in flying leaps that landed in splits. They glided instead of walked, so that you'd think the floors on the movie sets were greased, except that they exercised such perfect control and precision. When the Nicholas Brothers appeared in person, the audience at BAM went wild. Harold, small and grizzled, protested that they'd given up on those splits ("They hurt!"), but he sneaked one in anyway a little later. Epitomes of smoothness and fast repartee, they glided on the BAM stage too, and charmed us all with their buoyancy.

In the dance world, performers are so often thought to have limited careers on stage, retiring young to teach or to find second careers less demanding on bodies that begin to age at thirty. And then there's tap dancing, breaking the rules, teaching us not only about control and precision, but also about resiliency and about the way some performers gain a deeper, mellower flavor as they age.

Awhirl in Every Port

Fancy Free
New York State Theater, New York City
January 31–February 3

Fancy Free, choreographed in 1944, was Jerome Robbins's first ballet. It was made for the Ballet Theatre, of which the twenty-five-year-old Robbins had been a member for four years. The ballet was also a triumph for the young Leonard Bernstein, Robbins's exact contemporary and the composer of the ballet's lauded jazz score. In fact, everything about the ballet was praised: its set by Oliver Smith, the women's costumes by Kermit Love, the way Robbins mixed social dance steps with ballet steps to make an American ballet that, unlike its contemporary Americana ballets, was not a nostalgic period piece but a piece of the present—a scene of three sailors on the town, picking up two women and dancing with and for them in a bar.

The clothing, the dances, and the behavior were based not only on what Robbins saw around him as he "researched" his ballet by watching sailors on shore leave in wartime New York, but also on the sense of camaraderie between himself and the five other young dancers he chose for the roles. They had toured the country together, shared hotel rooms,

SOURCE: *SoHo Weekly News*, February 6, 1980

palled around and danced together in bars as well as on the stage. Edwin Denby called the ballet "a direct, manly piece." And indeed, the dancing embodies an athletic muscularity that had only recently begun to enter the public eye in elite and popular art. In 1933 Ted Shawn had begun his all-male modern dance company partly to prove men could project a "masculine" image on stage. In the early 1940s Gene Kelly brought a powerhouse style to male dancing on the screen.

But last Thursday night what had once been hailed as earthy and vital seemed like this year's nostalgic period piece, thirty-five years old, and aging rather stiffly. Though the piece has been in the repertory of the American Ballet Theatre since its premiere, Robbins staged it for his company, the New York City Ballet, from a film of the original cast and with the help of Terry Orr, a sailor from an early cast. Maybe the cool classicism I always admire in the New York City Ballet's dancing style has frozen a certain kind of expression out of the dancers' bodies. Maybe ballet dancers can never look like anyone but ballet dancers, whether they do a jeté or a lindy. But the ballet just didn't sit right.

Peter Martins as the sailor played originally by Jerome Robbins—the one who stays behind when his buddies run after the first "passer-by," then meets a second woman and dances a sweetly passionate tango kind of dance with her; the one who dances a rhumba with an imaginary partner in the sequence of sailors' variations and then beats his chest in rhythm—could barely crack a smile, let alone loosen his hips to swing them in a Latin mood. Jean-Pierre Frohlich as the first sailor, with the exuberant pyrotechnical variation full of splits and acrobatic turns, performed every stunt with a studied tone.

Only Bart Cook managed to look like he really meant the things he did, the high-jumping heel-clicking in the sailors' opening dance and later, in his more whimsical variation, the leg swings, knee drops, and come-hither hand gestures, right down to the final swoon at Stephanie Saland's feet. Cook is the mild, lovable sailor, the part made originally on John Kriza (to whose memory the ballet is now dedicated) who apparently was like that in life.

After the three sailors fight over the two women—and the two women leave in the course of the fisticuffs that ensue—they cool off, drink another beer, chew another stick of gum, and play another game to see who can throw the wrapper farthest. A third woman walks by and, though they remind each other about the fight they just had, as the curtain lowers all three run out after her.

The final skidding run after the woman somehow reminded me of the Roadrunner, and the whole ballet suddenly seemed like a cartoon. It's stylized to the point where the gestures are exaggerated and stereotypical, the timing too conscious. The story is perhaps overly sentimental for us now—how many women stand around reading newspapers under streetlamps outside bars?—and that glaring innocence adds to the flat, childlike mood.

Saturday afternoon's cast, with Joseph Duell, Christopher Fleming, and Douglas Hay as the sailors, and Delia Peters, Judith Fugate, and Maria Calegari as the passers-by, was more pleasant in certain ways. These younger dancers looked like they were actually having fun as well as dancing steps, and there was something infectious about their smiles. Duell grinned with joyous lust as he swung his ass at us in the third sailor's variation, and it seemed to me all the dancers added small details of characterization that made everything more naturalistic. Fugate looked askance at Duell's arm as it crossed her chest during their pas de deux. All five played musical chairs at the table with bright vigor.

When I saw the first cast again on Sunday, I felt better about it. Maybe *Fancy* is growing on me. But I also think it's growing on its dancers. Bart Cook even stole a kiss from Saland and Peter Martins smiled twice.

Under Glass

Bill T. Jones and Arnie Zane
Blauvelt Mountain
American Theater Laboratory
February 5–26

Everything about *Blauvelt Mountain* is finely crafted and compelling. It's almost too beautiful, too refined. I watched it mesmerized and now I can't remember very much about it, except the crystalline perfection that gives its athleticism and roughhouse moments a rarified quality, like dried flowers.

In Act I, "A Fiction," Bill T. Jones and Arnie Zane are dressed in black jumpsuits. There's a half-built wall of cinder blocks in the back of the wide, shallow performing space, and a pale blue light suffuses the back wall, décor designed by William Katz.

The air is suffused, too, with sound. The two men speak quietly to each other or murmur individually, and there are unobtrusive electronic noises controlled on the spot by composer Helen Thorington.

The two dancers repeat over and over again certain movement sequences: Jones, whose physical beauty and precise coordination draw you (or me, anyway) to watch him more often than Zane, sits on a small cube and makes intricate hand gestures; Zane, a small wiry man, runs

SOURCE: *SoHo Weekly News*, February 20, 1980

84

around and around in circles, embroidered with small leaps. Both lift, hold, support, balance, jump onto each other. All these activities are simultaneously rough and smooth, violent and affectionate, athletic and graceful. They build up, with the repetition, into a rhythmic fabric that gives the disparate activities a smooth and sensible shape, which soon becomes familiar. This ironically unwrinkled surface, full of rugged actions, gets broken from time to time as Jones and Zane stop to consult quietly about how the preceding round felt. The reflexive commentary just avoids coyness by taking place at the volume level so low it is usually inaudible. A sporadic verbal game of free-association is less interesting, though more audible.

Act II, "An Interview," contrasts in every way with the first act. Where the costumes were black, they are now white. The back wall too is a brilliant white. The electronic music is gone; instead, the soundtrack comes from a portable tape recorder Jones sets on the cinder block wall. His voice asks questions like: Where will we go? What will it look like there? Who will be the first person we meet? And later Zane's voice is heard, giving a whole series of answers we match in our minds to the questions. Finally, after a long silence, the two monologues are intercut to fit together as a single "interview."

And the movements have changed from a rolling fabric full of wild details and covering all the space, to two singular actions. Zane, wearing workman's gloves, deconstructs the wall and rebuilds it perpendicular to its original position. Jones dances up and down a corridor parallel to the new wall but wider than and including it. Sometimes he has to jump over the wall that's under construction. When the wall's completed, he dances forward and back along a single line, launching into a paroxysm of motion, arms and legs sputtering in every direction, while delivering a half-melancholy, half-comic, fantastical monologue about his own death.

It's that final, agitated death jig that stays with me now, days later, even though I remember feeling beguiled by all the actions in "A Fiction." I wonder what would happen if this collaboration let itself get messier.

Trisha Brown and Fujiko Nakaya Play Misty

Trisha Brown's dances always seem to me like docks along different channels of investigation. The dancing and the process of choreographing go on. The performances fix the flow, long enough to let the world catch a glimpse.

Brown's earliest dances were based on structured improvisation. Later she became intrigued with the distortion of movement over time or distance, as in *Roof Piece* (1971), in which a group of dancers transmitted movement over a twelve-block area in SoHo and Tribeca. In the late 1960s and early 1970s many of her dances clustered around the use of equipment to explore the mechanics of ordinary movements, like walking or dressing, in extraordinary relationships to gravity. In *Man Walking Down the Side of a Building* (1969) she created the illusion of a natural walk done perpendicular to the earth. In *Rummage Sale and the Floor of the Forest* (1971) dancers dressed and undressed their way through a grid of clothing suspended above the heads of spectators who also found themselves involved in a full-scale rummage sale. Beginning in 1971

SOURCE: *Village Voice*, June 16, 1980

Brown made dances of simplex body gestures glued together by logical systems like mathematical accumulation and palindromes. Recently her dancing has mixed functional movement with imagery, while her choreographic structures have explored the boundaries between order and disorder, as in *Line Up* (1977).

Brown's latest docking point is *Opal Loop / Cloud Installation #72053 City*, a collaboration with Japanese cloud sculptor Fujiko Nakaya, performed in a raw SoHo loft this week (through Saturday, with *Locus* and *Decoy*). The second part of the title refers to the fog Nakaya has built, the first to the dance Brown has constructed with members of her company—Lisa Kraus, Eva Karczag, Stephen Petronio, and Vicky Shick.

Opal Loop takes place at the intersection of several of Brown's enduring fascinations. The elusive movements look like the kinds of shrugs, flings, swings, and jerks that are reflex actions rather than planned, repeatable dance phrases. There is also a liquid look to the dancing that's not just metaphoric, but full of water images, which have coursed through other Brown dances from *Skunk Cabbage, Salt Grass, and Waders* (1967), in which being wet was part of her costume, to *Water Motor* (1978), a kind of flash flood solo. When I watched Brown's company rehearse part of *Opal Loop*, words like squirt, slither, spurt, dissolve, cascade came to me. The four dancers begin at the back of the space, stationed at even intervals, then work their way forward, paths crossing and clumping, their bodies rippling with small, sudden movements that seem like the spray off a steady wave. They move in and out of canon, in and out of sudden clear unison.

For some time now, Brown has been splicing different dances together—she does a tour de force these days called *Accumulation (1971) with Talking (1973) plus Water Motor (1978)* in which she tells three or four stories while interrupting one dance with another. At one point in *Opal Loop* the dancers insert a variation on *Message to Steve*, a dance Brown made in 1979 by reconstituting a short segment of Steve Paxton's improvisation. Paxton and Brown danced in each other's works in the early 1960s, and from 1970 to 1976 were members of the improvisatory group Grand Union.

"Steve said he didn't remember what he did when he improvised," Brown explains. "Around the time he told me this, I was working at trying to bring instinctual movement, not improvised, into my movement vocabulary. I got a videotape of one of Steve's performances, took a three-minute section, and had Lisa Kraus learn it. She performed it on a program in Dartington, England, in which Steve also danced." Originally a solo, *Message to Steve* has become a movement score that Brown reworks with four dancers in *Opal Loop*.

Brown's preoccupation with the use of space also shows up in the new dance. "I started with the idea of the endless phrase that doesn't have to be corrected toward the center of the space. All dances have to stay on a stage. If you do something that moves to the right, eventually you have to move to the left. I wanted to make a phrase that could go where it wanted without constraints, in a large open space. But we work in a stage space. So I decided that an endless phrase would happen at the edges. I connected up the end of the phrase with its beginning—in my mind—and made a movement loop.

"Now my company and I are building the dance very slowly and carefully, basing the phrasing on crossings of the space, as well as diagonals and circles, which let us have access to the entire space. We make very small loops—replays and previews of a limited amount of movement material—so that what you see is a boiling out of a phrase by four people."

Brown, Kraus, Karczag, and Petronio have been working closely with video recordings in order to copy precisely "those little coagulations, so fleeting they would be impossible otherwise to repeat exactly as they were arrived at." The effect is a constant flow of activity with an ever-changing shape.

Last year Brown collaborated with Robert Rauschenberg on *Glacial Decoy*, a new direction for a choreographer who for nearly twenty years has been presenting dances in a neutral context, without theatrical trappings. "The dancing has had its chance, and now it seems possible again to take on these other elements," Brown says. The photographic images that glide along a series of screens and the white, translucent, fluted dresses that swirl around the dancers' bodies will not, however, be used in this week's performance. The space, one hundred feet deep and only twenty-one feet wide, can't house the massive set. The dance in its stripped down version is called *Decoy*.

In *Opal Loop/Cloud Installation #72053 City*, Brown wanted to achieve "a tactile involvement with the décor that would not interfere with what we do. The set couldn't be closer to the dancers than this."

The space at 55 Crosby Street, a ground level loft with a concrete floor, once housed a direct current generator that supplied energy to SoHo factories. Now it's serving as a workplace in which Brown and Nakaya try to solve practical problems—like controlling the density of the fog and the wetness of the floor. The dance will eventually be performed in a theater; this series of performances is a process of refining the fog system, until now always used outdoors, as well as finding out how to dance in it.

Brown and Nakaya have known each other since the early 1960s, when the sculptor saw Trisha Brown dance at Judson Church concerts. "I was so impressed by her control of the body," Nakaya remembers. In 1964 when the Merce Cunningham Dance Company toured Japan, Nakaya got to know company members who were also active in Judson Dance Theater, like Deborah Hay, and Robert Rauschenberg, who did Cunningham's lights, décor, and costumes. At that time she was painting clouds and "rotting processes, using the colors of rotting—earth colors." She was also physically decomposing the paintings by removing layers of paint from the canvas. Not long after that, Nakaya became interested in actually creating clouds, not just representing them, and she experimented with dry ice and hotplates.

In 1970 through Billy Kluver, Julie Martin, and Experiments in Art and Technology (E.A.T.), Nakaya built a large-scale cloud installation at the Pepsi-Cola pavilion at Expo '70 in Osaka. She looked for a system to create pure water fog and finally worked with Tom Mee, a California engineer who had made chemical fog machines, on the apparatus she has used for ten years. Units of different sizes are arranged to supply the layers of vapor that accumulate to form clouds. The three units in *Opal Loop/Cloud Installation #72053 City* are the smallest she has used so far. This project is Nakaya's first collaboration with another artist, although plans are in the works to create a fog environment for a David Tudor concert on a Swedish island. In 1972 Nakaya began to record her ephemeral constructions, and then started to use the video camera to capture other forms of water—like rivers and waterfalls. She also uses video for community and feminist organizing in Japan.

She was pleased when Brown suggested they work together, Nakaya told me, because "Trisha's from Aberdeen, she's used to the cloud banks, and she feels very close to fog. We began work together last May when I was in the U.S. We met to discuss our ideas of fog."

"Water is omnipresent in the atmosphere and artificial fog simply emphasizes one phase of water. Anywhere you suddenly lower temperature fog can be formed. I'm creating a phenomenon by pushing nature just a bit further. I'm not trying to make a form but to reveal a structure."

Last week while working on the installation in the Crosby Street loft with Brown and Judith Shea (whose costumes also interact with the vapor), Nakaya commuted between New York and Washington, D.C. There she participated in the Eleventh International Sculpture Conference constructing a cloud sculpture in the Botanical Gardens. "They gave me the windiest spot in the city," she says, laughing, "so I had to make an environment about taming the wind. The nice thing about fog is that breezes go right through it. But wind can be a problem." (Nakaya dug a crater out of which fog billowed, like an erupting volcano.)

"Wind can also be such a problem in cities, where energy gets built up between buildings. The shapes we use in cities are completely arbitrary if you look at them in terms of wind, if we started with an idea of wind instead of gravity. But we didn't.

"You know," she muses, "fog has a very democratic status. It's constantly moving, and when two droplets collide they each go off a little, making room for each other. It makes the world a little bigger—for everyone to live in.

"For me, fog is all about revealing the structures of nature, the interrelationships of elements like temperature, wind, humidity, topography, and various obstacles. Even one tree can make a difference. Fog makes visible things invisible and invisible things, like wind, apparent. It gives people a different experience of a particular environment. And it seems to me that Trisha's dances are about revealing structures too—of space, of the dance."

"Men Together" and Bloolips

The persistent myth about the male dancer in Western culture is that he is gay. Sometimes the "myth" is true and sometimes it isn't. Can you tell a person's sexuality by the way he/she moves? The standard stereotype ignores the fact that some of the strongest, most muscular presences on the dance stage, in this century at least, have been men the public knew and knows are gay. And what about those still in the closet?

Ballet and modern dance have traditionally expressed human relationships in terms of heterosexuality. Although men have danced with men and women with women, not until recently has that partnering become explicitly erotic. Homoeroticism is still as shocking on stage as nudity was a generation ago. On the dance stage, to break that taboo is even more difficult than in film or drama. To talk about gayness is one thing; to express it bodily is quite another, because it is precisely at the overt physicality of gay culture that the straight world purses its lips.

—m—

SOURCE: *Dance Magazine*, March 1981

"Men Together," a festival of gay performance organized by Tim Miller (November 14–16 at P.S. 122), explored a number of aspects of male relationships, bringing together diverse artists, not all of whom ordinarily deal with gay content in their work. For me, the festival was striking in several ways. First, the artists were primarily young men of the post-Stonewall generation. Unlike past generations of gay men in America, they confront mainstream culture with a sense of pride and they are aware of their shared culture and history. Still, the verbal and nonverbal signals a covert gay community developed out of necessity are no less vital for the current generation just because the culture has emerged from underground. Second, the styles and means of expression at the festival varied widely, even though all six items in the festival began with the notion of performance art as an arena stripped of theatrical conventions. Third, a sympathetic, often enthusiastic audience gave the event a sense of community involvement and validation of both content and intent.

John Bernd and Tim Miller collaborated on a piece called *We Had Tea. We Ate Cashew Chicken.* Bernd is a dancer who has been performing solos mixing dance movements, texts, and objects; Miller doesn't call himself a dancer, but he had just finished several months of weekly performances involving meditations on history, reading poetry, cooking, amateur arson, and some movement. Both men manufacture meaning obliquely, through correspondences and juxtapositions. Bernd and Miller met at one of the latter's Monday evening performances and decided to make a dance together, which they originally titled *Post-Modern Faggot.* At one point during *We Had Tea,* Miller (who is fond of writing on things with spray paint) wrote "F-A-G" in big letters across his chest. "I prefer the word 'faggot,'" he confided to the audience, "but it doesn't fit." Bernd obligingly took the can of paint and wrote the remaining three letters on Miller's back. The mixture of roughness and attentiveness matched the tone of Miller's erotic poetry, which Bernd read later.

We Had Tea opened with the two men running in large circles in the vast gym of P.S. 122. Their black overcoats and pants gave them both an anonymous and an antique look. At times jogging together, at times overtaking one another, they set up an uneven rhythm of unity, leading, following, and gentle competition. They traded coats while running: gestures of sharing and aid. Bernd danced solo while Miller read from Proust about the beginnings of a friendship. Miller took his turn while Bernd read writings by Miller. Finally, the two again jogged together, this time along a diagonal, circling arms, advancing and retreating, and talking about their own relationship in parallel, echoing phrases.

The two have similar movement styles: Both hold their torsos straight, gesturing abstractly with the arms while stepping in easy rhythms. But Bernd has a chunky, solid quality, while Miller bounces and skitters, always veering off balance. The two made pleasing formal contrasts. "We had tea." "We had tea." "We ate cashew chicken." "Then we came here and did this dance." The collaboration, we came to understand, not only resulted in a product—the dance—but was also a process of two people discovering things about each other, becoming friends, perhaps also lovers. Threaded with ambiguities, the gentle dance transcended the personal.

(More) Short Lessons in Socially Restricted Sign Language, by Bruce Hlibok and Norman Frisch, was a parody of an academic lecture on "dirty words" in sign language that was witty, instructive, and quite moving. A tape-recorded, stuffy, male professorial voice explained how limited the deaf person's acquisition of sexual knowledge can be—both because we learn about sex through various oral/aural communicative channels as well as sight and touch, and also because so many deaf children are raised in institutions, where sexual expression is suppressed. Meanwhile, Tavoria Rae Kellam, dressed in a man's suit, gave a simultaneous translation of the lecture in sign language. She gestured voluptuously as the voice pedantically described (with slide illustrations) the signs for sexual organs, acts, and positions. A slight change in facial expression, for instance, can transform the sign for "testicles" into "wellhung." Small shifts of finger articulation make the difference between "breast," "nipple," "erect nipple." In fact, an entire range of sexual expression, including gay and lesbian slang, can be communicated through signing.

During the lecture, Hlibok, who is deaf, mimed a personal odyssey of sexual exploration, reading a newspaper, cutting out paper hearts, watching a film of men having intercourse. When the lecture was over, Hlibok, Kellam, and Tom Schoenherr signed a taped conversation between a married couple and their marriage counselor/physician. In this section, deadpan humor arose from two sources: the act of translation, which made the descriptions of mutual excitation purely clinical; and the sexual role reversal, in which Kellam played the male doctor while the naïve, bright-eyed couple was played by the two men. At the beginning and end of *(More) Short Lessons,* Hlibok performed a gestural dance to the song "Every Little Movement Has a Meaning All Its Own," a piece he has danced before with Remy Charlip. As Schoenherr sang the words, Hlibok signed their meanings. But the second time around, his interpretation was spiced with the facial expressions and the full, lusty gestures we had learned during the performance. Suddenly it seemed that perhaps sign language need not be restrictive. And it had become clear that much sexual meaning is produced in the paralinguistic "grease" that gives nuance to any language.

The gay men's movement, like the women's movement of the 1960s and 1970s, has stressed a connection between the personal and the political. This idea was expressed in *Three Short Pieces in Progress* by the Philadelphia men's dance collective Two Men Dancing in two ways. One was that the very act of expressing one's sexual feelings in public—making oneself vulnerable and stating what is usually unsaid—is a political act of consciousness-raising. The second, related notion was that to reveal the process of a work of art—to show a work in progress or to talk about the making of the piece—is political in that it demystifies art, reducing the gap between artist and audience and thus erasing false authority.

Two Men Dancing now has three members—Michael Biello, Daniel Martin, and Ishmael Houston-Jones. They were joined here by guest performers Warren Muller, Robin Epstein, and Charles Cohen. Biello's *Masked Mass* was a priapic ceremony that, for my taste, perpetuated negative, perverse stereotypes without adding any new insights. Martin's *Scenes from a Future Musical* was a sketch that suffered not so much from incompleteness as from poverty of conception. Can a banal soap opera about an adolescent leaving home, even when performed tongue-in-cheek, be salvaged by the subversive plot twist that makes him grow up gay?

Houston-Jones's *Part Three—Friction, Friction* was more successful as a work-in-progress, partly because of the choreographer's own electrifying stage presence, which makes even a fragment compelling, and partly because the gestures in the dance were so graphic their shock value was immense, ultimately transcending the confessional tone of the piece and adding a note of humor. Explaining that he usually works improvisationally, Houston-Jones announced that he would tonight teach Biello and Martin a set movement combination. He demonstrated three basic, mimetic gestures, identifying each one by the slang words for fellatio and active and passive intercourse. The dancers ran through the combination until it reached a frenzied pace, appropriately enough to Martha and the Vandellas singing "Heat Wave." Later, Houston-Jones spoke about his adolescence while Biello and Martin kissed and caressed for real. For the audience, transformed into voyeurs, this action was a shock—but transgression of the limits of sexual expression onstage is certainly not restricted to gay art. Carolee Schneemann's *Meat Joy* of 1964 raised the same issues, and so, in fact, did Marius Petipa's smacks on the cheek of a Spanish ballerina in the middle of the nineteenth century.

The other three items in the festival were primarily text-oriented. Jeff McMahon's *Smile at Knife*, a chilling stream-of-consciousness monologue about fear, crisis, and danger, was a kind of dance of stillness. Riveted in his chair, face impassive except for blazing eyes and the moving mouth that rendered a multiplicity of urgent voices, McMahon's "active text" sliced like a blade, grated like a shriek. Its absence of movement—its utter rigidity—made this performance as eloquent physically as it was verbally.

The political meanings in "Men Together" were general and implicit: The freedom of expression of gay feelings—and of feelings in general—was the festival's central, cumulative, and often very touching theme. A range of movement styles, from gentle and tender to boldly lascivious, proclaimed a sense of liberation from stereotypes both of effeminacy and machismo.

—m—

Lust in Space, a drag show by the British group Bloolips (Theater for the New City, November 8–23; Orpheum Theatre, November 28–December 14), was political in another sense. Using androgyny as a vantage point totally outside straight society (straight in both senses—as opposed to hip *and* gay), these men take on the personae of female caricatures. Wearing gaudy costumes made of junk, sporting make-up and hairdos so stylized a Kabuki actor would do a double-take, the Bloolips are not so much imitations of women as creatures betwixt and between sexual roles, free from social rules. Even their names are outrageous: Lavinia Co-op, Precious Pearl, Dizzy Danny, Bossy Bette Bourne, Naughty Nicky, and Gretel Feather. Clowns and tricksters, they dance outside social structure, commenting on and criticizing not only sexual roles and stereotypes, but also the arms race, American electoral politics, political repression, rampant consumerism, and an entire "parade of Western culture."

A plot of sorts is a loose skeleton on which to hang song and dance numbers that derive as much from the humor of British music hall traditions (including that of the heterosexual drag performer) as from the tradition of gay camp and the politics of gay liberation. The Bloolips group runs a laundromat that looks like a set for a science-fiction film. The Queen of England sends them to perform on the moon hoping to outdo the Russians. While getting ready for the big night, the Bloolips run into an evil computer (at the local Lunar disco bingo) that turns people's minds to malleable mush. Luckily, they finally break its power.

Bloolips, a group of consummate performers, blends popular culture and reflexive meditations on performance to create a piece of show business that is flashy, entertaining, funny, and at the same time wryly agitprop. They subvert the banality of hit songs by setting lyrics that really mean something to familiar tunes. Some of the lines are old hat; still, one can admire the proficiency of Bloolips' turn of phrase, sense of timing, or tap dancing rhythm along with its political wallop. In fact, all that entertaining, singing, and dancing, far from sugarcoating the message, speeds it along. And the dancing—not just tap, but bits of ballet aesthetic dancing, cancan, girlie revue, Weimar cabaret, and floating in space—is integral to the production.

Presenting "Folk Dances from the Migraine," several Bloolips in peasant skirts and babushkas galumph, brandishing scarves and singing about Soviet censorship. They discuss the possibility of performing *Swan Lake* on the moon (Aleksandr Godunov has sent them a request written on a gargantuan ballet slipper, to stand in for him), but they decide that audiences would never stand for a plot based on ornithophilia. Still, they get away with a fragment of the four cygnets. They dress up as cheeses to disguise themselves as part of the moon's landscape. And, if they nearly blow up the world a few times, in the end we all survive—at least for one more show. Bloolips' anarchic black humor is a welcome anodyne in these dark times.

"Men Together" and Bloolips' *Lust in Space* pointed toward two tendencies in recent gay art. One is the acknowledgment that the body is both subject and purveyor of a social message. The other is a parodic thrust, from the vantage point of a subculture outside the mainstream, aimed not only at sexual mores but also at the world at large.

Paul Taylor
Dance Company

I met someone at an intermission during the Paul Taylor season at City Center (April 14–May 3) who told me how excited she was by the concert. "It's the first time I've seen avant-garde dance," she confessed. The same night, a friend complained, "Why doesn't he just go ahead and make ballets?" To some, Taylor is the most accessible of the (older) avant-garde; to others, he long ago entered the mainstream of modern dance. To still others, Taylor is a fine craftsman as well as a showman who understands not only how to make a legible dance, but also how to put together a concert with tastefulness and variety.

Taylor caters to every dance constituency. While this versatility might be a virtue for a politician, it leaves a curious vacuum at the core of a choreographer's style. It's not that Taylor has no movement style; you can look at a phrase and know that he made it. But the movements and postures that are distinctively Taylor's form a limited, neutral vocabulary. The expressive qualities in a particular dance come not so much from the dancing itself as from the context the movement finds itself

SOURCE: *Dance Magazine*, August 1981

in: the lighting, the costumes, the props, and above all, the music. Of course, every dance uses such elements to create its meaning. But with Taylor's work you often feel that these are the strongest and most reliable means of expression. While it's true that part of the power and complexity of dance comes from the multiple meaning potential of gesture and movement, in Taylor's case this kind of ambiguity causes problems. It doesn't make the dances hard to watch; on the contrary, they're highly accessible precisely because the spectator doesn't need to "read" meaning in the movement. The dancing is a bland, homogeneous skeleton fleshed out with the expressive qualities the nondance elements provide. One might argue that classical ballet also uses a neutral, limited vocabulary to mean a range of different things. But even the most musical of choreographers find ways to use movement distinctively, matching strong choreographic statements to the music's substance.

Taylor's *Polaris* (1976), revived this season, more or less acknowledges these points. Taylor himself presents the dance as a small exercise in dance theory: If you change the dancers, the lighting, and the music, but you keep the steps the same, do you get two different dances, or two instances of the same dance? The glacial quality of the dance is already given by its title. Five dancers dressed in pastel patterned leotards (originally, they wore bathing suits) enter to take their places inside a coolly gleaming chromium frame. Illuminated by pale lighting and motivated by fairly uninflected music, the solos and group interactions that occur as the dancers emerge from their confinement take on a frosty sheen. In the second half, the lighting is more dramatic, the music more suspenseful (reminiscent of a Bernard Hermann movie score), and the dancing seems to take on a more forceful attack. The dance heats up, so to speak. Is it an optical illusion, or do all the theatrical cues for drama and urgency accompany an accelerating energy powering the movement?

Public Domain (1968), another revival this season, is like an exercise in making dances to the widest variety of musical examples. Here Taylor recycles his own material, bits from Graham, and various other dance images so familiar they seem to exist in the public domain. To a collage score (by John Herbert McDowell) of snippets of music and dialogue, Taylor whips up one choreographic fragment after another, like a short-order cook. *Public Domain* is a comic dance, but its humor comes not from the dancing itself—which tends to "mickey-mouse" the music—as from the abruptness with which the collage shifts from one musical style (with its dance accompaniment) to another. Dressed in bright leotards, the dancers move from gothic poses (accompanied by a Gregorian chant) to cheerleader strutting (accompanied by Sousa) to various folk dance motifs to Graham's *Primitive Mysteries*. Three men repeat the same solo—an essay in tangling the body—to two different pieces of music and a monologue. From time to time, small balls roll across the stage and finally, like a punch line, a woman rolls across the stage—like a ball. Lila York lies on the floor throughout most of the dance; at one point she stands up to gesture weakly with a white flag to a German cabaret song. The importance of the music is especially evident in one section in which a group of women dance together, then all but one leave the stage. She is left dancing alone. The fact that the music has ended, leaving her dancing in silence, underscores not only the fact that she is "out of step" with the others, but also that she is oblivious to being alone on stage. In general, the lurching of the music from theme to theme makes the dancers seem to have little control over their material, and loss of control is always fair game for comedy. The satire on Graham is genuinely funny. But there are also moments in *Public Domain* when the literal-mindedness of the correspondence between music and movement makes Taylor appear to satirize himself.

The most interesting piece in Taylor's current repertory is the oldest, *Three Epitaphs* (1956), in which everything seems raw, original, almost unthinkable. The configurations of the body are so peculiar that when Taylor uses them again in *Dust* it seems a violation. Five dancers (Linda Kent, Christopher Gillis, Susan McGuire, Cathy McCann, and Daniel Ezralow) shamble across the stage in various groupings, to ancient, ponderous, rusty-sounding blues. Dressed in black costumes (by Robert Rauschenberg) that cover their entire bodies, so that they look somewhat like five lumps of lead, with bits of mirrors on their heads and palms, the dancers take on a musty greenish glow under Jennifer Tipton's lighting. Every part of the body is set at an oblique angle to its neighbor, until hands, arms, head, neck, chest, pelvis, thighs, and feet all seem nothing more than a series of slipping planes, collapsing toward a single center. These faceless creatures of assorted sizes rotate their arms madly like motors revving up; they lumber about in what for humans would be a frisky manner; they bump into one another; one of them admires himself in a mirrored hand. A large creature picks up a smaller creature with the greatest effort, then drops her with a thud. A climax occurs when the brutes essay a low leaden leap, their heads and chests hunching downwards. Part of the delight of *Three Epitaphs* is its conciseness. Just as the misshapen, slouching bodies, their strange antics, the baleful music, and the moldy lighting fuse into a single image, the dance is over. But part of its delight must also lie in its utter recalcitrance to everything dance has traditionally meant.

Taylor has a special flair for imagery—haunting tableaux that stay with you long after the choreography has faded from memory. *From Sea to Shining Sea* (1965), another revival this season, is a string of such tableaux. Performed to another whimsical score by McDowell that quotes various patriotic songs, the dance is a conflation of American myths and legends, treated with an ironic flippancy that turns the American dream into a comic nightmare, a performance gone awry. Weary performers in bathrobes stumble onto a raggedy red-white-and-blue set, then gradually don costumes to form living pictures: the Statue of Liberty, the Pilgrims landing at Plymouth Rock, Washington crossing the Delaware. But these proud emblems of Americana are undermined comically and with heightening ferocity. Mighty Mouse strangles a flapper; the violent underbelly of American history protrudes prophetically in this dance made on the brink of Vietnam, student upheaval, and a decade of "law and order." With bold strokes, Taylor portrays America's history and destiny, finally, as a circus. In the last section of the dance, the dancers become circus performers who can't get their acts together. We Americans are seen as vacillating between boredom on the one hand, and murder and strife on the other.

Nightshade (1979), to brooding music by Scriabin, is a murkier brew of American types: pilgrims or pioneers, a woman in a filmy black peignoir, a dusky man in black tails and a fright wig, a figure who might be an American Indian shaman. It is a dance of quietly sporadic violence, shocking in some vague and indefinable way. The night I saw it, part of the audience laughed heartily at what I took to be a rather grim rape scene. Perhaps they saw something in the dance that I missed. But I think their laughter stemmed from that ambiguity of Taylor's work; primed to laugh at certain kinds of movements, the spectators did not shift gears with the deepening dramatic context.

In *Dust* (1977), as in his earlier *Churchyard* (1969), Taylor uses the popular image of a medieval dance of death to structure the work. With its sinister black rope hanging on one side of the stage, its snaking line of flagellants, its spasms of rapid footwork that make you think of exotic plagues like St. Vitus's dance and ergotism, *Dust* is in some ways a powerful piece. It is full of terror and pathos; over and over, figures drop into black cloths other dancers hold open for them. Susan McGuire dances an extraordinary solo, twisting about an arm that is held to her side, maimed. The shiny nude leotards, with their bright mandalas (by Gene Moore), seem like diseased skin blistered with sores. There is even a grisly strand of humor threading through the piece. But in the end I find *Dust*'s power cheap. All its imagery is based on sets of cultural clichés.

Runes (1975) suffers from the same ailment. It is neither a recreation of an authentic ritual nor an imaginative reworking of ritual themes, as in, for instance, Humphrey's *The Shakers*, Nijinska's *Les Noces*, or Monk's *Education of the Girlchild*. Where these choreographers make the vitality and specificity of ritual action clear, matching expressive movement to social function, Taylor merely presents the trappings of mysticism, a set of commonplaces about the magic. Shorn of time, place, or culture, the rites in *Rune* lose their meaning. An eerie moon and a darkened stage; a person lying at the center of the group who is replaced by another, then another; strange couplings; a flattened, archaic, Nijinskyesque walk— all are elements that trigger predictable associations. But this is nothing more than a fanciful depiction of ritual, a contrived and obscure set of action divorced from symbolic import.

Even the more abstract pieces seem like cartoons or caricatures of something else. *Aureole* (1962) is a series of throwaway allusions to ballet; *Airs* (1978) and *Arden Court* (given its premiere this season) refer to court dances. The sideways movement that recurs throughout *Aureole* is a hyperbolic instance of turnout, one of ballet's most fundamental principles. The bouncy jumps stretch the body past ballet's noble elongation into a strictly vertical line. The embraces in the adagio fourth movement are nothing like the partnering of classical ballet, although they're supposed to mean the same thing. While the rapid footwork recalls the rhythms of ballet steps, the bare feet of the dancers aren't pointed and stretched according to the ballet aesthetic. The men jump with the proud virtuosity of ballet danseurs, but their legs are intricately and awkwardly snarled.

The abstract pieces pose a special problem. They're not presented as satiric or particularly comic dances. We know from the music and other theatrical elements that we are meant to take them seriously. Yet everything about Taylor's work—including the potency of the images, of the music, lighting, costumes, etc.—places him as a choreographer in an expressive rather than abstract ballpark. Unlike a Balanchine or a Cunningham, he doesn't connect movements in a particularly perspicuous manner. When his dances work, it is on the level of meaning rather than formal movement inventions. This makes the action in a piece like *Aureole* or *Esplanade* (1975) seem bunched into discontinuous moments, clusters of images that often dangle, with no place to go.

Taylor's newest dance, *Arden Court,* to music by the English Baroque composer William Boyce, is an expansion on the court dance theme of Taylor's *Airs* to Handel. But again, Taylor's exercises in baroque style are neither replicas of some antique original nor are they meditations on form. They depend on stereotypes and expectations already held by the viewer, which start to resonate even before the dance begins, as chords are struck by the title, then the décor, costumes, and other expressive elements. At times it seems that the task of the spectator is to crack the code. But the code is never all that complex. In the Forest of Arden, of course, the characters in Shakespeare's *As You Like It* found a free terrain in which to play and love, stripped of the constraints of their social identities. Playing and loving are the double themes in *Arden Court* as well. But a court is a condensed area, smaller than a forest. Nature has been distilled here to a single immense rose, painted on the backdrop. And the center of the dance has an almost simple-minded choreographic structure: Nearly every configuration, though densely embroidered, replicates the layered, wrapped circularity of that rose. Like a courtyard, the dance has its borders; before and after the circular motifs, the dancers trace straight diagonal lines through space. Thus Taylor also begins a series of verbal puns on the word court. The first meaning is of a court as a physical, formally arranged, and enclosed space. As the five men (Elie Chaib, Robert Kahn, Kenneth Tosti, Daniel Ezralow, and David Parsons) enter this space, they process along the diagonal in a stately way, dressed in blue and magenta patterned tights, with bare chests; they jump, folding legs into knots underneath them; they run with arms outstretched overhead in alternating opposition to their legs. The second sense of court—as a verb—is played out next in a series of pas de deux, in which the men and the women take turns wooing one another, always circling close, suggesting not only the rose petals, but also an embrace extended in space. Two men seem like court buffoons as they perform a set of broad, elastic capers. They lead all the couples in a procession, and in the next section—with the couples circling a central couple, and the men showing off for the women—we see, always informed by the circling and enfolding theme, a society of noble couples going through their rituals of courtly love. In this society, as in the antique Europe Taylor refers to in the dance, power and mobility are reserved to the men. After they spin one of the women in helpless, nearly tortuous somersaults, the men carry all of the women offstage. Then they return to indulge in their most virtuosic aerial hijinks, leaping and turning as the women run demurely across the stage and the curtain falls.

Taylor's dancers performed *Arden Court* with the same bright energy and aplomb they invested in the rest of the season's repertory. What a pity, I thought after *Arden Court*'s empty fireworks, for so much sound and fury to have nowhere to go.

10¢ a Dance
The Funds Over

In the late 1950s the Ford Foundation began a robust program of arts granting that stimulated the formation of the National Endowment for the Arts (NEA) in 1965. Through the 1960s and 1970s, this blend of corporate and government support fueled a veritable dance boom in America, centered in the vibrant hub of New York City. However, in the early 1980s, a combination of economic recession and fiscal policy slashed arts funding, restructuring many aspects of the dance community in the process. In this article Banes documents how these cuts specifically affected dance, many reverberations of which are still felt in the field today.

All the arts have taken a beating from the recession, inflation, and Reaganism, but dance's black and blue marks feel especially cruel—the result of fate's ironies. Perhaps no other art has grown so prodigiously in recent memory. Americans have always danced, and since the beginning of the twentieth century, Americans have led the vanguard of

SOURCE: *Village Voice*, April 24, 1983

dancing, but not until it won solid financial backing could a truly professional dance world with a stable infrastructure emerge here. In the 1960s and 1970s, largely through the fiscal efforts of the Ford Foundation and the NEA, an American dance tradition—replete with companies, presenters, individual choreographers, well-trained dancers, teachers, schools, and all the other jobs and institutions associated with the field— was established. The economic push, combined with the post-World War II shift of the center of the art world from Europe to the United States, fixed New York as the dance capital of the world.

In some ways, the demands of the funding agencies have shaped the inner-workings of the dance world. Cynics say that companies have been formed, boards appointed, development directors hired, tours arranged, even styles built to satisfy the various panels. An artificial network of bureaucracy has been the legacy of the dance boom, they claim. Seen from another perspective, the funding agencies have stimulated and administratively strengthened a field notoriously weak in organization and short on dollars. Most importantly, those agencies have built and educated audiences that in turn created a need for more, bigger, and better dance companies, more dance teachers, more dance on television, more dance books, more service organizations, and on and on. Created—in the past tense. The irony is that once the demand and supplies were in place, the bottom fell out of the market.

Although there are various sources of funding for dancers and dance companies, and although the government grants account for only a small part of any dance organization's budget, in thinking about funding the NEA and the New York State Council on the Arts (NYSCA) spring immediately to mind. The Dance Program at the NEA suffered its first cut in fiscal year 1981—although the overall cuts in the NEA budget turned out to be less than had been threatened. In order to cope with the cuts, the dance panel (a group of experts culled from the field, who serve three-year terms and set policy as well as evaluate grant proposals) set new priorities. It phased out the Dance Touring Program— a blow many companies have found crippling—and in general concentrated on making support to dance companies its central role. Individual grants to choreographers, however, have not only been protected but increased in terms of the percentage of the program's total allocations.

The NEA Dance Program's total allocation in 1982 was $8,457,000. In 1983 it was $8,949,000—still under the $9 million it totaled in 1981. The result, after taking inflation into account, is that 1983 activity and 1983 costs must be met with 1979 levels of funding. Nigel Redden, the director of the NEA Dance Program, underscores the absurdity of this situation, pointing out that until last year, expectations and actual growth spiraled. "In the '60s, no one expected to make a living dancing; they did it by the skin of their teeth. Now people are making a living at it, and a different kind of creativity and professionalism exist. Now is the time when a lot of younger companies could get started—except that it's tougher than ever before for a young choreographer or a young company to have the financial freedom to get their sea legs."

From 1970 to 1976 the Dance Program's total budget grew 40 percent a year. NEA support of dance companies increased from twenty grants in 1972 to one hundred grants in 1982. Companies have also been indirectly supported by the other aspects of the Dance Program. Of the companies the NEA supports, Redden maintains, none has gone out of business. But those one hundred companies, he estimates, are only a quarter of the formally organized dance companies in the United States and perhaps only one-tenth of the number of companies in a broader sense.

Although the NEA is hopeful that its allocation for next year will be increased, the Dance Program still looks for ways to cut corners. In an attempt to ameliorate the touring situation, it has started a tutoring-initiative program that requires matching funds from state organizations. Redden has placed the responsibility for coming up with solutions to financial troubles on the companies. "They've got to have more flexibility," he explains. "Some will have to find ways of producing more money at home. Some will be able to continue to tour. There's no single answer to the problem." Still, Redden is sanguine about the future. And he thinks that the dance world can survive. "Dancers are used to unemployment; steelworkers are not. Dancers are more resilient than people in other professions."

But others—on both sides of the funding process—disagree. Beverly D'Anne, director of NYSCA's dance program, and Larry Greene, program analyst, were given a reprieve in March when the legislature overturned Governor Cuomo's proposed budget, which would have reduced NYSCA's funding by 13.8 percent and added a tax on ticket sales. Although they feel safe now from "major disaster," their allocation for next year is still unknown, and they grumble that NYSCA's total allocation hasn't really risen since the mid-1970s, while the dance program has been faced with increasingly greater needs. The cutback of the NEA touring program has created a domino effect, leading companies to apply to NYSCA instead. As the government pulls out of funding, D'Anne points out, the question of who's going to take over is left open. And with funds in every area cut, corporations and foundations are hard-pressed to finance not only education, health care, and other social service needs, but also the arts. Meanwhile, the number of applications to the dance program and amounts of requests have increased.

NYSCA's response to funding cuts will probably be to help more vulnerable organizations survive, at the expense of larger institutions. "You can't cut someone's $3,000 grant," D'Anne explains. "But in dance, the major institutions can't afford to be cut either. There's no such thing as a rich dance company." With touring both more expensive and less possible, with grants remaining at low levels, ticket sales and subscriptions down, and with more and more dancers and companies born each year, "these are bad times for the dance field, and we haven't seen the hardest times yet," D'Anne predicts. "A lot of dance companies haven't yet faced reality."

David White, director of Dance Theater Workshop (DTW) and outspoken activist for dance, paraphrases Henry Geldzahler: "Funding is a six pocket accordion; there's money from federal, state, city, corporate, foundation, and individual sources. But you need air in all the pockets in order to make music." White supports this notion both because this way one won't rely on a single source that could collapse, and because with decentralized funding, no single source controls aesthetic judgment. Still, White puts the responsibility for problems in the market place on the shoulders of the government. The cuts, he says, are partly the result of overt neglect. "While the state budget doubled in New York, NYSCA hasn't had a real dollar increase. Yet when the city went through its fiscal crisis, the arts proved to be the core of New York's cultural life. People are simply shortsighted about the way money spent on the arts is returned. It's not simply box-office; it's all the jobs in the industry and in related things—restaurants, printing, everything."

Funding is subject to both trickle-down and ripple effects. When education budgets are slashed, as they have been in New York, the dance field is also affected. The dancers who support themselves and their companies with teaching jobs find one of their funding "pockets" empty. The quality of education for future dancers is diminished, and training for related professions—history, criticism, notation, therapy, pedagogy—is also damaged. When people everywhere have less money to spend, they are less likely to buy tickets to dance concerts. White points out, "The field is not just a set of choreographers and performers, although these are the funding priorities. The field is a network of relationships that need to be maintained." But also, as Don Moore, director of Dance/USA, the D.C.-based advocacy organization, explains, cutbacks in one place tend to ripple out to other places for no good reason. "When Washington, D.C., planned to cut its arts budget by 50 percent, Washington State followed suit. But when the city toned down and made a 10 percent cut, the state also followed suit. Sometimes it's not so much a question of economics as a question of leadership."

Although most companies haven't actually gone out of business, their operations have changed and will continue to change to accommodate rising costs and funding cutbacks. The demise of the New York Dance Umbrella and the New York Dance Festival in Central Park has cut down on New York seasonal appearances for many companies. Alternative spaces—including DTW, Danspace, and The Kitchen—find themselves under siege. Martha Graham canceled her spring season this year, and the Joffrey Ballet will now look to Los Angeles for its base of support. Many companies are planning seasons only every eighteen months, instead of yearly. And as the recession hits Europe, smaller companies and avant-garde choreographers who previously found support there for part of the year have hit another empty pocket. White, faced with higher rents, refuses to pass DTW's higher costs on to either the artist members or to the audience. "Whether DTW will find some way to absorb costs or just go under is a question right now," he says.

Cynthia Hedstrom, director of Danspace at St. Mark's-in-the-Bowery Church, echoes White's pessimism. "A small organization like Danspace is never going to be part of the mainstream, and is never going to have a big budget. As the NEA preserves funding to companies and cuts other categories, an organization like ours is put in an awkward position. Without the government's seal of approval, it's hard to raise funds from other institutions. Since our budget is under $100,000, we don't qualify for most foundation grants. As the economy gets worse, attitudes get more conservative. It's hard and it's going to get worse," she declares. "It makes me question whether Danspace is viable. I think that some people in dance will have to go into other fields, myself included.

"It doesn't speak well for our city or our country that artists are not respected here; it's detrimental to our social fabric and to people's lives."

What is to be done? Most people in the dance field agree that dancers will have to rally together to go on dancing. An organization like Dance/USA, founded to be an advocate for dance in both the public and private sector, may be one answer. But Don Moore suggests additional avenues. "There is a growing sense of urgency in New York State, and much more needs to be done," he counsels. Arts institutions need to form a statewide coalition to monitor the government before another crisis hits. And both the dancers and the concerned public need to continue to voice their opposition to cuts, while facing the reality that for the near future, there will simply be less dance in the world. "The next six to eight months will be crucial for everyone in dance," Moore says. "Right now we're in the eye of the storm."

Nearly Sort of
Not Dance Maybe

Almost Dance
The Kitchen
November 16–25

Almost Dance was a curious conglomeration of performance art, music, and dance. On the one hand, it represents a new movement, in the 1980s, away from the purism of genres that dominated the 1970s, toward hybrid forms. As in the 1960s, the blurring of boundaries and forms immediately poses the question of what constitutes the separate genres whose identities are being challenged. The vexing question of what dance is, exactly, and how it differs from performance art, from theater, from music, from play and games, from sports, from language, and so on, has been at the basis of much (if not all) postmodern dance. But on the other hand, so many of the rules for doing, watching, and understanding dance were broken—or at least tested—in the 1960s that to group these current hybrids as falling outside of dance seems like beating a dead horse. Today we no longer have the seemingly monolithic academy of dance tradition that the dancers of the Judson group, for instance, felt moved to repudiate. Today, when anything is possible on the dance stage, whether in a SoHo loft, a Lower East Side cabaret, or

SOURCE: *Village Voice*, December 16, 1984

110

the New York State Theater, and when, with the reemergence of narrative and virtuosic technique among the avant-garde (and the simultaneous use by the mainstream of what once could only be considered
avant-garde terrain), it is sometimes hard to say what differentiates the
mainstream from its alternatives stylistically. It hardly seems original to
fall just outside the genre.

The result of the recent history of postmodern dance is that while
our fundamental ideas of what dance is have been shaken, we are left
feeling that lines should be firmly drawn *somewhere* and redefinitions attempted: if *anything* can be dance, what's the point of making distinctions
between dance and nondance at all? Paradoxically, at the same time,
we revel in dances that open their borders to embrace a variety of elements from the other arts, from popular media, and from all sorts of
other aspects of everyday life, ranging from diaries to politics.

With its mix of downtown artists who work in that dimly defined area
between dance, performance, and music, The Kitchen series promised
to shed more light on differences while also suggesting lines of overlap,
congruence, and divergence. The provocative title and the array of performers alone did not, however, provide enough of a conceptual framework for the issues that one felt or hoped might be addressed. I saw
nearly every performance either live or on videotape, and, despite my
interest in and enjoyment of many of the pieces—quite a few of which
I'd seen elsewhere this season or last—I ended up regretting the lack of a
clear rationale behind the programming, or perhaps more accurately,
the failure to carry out the original impulse for a rationale.

For one thing, I wondered whether the choreographers in the series
felt insulted at being labeled "almost dancemakers." There was an un-
necessarily belligerent tone about this term of denial—or even failure—
a feeling that one was witnessing an artificially assembled Salon des
Réfusés, populated in fact by some of the favorite acceptés of the avant-
garde, like Pooh Kaye, Ishmael Houston-Jones, and Wendy Perron.
And since so many of the choreographers chose as methods for moving
their contributions away from pure dance either narrative (such as
Barbara Allen in her parodic *Savage Bliss* and Hope Gillerman in her
skewed fairytale *The Princess Story*) or spoken commentary (Stephanie
Skura in *Chase Scene*, a tongue-in-cheek exploration of videodance techniques), one began to feel as though an extremely narrow definition of

dance were being proposed—that is, if it's got words it may no longer be dance. On the whole, the "real" dance works seemed slightly diminished in this context.

Yet it was heartening to note that, in contrast, the works presented by nonchoreographers were enhanced by the series' suggestive title. Peter Rose, for instance, who works with movement but doesn't design it choreographically, became a dancer as one paid attention to the strong literal gestures that corresponded quite specifically to the auto-biographical adolescent adventures of *Loyaltown, USA!* Perhaps in the end, choreography is defined by the eye of the beholder or even by her attitude; perhaps it's more useful to let dance be a pluralistic, inclusive category than to worry about criteria for exclusion.

Or maybe dance is defined by the body of the beholder. Arto Lindsay didn't move around much (a lot of head motions, but in Western dance we tend to discount that as dancing), but his wonderfully off-kilter fake Brazilian songs (almost folk music?) certainly made you feel like dancing up a storm in your seat.

One of my favorite works in the series was *Stalin and Alliluyeva* (Part II of *The Life of Stalin*), a collaboration between the Soviet émigré artists Komar and Melamid and choreographer Meg Eginton (who also danced Stalin, partnering Hillary Harper who danced the role of his daughter on point). With its mock-heroic soundtrack of political anthems and Tchaikovsky ballets and its use of the ballet vocabulary for triumphant posturing rubbing against Eginton's tiny figure of Stalin and our knowledge of the vicious, sordid facts of his regime, it presented a clever, biting parody of socialist realist ballet.

Choreographer Steps Spryly into Television

David Gordon is a New York choreographer who shuttles between avant-garde loft performances and opera house ballets. In 1986 Gordon made the ballet *Murder*, his second commission by Mikhail Baryshnikov for the American Ballet Theatre.

Now Gordon has made television his territory, too. An hour-long program, "David Gordon's Made in U.S.A.," featuring *Murder* and two other works by Gordon, will be shown tonight at ten o'clock on "Great Performances" on Connecticut Public Television (Channel 24 in the Hartford area).

"Made in U.S.A." is a showcase not just for Baryshnikov—whose dramatic gifts Gordon sets like a jewel in his own wittily sparkling structures—and the ABT cast, but also for Gordon's own Pick-Up Company, featuring his wife, the elegant Valda Setterfield, formerly a dancer with Merce Cunningham.

Taking advantage of television's intimacy as well as its capacity for visual magic, and mixing dancers from two quite different companies

SOURCE: *Hartford Courant*, October 23, 1987

who wouldn't ordinarily share a stage, "Made in U.S.A." is a dance event that couldn't happen live.

The first segment of the show, *Valda and Misha,* is a variation on an earlier live duet Gordon made, in which Setterfield and another woman dance while reminiscing about their mothers. Here Setterfield and Baryshnikov perform a quiet pas de deux in a cartoon dance studio while discussing the pros and cons of life in America.

He moved from Russia, she from England—both, as their stories make clear, to find a place for themselves as idiosyncratic dancers. They discuss their families, favorite movies, and beloved theaters, as the music quotes movie music and ballet music, from Disney soundtracks to "Swan Lake," and as animated illustrations float by.

As they agree, gently disagree, and help one another excavate memories and traits, their dancing similarly shapes its own conversation. They dance side by side, move apart, show off a little, offer one another a hand for support.

Deceptively Effortless

It all looks so simple, until you remember that dancing is difficult. The dancers' effortless chatter belies their physical exertion, so the dancing and the conversation achieve a disarmingly unpretentious grace.

It is not only Valda and Misha who, in learning about one another, are becoming friends; as the title itself suggests, we are becoming friends with them, too.

Gordon's wit partly comes from the way, even in the dances without texts, he plays with movements as if they were words. He loves puns and double entendres. He delights in showing how meanings change with new contexts, and this carries over from dance to dance.

In *TV Nine Lives* some of the same movements appear again, but the scene is entirely different. Baryshnikov and Setterfield are no longer a genteel man and woman getting acquainted, but cowboys (she with a fake mustache) with Pick-Up Company members Keith Marshall, Dean Moss, Chuck Finlon, Robert Wood, and Scott Cunningham.

In this vaudevillian salute to the myth of the Wild West, set to a music collage of country-western songs from the past and present, barroom brawls are as stylized as a grand pas de deux.

People step on, over, and through a folding chair (now a signature that crops up in many of Gordon's pieces, the chair phrase was originally a quote from an earlier long duet danced by Gordon and Setterfield). They knock one another over, sock each other in the jaw, get shot, somersault, and pick themselves and one another up—fluently, in time to the music.

TV Nine Lives constantly surprises—not just because, as in Western movies, these clown cowboys are indestructible. The movements themselves begin by looking quite abstract. Much of their pugnaciousness comes from the context—the cowboy costumes, Western music and (well, almost) all-male cast.

Gordon's use of a well-defined, repeatable but flexible vocabulary—though it is not at all classical—is well suited to the requirements of the ballet. He is a master of variation and repetition, two of ballet's cherished devices.

Murder, to music by Louis-Hector Berlioz, adds the detail of period costumes and the specificity of narrative to the dancing, but still partakes of the dry humor—this time in a macabre vein—one could call the Gordonian knot.

With sets and costumes by the grim humorist Edward Gorey, the ballet is a spoof on murder mysteries. Baryshnikov as quick-change artist plays a number of comic roles in stories both historical and fictional, told in words as well as dancing. He is a butler named Smith in a murder case, narrated by Setterfield, where all the other suspects also are named Smith. He is Dr. Jekyll, Anna Pavlova dancing a coughing Camille, and Mata Hari's accomplice who is shot in a duel. The cast of *Murder* includes twenty-three members of the American Ballet Theatre.

As one narrative rolls seamlessly into another and Baryshnikov reappears instantly in a new disguise, his ubiquitousness itself becomes funny.

In *Murder* the narrative wanders, only to wind up neatly where it began. Suddenly all the stories can be seen as nested, one within the others. And just so, in "Made in U.S.A.," we end up watching Valda and Misha watching themselves in the theater, then hailing a boat home.

Made in U.S.A." was broadcast on PBS's "Great Performances" on October 23, 1987.

Between the Arts

*Interdisciplinary Writings
on the Arts in Culture*

From "Messin' Around" to "Funky Western Civilization"

The Rise and Fall of Dance Instruction Songs

WITH JOHN F. SZWED

Listen while I talk to you
I tell you what we're gonna do
There's a new thing that's goin' around
And I'll tell you what they're puttin' down
Just move your body all around
And just shake. . . .

Sam Cooke, "Shake"

SOURCE: *New Formations* 27 (Winter 1995–96): 59–79

"Shake," by Sam Cooke, was recorded at the height of the dance instruction song craze of the 1960s. In this genre—which originated in
African American dance and music traditions—choreographic instructions are given or "called" while the dance is in progress. This article
will focus on the dance instruction song wave of the 1960s, tracing its
roots and its decline. Along the way we will analyze the rhetoric of the
song, both in terms of its lyrics and its music.

In her book *Dance Notation*, Ann Hutchinson Guest calls notation
"the process of recording movement on paper."[1] The development of
written notation for dance since the Renaissance in Europe has been a
fluctuating process of analysis in which the dance is described in terms
of a body of shared dance values. For instance, Baroque dancing masters in Europe wrote down floor patterns and the ornamentation of
footwork and turns with the assumption that arm movements, carriage,
and other aspects of dance style were common knowledge, while [Ru-
dolf] Laban sought ways to describe scientifically information that was
not only quantitative (body parts in use, divisions of time and space) but
also qualitative (for example, energy use).

The use of notation for theatrical dancing requires a system that is
fully descriptive, since the choreographer's patterns are not necessarily
shared by others. Social dancing, however, may be encoded in much
more abbreviated ways, partly because of its close relationship with its
music and partly because its sequences are redundant in several ways.

However, the dance instruction song is a form of dance "notation"
that is part of an oral, rather than written, tradition and is popular rather
than elite.[2] This popular genre of American song, which clearly has African roots, has appeared in mainstream culture in successive waves, beginning just before World War I with songs such as "Messin' Around"
and "Ballin' the Jack." It has spread from the United States to become an
internationally known phenomenon. Thus, in the twentieth century, the
broad dissemination of African American social dance instruction to audiences of all ethnicities and classes through the mass media—by means
of sheet music, records, radio, television, and cinema—has taken its
place alongside the dance manual and the private lesson of the Euro-
American elite that dated at least from the Renaissance.

The dance instruction song, spread via these modern mass technologies, has a privileged place for the historian of culture and performance, because it is *about* the mass distribution of dance and bodily knowledge and thus has served crucial aesthetic, social, and political functions.

It has played an important part in the democratization of social dancing; it has spread African American dance forms and styles throughout Euro-American culture and other, subaltern cultures; and it has helped create a mass market for the work of black artists. In short, the dance instruction song has contributed to the formation of a syncretic dance culture—and bodily culture—in multicultural America.

The dance instruction song in mass culture may be traced at least to the beginning of the twentieth century, although it has longer vernacular roots in the African American community. Even though songs have occasionally been used to teach European dances—the Beer Barrel Polka or the Lambeth Walk—it is important to note that the dance instruction song primarily comprises African American dances, from Ballin' the Jack and the Black Bottom to the Twist, the Loco-Motion, the Mashed Potato, and the Funky Broadway to the Hustle, the Smurf, and the Vogue. The song/dance titles range from the internationally recognizable, like the Charleston, the Shimmy, the Madison, the Boogaloo, the Frug, the Limbo, the Jerk, the Watusi, and the Bump, to the more obscure, like the Georgia Crawl, Stewin' the Rice, the Clam, the 81, the Lurch, the Bounce, and the Boomerang. As well, in the African American dance and song tradition, many of these dance instruction songs make reference to "animal" dances: the Bird, the Duck, the Funky Chicken, the Horse, the Pony, the Raccoon, the Dog, the Funky Penguin, the Monkey, and so on.

This genre is so powerful that it has not only spawned various series of dances, like the entire Twist, Jerk, or Dog successions,[3] it has also given rise to a metagenre—a group of songs commenting on or parodying the dance instruction song. These songs create instructions for dances that are physically impossible, either because of the limitations of human physiognomy—for instance, Dr. Hook's "Levitate" (1975), which commands the listener, "I want you to raise your right foot. . . . / Alright, now raise your left foot. / No no no no, don't put your right foot back down!"—or because they are far too general and large-scale—for example, Tonio K's "Funky Western Civilization," which, after cataloging the evils of western history, instructs its dancers to do all sorts of nasty things to one another: "You just grab your partner by the hair / Throw her down and leave her there" or "You just drag your partner through the dirt / Put him in a world of hurt." And Loudon Wainwright III's "The Suicide Song" (1975) gives new meaning to the dance of death by mixing instructions for shaking one's hips with those for cutting one's wrists. It seems that the parodic dance instruction song has been around nearly as long as the genre itself. However, we also want to suggest that one symptom of the dance instruction song's decline during the disco era—the late 1970s and early 1980s—was a disproportionate increase of parodies compared to the number of "actual" or "serious" dance instruction songs.[4]

Roots of the Dance Instruction Song

Dance instruction songs, in the form of dance rhymes and rhythmic verbal-movement games, were already long-established practices when they were first recorded in African American communities as early as the mid-nineteenth century. One of the fullest and earliest accounts of slave dancing records a portion of a dance song from Virginia: "She *bin* to the north / she *bin* to the south / she *bin* to the east / she *bin* to the west / she *bin* so far *beyond* the sun / and she is the *gal* for me."[5] Thomas W. Talley collected a number of what he called "dance song rhymes" in *Negro Folk Rhymes*, and typical is "Jonah's Band Party," which he saw developed at various occasions as a child:

> Setch a kickin' up san'! Jonah's Ban'!
> Setch a kickin' up san'! Jonah's Ban'!
> "Raise yo' right foot, kick it up high,
> Knock dat Mobile Buck in de eye."
>
> Setch a kickin' up san'! Jonah's Ban'!
> Setch a kickin' up san'! Jonah's Ban'!
> "Stan' up, flat foot, Jump dem Bars!
> Karo back'ards lak a train o'kyars."

(Talley notes that "Jonah's Ban'," "Mobile Buck," "Jump dem Bars," and "Karo" were dance steps.[6])

The roots of this genre reach back to the instructions and commentary by slave musicians at both slave gatherings and white plantation balls, to the African American folk song, game, and dance tradition, and earlier to the close relationship between West African dancing and the musicians' cues.[7] There is a link here with Euro-American forms such as square dancing, quadrilles, and play party games, but there is also strong evidence that there is a hidden history of these Euro-American forms—that in the United States, they were partly shaped by

African American interventions, including black musicians, callers, and prompters at square dances and contra dances, as well as African American games or styles of game playing.[8]

That the dance instruction songs are related to rhythmic games synthesizing Euro-American and African American traditions is nicely illustrated in a song from the 1960s—Rufus Thomas's "Little Sally Walker," which is a virtual catalog of free-floating, recombinative, formulaic game and song phrases, mixing an Anglo-American traditional children's chanting game with standard African American vernacular dance-calling phrases such as "Put your hand on your hip / Let your backbone slip," all set to a rhythm-and-blues beat.

> Little Sally Walker
> Sittin' in a saucer
> Rise, Sally, rise
> Wipe your weepin' eyes
> Put your hand on your hip
> Let your backbone slip
> (I want you to)
> Shake it to the east
> Shake it to the west
> Shake it to the very one that you love best . . .
> Little Sally Walker
> I see you sittin' in your saucer
> Rise and do the jerk
> I love to see you work . . .[9]

Roger D. Abrahams recorded girls' jump-rope rhymes from Philadelphia in the early 1960s that were parallel to or derivative of dances of the period, such as the Madison and the Baltimore.[10] Since these girls taught their younger brothers and sisters how to play these games, the interaction between dance and games is difficult to unravel.

There is also a connection between these songs and military marching chants—or cadence counting, or "Jody calls," introduced to the U.S. Army by African Americans—which help coordinate the drill movements of large numbers of troops: "Jody was here when I *left* / You're *right*."

Sheet music renditions of dance instruction songs were printed before the turn of this century. Nearly twenty years before "Ballin' the Jack" (1913), which Alec Wilder calls the first dance instruction song, black audiences were dancing to "La Pas Ma La," introduced by the

African American dancer-comedian Ernest Hogan in his Georgia Graduates minstrel show and published in 1895.[11] Less explicit in its choreographic instructions than later songs marketed to whites, "La Pas Ma La" often simply names or calls other dances to be performed, like the Bombashay and the Turkey Trot. According to Marshall and Jean Stearns, this served as a shorthand for those who knew black dance conventions. But the choreography for the Pas Ma La itself *was* given, if somewhat elliptically, in the chorus:

> Hand upon yo' head, let your mind roll far,
> Back, back, back and look at the stars,
> Stand up rightly, dance it brightly,
> That's the Pas Ma La.[12]

But if "La Pas Ma La" was marketed primarily to black audiences, during the first American mass dance craze "season" of 1912–14, many other dances and their notation—in the form of music and lyrics published in sheet music, as well as live demonstrations in Broadway revues and musicals—began to find commercial viability among mass white audiences (that is, both consumers at theatrical spectacles and participants at parties and dance halls). In fact, live performances and sheet music (or instructions, with pictures, published in newspapers and magazines) all formed part of a package that provided a network of verbal, aural, and visual demonstrations of the dance.

There were occasional early efforts to reach Euro-American audiences with conventional oral instruction—as in "One Step Instruction" (ca. 1915), a Columbia record of dance music with an instructor interrupting the music to describe the steps. But these were short-lived failures.[13]

The song "Ballin' the Jack," written for the *Ziegfeld Follies of 1913* by two African American musicians, Chris Smith and Jim Burris, describes traditional African American vernacular dance steps, and it is a paradigm of the early dance instruction song. It contains a great deal of information about various aspects of the choreography.

> First you put your two knees close up tight
> Then you sway 'em to the left, then you sway 'em to the right
> Step around the floor kind of nice and light
> Then you twis' around and twis' around with all your might
> Stretch your lovin' arms straight out in space
> Then you do the Eagle Rock with style and grace

> Swing your foot way 'round then bring it back
> Now that's what I call "Ballin' the Jack."[14]

Here we have choreographic instructions that describe the structure of the step, call a figure (in the form of an already known dance, the Eagle Rock), and also give advice on style and energy use ("nice and light," "with all your might," "with style and grace").

Similarly, Perry Bradford's songs "Bullfrog Hop" (1909) and "Messin' Around" (1912) provide explicit choreographic instructions, including some similarities to the later, more widely disseminated "Ballin' the Jack." In "Messin' Around," for instance, Bradford explains:

> Now anyone can learn the knack
> Put your hands on your hips and bend your back,
> Stand in one spot, nice and light
> Twist around with all your might
> Messin' round, they call that messin' round.[15]

Bradford's "The Original Black Bottom Dance" (1919) encodes instructions in a catalog of other figures, including previous dances by the songwriter:

> Hop down front and then you Doodle back,
> Mooch to your left and then you Mooch to the right
> Hands on your hips and do the Mess Around,
> Break a Leg until you're near the ground
> Now that's the Old Black Bottom Dance.
>
> Now listen folks, open your ears,
> This rhythm you will hear—
> Charleston was on the afterbeat—
> Old Black Bottom'll make you shake your feet,
> Believe me it's a wow
> Now learn this dance somehow
> Started in Georgia and it went to France
> It's got everybody in a trance
> It's a wing, that Old Black Bottom Dance.[16]

In addition to the description of the steps and the calling of other figures or dances, the dance explains the timing (like the Charleston, it is on the "afterbeat"), promises positive psychological affect, and makes reference to altered states of consciousness.

Even though these dance instruction songs were published in the form of sheet music, prior to the introduction of recording and broadcast technologies they were part of an oral tradition of instruction through popular performance, at first in minstrel shows and black vaudeville, and then in both black and white revues and musicals. The African American musician Clyde Bernhardt describes a 1917 performance by Ma Rainey and her black minstrel company. In the finale, Bernhardt remembers:

> The whole chorus line come stepping out behind her and she dance along, kicking up her heels. The song had dance instructions in the lyrics, and as she call a step, everybody would do it. Soon the whole cast was out on stage, jugglers, riders, singers, comedians, all dancing wild with Ma Rainey shouting and stomping. She call "WALK!" and everybody walked together before breaking out fast. She call "STOP!" and everybody froze. After many calls she finally holler "SQUAT!" and the whole group squatted down with a roar. Including Ma Rainey.[17]

Audiences, that is, learned the dance visually and aurally in public performances, rather than by learning to read cryptographic notation or taking private lessons. Accessible to all, this was a democratic form of dance pedagogy. Eventually, as the mass medium of television edged out live popular entertainments like vaudeville and traveling shows, broadcast programs such as *American Bandstand* and networks such as MTV replaced the live visual demonstrations.

The Rise of the Dance Instruction Song

By the 1920s, Broadway musicals with all-black casts regularly introduced new dance crazes to whites by demonstrating the steps and singing songs exhorting spectators to do the dance, such as the Charleston, danced to the song by James P. Johnson in *Runnin' Wild* (1923).[18]

The Stearnses give an account of the process by which the African American dance rhyme, a folk form, was transformed into the commercial dance instruction song. At first the structure was "a *group* dance performed in a circle with a few 'experts' in the center." As these experts improvised, inserted, and invented steps, the chorus on the outside repeatedly executed the steps named in the title of the dance. Often, the dance was simply named, rather than described, and if there was description, it was cursory. Later, however, as the dances reached the commercial market, "editorializing . . . as to its purported origin, nature, or popularity" began to appear as part of the song's format. The group dance with improvised steps metamorphosed into a couple dance with a fixed choreographic structure and order. "Although the verse names new steps, and the chorus describes the main step, the aim is simply to sell the dance," the Stearnses lament.[19]

According to the Stearnses, it was the Tin Pan Alley appropriation of these vernacular African American dances, in the form of the dance instruction song, that fostered their surfacing to the mainstream from black folk culture and, indeed, their survival. But oddly enough, although they were writing at the height of a new dance instruction song craze in the 1960s, the Stearnses claim that by the end of the 1920s, "the days of the dance-song with folk material were passing" and "the demand for dance-songs faded. The practice of including instructions in the lyrics of a song dwindled and gradually hardened into a meaningless formula." They claim that, with the advent of the blues, "dance-songs were forgotten" although the dances themselves persisted.[20]

However, it is our contention that, far from being forgotten or hardening into "a meaningless formula," dance instruction continued in the blues (and beyond). William Moore's "Old Country Rock" (1928) has shouted instructions sprinkled through the record:

> Young folks rock.
> Boys rock.
> Girls rock.
> Drop back, man, and let me rock.
>
> Now let's go back to the country again
> on that old rock.
> Rappahannac, Rappahannac,
> Cross that river, boys, cross that river.

And boogie-woogie pianists continued to simulate the ambience of live dances on recordings up until the 1950s.[21] During the course of the twentieth century the dance instruction song consistently reemerged in times of heightened racial consciousness or change—times like the 1920s, the 1940s, and the 1960s—as a subtle component of an ongoing cultural struggle between black and white America that includes provisional and partial reconciliations. Even as white America violently resists political and social progress by African Americans, a steady, subterranean Africanization of American culture continues, and emerging generations of white youth eagerly learn the bodily and cultural codes of black America by practicing its dances. And even where whites sang songs that presented black dances derisively or stereotypically—as in the case of rockabilly Carl Mann's "Ubangi Stomp" or Johnny Sharpe and the Yellow Jackets' "Bombie," both of which apply the "n-word" to Africans—the description and instructional elements were there nonetheless.[22]

While European Americans had danced to music performed by African Americans for generations, they did not as a group perform black moves or dance to exactly the same music enjoyed in the black community. When whites did so, it was either in an exaggerated, stereotyped way, in the context of the blackface minstrel show, or it was an individual matter, done either in the black community or in private. The dance instruction song "crazes" seem repeatedly to have served the function of both teaching and licensing whites to do black dance movements wholesale, to African American music, in public spaces in mainstream Euro-American culture.[23] That an African American movement style, done to a $\frac{4}{4}$ beat, was utterly alien to whites accounts for the necessity of these songs explicating not only steps, but also aspects of dance style, even bodily style. (It must be noted, however, that the dances are doubly coded, for embedded in the instructions are often allusions to aspects of black culture—particularly to religious experience—that would not necessarily be understood by the average white listener.) The repeated infusions of black style into white mass culture, which dance instruction songs enable, have allowed for temporary resolutions of racial conflict to take place on a deeply embodied cultural level, paralleling shifts in political and legal strata. The (as yet uncompleted) democratization of American culture has depended, in part, on the Africanization of American culture. The dance instruction song has been both a reflection and an agent of that process, although this has not been unproblematic, as we will discuss below.

Taxonomy: Structure and Function of the Dance Instruction Song

In order to analyze the dance instruction song in more depth, it is useful to establish a taxonomy of the structure and function of the songs and their component parts. For example, some songs do little more than urge the listener to perform the dance by naming it, like Rufus Thomas's "The Dog" and Van McCoy's "The Hustle." However, the majority of the songs begin with the premise that the listener has to be instructed in at least one or more categories—not only in the steps, spacing, timing, or other particulars of the dance but also in the style as well (that is, in a specifically African American dance style). Although in this section we concentrate on the directions given in the lyrics, a great deal of instruction in these songs takes place through aspects of the musical as well as verbal text.

In the beginning stages of the waves of the 1920s and 1960s at least, the detailed instructions of the songs seem to indicate that the white mass audience/participants needed tutoring in all the moves, postures, and rhythms of black dance. However, in each wave, as it progressed, the songs begin to assume some mastery of the black dance style, naming only figures or other coded instructions; sometimes they even assume mastery of previous dances, naming them specifically as comparative references, as we will illustrate below.

Most of the song structures, despite their apparent simplicity and their repetitions, are quite complex. They contain information about the quantitative and qualitative content of the dance—its steps, gestures, and style—but they also make reference to its novelty, popularity, and/or venerable history; to the dance's psychological affect to other practitioners of the dance; to the dancer's agency; and to aspects of teaching or learning the dance. They may also make reference to religious practices, sexual pleasure, or altered states of consciousness. Sometimes the songs use the dance as a mask or metaphor for those other experiences; sometimes they overtly frame the dance as a social activity connected with courtship; but at other times they simply offer the listener the chance to learn the dance, with no strings attached. (Strangely, the wording of the instructions given in Irene and Vernon Castle's 1914 book, *Modern Dancing,* seems very similar to that of dance instruction songs, perhaps suggesting that in the process of learning these dances from African Americans, they also absorbed the pedagogical rhetoric.[24])

The dance instruction songs usually begin, almost obligatorily, with a formulaic *exhortation* to learn or perform the dance. These range from the paternalistic ("Listen while I talk to you / I tell you what we're gonna do" ["Shake"]) to the pedagogical ("C'mon baby, gonna teach it to you" ["Mashed Potato Time"]) to the factual ("Come, let's stroll / stroll across the floor" ["The Stroll"]); from the encouraging ("Come on baby, do the Bird with me" ["Do the Bird"]) to the wheedling ("Come on mama, do that dance for me" ["Come on Mama"]) to the aggressive ("Hey you. Come out here on the floor / Let's rock some more" ["Baby Workout"]) to the tender ("Come on baby, let's do the Twist. . . . Take me by my little hand / And go like this" ["The Twist"]).

It is striking that when inviting the listener to do the dance, narrators of the dance instruction song often sweeten the offer with the promise that the dance will be easy to do. Sometimes this assurance comes in the form of pointing out that other people have already mastered the dance: "I wish I could shimmy like my sister Kate"; "My little baby sister can do it with ease"; "Goin' to see little Susie / Who lives next door / She's doin' the Pony / She's takin' the floor"; "You should see my little sis / She knows how to rock / She knows how to twist"; "Mama Hully Gully, Papa Hully Gully, Baby Hully Gully too"; "Pappy knows how. . . ." These are aspects of the formulaic part of the song that reflexively call attention to its *pedagogical function*. In fact, in "The Loco-Motion," Little Eva makes literal the connection with learning, simultaneously guaranteeing user-friendliness, when she remarks that the dance is "easier to learn than your ABC's." And the many allusions to little sisters also seem to literalize the idiom that these dances will be child's play. At least as early as "Doin' the Scraunch" (1930), Robert Hicks (a.k.a. Barbecue Bob) promised that "Ain't much to it an' it's easy to do."

These references to teaching and learning also come simply, without any warranties of easy mastery: "Bobby's going to show you how to do the Swim"; "C'mon now, take a lesson now"; "Now if you don't know what it's all about / Come to me, I'll show you how / We'll do it fast, we'll do it slow / Then you'll know the Walk everywhere you go." As the song progresses, words of encouragement and positive feedback are frequent: "Oh, you're lookin' good, now"; "That's the way to do it"; "Well, I think you've got the knack."

The promise that the dance will be user-friendly and the positive feedback offered as coaching is the part of the song—not obligatory but still quite frequent—that speaks to *psychological affect*, either that of the listener or that of the narrator. In "Finger Poppin' Time," Hank Ballard sings, "I feel so good / And that's a real good sign," and in "Bristol Stomp," the Dovells predict, "Gonna feel fine," and conclude the song by noting, "I feel fine." Sam Cooke, in "Shake," claims, "Oh I like to do it. . . . Make me feel good now," and Little Eva, in "The Loco-Motion," guarantees, "It even makes you happy when you're feeling blue." The lyric "Twist and fly / To the sky" is one of many invocations of euphoria in "Do the Bird." There is a connection here, to be sure, between the kinetic pleasure of the dance and other forms of ecstasy—sexual, romantic, drug-induced, and religious.

On the other hand, a few songs tell of failures to learn the dances, but always within special circumstances. Some blame their partners, as in "My Baby Couldn't Do the Cha Cha," or in Buddy Sharpe and the Shakers' "Fat Mama Twist," where the singer's girlfriend is too fat to do it. In other songs, the singer is culturally unprepared for the dance: in Frankie Davidson and the Sapphires' "I Can't Do the Twist," the singer (in a fake Spanish accent) confesses he can't do it, though he can do all of the Latin dances; Benny Bell & His Pretzel Twisters' "Kosher Twist" follows much the same pattern, but in Borscht Belt dialect.

Sometimes, at or near the beginning of the song, the narrator makes references to the *popularity, novelty, and / or venerability* of the dance. Although the Stearnses consider this aspect of the song a symptom of commercialization and decline, we see it quite otherwise. This is an African-derived practice, clearly in the tradition of the African American praise song. (Indeed, some of the dance instruction songs—like the "Ali Shuffle"—also function as praise songs for other objects than the dance itself. Similarly, in "It's Madison Time," both Wilt Chamberlain and Jackie Gleason are celebrated with a step.) "Down in Dixie, there's a dance that's new," Barbecue Bob announces in "Doin' the Scraunch"; Blind Willie McTell's "Georgia Rag" sets the scene "Down in Atlanta on Harris Street," and insists that "Every little kid, that you meet, / Doin' that rag, that Georgia Rag. . . . Come all the way from Paris, France / Come to Atlanta to get a chance. . . . Peoples come from miles around / Get into Darktown t' break 'em down." In "The Loco-Motion" Little Eva notes that "Everybody's doing a brand new dance now," while in the background the chorus exhorts "Come on baby, do the Loco-Motion." In "Popeye" Huey Smith and the Clowns tell us that "Everywhere we go, people jump and shout / They all want to know what the Popeye's all about." In "Peppermint Twist" Joey Dee and the Starliters announce, "They got a new dance and it goes like this / The name of the dance is the Peppermint Twist." In "The Bounce" the Olympics assert, "You know there's a dance / That's spreading around / In every city / In every little town." In "Hully-Gully Baby" the Dovells characterize the dance's popularity somewhat ominously: "There's

a dance spreadin' round like an awful disease." Perhaps in "Mashed Potato Time" Dee Dee Sharp puts the praise of the dance most succinctly:
"It's the latest / It's the greatest / Mashed Potato / Yeah yeah yeah
yeah." She then goes on to trace the roots of the dance and to bring the
listener up to date on its vicissitudes. Similarly, "The Original Black
Bottom Dance," "Bristol Stomp," and "Popeye" provide mythic accounts of origins.

One the dance has been invoked and/or praised, the lyrics indicate
the *steps, gestures, and postures.* Usually this information is stated in the imperative mode, as a command: "Just move your body all around / And
just shake" ("Shake"); "You gotta swing your hips now / . . . jump up,
jump back" ("The Loco-Motion"); "All right, now, shake your shoulders now / All right, wiggle your knees now" ("Hully Gully Baby");
"You just shake your hips and close your eyes / And then you walk"
("The Walk"); "Shake it up baby" ("Twist and Shout"); "Now you sway
at the knees like a tree in the breeze / Then buzz around just like the
bumblebees" ("Scratchin' the Gravel"); "Oh, shout you cats, do it,
stomp it, step you rats, / Shake your shimmy, break a leg, / Grab your
gal and knock 'em dead" ("Shout You Cats"). Sometimes, however, the
instructions are more in the manner of a description: "'Round and
around / Up and down" ("Peppermint Twist"); "We're moving in,
we're moving out" ("Baby Workout"). Occasionally this is stated as
an invitation: "Now turn around baby, let's stroll once more" ("The
Stroll"). At times the narrator actually counts out the sequence: "One,
two, three, kick / One, two, three, jump" ("Peppermint Twist"); "Oh
my mama move up (first step) / Honey move back (second step) /
Shuffle to the left (third step) / Wobble to the right (fourth step)" ("Baby
Workout"). In Charles LaVerne's "Shoot 'Em Up Twist" a freeze is ordered every time a gunshot is heard on the record.

One subcategory of this part of the dance is what might be termed
calling the figure. As in contra dancing or square dancing, the narrator instructs the dancers to perform a phrase or move that itself has already
been named, either during the current dance or by common knowledge
because it exists in other cultural arenas (like the dog paddle or back
stroke, or hula hoop, or "a chugga-chugga motion like a railroad train").
"It's Pony Time" is a very good example of first teaching, then calling
the figure. The narrator explains: "Now you turn to the left when I say
'gee' / You turn to the right when I say 'haw.'" Then he sings, "Now
gee / Yeah, yeah little baby / Now haw."[25] Or, in "It's Madison Time,"

the narrator commands, "When I say 'Hit it!' I want you to go two up and two back, with a big strong turn, and back to the Madison."

As suggested earlier, one way of calling the figure is actually to invoke another dance already popular and, presumably, known and available as a standard measurement. The dance may then simply be repeated: "Let's Twist again / Like we did last summer." Or in a mise-en-abyme structure, the song may direct the listener to do other dances as part of the dance being taught (as noted above in "Jonah's Band Party" and "The Original Black Bottom Dance"): "Do that Slow Drag 'round the hall / Do that step the Texas Tommy" ("Walkin' the Dog," 1917); "When I say 'Hold it!' this time, I want everybody to Gully . . . / When I say hold it this time I want everybody to Sally Long" ("Fat Fanny Stomp"); "Do the Shimmy Shimmy" ("Do the Bird"); "Do a little Cha-cha, then you do the Buzz-saw" ("Hully-Gully Baby"); "Do a little wiggle and you do the Mess Around" ("Popeye"); "Hitchhike baby across the floor" ("The Harlem Shuffle"); "We Ponyed and Twisted" ("Bristol Stomp"); "Think we'll step back now / And end this with a Shout" ("Baby Workout").[26] Indeed, Bradford's "Bullfrog Hop" is a veritable catalogue of other dance titles:

> First you commence to wiggle from side to side
> Get 'way back and do the Jazzbo Glide
> Then you do the shimmy with plenty of pep
> Stoop low, yeah Bo', and watch your step
> Do the Seven Years' Itch and the Possum Trot
> Scratch the Gravel in the vacant lot
> Then you drop like Johnny on the Spot
> That's the Bullfrog Hop.[27]

Sometimes the called dance may serve as a model from which to deviate. For instance, in "The Swim," Bobby Freeman explains how to do it: "Just like the Dog, but not so low / Like the Hully Gully, but not so slow." "The Walk" mentions the Texas Hop, the Fox Trot, the Mambo, and the Congo, but all as dances that are now out of fashion. In a very complex example, Junior and the Classics' "The Dog," the dancer is asked to "do" various breeds of dog—the poodle, the scotty, and others.

Oddly enough for songs that were usually distributed over nonvisual channels such as radio or records, sometimes the lyrics indicate that the narrator is also demonstrating the dance along the visual channel, as in

"The Swim" ("Kind of like the Monkey, kind of like the Twist / Pretend you're in the water and you go like this") or as in "The Twist" ("Come on and twist / Yeah, baby twist / Oooh yeah, just like this").[28] The radio or record listener has to fill in the visuals, based on a general knowledge of the appropriate vocabulary and style.

This indication of visual demonstration seems to make reference to earlier times, when dance instruction was routinely done as part of live entertainment in black vaudeville and tent shows, as described above. Long before he became a recording artist, Rufus Thomas was a member of the Rabbit's Foot Minstrels, a black vaudeville group that showed its audiences the latest steps. "I sing, I do a step or two, and I'm a comedian," Thomas later described his act.[29]

On the recordings, the residue of a live show with visual demonstration is evident during the musical break, when the time seems right either for the listener to watch the narrator demonstrate the dance (saving the breath he or she would otherwise need to sing) and/or for the listener to practice the movements just learned. Then, when the lyrics are repeated after the musical break, the listener does not find the repetition boring or redundant, because he or she is ready to test the progress made during the (nonverbal) practice time against the instructions once again.

This is nicely illustrated in the Pearl Bailey/Hot Lips Page version of "The Hucklebuck," in which, partly because of the duet form and the dialogic patter, we have the distinct sense that Bailey is teaching Page how to do the dance. In fact, even before she begins singing, Bailey formulaically initiates the dance event by confiding in Page that she has learned a great new dance. According to their conversation, they are in a club, and not only do they comment on the abilities and looks of the musicians, but also Bailey at one point complains that Page is dancing right on her feet. This song seems to record a performance within a performance, for certain lines cue the listener to set up a scene visually that puts Bailey and Page onstage in the club, teaching the audience how to do the dance. That is, in the fictional drama of the song they are a couple getting together on the dance floor in a club, but in the frame they are the featured club performers singing the fictional romance narrative. In any case, they repeatedly sing the chorus together, exhorting the listener to do the dance and describing the steps and other movements:

Do the Hucklebuck
Do the Hucklebuck
If you don't know how to do it, boy you're out of luck
Push your partner out
Then you hunch your back
Start a little movement in your sacroiliac
Wiggle like a snake
Waddle like a duck
That's the way you do it when you do the Hucklebuck.

As the band plays in between the stanzas, and Bailey and Page trade patter, it is clear that they are *doing* the dance, especially when Bailey scolds Page: "No, not now! I'll tell you when. Right here!"

As noted earlier, dance instruction songs teach not only the quantitative aspects of the dance (the steps, postures, and gestures) but also the qualitative aspects. One of these aspects is *timing*. For instance, "The Walk" is very specific in teaching the proper timing for the moves. Walking may be an ordinary act, but turning it into a dance requires the proper rhythmic sequence. So Jimmy McCracklin notes that "We'll do it fast, we'll do it slow," and later regulates the speed even further as he marks the exact moment in the music when the dancer should take his or her step: "You'll then walk / And you'll walk / *Now* you walk." In "The Harlem Shuffle," Bob and Earl often qualify a step by indicating its proper speed (which, of course, the slow and steady music underscores): "You move it to the right (yeah) / If it takes all night" and they frequently admonish the dancer: "Don't move it too fast / Make it last." In "Slow Twistin'," reminiscent of the "Slow Drag," Chubby Checker and Dee Dee Sharp recommend: "Baby baby baby take it easy / Let's do it right / Aw, baby take it easy / Don't you know we got all night. . . . Let's twist all night! / You're gonna last longer, longer / Just take your time."[30] The music, especially its percussive beat, plays an important role in all the songs in indicating timing.

Another qualitative aspect of the dance is its *spacing;* this too serves as an aspect of instruction. Again in "Slow Twistin'," Chubby Checker and Dee Dee Sharp advise the listener that all one needs is "Just a little bit of room, now baby." Spacing refers not only to ambient space, but also to levels of space, as in "The Swim": "Just like the Dog, but not so low." It also refers to relations with one's partner, which can be difficult to negotiate. In "The Walk" the narrator warns: "But when you walk,

you stand in close / And don't step on your partner's toes." Several
songs recommend, once one has learned a step, doing it in "a big boss
line" or "a big strong line." In "The Loco-Motion" Little Eva instructs
the listeners, once they have mastered the step, to make a chain. This
clearly invokes earlier African American vernacular and communal
roots, when the dances were done as group folk forms, rather than as
couple forms in the dance hall.

Yet another aspect of style is the category of *energy use*—what Laban
movement analysts refer to as effort qualities, such as strength and lightness, boundedness and unboundedness, directness and indirectness.
This too is a stylistic characteristic that the dance instruction song sometimes teaches. For instance, "The Loco-Motion" tells us to "Do it nice
and easy now / Don't lose control," while in "Shake" Sam Cooke gives
us quite a few clues: "Shake shake with all your might / Oh if you do it
do it right / Just make your body loose and light / You just shake." In
"The Duck" Jackie Lee gives some sense of the energy invested in the
dance when he describes performing it as "like working on a chain
gang" or "busting rocks." Less easy to characterize are other references
to *overall style:* the many songs that recommend, for instance, that the
dance be performed "with soul."

One of the oldest forms of African American dance instruction is
that given by the instruments themselves. The role of drums, for instance, in "talking" to dancers, or in signaling states of possession is a
well-known phenomenon, both in Africa and the Americas.[31] The role
of instrument as caller or instructor is not so well understood in American dance music, but its presence is undeniable. Barry Michael Cooper
describes both horns and singers calling instructions to dancers at
Washington, D.C., go-go dances in the 1980s.[32] Dance music critic Michael Freedberg suggests that instruments enact gender roles, both in
the blues and in dance music performances.[33]

Dance instruction songs vary in the amount of choreographic information they impart, and they obviously serve a range of functions.
Some actually teach the dance from scratch; some serve as prompts
or mnemonics, recalling for the listener previously demonstrated and
learned dances; some serve to coordinate ensemble dancing; some
merely praise a dance or exhort the listener to perform it. It is possible for
a dance instruction song to "notate" all ten elements in the taxonomy:
exhortation; pedagogical function; psychological affect; popularity,
novelty, and/or venerability; steps, gestures, and postures; calling the

figure; timing; spacing; energy use; and style. Thus, the amount of information can be quite complete.

Doin' the Hermeneutics

Certain aspects of the dance instruction song have nothing to do with learning or remembering to perform the dance. In fact, sometimes even what serves as explicit instructions seems also to have subtextual, metaphoric, or "secret" meanings. While the dance instruction songs have partly served to teach the rest of the world African American dances and dance styles, they also allude to other aspects of knowledge and experience. Some of these allusions are highly encoded in terms of African American custom, emerging for white consumers and participants only through familiarity with African American history and culture. That these references are also formulaic and appear repeatedly in the songs, in succeeding generations, shows the extent and tenacity of their roots. They are often unrecognized, sturdy traces of longstanding cultural traditions.

Some of the metaphors of African American dance instruction songs are merely pedagogical in function, since traditional dance language lacks names for the steps. So "mashed potatoes," "ride your pony," "walk like a duck," "walk pigeon-toed" and the like are means of directing the dancers away from the received, conventional steps of western dance.

Not all the extrachoreographic references have to do with experiences that are uniquely African American. Often, social dancing serves as a metaphor in these narratives for other kinds of partnering—either romantic or sexual. And since dancing—especially to slow music— often involves sustained body-to-body contact between partners, the metaphoric leap can be but a tiny one. When white teenagers danced the Twist, they were accused of moving in overly erotic ways and raised the ire of their parents. The lyrics of "Slow Twistin'" are full of double entendres, underscored by the male–female vocal duet: "Don't you know we got all night. . . . Let's twist all night / You're gonna last longer, longer / Just take your time." Perhaps the extreme case is Ronnie Fuller's "Do the Dive," where cunnilingus appears to be the move taught. In some songs, however, the dance serves not as a metaphor for sex, but as a love potion. Performing the dance itself is guaranteed to bond the partners romantically, as in "Bristol Stomp": "We'll fall in love you see / The Bristol Stomp will make you mine, all mine."

The ecstatic body consciousness of sex, however, is easily conflated with that of another high—from drugs or alcohol. The word "trance" does not only show up in these songs because it rhymes with "dance." Thus, in "Do the Bird," as we have seen, it is not clear whether romance or drugs, or both at once, are in effect when the singer urges:

> Come on take me to the sky above (fly-y-y-y-y)
> Come on baby we can fall in love (fly-y-y-y-y)
> (Do the bird do the bird) You're a-crazy flying
> (Do the bird do the bird) You're going to fly higher.

Similarly, the lines "Let's go strolling in Wonderland," or "Baby, let's go strolling by the candy store," in "The Stroll," also ambiguously suggest some kind of euphoria, whether sexual, drug-induced, or religious.

Yet "Doin' the New Low-Down," while acknowledging rapture— even invoking dreams and trances—specifically rejects other, non-dance forms of euphoria, either chemical or sensual, insisting on a surface reading: for "It isn't alcohol / No yaller girl at all! Thrills me, fills me with the pep I've got / I've got a pair of feet / That found a low-down beat. . . . Heigh! Ho! doin' the New Low-Down."

Another line in "Doin' the New Low-Down" invokes a crucial category of cultural invocations: specifically, African American signs of *religious* references. "I got a soul that's not for savin' now," this song's narrator admits, since his feet are "misbehavin' now." But more often, dance and religion are seen in the dance instruction song not as exclusionary opposites but as integrally linked. In fact, the frequent references in the songs to black religious practices, in particular the shaking or trembling associated with religious possession, suggest that many secular African American folk dances or social dances are derived directly from religious dances; they may even be the same dances performed in a different context. These are movements that originated in sacred rituals in West Africa, were associated with Yoruba, Ashanti, Congo, and other West African spirits, and shaped the syncretic worship formations of the African American church. In fact, instruction in appropriate physical response among Afro-Protestants is seen when ministers direct the congregation verbally ("Everybody raise your right hand and say 'Praise Jesus!'"), and in eighteenth-century Cuba, among Afro-Cuban religious orders, when leaders directed initiates to "open their ears, stand straight and put their left hand on their hip."[34]

Thus the Eagle Rock, mentioned in many of the songs beginning with "Ballin' the Jack," and described by the Stearnses as "thrusting the arms high over the head with a variety of shuffle steps," actually took its name from the Eagle Rock Baptist Church in Kansas City. According to musician Wilbur Sweatman, worshipers at the church "were famous for dancing it during religious service in the years following the Civil War," and the Stearnses note that although the Eagle Rock eventually adapted itself to rent parties and other secular venues, "it has the high arm gestures associated with evangelical dances and religious trance."[35]

Similarly, the Shout often crops up in the steps invoked by dance instruction songs, from "Twist and Shout" to "Do the Bird" to "Baby Workout." Also known as the Ring Shout when done in a group form, this was not a strictly vocal performance, but a religious dance with chants. It involved a rhythmic walk or shuffle in a circle, tapping the heels, swaying, and clapping as one advanced. In several accounts, observers noted that the shouters moved increasingly faster working themselves into a trance.[36]

Indeed, Jones and Hawes explicitly make the connection among children's ring plays, adult secular dances, and religious ring shouts in the African American tradition. They include in their chapter on dances the religious ring shout "Daniel," which includes lyrics, sung by the leader, strikingly reminiscent of several dance instruction songs:

> Walk, believer, walk,
> Walk, believer, walk,
> Walk, I tell you, walk,
> Shout, believer, shout.
> Shout, believer, shout.
> On the eagle wing,
> On the eagle wing,
> Fly, I tell you, fly
> Rock, I tell you, rock
> Fly the other way,
> Shout, I tell you, shout,
> Give me the kneebone bend,
> On the eagle wing,
> Fly, I tell you, fly
> Fly back home.[37]

Finally, the all-over body trembling called for and described in various songs—and known as the Shake, the Shimmy, and the Quiver, among other dances—bears a striking resemblance to the movements seen, especially among women, during religious possession in gospel churches.[38] Terms like "workout," "work it on out," "rock my soul," "turn the joint out," and "tear the house down," as well as the instruction to "go down to the river" ("The Duck"), all make explicit reference to ecstatic forms of African American religious worship.

In addition to these markedly African-derived dance practices, yet another set of associations reveal the presence of African cultural practices in dance instruction songs. Although the songs do give choreographic directions to the dancer, space is often made for *improvisation*. Thus, in "Shake" we are told, "Dance what you wanna"; in "The Swim" we are assured, "Do what you wanna, it's all right"; in "The Loco-Motion" we are instructed, "Do it holding hands if you get the notion"; and in "It's Pony Time" we learn that "Any way you do it / You're gonna look real fine." These lyrics not only reveal improvisation as a standard component of African American dance, suggesting that during the musical break it will be perfectly appropriate to "go crazy folks for a minute."[39] They also suggest, in a deeper vein, the metaphoric meaning of that improvisation. That is, the songs promise more than simply feeling good; they imply freedom and agency.

It should be acknowledged that the cross-cultural pedagogy of dance has been neither static nor one-way. Hip-hop, go-go, and ska are only the latest African American dance forms assimilated by white America. On the other hand, European dances like the quadrille have been absorbed, albeit in modified form, into the African American repertory.[40] For instance, the Stroll involves forming two facing longways rows of dance partners, as in a European contra dance configuration. However, there is a difference. When each couple goes down the column of space between the rows, they improvise virtuosic inventions in a characteristically African American vein.

One way to understand dance instruction songs is as a summing-up of a musical period. There is considerable self-consciousness about them, and by the time the songs are commercially available it is likely that the original people involved with the dance have moved on to other dances, or will soon do so as popularization sets in.

What is striking about most of these songs is that they offer a thin reading of the dance that lay behind them. Especially among Euro-Americans, there is a tendency to reduce a complex physical-verbal-musical phenomenon to the merely verbal. Thus, the Shout is often discussed as a kind of folk song. And the same reduction has been worked on rap, where the dance components of the form are almost always ignored in favor of the verbal.[41]

The Decline of the Dance Instruction Song

At the end of the 1960s popular music was developing at a remarkable rate. Yet dance per se was not the focus of forms such as psychedelic music, heavy metal, and art rock. Increasingly, songs about dances became not merely wannabe dances, but conceptual dance instruction songs—songs about dances that did not exist. The genre became something of a joke. *Mad Magazine*'s "Let's Do the Fink," by Alfred E. Neuman, which came with illustrated dance steps, was typical.[42] At the same time, however, black and Latin music continued a commitment to "the beat," so that when the white gay community encountered strongly grounded dance music in clubs and ballrooms in the 1970s, it seemed a totally new phenomenon. It was as if rock had never happened.

When dance music made its comeback as disco, it did so with a vengeance. New dances were developed apace, but instructional songs were minimal at best, with exhortation and novelty/praise functions carrying the weight of the lyrics. The names of dances were repeated rifflike in songs: "Do the Hustle," "Do the Jaws." Professional dance teachers returned, and a ballroom formality replaced the homemade, self-help atmosphere of many earlier dance eras.

The 1990s are certainly a time of acute racial tension and heightened race awareness in the United States. And yet, dances are being invented and reinvented at a slower rate, and no dance instruction song craze has emerged thus far in this generation. The Electric Slide, one of the few to have appeared in recent years (accompanied by a song of the same name by Marcia Griffith [1989]), was immediately challenged by an older generation of dancers as a thinly disguised remake of the Madison, especially as it, too, emerged from the Baltimore–Washington, D.C., area.[43] Similarly, the Lambada was attacked as a commercially fabricated generic Latin dance, and its accompanying song debunked as plagiarism. The current generation of African American kids still knows some dance instruction songs, like the currently popular "Tootsie Roll" by the 69 Boys. But these have not crossed over into the mainstream. In hip hop, one of the few distinctive music forms of the current era, MCs (especially in the early days of the form) may direct dancing and crowd behavior, but usually in an improvised rap, with routinized calls, and seldom in the form of a fully structured song for a distinctive dance. Madonna's appropriation of Voguing from the black gay community in the early 1990s was a sudden, singular—and spectacularly popular— resuscitation of the genre, but it did not spark a new wave.[44]

Dance instruction songs are still with us, though, in truncated, restricted forms. Country and western line dances—a remarkable case of cultural lag—still retain something of the calling of steps used in black popular dancing of the late 1950s and early 1960s (at least in the instructional videos), and aerobics and jazzercise do struggle mightily to get the feel of the discotheque into their routines. But there is a sense here of the end of an era. Two items of nostalgia—"Time Warp" (a camp parody of "Ballin' the Jack") from *The Rocky Horror Picture Show* (1975) and the commemorative scenes from John Waters's 1988 film *Hairspray* indicate that, for the mainstream, the dance instruction song is truly a relic from the past.

Conclusions

There is a school of mass culture criticism, most notoriously represented by Adorno, that condemns popular music as an opiate.[45] The dance instruction song, however, clearly contradicts that position. Far from assuming a docile listener, it galvanizes audiences into action with both its swinging beat and its lyrics. It is a dialogic form, requiring interaction between artist and auditor. Thus, even though the form of dissemination—especially after the invention of the phonograph—has been mass production or broadcast, the dance instruction song does not promote passivity. Rather, it provides a means for individual agency and creativity, especially with its improvisational component. Moreover, it insists that listener response can be bodily, not just intellectual, participation. Unlike the Castles' gendered ballroom choreography instructions, the dance instruction songs make no gender distinctions in the movements. In fact, unlike the Euro-American style of couple dancing, where the man leads and the woman follows, in the pedagogy proposed by dance instruction songs, women and even girls are often cited as authorities.

The question arises as to whether people actually *listen* to the lyrics and, further, whether listening to the lyrics enables people to learn to do the dance. Several theorists of popular culture claim that people screen out the words in popular music and hear only the rhythm, or the emotional contours.[46] Many cultural critics condemn the lyrics of popular songs, claiming that since the words are banal and predictable to begin with, auditors do not need to pay attention to them.[47] The dance instruction song seems unlike other genres of popular music in that here it *is* important to listen to the words, and not just to sense the beat, melody, or emotional content of the song. This is not to say that the words alone supply the entire set of choreographic instructions, for as we have pointed out, the music also directs the dancer. The words are important, even if not all of them need to be heard or understood, because the dance is "overdetermined." That is, listeners may not hear or comprehend every single word (and indeed, not every song makes every word clear enough to understand). But given the various ways people learn to dance, the redundancies, both in terms of the repetition of the lyrics and the parallel teaching across various channels—verbal, rhythmic, melodic, and visual—allow for successful instruction.

The dance instruction song is laced with esoteric references to African American culture—especially to ecstatic religious experiences—that have been inaccessible to most Euro-Americans. Nevertheless, during the course of the twentieth century the dance instruction song, while keeping black vernacular dances alive, has had a mass appeal to white audiences. Through the dance instruction song, white bodies have learned—and loved—black moves, from the practice of performing separate rhythms with diverse body parts, to stances like akimbo arms and bent knees, to specific movements like all-over body quivers or hip rotations. Despite the recondite allusions, there is enough accessible material in the songs, both in the music and the lyrics, for Euro-Americans to learn the dances and the dance style. The genre has become part of mainstream American culture.

We want to close by raising the issue of cultural appropriation. On the one hand, the dance instruction song, besides its own formal pleasures, is an attractive genre for all the reasons we have already mentioned—not only its preservation of vernacular black dance but also its dialogic character, its role in the democratization and Africanization of American culture, and the economic opportunities it has created for African American musicians. By introducing an African American bodily habitus into mass white culture, thereby stirring up racial, generational, and sexual threats, it has even been subversive. On the other hand, the dance instruction song *crazes* have been problematic. They commodified and naturalized the dances, appropriating them for white culture without fully acknowledging their cultural source—their African roots—and sometimes totally detaching them from black bodies and black communities. The dance instruction song crazes created the impression that these dances have no roots—that they always have been and always will be. We hope that this article will in part redress that misperception.[48]

NOTES

1. Ann Hutchinson Guest, *Dance Notation: The Process of Reading Movement on Paper* (New York: Dance Horizons, 1984).

2. Alec Wilder, *American Popular Song* (New York: Oxford University Press, 1972), uses the term "dance instruction song." We use his term, but without the quotation marks. Marshall Stearns and Jean Stearns, *Jazz Dance: The Story of American Vernacular Dance* (New York: Macmillan, 1968), call these "dance songs with instructions."

3. "The Jerk," for example, originally recorded by the Larks in 1964, gave rise to a long line of successors: for instance, Clyde and the Blue Jays' "The Big Jerk," Bob and Earl's "Everybody Jerk," and even the Larks' follow-up, "Mickey's East Coast Jerk." See Steve Propes, "The Larks and the Jerk," *Goldmine* 26 (August 1988).

4. For further comments on dance crazes, see Katrina Hazzard-Gordon, *Jookin': The Rise of Social Dance Formations in African American Culture* (Philadelphia: Temple University Press, 1990); and Stuart Cosgrove, "The Erotic Pleasures of the Dance-Craze Disc," *Collusion* (February–April 1983): 4–6. Also, see Jim Dawson, *The Twist: The Story of the Song and Dance That Changed the World* (London: Faber and Faber, 1995); and the 1993 documentary film *The Twist* by Ron Mann (New Line Pictures).

5. William B. Smith, "The Persimmon Tree and the Beer Dance" (1838), reprinted in Bruce Jackson, *The Negro and His Folklore in Nineteenth-Century Periodicals* (Austin: University of Texas Press, 1967), 3–9.

6. Thomas W. Talley, *Negro Folk Rhymes* (New York: Macmillan, 1922), 258–62.

7. Dance instruction songs have also been noted in the carnivals of Haiti and Trinidad, and in Argentinean tango, areas with either a majority of peoples of African descent or with a history of significant African cultural influence.

8. On African American musicians and callers, see Paul Oliver, *Songsters and Saints: Vocal Traditions on Race Records* (Cambridge: Cambridge University Press, 1984), 22.

9. Bessie Jones and Bess Lomax Hawes, *Step It Down: Games, Plays, Songs, and Stories from the Afro-American Heritage* (New York: Harper and Row, 1972), discuss the African American version of this "ring play" song.

10. Roger D. Abrahams, "There's a Brown Girl in the Ring," in *Two Penny Ballads and Four Dollar Whiskey*, ed. Kenneth S. Goldstein and Robert H. Byington (Hatboro, Pa.: Folklore Associates, 1966), 121–35.

11. Stearns and Stearns, *Jazz Dance*, 100–102; and Oliver, *Songsters and Saints*, 33–34.

12. Stearns and Stearns, *Jazz Dance*, 100–101, 117. The Stearnses spell the name of the first dance invoked as the "Bumbishay," while Oliver spells it "Bombashay."

13. "One Step Instruction" was part of a newspaper promotion give-away. See *Early Syncopated Dance Music*, Folkways Records RBF 37.

14. Stearns and Stearns, *Jazz Dance*, 98–99.

15. Ibid., 107.

16. Ibid., 110–11.

17. Clyde E. B. Bernhardt, as told to Sheldon Harris, *I Remember: Eighty Years of Black Entertainment, Big Bands, and the Blues*, foreword by John F. Szwed (Philadelphia: University of Pennsylvania Press, 1986), 26.

18. See Stearns and Stearns, *Jazz Dance*, 140–59 on black musicals in the 1920s. See also Allen Woll, *Black Musical Theatre: From Coontown to Dreamgirls* (Baton Rouge: Louisiana State University Press, 1989).

19. Stearns and Stearns, *Jazz Dance*, 100–101.

20. Ibid., 113–14.

21. Rod Gruver, "The Origins of the Blues," in *Down Beat Music* 71 (1971): 16–19.

22. But see also African American songs that describe animals dancing in Africa, such as The Ideals' "Mo' Gorilla."

23. "Public spaces," however, were, and to some degree still are, segregated: *American Bandstand*, the television show that did the most to spread new dances in the United States, was initially restricted to whites.

24. Mr. and Mrs. Vernon [Irene] Castle, *Modern Dancing* (New York: World Syndicate Co., by arrangement with Harper and Brothers, 1914). Reid Badger, in *A Life in Ragtime: A Biography of James Reese Europe* (New York: Oxford University Press, 1995), describes the relationship between the Euro-American Castles and James Europe, their African American bandleader, and names black dancers such as Johnny Peters and his partner Ethel Williams who taught the Castles African American dances.

25. "Gee" and "haw" (or "hoy") are commands used for horses or mules in the South. Their use in the 1950s and 1960s suggests that the influence of rural-based "animal" dances was still vital.

26. As we will discuss below, "The Shout," contrary to what its title might

suggest by way of vocalization, is actually an African American religious dance. See Lynn Fauley Emery, *Black Dance in the United States from 1619 to 1970* (New York: Dance Horizons, 1980).

27. Stearns and Stearns, *Jazz Dance*, 104.

28. There is an obvious sexual meaning here, to be discussed below.

29. Quoted in Roger St. Pierre, liner notes, Rufus Thomas, *Jump Back*, Edsel Records ED 134 (1984).

30. Again, there is an obvious sexual reference here.

31. Morton Marks, "You Can't Sing Unless You're Saved: Reliving the Call in Gospel Music," in *African Religious Groups and Beliefs*, ed. Simon Ottenberg (Meerut, India: Archana Publications, 1982), 305–31.

32. See Barry Michael Cooper, "Kiss Me before You Go-go," *Spin* (June 1985): 65–67.

33. Michael Freedberg, "Dust Their Blues," *Boston Phoenix*, October 16, 1992; and "Rising Expectations: Rick James Gets Down," *Village Voice*, October 11, 1983.

34. Ramón Guirao, *Orbita de la poesía afrocubana, 1928–37* (Havana: Talleres de Ucar, García y cía, 1938).

35. Stearns and Stearns, *Jazz Dance*, 27.

36. See Emery, *Black Dance*, 120–26. See also Jones and Hawes, *Step It Down*, 45–46, for the distinction between religious and secular shout steps.

37. Jones and Hawes, *Step It Down*, 144–45. After each line sung by the leader, the group responds, "Daniel," and performs a mimetic action.

38. See Stearns and Stearns, *Jazz Dance*, 105, on the various titles of the dances.

39. William Moore, "Ragtime Crazy," quoted in Oliver, *Songsters and Saints*, 33.

40. In fact, the earliest recorded dance calls for European set dances and dance suites were performed by African Americans. See John F. Szwed and Morton Marks, "The Afro-American Transformation of European Set Dances and Dance Suites," *Dance Research Journal* 20, no. 1 (1988): 29–36.

41. This has complex cross-cultural repercussions, especially since, as several theorists have argued, black music and dance (on both sides of the Atlantic) are key agents in the articulation of cultural memory. See, for instance, Paul Gilroy, *The Black Atlantic: Modernity and Double Consciousness* (London: Verso, 1993).

42. Conveniently collected together are the following sets of dance songs without dances: *It's Finking Time! '60s Punk vs. Dancing Junk* (Beware Records LP Fink 1); *Bug Out Volume One: Sixteen Itchy Twitchy Classics* (Candy Records LP4); *Bug Out Volume Two: Sixteen Itchy Twitchy Classics* (Candy Records LP5); *Land of 1,000 Dunces: Bug Out Volume 3* (Candy Records LP 7). A selection from the three Candy discs is available as *Best of the Bug Outs* (Candy CD7).

43. Lena Williams, "Three Steps Right, Three Steps Left: Sliding into the Hot New Dance," *New York Times*, April 22, 1990, sec. 1, 48.

44. On Madonna's appropriation of Voguing, see Cindy Patton, "Embodying Subaltern Memory: Kinesthesia and the Problematics of Gender and Race," in *The Madonna Connection: Representational Politics, Subcultural Identities, and Cultural Theory*, ed. Cathy Schwichtenberg (Boulder, Colo.: Westview Press, 1993), 81–105.

45. See Theodor W. Adorno, *The Culture Industry: Selected Essays on Mass Culture*, ed. and with an introduction by Jeremy M. Bernstein (London: Routledge, 1991).

46. In "Why Do Songs Have Words?" (in *Music for Pleasure: Essays in the Sociology of Pop* [New York: Routledge, 1988]), Simon Frith cites two such theorists: David Riesman, "Listening to Popular Music," *American Quarterly* 2 (1950), and Norman Denzin, "Problems in Analyzing Elements of Mass Culture: Notes on the Popular Song and Other Artistic Productions," *American Journal of Sociology* 75 (1969). Frith notes that this was the typical view of sociologists of rock and pop music in the 1970s.

47. Frith, in "Why Do Songs Have Words?" traces this view back to 1930s Leavisite mass-culture criticism.

48. The authors would like to thank Roger Abrahams, Robert F. Thompson, Noël Carroll, Laurence Senelick, Michael McDowell, David Krasner, Gerri Gurman and her Memorial High School dance class, Amy Seham, Toni Hull, Juliette Willis, and Margaret Keyes, as well as Brooks McNamara, Richard Schechner, and the faculty and students in the Department of Performance Studies, New York University, for their help with this article. [Minor changes have been made for consistency within the current volume.]

Theatre of Operations
Stuart Sherman's Fifteen Films

The following two essays, which were both originally published in Millennium
Film Journal, *showcase a descriptive style of writing that was commonly practiced
in film criticism during the early 1980s. Banes's writings chronicle both Stuart
Sherman's and Ericka Beckman's films, and are the only articles that discuss these
particular artists' films in that time period.*

—ɱ—

One of the dilemmas of modern theater and dance is their rivalry with
film. In the nineteenth century the stage was a venue for magic, a place
that bedazzled the theatergoer with spectacular apparitions and transformations, opulent landscapes, natural disasters, and all manner of impossible creatures from dragons to demons to ballet beauties who could
spin, fly, and in general defy the limitations of the human body. The
theater was a domain where reality could either be heightened or transcended. But film launched a powerful attack on theater's prerogative.

SOURCE: *Millennium Film Journal* 10/11 (Fall/Winter 1981–82): 87–101

How could the crowd scenes in even the most lavish play, ultimately still boxed in by the proscenium frame, hope to rival the effect of the limitless expanses and thousands of extras the cinema commanded? The old monsters and melodramas would never measure up to the diabolical aberrations of a film like *The Exorcist*. And a stage fight will no longer impress us when we regularly see plane crashes and murders on screen. But theater's move toward realism was also countered by film. How can we be touched by an actor's impassioned monologue when through the cinematic closeup we can watch his lips tremble and his eyes fill with tears? The vitality of live performance has been curiously flattened by the shadowy events of cinema.

The possibilities that film offers, not only in terms of creating spectacular effects, but—more radically—in terms of manipulating material reality, have consistently attracted theater artists as they approach the limits of performance. In "Through Theater to Cinema" Sergei Eisenstein recalls his own movement toward a barely existent Soviet cinema, from a no longer compelling theatrical reality. Eisenstein staged Tretiakov's "Gas Masks" (1923–24) in a real gas factory. "Theater accessories in the midst of real factory plastics appeared ridiculous. The element of 'play' was incompatible with the acrid smell of gas. The pitiful platform kept getting lost among the real platforms of labor activity. In short, the production was a failure. And we found ourselves in the cinema."[1] Fifty years later Yvonne Rainer, treading the line between fact and fiction in anti-illusionist postmodern dance performance, echoed Eisenstein's frustrations. "Dancing could no longer encompass or 'express' the new content in my work, i.e., the emotions," she wrote after making *Lives of Performers* (1972). "Dance was not as specific—meaning-wise—as language . . . Dance is ipso facto about me (the so-called kinesthetic response of the spectator notwithstanding, it only rarely transcends that narcissistic-voyeuristic duality of doer and looker); whereas the area of the emotions must necessarily directly concern both of us. This is what allowed me permission to start manipulating what at first seemed like blatantly personal and private material. But the more I get into it the more I see how such things as rage, terror, desire, conflict, et al., are not unique to my experience the way my body and its functioning are."[2]

Stuart Sherman's foray into film stems from an impulse he shares with these directors. Indeed, the irony of his title, *Spectacle,* for his solo performances in which he manipulates small ordinary objects is an index of his sensitivity to the precariousness of performance in our times. As a live performer, in fact, Sherman trades in magic. But as Noël Carroll has noted, his subject is not the illusionistic metamorphoses of the stage conjurer, nor the transformations of the stage technician, but a modernist baring of the devices of sleight of hand. The associative structures Sherman employs, as well as his stance in performance (like a prestidigitator, he stands at a small table with his suitcase full of props, focusing obsessively on the operations of his hands), reveal infantile themes of control and solipsism that gratify our fantasies of mastering the material world and that, further, locate "the basis of magic in our earliest and most submerged ways of thinking."[3] Sherman's tabletop is a kind of screen for the concrete projection of mental processes. Here objects collide in a realm akin to the imagination, freed of causal and ordinary logical constraints. Like a poet whose action is expressed on the blank page, Sherman uses the neutral rectangle of the table's surface to make metaphors and symbols, arranging the cognitive features of things in comparative and contrastive alliances. The analogy is one that he reflects on in the work itself; themes of writing, reading, and language continually appear in terms of both objects and actions. Sherman's task—the freeing of objects from necessity, setting them into associative play—and his solemn, focused attention on that task create the impression of a child mastering his toys, of a titan surveying a miniature universe.[4]

Through cinema Sherman amplifies his field of action and his command over that field of action a hundredfold. Camera movement and editing provide him with expanded means for systematic comparison and contrast. The repetition and accumulation of shots correspond to but also supersede the obsessive, meticulous operations that structure the live performances. The movie screen correlates directly with the tabletop and the page as an arena for imaginative action, but the use of the camera drastically magnifies the scale, scope, and focus of items to manipulate. Pencil sharpeners, toys, and sheets of paper give way to buildings, trees, cities. The use of film, Sherman says, allows him to enter into an active relationship with his environment, changing the seemingly god-given landscape into a storehouse of articles for use.[5]

Still, Sherman's style as a filmmaker is unique and closely related to his performance methods. Each shot is composed with such precision and clarity that one feels, watching these utterly concise works (the fifteen films total less than thirty minutes) that every detail is necessary to the work as a whole, that no aspect of the film appears without reason. This scrupulousness is rare in film. Usually the motion picture camera records the happenstance positions of things in the world. Even in fiction films, although usually everything within the frame has reason to be there, there is still the sense that the camera is recording the haphazard, indeterminate state of our everyday visual experience—either because the images shot are haphazard or are made to look that way. In Sherman's films the composed, determinate nature of each shot asserts itself very powerfully. Every object is strangely and insistently *there*. People stand gazing at the camera or enter the frame as if it were a stage on which every movement is carefully blocked. Sherman's films are more like a succession of stills than like a stream of imagery. On the one hand, this posedness and fixity, added to the silence of the films and the fact that they are primarily in black and white, give the films an antique look. On the other hand, Sherman's small formats, the use of black and white, silence, and the economy of imagery are integral to the themes of control and elegance that are basic to Sherman's aesthetic. It is not just because he works on a low budget that Sherman's films are short and silent. Silence and economy of means and action are crucial to Sherman's performances as well as his films, pinpointing focus and evoking a compelling, enigmatic presence.

Contra Bazin and Kracauer, Sherman makes films that are not slices of reality. His camera does not give us the sense that it is gliding over an endless continuum, recording objects and events that are everywhere connected to more off-screen data. Rather, Sherman returns to an earlier idea of cinema, composing pictures that suggest that proscenium arch of the theater. His frames are centripetal, focusing inward and calling attention to their own artifice. But unlike filmmakers such as Godard, Straub and Huillet, or Rainer who use artifice and theatricality to call attention to the conditions of cinema and to destroy illusion, Sherman calls attention to cinematic representation as an object of magic and awe. We know, as we watch his films, that they are machines for producing illusion, but at the same time, the illusion works. Like the Surrealists, with whom he shares both themes and methods, Sherman tampers with the ordinary in order to produce the uncannily marvelous. Through camera movement and editing, he not only arranges unlikely encounters between objects, but also prompts mental associations, very often in terms of metaphors or puns.

Because the films are so short, detailed, and elaborately composed, it is difficult to summarize them. Every element in the film is a significant aspect of the set of operations that Sherman puts into motion in the course of the film. Therefore I have chosen here to describe each film fully, not only to convey the relationships between objects and actions accurately, but also to animate the moment-to-moment phenomenological play that Sherman's work commands.

The perfect symbol of the controlled, contained, and orderly world that so fascinates Sherman is the globe; *Globes* is also the title of Sherman's first film (1977; camerawork: Babette Mangolte). The film is two and a half minutes long. It opens with a still life, in black and white: a hammer standing upright and a bucket with a paintbrush laid across it occupy the lower portion of the frame. They are set on an urban rooftop against a low wall, above which we see the tops of other buildings jutting into an expanse of sky. The precision of the placing of these objects and the clarity of the shot create a portentous aura. The next shot, in color, shows a closeup of blue shards lying on a dark ground. An unidentifiable object swiftly drops into the frame. The camera gazes upward, into a cloudless blue sky, then moves back down, showing a plaid shirt lying on top of the shards, which we now recognize as lying on the same roof we saw in the initial black and white shot. The blue shards, bits of shattered sky, recall the similar shards in Rene Magritte's paintings *Le domaine d'Arnheim* (1949) and *Le soir qui tombe* (1964). The film continues in color. We see a slight man, whose head is cut off at the top of the frame, enter from the left, pick up the shirt, and put it on top of a bundle he is carrying, then exit the frame on the right. If we know Sherman as a performer, we recognize the man as Sherman, even though—again à la Magritte—he is headless. When he picks up the shirt, the shards have disappeared. In the next shot the man is rounding a corner carrying the bundle. The sequence occurs again, with a slight variation: shards, object catapulting into frame, vertical camera movement up and then down, but now a woman's shoe, again on the roof. Sherman enters in the same way, adds the shoe to his bundle, then rounds a different corner. It is exactly this use of permutations of actions, objects, and places that gives Sherman's films their strong sense of unity and coherence. The sequence begins a third time, but now there is an ellipsis. We see the shards, then a catapulting object. But the next shot shows Sherman rounding a third corner with the item already topping his bundle. Next we see a store window filled with the blue and yellow globes, in front of which Sherman deposits the pile of clothing. Suddenly we see a man and a woman standing in front of the window, wearing the clothes that had constituted the bundle. They walk out of the frame to the right. Next we see Sherman squatting in front of the window, with empty arms outspread, as if he had just deposited the bundle that has already come to life and departed. He stands and faces the camera, his back to the window full of globes. This "found" image is utterly uncanny, suggesting that Sherman is an urban god who has created a world in a primeval couple. There is a sense of completeness afforded by the masses of globes and by the appearance in this shot of Sherman's face, a completeness that he acknowledges by looking over his shoulder at the globes as the camera zooms in to frame his face. The next shot provides an even fuller sense of closure, returning to the black-and-white imagery of the initial shot. We see, in black and white, the window full of globes; against a broad black swath at the bottom of the window, the hammer, bucket, and paintbrush have reappeared in their original configuration. The repetition and variation of images create a rhythmic structure, akin to a poem or a song, that pervades Sherman's films.

Globes is rich with the most elemental contrasts of perpetual and cultural categories: black and white versus color; up and down; man and woman; clothing versus living bodies. Although it is not a narrative in the sense of a linear, causal development, there is a progression in the film that occurs through spatial movement and through the rhythmic accumulation of events. At times causality is strongly suggested simply by juxtaposition, as when Sherman glances over his shoulder and seemingly turns a color image into black and white. Something clearly happens in the film, but what happens is structured more like a myth or fairy tale than like an ordinary narrative. Out of a heap of inanimate objects, a man and woman are born. The window full of globes that forms the backdrop to their creation makes them not just two individuals but a primordial couple. Further, Sherman's role in the process places him in a godlike relationship to the couple. He seems to construct them out of materials at hand, and the hammer and paintbrush underline this workaday attitude. In a sense, via the camera, that is exactly what he does.

In *Scotty and Stuart* (1977; camerawork/lighting: Ken Ross) a number of other categorical distinctions are explored. The film opens with a shot of a hand turning on a water faucet and filling a wine glass with water. A round-faced woman, Scotty Snyder, drinks the water; closeups of her face are intercut with shots of Sherman in a gym running toward the camera. The editing implies a relationship between the two images akin to a simile. The water, it is suggested, "races" down Snyder's throat. However, the water rushing inside one body is displaced by the next shot, which reverses the situation. Sherman, fully dressed, steps out of a full bathtub. He walks past Snyder, who still stands by the sink, into the doorway of a kitchen. Now that the two characters have been spatially located, one suspects that a narrative might begin. But the causal links continually go awry. Although there is a pile of towels in the kitchen, Sherman does not use them. Instead, as he stands dripping in the doorway, he glances at various points in the room. Typically Sherman brings normal situations or relations between objects to mind, imbuing them with a sense of order, but then subverting them. In this case, the scene shifts from inside to outside. The stack of towels now sits on a wooden dock. Snyder sits beside the stack of towels; she picks them up one by one and tosses them in the water, like a laundress performing the inverse of an ordinary operation. Sherman's cryptic glances in the kitchen are answered in the next shot, in which we see wet towels draped around the room. The theme of objects moving inexplicably from one setting to another, or in and out of an individual frame, is one that will recur throughout Sherman's films. The migration of objects not only provides a sense of unity in the film, but also charges the objects themselves with significance, endowing them with mystery and power. Sherman finally steps through the doorway, into the kitchen, where he sits at a table set with plates, silverware, two glasses filled with water, and a single candle. Snyder is already seated at the table. But instead of beginning a meal, the two immediately leave the table. Snyder lights the candle, stands up, and ceremoniously walks into the bathroom of the first shot. Sherman follows her, bearing a glass of water with equal solemnity. The faucet of the bathroom sink is running—still running, we tend to feel, from the time of the first shot. (Even though the events in the film flout any ordinary sense of temporality or causality, our tendency to associate an ongoing flow of time with the ongoingness of the film provides a very strong sense of linear narrative, giving *Scotty and Stuart* the quality of a surrealistic story, but a story nonetheless.) A lovely sequence follows. Snyder turns off the faucet. The lights go out, and in the darkness her face is illuminated by the candle's flame. Sherman pours water on the candle. Suddenly the black-and-white film turns to color. Snyder and Sherman, dressed in blue and black clothing, stand on a beach holding bentwood chairs, their backs toward the camera, facing the sea. They place their chairs side by side at the water's edge and sit down, watching the waves as the tide rolls in around their ankles. The structure of this film is rhythmic in an almost musical way, developing images of water from glass to tub to ocean, through clusters of oppositions such as water/fire, man/woman, turning on/turning off, inside/outside. The centrality of the water faucet makes it, rather than the human actors, seem the source of action in the film.

Several of Sherman's films make this type of rhythmicity palpable in a most physical manner by using the imagery of nonverbal rhythmic actions, such as dancing or sports. *Skating* (1978; camerawork: Ken Ross) systematically plays with the mental categories the act of skating arouses. The film is a two-minute long meditation on the ways in which the social act of skating uses the human body and its environment. This entire film is in black and white. It opens with a favorite Sherman composition: one sees a vast expanse of white, crisscrossed with white markings, and at the bottom of the frame, a horizontal stripe of railing. A file of three people appears at a break in the railing and one by one peel away from the line, holding a pair of boots up at eye level. The first two, a man (Power Boothe) and a woman (Judy Henry), hold up skates. The third, another man—Sherman—holds up an ordinary pair of shoes. Suddenly the man and woman have appeared behind Sherman, and each one skates to the right, leaving the frame. This action provides the necessary information to decipher the markings in the first shot, which we now perceive was a frozen pond. Sherman walks away to the left. Now that the word "ice" has entered the spectator's mind, the filmmaker moves on to a new set of operations with ice at their center. We see the man and the woman standing a few feet apart on a huge stone stairway. Posed thus, in their dark clothing and somber demeanor, they look like an antique photograph. Sherman walks up the stairs and stands between them, holding a large sack. He solemnly takes two ice cubes out of the bag and hands one each to the man and the woman. They put the ice cubes in their mouths. Sherman dumps the contents of the bag on the steps; hundreds of ice cubes form a heap on the staircase. This seems to prompt the man and the woman to lean over, take off their shoes, and hold them up to their eyes, just as Sherman had done with his shoes earlier. The next few shots are rapidly intercut, creating a series of images that suggest the mental flashes of memory or fantasy. Sherman, at the railing, skates out onto the pond; the man and the woman, still standing on the staircase, fold their arms behind their backs and step into a swaying motion that evokes skating; Sherman takes ice [cubes] out of his coat pockets and puts them in his mouth; suddenly he stands between the man and the woman again, on the stairs, takes the cubes out of his mouth, hands them to the couple. The man and the woman, who are holding both hands out, toss a cube from each hand onto the stairs. Finally we see all three actors in the same posture, but now standing on the ice, wearing skates. After the camera freezes them in this pose, they turn and skate away to the right, onto the expanse of ice. The final shot, from overhead, shows the three skating, equidistant, in a counter-clockwise circle.

There is a strange fitness to these juxtapositions, which at first glance might seem arbitrary. The ice cubes are miniature versions of the frozen pond we see in the first and final shots. The miniaturization allows the actors to perform the magical act of swallowing the pond. Like the water in *Scotty and Stuart,* the ice appears in large and small forms; it moves from outside the body to inside and then out again. Once the stairs are covered with ice cubes, the man and the woman can simulate ice skating by their swaying motions. Through editing the act of ice skating is broken down into its components and then reassembled.

In *Skating* Sherman plays with a number of contrasts: the skating body/stationary body; the body stable on ordinary shoes/balanced on the edge of skates; ice inside/outside the body; culture (the stairs)/nature (the pond). Once again, his main actors are a man and a woman. They are seen not as distinct in terms of a sexual division of action, but nevertheless they populate the otherwise deserted landscape like an urban Adam and Eve. Sherman, again, seems separate from them, again in the role of creator. Through his manipulations of the ice cubes, he appears to create a frozen landscape. Underlying the imagery of the film, as well, is the notion of frozenness, both in the literal and the figurative sense. The lucidity of this imagery and the conciseness and mysteriously logical illogic of the operations strike the spectator with the same sort of insistent, apparent flash of meaning one encounters in a Zen koan.

Tree Film (1978; camerawork: Babette Mangolte) is a black-and-white film, lasting about a minute and a half, that continues Sherman's surrealistic motif of rearranging nature and culture. The film involves Sherman as the central actor, assisted by a hat, a ladder, and a tree. Again the imagery is reminiscent of Magritte—not only in the permutations involving the hat, which sits successively on the ladder, a bundle of sticks, and then on empty space; but also in the contrast between live trees and wooden sticks (the cultural analog of the trees), and between a bare and shod foot. In the opening shot of the film Sherman stands by the tree, opens the metal ladder, but instead of climbing the ladder, puts his straw hat on top of it and holds the ladder above his head. In the five succeeding shots he pulls five sticks out of five large outdoor metal trashcans, at five different points in an urban landscape. The sticks are compared to the ladder, for the next shot shows Sherman holding the bundle of sticks up to the hat, which floats in the air above them. Suddenly he is outside, lying on the grass, ladder and hat beside him, as if he has fallen. But the next shot shows him pulling the hat down from the ceiling of a room and walking down the ladder, one foot bare and the other wearing a sneaker, until his bare foot comes to rest on a photograph of grass that lies on a wooden floor. In *Tree Film* Sherman manages to set up several different categories of objects with a striking economy of images. There is a kind of infantile delight in identifying tree, ladder, sticks, and the human body as members of a single set of objects: vertical things that reach up. But also, as in *Skating*, where the ice cubes are a miniature form of the frozen pond, the sticks are a smaller form of the tree. The shift in scale, also a favorite maneuver in the performances and films of Meredith Monk, increases Sherman's control over objects, making them literally "handleable"—just as the use of film makes the world handleable by reducing it to a set of small manipulable images. The final shot of *Tree Film* underscores Sherman's enchantment with the magic and power of representation. It is this sense of wonder that invests every isolated object in the films with latent meaning and that, especially, imbues meetings of objects with an animistic force.

Edwin (1978; camerawork/lighting: Jacob Burckhardt) is a one-minute-long, black-and-white work that uses writing as its dominant image. The one actor in the film is Edwin Denby, the venerable dance critic and poet. The film opens with a view of a white pressed tin ceiling. The camera moves down past an open window to show the fragile, white-haired Denby seated in profile at a table. Denby picks up a cup, very deliberately turns it over completely, but there is nothing in it. He replaces the cup and just as it touches the table a circular sheaf of papers appears underneath it. It is as if the papers had, in fact, fallen out of the overturned cup. As he lifts the cup to his mouth with his right hand, Denby brushes the papers off the table with his left forearm. He replaces the cup on the table, but it instantly disappears. Denby leans forward and scribbles on the far end of the table with his fingertip. Now the camera imitates his action, making a jerky scan of the room's interior, moving upward until it comes to rest on the tin ceiling. The use of the camera to imitate the motion of objects in this way is a favorite Sherman device that contributes to the sense of "primitive" animism in the films: In *Flying*, for instance, the camera imitates an airplane and in *Fountain / Car* it mimics the motion of a car. The oddness of the camera movement calls attention to itself in a way that is rare in film, even in avant-garde film. Stan Brakhage, for instance, employs unusual camera movements expressively—to embody intense emotions. But in *Edwin* Sherman uses the camera movement itself representationally, making it stand for—via mimesis—the movement of Denby's hand. Through camera movement, Sherman creates irresistible associations, extracting salient qualities of objects and transferring properties from object to object in a way that seems magical, rather than following any physical laws. In *Edwin* Sherman literally uses Astruc's metaphor: the *camera stylo*. The film very succinctly suggests that the filmmaker is like the poet who inscribes action on a blank page, making it full, like the squares of tin impressed with designs or like a table with its array of objects.

Camera / Cage (1978; camerawork: Babette Mangolte) also uses camera movement to establish a metaphor for a quite different view of the filmmaker's role. Here the camera is analogized to a cage, in which the filmmaker imprisons objects and bits of reality. *Camera / Cage* also adds another layer of representation to that of the film medium by introducing a drawing of a cage. And it moves from the hermetic locales, populated by at most three people, of the earlier films, to a crowd scene. It opens with a view of a busy intersection—to be precise, the corner of 14th Street and Sixth Avenue in Manhattan. The camera quickly moves in a zigzag line, drawing a rectangle that cordons off the area. Next the camera moves close to the ground in a jerky manner, confronting Sherman, who crawls toward it, a movie camera dangling from his mouth. He drops the instrument, opens his mouth, and the camera that is recording zooms into this dark cavity. The next shot shows us the schematic drawing of the cage, which is represented by two horizontal lines connected by five parallel vertical lines. As in *Scotty and Stuart* and *Skating*, a new piece of information allows the spectator to interpret an earlier ambiguity. In this case, we recognize in the drawing the shape the camera had traced over the crowd scene. Then we see another cage, as the camera jerkily approaches two owls in a metal pen. The bars fill the screen. Finally the camera pulls back for a long shot of a glade. Sherman rides in from the right on a bicycle, parks it, and picks up an object from the ground. He turns what seems to be a camera around and around, then puts it in the bicycle's saddlebag. He remounts the bike, rides in a circle (with the camera panning around to follow him), and then, as if having given the camera its cue, he rides off to the right, while the circular panning continues, catching Sherman on each go round riding into the distance.

Flying (1979; camerawork: Mark Daniels, Octavio Molina) is another extremely concise film, a minute long. An airplane takes off. The composition of the first shot repeats Sherman's favored design, a horizontal stripe of details at the bottom of the frame. In *Flying* the runway over which the airplane and camera both move (to the right) stretches out above an airport balcony that becomes the locus of the next operation. One of these details becomes recognizable as a railing, and the camera sweeps back over it, traveling left, in answer to the plane's swift takeoff to the right. It stops to focus on a hand clutching a handle, which converts the railing into a suitcase. Next the hand and handle appear above a city that the camera has been surveying from above. The scene freezes. The hand and handle then appear over an expanse of sky and a small airplane. The airplane begins to move. Finally the camera moves downward to a new runway, suggesting a landing. The camera is like an airplane, affording the filmmaker enormous mobility and a sweeping horizon; the camera is also a "handle" on the world, a way of framing and freezing visual experience.

In several ways, *Baseball/TV* (1979; camerawork: John Ligon, Octavio Molina, Paul Savage; lighting: Octavio Molina) recapitulates the concerns of *Globes*. But this film is more complicated, partly because it incorporates and contrasts different types of found TV imagery. Within the carefully composed and systematically arranged material of Sherman's films, these tiny snippets of video seem wildly disorderly. The film opens with another set of objects that seem to await imminent quickening. A T-shirt and a pair of dark pants are standing up in the shape of a body, with a TV set (that is broadcasting a baseball game) as a head. The objects are "disembodied," as in *Un Chien Andalou*. A sequence of ten shots follows, in which Sherman is first seen lying on grass or sand, and then springs up in all the various positions of ten players on a baseball diamond. He has created a baseball team plus a batter, we realize by the tenth shot, and our assumption is answered by the next image—a long shot of a baseball game in action. We see bits of unrelated television shows. Next, a baseball action—a pitch and a hit. The string of television imagery runs in reverse. Finally the camera returns to the T-shirt and pants, which now have a baseball glove for a head. A ball drops into the glove, and the outfit is transformed into a baseball uniform with a TV set atop its collar. Once again, Sherman is fascinated by the magic of representation—the ability of film and television to populate a world, to create something from nothing, to animate lifeless objects. A pun on the word "catch" is suggested here: the camera catches images, just as a baseball player catches a ball.

Fountain/Car (1980; camerawork: John Ligon, Art Feinberg) is a short set of permutations involving the actions of the objects in the title. First we see a spray of water gushing vertically out of a grassy ground. Next we view a horizontal jet of water spraying a car from left to right. The camera moves to the left over an expanse of grass, seemingly in answer to the previous motion of the jet from left to right. The next image is a closeup of a stop sign. The car backs up, from the left to the right of the frame, answering the previous answer. As it backs up, the vertical spray of the initial shot gushes forth from under the car. The entire film lasts forty seconds. Once again, objects seem to migrate without warning. And once again, the camera stands in for an object, supplying by its motion the missing link in a chain of events. The mental process of association is foregrounded through the clarity and preciseness of the imagery. In addition to the theme of control, the concision of the film and its statement-answer format evokes a sense of pure elegance.

Rock/String (1980; camerawork: John Ligon, Jacob Burckhardt) is a set of visual tricks that confounds spatial relationships as well as gravity. In another grassy, idyllic setting, the camera travels downward along a string. It moves from sky to treetops to full landscape, coming to rest on Sherman, who holds the string in his left hand and looks up, as if toward a kite. He raises his right hand and holds it palm up. Presently a small rock drops into it. Immediately we see him lying on the ground, eyes closed, with the rock lying next to him, and the string, attached to the rock, leading up out of the frame. The camera travels up the string along the ground, rather slowly. Finally it reaches Sherman, who stands on the end of the string. Five times in a row, he opens and closes his extended right hand. The camera travels up the string, which he now holds with his left hand, in between each clenching of the hand, repeating in discrete increments the initial downward path of the camera. Finally on the fifth movement, the camera reaches the top of the string, where we see the rock, held up by Sherman's hand. The ability of objects, in this case a rock and a human body, to migrate from one place to another during a continuous panning shot is, if one stops to think about it, not at all difficult. However, it is so contrary to our expectations of filmic logic that it strikes us as uncanny, even marvelous. It is because we understand the cinema of Stuart Sherman to be a series of precisely fixed frames that we are startled when an object seems to jump from one frame to another or when it seems to be in two different places in a single frame. The space that Sherman creates in *Rock/String* appears, through camera movement, to be a long, vertical yet limited space that the lens cannot entirely encompass, but, rather, must move up. Thus an entirely plausible rearrangement of things becomes, through representation, pure magic.

Elevator/Dance (1980; camerawork/lighting: Mark Daniels) is the most complicated film in terms of rhythmic variety. At three and a half minutes, it is also the longest of the fifteen films. A man and a woman (Power Boothe and Judy Henry) stand with their backs to the camera, facing an elevator with a small circular window at face level. The elevator door opens, the man steps in, and the woman steps to the side to directly face the window. We see each one's face, in two successive shots, framed by the window. Next, the image of a massive dark jukebox appears. Now the elevator begins to move. However, it follows no logic in terms of its direction or occupant, although it does follow a perfect logic in terms of rhythm. First the man goes up. Then he goes up again. The next time, he goes down. Next we see the woman's face as she goes up once, then down, and down again. The jukebox appears again. This entire sequence is repeated a second time, again punctuated by a view of the jukebox. The third set of moves, however, is more complex. The man moves up, the woman moves up, the man moves down; the woman moves up, the man moves down, the woman moves down. Finally, an empty elevator moves up, then down. The whole sequence is as intricate and symmetrical as a foxtrot. And the jukebox suggests that dance music is being played—although, because the film is silent, we never hear it—which makes the metaphor for the rhythmic partnering even more salient. Now the scene shifts to an escalator, which faces the camera and moves down, bringing the man into view feet first. The scene changes again, to an up escalator, which brings the woman in to view headfirst. Again we see the jukebox. Now a new couple enters and stands in front of the jukebox. In quick succession, we see the jukebox, the two escalators, the two portholes, and, finally, a shot of the two elevators, with the two couples arranged one in front of each elevator. The suggestion is that the dance is about to begin again in a double version, like a multiplication dance.

In *Elevator/Dance* the permutations on a directional grid are essential to establishing the rhythm of the film. They also provide a sense of unity and closure, as they do in the other films and especially in the live *Spectacles*. Unity is also created by the use of similar operations in different places—as when both elevators and escalators move up and down. The suggestion of metaphor is entirely created through concision, a quality that is important in Sherman's films not only in terms of clarity of content but also in terms of elegance of style.

Hand/Water (1979; camerawork/lighting: Art Feinberg) is a reflection on two of Sherman's preferred and highly resonant themes. Various images of the hand and the water are plied in terms of contrasts of scale and of representation. The film opens with a view of a large steamship, which impressively fills the frame. As the camera zooms in, we see its name on a sign—"the Statendam"—and then we see Sherman on board. He is waving, and the camera keeps zooming until it frames his open, vertically extended palm. The hand freezes. This is followed by a shot of a cutout hand in the same position, floating in water. It is as if the camera, by "catching" or "freezing" the live hand—that is, making a representation of it—had transformed it into a flat, lifeless object. The camera moves upward, and as Sherman descends into the frame, we see that he is seated in a towboat with a small bowl of water (with the hand floating in it) on the seat opposite him. He rows away, out of the top of the frame. Next, he rows back into the frame on a horizontal plane, from the left. When he reaches center, he puts down the oars, lifts the bowl ceremoniously with two hands, and lowers it over the side of the rowboat until it floats in the water, prompting a comparison between the large body of water outside the bowl and the small body of water inside the bowl, and, further, between the hand floating in the water and the water floating in the water. The hand that is a representation of Sherman's hand also seems to wave, an activity that is partly activated by a pun: the water's waves rock the hand, making it seem to wave as if in greeting. We see another closeup of the hand; backlit, it becomes a large black shape against a luminous circle. Water splashes over this image, and we see the bowl, now empty. Next it appears as a white, gleaming moon-like circle. Another splash and the bowl disappears. The next image shows the Statendam and a tugboat moving out of the frame to the left. Finally we see Sherman, looking down at the water, waving and floating in his rowboat toward the top of the frame. This time it seems as if he is waving at the departed bowl with the hand inside it.

As in *Scotty and Stuart*, water is the extremely potent, evocative image that flows through every frame of *Hand/Water*. Through the different water/boat images, Sherman creates a set of specified, precise associations. Scale plays an important part in this associative structure. At first, one sees a large boat in a body of water that is even larger. Next we see a body of water (in the bowl) that is smaller than the boat, and a miniature version of the ocean. In the bowl of water the hand floats as if it were a boat. And, finally, the bowl of water floats in the ocean as if it, too, were a boat. This chain of relationships creates a structure without a single, specific meaning that is compelling partly because of its allusiveness. Objects seem to transfer qualities to other objects, live things to dead things, in a way that is quite magical. Water seems to animate things, and, like water, the nature of objects—their size and their identity—becomes fluid as well.

Piano/Music (1980; camerawork: Jacob Burckhardt, Mark Daniels, John McNulty, and Leonard Puzzo; lighting: Daniels, McNulty, and Puzzo) is another film "about" rhythmicity. It interweaves the act of piano playing with the act of handball playing in a very satisfying series of maneuvers. Sherman is seated at a piano with his back to the camera. He lifts his hands, which begin to crash down to the keys. Before the action is completed, the scene shifts to a brick wall, at which Sherman stands (still with his back to the camera). His hands are on two strips of paper representing piano keys, which immediately fall down as he lifts his hands. The shapes of the bricks echo the piano keys. Sherman wears formal dress; he attaches white cuffs around his wrists and then around his ankles. We see that his feet are bare. The hands and feet have been framed by this action but this is an odd act of framing—we would expect a pianist's hands to be emphasized, but not his feet. This reversal of expectations is like the scene in *Scotty and Stuart* when Sherman gets out of the bathtub dripping wet but fully clothed.

An associative leap structures the following shot, in which we see a pair of gloves and a pair of shoes taped to the brick wall. We understand these objects to be representations, through metonymy, of Sherman's hands and feet. As with many Sherman images—for instance, the handle of the suitcase in *Flying*—this use of a figure of speech through imagery supplies an expressive edge to the film, suggesting a ghostly absence of people while at the same time supplying an unearthly power to objects. Four pairs of shots follow rapidly. A ball hits the righthand glove; we see the piano with the righthand keys depressed by pieces of tape. A ball hits the lefthand glove; the lefthand keys of the piano are taped down. The same operation happens with the two shoes. In four more pairs of shots, Sherman stands at the wall and makes four quarter turns, bouncing the ball to the ground after each turn, which is immediately followed by a nearly indiscernible frontal shot of a dark, gleaming, upright piano. He throws the ball against the wall, and, suddenly, he is seated at the piano again, as in the first shot, but this time he lifts his hands up from the keyboard. It is as if all the action between this shot and the first shot were a split-second fantasy in the mind of the piano player. But this completing image is followed by a coda: we see the gloves and shoes again, this time resting on four paper diagrams of piano keys that form a diamond shape. Inside the diamond is a tiny white toy grand piano. A white runway leads up to the whole arrangement. We see all of this in a single instant, as a ball rolls up the runway and knocks over the piano. Once again the causality in the film is seen as coming from an object (the ball) rather than from a person.

In *Roller Coaster/Reading* (1979; camerawork/lighting: Mark Daniels) Sherman proposes, through editing and parallel camera movement, that the act of reading is exhilarating, like riding a roller coaster. The conjunction of the two actions is established in the first shot, in which Sherman gets into the car of the roller coaster without looking up from the book he is engrossed in reading. In a series of symmetrical camera movements and compositions, a bookcase and the white wooden structure of the roller coaster are scanned and compared, with the camera moving upward, or to the right (as if in reading), or zooming in and out. The final pair of shots shows Sherman, still reading, walking into the enormous roller coaster structure (whose double doorway resembles an open book) as the bookcase recedes. The movement oppositions instill a sense of a machine behind not only the roller coaster, but the representation of both roller coaster and bookcases. Each shot and each object, in a highly structured set of representations, from small to large, and scanned side to side and up and down, seem like moving cogs and gears in a unifying, sensible engine. At the same time, the juxtaposition of the roller coaster and the books prompt one to think of the phrase "mental machinery."

Sherman's fifteenth film, *Theatre Piece* (1980; camerawork: Mark Daniels; lighting: Daniels and Jan Croeze with Ric Greenwald), returns us to the theater. But again, Sherman populates a world by his solipsistic, demiurgic actions. He sits in an audience seat, then a chair on the stage, then stands at the door to the theater. Back inside the deserted theater, we see Sherman from behind sitting in the auditorium. His body becomes transparent and he rises from another chair. It is as if he is peopling the building by leaving his trace everywhere. But, also, this creative act seems to constitute his lonely performance, for we also see him, small and at a distance, bowing on the stage. This is a melancholy version of Buster Keaton's *The Playhouse*. The nearer figure disappears. But Sherman's ghostly traces come to life in the final shot, which shows a bustling crowd at the theater's door.

The determined schematism of Sherman's films, approaching didacticism, and the reflective cogitations on the use of the camera and the role of the filmmaker tempt one to view his work as part of the Structuralist trend. Each film is constructed in an extremely methodical fashion, creating and emphasizing a range of oppositions between qualities, objects, and actions. In the course of watching the fifteen films, one is led to consider that, through the use of the camera, the filmmaker can create worlds, imprison things, write, freeze things, get a handle on things, choreograph, imagine. The recurrent focus on the hand suggests a down-to-earth view of filmmaking as a kind of manual labor or craft. Both the imagery and the incessant left to right camera movement elicit the inevitable analogy between film and language.

However, to view Sherman's fifteen films in this way is to overlook two critical aspects of the work: wit and magic. There is a deadpan humor that lurks behind all the improbable juxtapositions and reversals, a humor that results from the subversions of causality and the transgressions of all the categories that have been so painstakingly laid out. As in the activities of childhood, as in the symbolic action of certain ritual situations, categories are set into free play, not binding the world according to laws of causation. Unlike the positivism that informs the films of the Structuralists, an absolute certainty of the marvelous is intrinsic in Sherman's work. The hand not only crafts; it also works wonders. Glances cast spells. Objects have wills of their own; they are fetishes in the magical sense. And it seems to me that this is exactly how Sherman intends these objects to be perceived—not as fetishes in the psycho-analytic or Marxist sense. The magic of Sherman's films is not unprecedented. Indeed, they fit into the genre of trick films that preoccupied the earliest filmmakers, most notably Méliès. But they are striking and delightful precisely because they locate magic and mystery firmly in the everyday world. The tangible deliberateness of the composition of Sherman's films and the economy of his juxtapositions are worked out in a gesture of concision. Through the simplicity, clarity, and brevity of the images an acute sense of elegance and rightness is created. Like riddles, jokes, koans, and paradoxes, Sherman's films operate on the edge of sense, in a world of wonder.

NOTES

1. Sergei Eisenstein, "Through Theater to Cinema," in *Film Form: Essays in Film Theory*, translated by Jay Leyda (New York: Harcourt, Brace, 1949), 16.

2. Yvonne Rainer, *Work 1961–73* (New York: New York University Press, 1974), 238.

3. Noël Carroll, "Modernist Magic," *SoHo Weekly News*, September 28, 1978, 81.

4. For descriptions of Sherman's *Spectacles*, see Carroll, "Modernist Magic"; Berenice Reynaud, "Stuart Sherman: Object Ritual," October 8 (Spring 1979): 59–74; Trudy Scott, "Stuart Sherman's Singular Spectacles," *The Drama Review* 23 (T81, March 1979): 69–78.

5. Conversation with Stuart Sherman, New York City, March 1, 1981.

Imagination and Play
The Films of Ericka Beckman

Ericka Beckman was trained as a visual artist. While an MFA student at California Institute of the Arts in 1974–76, she moved from painting into filmmaking. The environment at CalArts was permissive and supportive of interdisciplinary art; Beckman's mentor, John Baldessari, headed a program called Post–Studio Art. Beckmann's projects at CalArts began with black-and-white Super-8 films shot from the monitor image of videotapes that she had produced. Her technique used the Super-8 camera as a kind of optical printer that altered the timing and framing of the video image. Her subject for these films was the production of personal and visual "icons," single images on a black ground composed of multiple exposures of matted black-and-white video images. It was at CalArts that she met Brooke Halpin, a music student, with whom she has collaborated on the soundtracks of her films.

Beckman produced ten short films as a student and gave her first New York City show at the Fine Arts Building in 1975. Her films were shown with the work of such artists as Richard Serra, Yvonne Rainer,

SOURCE: *Millennium Film Journal* 13 (Fall/Winter 1983–84): 98–112

Vito Acconci, Judy Pfaff, Robert Mangold, and others. Of her early film influences, Beckman has said that the work of Warhol and Snow perturbed her and prompted her own investigations, although her strong influences at the time came from visual/performing artists: John Cage, Rainer, Acconci, Joseph Beuys, and Phillip Glass. Following Cage, she set up systems (including chance) that would manufacture the work. She was also attracted to Cage's sense of playfulness and his willingness both to take risks and to use mistakes in his work. Beckman's work started with establishing actions based on game structures, often involving the manipulation of objects, her own construction of props and materials, and songs and texts that she performs herself or with a few assistants.[1]

Since moving to New York in 1977, Beckman has made five Super-8 color films with sound. All but one of the films is about one-half hour long (*Hit and Run* is only seventeen minutes long). In these films Beckman has developed a distinctive style in terms of the visual appearance, the sound, and the content. In 1983 she completed her first 16-millimeter film, *You the Better,* also thirty minutes long, which expands on these themes and effects. Beckman's films make use of dark backgrounds, giving the impression either of nighttime skies or a featureless, hermetic space devoid of landmarks for spatial orientation. The result is a mythic quality of a timeless, spaceless domain, a region of the imagination. But the dark background also has a practical origin. The superimpositions and double exposures that are a central feature of Beckman's style are created by shooting actors and objects against a dark field. On this dark ground, certain actions take place, often involving special props and constructions, enacted in a vivid, graphic manner. Objects and clothing are either brightly colored or brilliant white. Shapes are simple and instantly recognizable: a circle, a square, a door, a house. Very often the objects and symbols are like toys—bright red, orange, blue, and green blocks; white and yellow hoops; a red toolbench; bright yellow briefcases. Actions predominate over such elements as plot, narrative, or character, and these actions are both basic and recurrent: falling, running, gesturing, and—notably—all sorts of actions that come from games and play.

The childlike, often homemade appearance and the buoyant, cheerful tone of Beckman's films are related to a tendency in performance art that delights in the infantile. Stuart Sherman's play with small objects and verbal images, David Van Tieghem's musical adventures with various toys, and the polymorphous perverse physicality of Pooh Kaye's dances are only a few examples. The recent movement of performance

art toward music—especially toward the rhythmic, high-energy percussion of punk and new wave music—provides an important context
for understanding Beckman's work, because her films are either structured like songs or use repetitive, childlike incantations (composed with
Brooke Halpin) to carry narrative information as well as atmospheric
qualities, such as the excitement of a repeating percussive line. Another
aspect of the films that is childlike is the rich counterpoint of a light,
whimsical, innocent tone to content that is often violent, even morbid.
As in many fairy tales, the world of mundane reality is contrasted with
the realm of the fantastic in expressions that range from the sublime and
delightful to the harsh and cruel. Categories such as work and play,
male and female are set into stark contrast. The bifurcation of experience caused by the processes of representation, symbol-making, and
language are poetically explored. Especially important to the work are
the many levels of meaning present in both children's lore and folklore,
in which seemingly simple meanings also embrace layers of social,
psychological, political, and philosophical significance. In this regard, as
Beckman herself has pointed out, the double exposure becomes both
method and meaning in her films.[2] The films are much more complicated than they might seem at first glance because below their bright,
light, charming surfaces and the apparently disconnected streams of
imaginative icons one finds the most profound issues: questions of
ethics, identity, gender, sexuality, acculturation, destiny, power, knowledge. Subtle ambiguities arising from plays on words, from verbal images,[3] from elusive metaphors, or from arbitrary systems of rules and
abstractions generate both the quality of fanciful play and the possibility
of serious, double meanings. For instance, many of Beckman's titles can
be read in at least two ways. *Hit and Run* is partly a description of two separate activities that occur in the film; it also refers to the most reprehen-
sible, violent sort of automobile accident. Similarly, *We Imitate; We Break-
Up* refers literally to actions in the film (mimicking activities and
breaking up arrangements of objects) and more idiomatically to a friendship or love affair. Yet it also refers to the development of the mental
process of abstraction.

White Man Has Clean Hands (1977) juxtaposes language to images in
ways that only partially correspond. It pokes fun at American consumer
society by using the format of the consumer survey with a subversive
twist. At the same time, it is a devastating indictment of the power of
advertising. And further, it takes infantile delight in wholesale chaos.

Images from advertisements are intercut with images of both clumsiness and violence, so that one aspect of the film is its moral commentary, constructed through montage. But another aspect of the film is its formal play with words, colors, and representations, using such devices as repetition, variation, and statement-answer. Because the formal play is more immediately apparent than the commentary, the film appears playful rather than solemn or cautionary. But it is playful in the way that many children's games, songs, and stories are—under its lilting surface one finds all sorts of brutal imaginings.

The film begins with running titles rhythmically intercut with footage of a few activities. The titles exhort one to "Make a cross on the first thing you see." The image is a set of concentric circles, then a pair of clasped hands. "Make a cross before it leaves you." The hands open in a gesture of offering. A blindfolded man moves tentatively against a grid of horizontal stripes, "Make a cross on the mistake." A man runs in circles, in place. "Make a cross off the record." The man is now seen running on a superimposed image of concentric circles, like a huge record album, which revolves under his feet. "Make a cross on the correction." A woman in white pants paces in a circle; a label dangles from her waist and, when the camera zooms in, we see that the label shows the man we saw running in circles earlier. Drum rolls introduce each entry in this list, creating an atmosphere of circus-like spectacle and building suspense. The format is part survey, part game. As the list continues, one finds oneself prompted to puzzle out the connections between the instruction and the image; because of the powerful format—the rhythmic statement-response that is further divided into word-image—there is a palpable sense of necessary correspondences, even in the most obscure, seemingly arbitrary cases.

The list goes on. The activities recur or vary. The blindfolded man walks along, arms outstretched, in a game of blindman's bluff. Sometimes he falls or knocks things over. The other man repeatedly takes a pack of Tareytons out of his breast pocket. Eventually, when he puts a cigarette to his mouth, the black-and-white picture turns into color, as red flames blaze. A woman's voice cries, "NO!" In a later sequence the man puts a gun to the roof of his mouth, a woman throws laundry out a window, and a woman falls down a flight of red-lit stairs in another flash of color. A notebook falls open, echoing the movement of the hands in the second shot. The blindman stumbles onto two tall stools and falls when he tries to sit between them. One finds oneself responding to the images with words, labels, figures of speech (such as "falling between two stools"); the urge is to complete the word-image statement-response with another response, in words.

After about twenty-five shots the drumming stops and the rhythm of the film changes. Now the shots are longer; they show more of the actions, and they show them in recognizable, sensible sequences. But as the film becomes more orderly and comprehensible, the actions it depicts become progressively chaotic and violent. The blindman climbs a ladder that falls apart and knocks over a table set with flowers and glasses of water. The man shoots himself over and over. The woman falls again and again.

White Man Has Clean Hands is structured more like a song or dream than like a narrative. Its meaning is constructed by juxtaposition and as-sociation, rather than by causal relations. But if it is a song, it is like a child's made-up ditty that courses from theme to theme, returns obses-sively to favorite verses, makes use of arbitrary time divisions, rhymes only intermittently, and, as I have suggested above, revels in gory fanta-sies as well as in abstract wordplay.[4] A feeling of play is engendered by the associations that skip from one level of meaning or appearance to another, by the actions that are rhythmically answered by succeeding but disparate actions, and by the tensions between the literal and figura-tive meanings of words as well as images. Sometimes this playfulness takes the form of a series of abstractions, codes, and representations. For instance, the circles traced by the running man and the pacing woman are echoed in the concentric circles, which we can understand as a record, and then the circles later appear in a drawing tacked to a wall. Color shots are reserved for danger: fire and falling down stairs. When in one color shot we see two red buckets, we read them as fire buckets because of the code. A person standing in the buckets raises one foot, which is coated with a black liquid. This odd image is answered a few shots later when, in a black-and-white image, the blindman plunges his hands into two glasses of water (recalling the film's title). At the end of the film, the camera comes to rest on the two glasses of water standing on the floor in their original position, despite the fact that the blindman has just knocked them off the table. Their symmetry echoes that of the two red buckets and also that of the two stools. Another movement-rhyme is that of the opening of the clasped hands and of the spiral note-book, an association rich with implications, especially in light of the "clean hands" of the title.

Thus on the one hand, the film creates a feeling of pleasurable non-sense as it manipulates basic elements and categories such as fire and water, stripes and circles, walking and falling, in a vertiginous game that nevertheless displays a rigorous sense of order—a feeling that every image has its place in the developing pattern, every statement has its answer—and the unassailable logic of an insistent rhythm. One is re-minded of such children's chants as "Little Sally Saucer / Sitting in the water . . . / Ashes, ashes, we all fall down!" On the other hand, there is much in *White Man* that comments on the adult world, beginning with the irony of its title. The glamour of the advertising media is shown as both endlessly repetitive and destructive, a distorting abstraction of reality. More specifically, the film suggests that to smoke is to commit suicide. As in several of Beckman's films, men are associated with both games and violence, while women are shown in several roles: worker, victim, sexual commodity.

Hit and Run (1977) shows how appearances and actions that seem simple or innocent can take on more sinister meanings in new contexts. This is first stated in the title, as I have pointed out above. The opening shots of the film show first a running woman, dressed in turquoise, red and yellow, then a man, dressed all in white, who swings a white stick. The gaudy colors of her costume and the stylized abstraction of his make them seem toy-like or like cartoon characters; their activities are as innocuous as child's play. However, when the two images are super-imposed, we see their synthesis as an ominous event: a woman running from an attacker. The music changes from an a cappella, high-pitched song to a batting noise and then to percussive, harsh sounds like shots and slaps, underscoring the darkening tone. Later in the film, Beckman, dressed in a red leotard, tights, and red gloves, does a series of sexy poses against a wall. The jazzy guitar music slows down, and the dance seems to change from provocation to surprise. Next we see a man with a long-barreled shotgun. Again, the juxtaposition makes us interpret the woman's action in a new light.

In between these two significant juxtapositions, we see a number of different images and aural rhyming patterns. First, in black and white, a man walks down a city street. He walks in an ordinary way, except that his hand forms an O. A childlike voice sings, "Oh oh oh oh. / We say." The picture is replaced by a white hollow circle that, following the tempo of the song, grows rhythmically several times. It changes color, then magically is filled with an image of a domestic scene, again gaily colored, like a cartoon version of reality or an illustration from a children's book. A man and a woman play a game at a dinner table. He sits at the table and repeatedly drops a white plate. Every time he drops it, she, standing behind him, spins in place. When the plate breaks, a new sequence begins. Four images—white animated circles, a pair of jumping, sneakered feet; stripes of light; a gloved hand—alternate in rhythmic patterns, accompanied by snatches of song, drumbeats, and brittle, syncopated clatters. The ten shots in this sequence play out ten different permutations of sound and image, building and breaking suspenseful motifs. It is as if the forward motion of the film's theme were interrupted by a central section of pure play with key elements from its iconography, in much the same way that a melodic line in jazz may be suspended for a section of pure improvisation. But this nearly abstract section of pure play also harks back to the title of the film, since the action of the white circles is to hit the ground, while the feet enact an ornamented version of a run. In the final sequences of the film, a pair of feet treads steadily across the floor of a barren loft, leaving small black-and-white drawings of houses instead of footprints in its wake. The image is a pun: the feet leave "tract" homes instead of tracks, Beckman's first use of the idea of subdivision. The feet then step into three pairs of white circles and, as a foot leaves each circle, it flies upward out of the frame, not only reversing the downward flight of the circles in the central section of the film, but also echoing in its rhythm the hesitations and disappearances of the musical accompaniment.

As in *White Man Has Clean Hands,* the images in *Hit and Run* evoke many ambiguous meanings. In one view, the film is a series of game-like maneuvers, as shapes, colors, sounds, and motions are set into sprightly relations of opposition, imitation, contrast, and statement-response. The combination of recognizable objects into abstract formal patterns, in which one image or act calls another into being with all the appearances of causality but without narrative meaning imbues the chain of images with an odd combination of inevitability and arbitrariness, giving the film the look, even the structure, of a game. The bright colors add to the antic, homespun tone. And the domestic images—the man and woman at the table as well as the house-footprints—lodge the rest of the disparate, at times dangerous elements in safe and comfortable frame. As in many folktales, the dangers and darkness of the world beyond hearth and home are hedged about with memories or symbols of cozy domesticity. The result is not a sugarcoated version of a tale of hardship and suffering, but rather, an account of the world made conceivable by its mix of horror and pleasure, the unimaginable and the mundane, the serious and the frivolous, and made wieldy by schematic abstractions of cultural categories. Another view of the film would suggest a serious analysis of sex roles in which women are seen as playful, innocent, and domesticized, while men are seen as violent, even in their sports and games. Yet, as I have suggested, these two views are not necessarily irreconcilable, for very often even the most abstract, nonsensical-seeming children's games and tales in fact, on close examination, clearly reflect and even effect various stages of socialization of gender roles. It might be argued that *Hit and Run* takes a feminist position in this regard. But to do so would be to attribute a stronger political critique to the work and a more ironic tone than is actually there. Rather than staking out a doctrinaire feminist position, Beckman seems here to be commenting on the ways in which cultural expressions such as games carve out stereotypical roles because they abstract and exaggerate social relations.

We Imitate; We Break-Up (1978) is about two different kinds of imitation: the simple process of copying actions (mimicry) and the more complex analytic processes of abstraction and representation. The film grows directly out of Beckman's interest in the writings of the psychologist Jean Piaget and his views on the acquisition of language, on the importance of sensory-motor activities in developing pre-language symbolic functions, and on imitation as a key element in the development of human intelligence. Piaget isolates six stages in the development of imitation in children prior to the acquisition of language; this developmental process is linked to the process of representation, so that by the sixth stage imitation takes place at two levels of representation: that of concepts or abstract schema, and that of images or symbols, both of which appear in the child's development simultaneously with speech and the change of sensory-motor intelligence into representation and conceptualization.[5] Beckman has subsumed these six stages under two larger stages: in the first, imitation consists of simple mimicry, and in the second, it takes place through symbolic representation.

In the first section of the film, Beckman, dressed in a schoolgirl's outfit, imitates the movements of Mario, a pair of white constructed legs suspended by strings. The opening title tells us: "Mario and I are equal. At first we imitate each other." The legs walk into the camera frame, then Beckman walks into the frame and turns to face the camera with a triumphant smile. Mario taps a foot and lifts a leg, then Beckman turns a sequence into a little dance, to the accompaniment of a tinkly piano tune. Presently it is Beckman who turns a cartwheel; when Mario imitates her, the camera takes on his point of view and the entire room revolves. After Beckman and Mario play a ballgame that combines kickball, dodge, and basketball, their friendship sours. She bounces the ball against the puppet-legs and runs away, while on the soundtrack a girl's voice sings, "Mario's against me. He chases me." Drum rolls underscore the ominous, suspenseful sequence that follows, as Beckman carries an orange duffle bag, while a voice-over song says, "He's acting like I've got the loot." Later she repeatedly runs toward the camera, falls and runs, falls and runs.

The second section of the film shows a stream of rapidly changing, symbolic imagery. A white door appears, opens, closes, and revolves. A figure in white plays a bowling game with a white ball and white chairs (instead of pins), then carries a pile of shiny, gaudy boxes or blocks of different shapes and colors. We understand these as verbal images for the mental processes of breaking down and building concepts. We see a boxer, a stage, Beckman perkily aiming her rear end at the camera, a spoon, a clown holding the spoon, a title that states "This is your share of trouble," women, and a cake. The images prompt all sorts of verbal associations and rhymes, such as moon/spoon. Beckman runs toward a goal, but suddenly we see the boxer, who is now a runner, bursting through a curtain of crepe-paper streamers. Again, one understands this physical action as mental action, as if the mind were rushing toward the formation of an idea; the burst through the goal is equivalent to the proverbial lightbulb over a comic-book character's head, and signals a "breakthrough." Next we see objects that stand for other objects, a correspondence shown through magical transformations, such as white eyeglasses that become steering wheels as a helmeted figure sits down to guide them, while footage of a rushing train flashes on a screen above them. It is the context that gives the objects meaning, just as words are only sounds until they are combined with other words in appropriate patterns to form meaningful utterances. White drawings of boxes turn into the colorful, three-dimensional boxes seen earlier. Other actions and objects appear in a number of variations, as if the camera were making visible the operations of a mind endlessly assimilating reality and repackaging it as a series of abstractions.

Now we see a headless figure on the stage against a backdrop that is a glowing circle—part mask, part Halloween pumpkin, part moon. It is a typical Beckman image, a recombination of several elements into a single, hard-to-define synthesis that juxtaposes childish innocence to subterranean malevolence. The reference to Halloween, with its mythic, demonic substratum barely masked by its surface of sweet childish pranks, intensifies the cosmic ambiguities that Beckman calls into play on many levels in all her films; so does the chilling image of a headless body that on a gut level disturbs us, but on an intellectual level symbolizes the split between sensory-motor and conceptual activities that is the subject of the film. The circle sways, and the figure throws the mask's teeth out of the circle. We see that they are the colored blocks. The blocks migrate across the frame and rearrange themselves to form the windows and doors of a playhouse. Finally an invisible figure, of which we see only the bow tie and the drumsticks it wields, drums a tattoo, while the colored blocks again migrate, this time to form a face. The interchangeability of house and face is another aspect of the fantastical, child's-eye view quality of Beckman's work, in which conceptual correspondences—in this case, the connotation of domesticity, intimacy, comfort, and identity—have the magical power to change physical appearances.

We Imitate; We Break-Up seems to be not only about mental processes, but also about the social meanings play has for children. Here a relationship of cooperation and equality, expressed through mutual play, becomes competitive, antagonistic, and destructive. But these dynamics are negotiated through the symbolism of play, which provides a free realm in which various skills may be rehearsed and tested without fear of failure and where, further, violence may be indulged in without lasting repercussions. The ease with which the breakup occurs—the flight, which is transformed into a mere running race, and then the abrupt shift of subject to the imagery that prompts verbal associations in the second part of the film—as well as the fact that Mario is, literally, a construction, suggest that the relationship depicted here is that of the imaginary playmate that appears suddenly in the lives of many children. The imaginary playmate occupies an important role in the child's fantasy life, provides material for stories, and fulfills the necessary role of coactor in what would otherwise be solitary games. But then, having satisfied certain needs, the playmate disappears as suddenly as she/he appeared, without regret on the part of the child, who is ready to move on to new stages of play, usually involving real children as partners.[6]

The Broken Rule (1979) is more concise in terms of its action. It draws a contrast between a woman who hangs laundry from an old-fashioned revolving clothesline and a group of men who play a relay race. At first, their race involves pulling laundry down from the clothesline, but then the action moves to a blacktop outdoors at night, where the men line up in two teams, form huddles, run to and from a lit screen, and pass yellow briefcases over their heads and under their legs. One man always makes a mistake and breaks the rules of this strange game. He fails in his attempt to break through the intertwined arms of the opposite team, he passes the briefcase over when it should have gone under, he drops the briefcase as he runs along the playing field. Like Harold Lloyd, he is an incorrigible schlemiel. Meanwhile, a group of women cheerleaders appears. Lights flash on and off as they shout "Compete! Compete!" into lighted megaphones. As the relay race progresses, a song underscored by rhythmic clapping and drumming eggs the runners on; the chant ascends to a climax as the men reach their goals. Finally, the men run around the clothesline of the earlier shots, which has migrated to the blacktop to appear in front of the lit screen. Now the rules of the game shift again. This time the men take turns switching hats and briefcases. A woman waves a red kerchief in an image that fluctuates between approval and dismissal, symbolically indicating a winner and saying goodbye. Finally vertical panels with the image of a man in a suit running with a large briefcase alternate with red panels containing a black silhouette of a man—a target figure.

As with Beckman's other films, *The Broken Rule* sets up shifting meanings and correspondences. When men take over the activity that was a woman's (handling laundry), the activity changes social meaning—from work to play. When later the game switches between running toward a goal to switching hats and briefcases, it seems as though the men are no longer involved in playing a game, but have entered a work mode. Even so, their motions are as nonproductive as play; thus, their work is shown as lacking in seriousness or significance. By the final series of shots, we have come to equate the game with the stereotypical American rat race, in which the women stand at the sidelines to cheer on their men, who from boyhood are preoccupied with competitive sports that merely serve as a training ground for the rushed, goal-oriented, competitive life of the American businessman. The slipperiness of the metaphor creates a sense of the marvelous, since one thing (play) stands for its opposite (work). This irony is possible because, depending on the context, games and sports can be considered either work or play. A sense of the marvelous also stems from the folklore imagery: the idyllic colors and sounds (including bird songs) of the opening scene, when the woman is hanging her wash; the man all in white, who hangs up his wash, prompting the woman to gaze at him and stroke her laundry tenderly; the beginning of the men's game, in which each takes down laundry that matches the color of his clothing (orange, green, or white); the clapping, drumming, and chanting of the relay race section; the waving of the red kerchief. Beckman does not draw on any specific folklore tradition; rather, she creates new forms of songs, chants, games, costumes, and rules and symbols, all of which are arranged in patterns that recall the archetypal characters and functions of folk and children's lore.

Out of Hand (1980) is Beckman's most magical and mythic film, making use of her immediately recognizable stylistic elements—the superimpositions and animations, the juxtapositions of "real" objects with their abstractions, the bright colors and simple, toy-like shapes, the use of songs to supply information, the nighttime setting—in a structure that comes close to a narrative about a quest. A boy is dressed all in white; he lies on a grid of white stripes. The next image is that of a white, stately house, all its windows alight, against a black sky. As the camera moves in and we hear voices singing "Stea-dy. Stea-dy," the front door of the house buckles and bursts. The imagery recalls that of recent commercial horror films. Next we see a green door barred by red strips, an officer with a flashlight whose large, warm hand beckons, and a circle studded with five brightly colored blocks that revolve under a white stick. All of this is accompanied by a steady, percussive, brittle beat.

Suddenly the noise changes to a loud clunking sound and the boy is surrounded by the boxes, now open, changing colors, and each containing the eagle previously seen over the door of the white house. The eagles are now alive. Two men break through the green door. The boy shudders and wakes up. A title reads: "Something is missing. Something still lingers in the house he left behind." We see the boy running toward the house, which floats in the dark, to the sound of loud, ominous footfalls—even though he runs past leafy trees, down a dirt path, in sneakered feet. A second title reads: "He does not know where he put it, and he does not know exactly what it is." We see the image of the clock-like object again, but this time the blocks are white and the disc black. To a repetitive incantation of the phrase "Where is it?" a sequence of images unrolls. We see a paintbrush, a tool bench, a red shirt, a shovel, a blue toy house, the white house, and a yellow rocking horse. It is as if the boy is consulting a mental catalog in his search for the unknown object. He puts on the red shirt, as though it were a magic mantle. He takes the clock off the wall and arranges the colored blocks and the yellow suitcase so that at their center is a five-sided, coffin-shaped hole. The white stick moves from one block to another, while voices sing, "This . . . this . . . this . . . this . . ." The next sequence shows us what these blocks stand for by virtue of their colors: a large yellow trunk, the blue house, and the red tool bench with its tools.

The boy bends over the yellow trunk, takes out various objects, and throws them away over his shoulder. We see them hurtling for- ever through infinite space. When he finally takes out the yellow rock- ing horse and throws it away, it returns like a boomerang and hovers near him. He is attracted to it, a state made literal by the next image, in which a large blue magnet pulls the boy. The childlike quality of Beck- man's style is evident here in the pleasurably crude, homemade look of the objects. As in children's pretend play, what is important is the con- cept behind the construction and the graphic, diagrammatic shape of the symbolic, rather than complex details of realistic representation. When a child makes a pencil stand for, or "become" a soldier, it is enough that certain qualities (e.g., uprightness, rigidity) are shared by both; the child has no need to supply the pencil with a face or a uniform. Like the flimsy white puppet legs that stand for Mario in *We Imitate; We Break-Up*, the magnet, the blue house, and various other objects in *Out of Hand* are magical and meaningful exactly because they are so obviously figments. The boy picks up the horse and, mesmerized, rocks it. This ac- tion is intercut with a series of images involving a white steering wheel and the white stick (now functioning as a windshield wiper). With each succeeding image, the blurred shapes on the windshield come into focus, until we perceive that they are tiny replicas of the blue house. Like a video game, the screen above the steering wheel scans a landscape pop- ulated with graphic symbols. Next the screen simulates an accident in which the "car" runs into a white fence. The boy throws away the horse. The windshield/screen shows the blue magnet, and the boy turns to the blue house. Once again, the imagery depicts a mental process: the boy reaches deep into the fog of his consciousness and gradually focuses on the object of his quest.

But before he enters the house, he must explore the red tool bench. It is here that he meets what we can only interpret as his second set of archetypal obstacles or trials, required of a folktale hero, before his third attempt to reach his goal. Over the tool bench a red fan revolves, suspended from the ceiling. Each of its blades is shaped like a coffin. A battle ensues, in which the boy, after performing a dance over the trunk, seems to let loose the tools and the blocks and suitcases in a fusillade against another officer, who blows a whistle and wields a red shield. The boy takes the door of the blue house for his shield. The officer directs the flow of objects like traffic, nodding to the blocks but putting a halt to the tools. A song that begins with the dance over the trunk slowly builds its message, from "Gotta get a . . ." to "Got to get home." Now objects are divided into two piles: a blue one and a yellow one. The image seems to stand for a mental process of classification. The whistle blows as the boy reaches for the yellow pile. The officer's hand beckons him to the blue house. "Con-con-centrate!" singing voices admonish. The boy's action seems to stand for the making of a decision. "Take a note of it!" the voices advise. Now the boy again dances over the trunk, alternating hands as he reaches into it, while a song describes his action: "Dip, dive, go deep into it. I go deep into it." He takes a shovel and looks at the blue house, which is now filled with light that casts a reflection on the floor and refracts again, as if through water, in pale veins on the house's façade. "Look! Look! Look!" the voices urge.

Now the boy begins the final stage of his quest. He looks through the arch of the house, which is now a furnace. His hand, held up to the bright light from within, alternates with the image of the shield that had been the door covering the arch. A heartbeat sounds. Then, as if the point of view had shifted to looking out from inside the blue house, we see the silhouette of the shield with the white house at night superimposed on it. The boy reaches into the arch but looks blinded by the light. As he reaches into the arch, a woman's hand grasps his arm, which instantly turns into a red baton. There is a bifurcation of function of the two arms and hands: the right hand, extending, explores and the left hand, retracting, protects. Drums and cymbals play marching-band music, and as voices sing "Let it slip, pass over," we see, inside the house, three enchanted majorettes, with hips, legs, and booted feet in a row, but with only red revolving fans for upper bodies. We hear the sound of a motor and see the white house, with three red fans revolving in front of it on the lawn. The house backs up until it is miniscule. The final image shows the boy's hand grasping the handle of his shield: a small version of the blue house/furnace. Beckman explains, "He thought he would find it with the exploring arm—but it was always close at hand."[7]

Out of Hand is magical for a number of reasons. It combines and condenses formats and images from both myths and children's fantasies. Its rhetoric is sophisticated, creating metaphors for consciousness, memory, and symbol-making processes, but at the same time it is basic and childlike. The yellow trunk is, on the one hand, a metaphor for the mind, like David Hume's idea that the mind is "a heap or collection of different perceptions."[8] On the other hand, the shifting viewpoint of the camera turns the trunk into a gateway for another universe, peopled by toys, tools, and other objects, in which the guardian is another incarnation of the child himself (Paul McMahon plays both the boy and the second officer in the film). Both the trunk and the blue house are thresholds from the ordinary world to the imaginary world, which figure in many children's stories, from C. S. Lewis's *The Chronicles of Narnia* (especially *The Lion, the Witch, and the Wardrobe*) to Lewis Carroll's *Through the Looking-Glass*. As in such stories, objects here have animistic powers; for instance, they move by themselves. The double imagery of the house suggests a psychoanalytic interpretation, as does the fact that the boy-hero is played by a grown man. That is, the object of the hero's quest is self-knowledge—the blinding light—which he can only reach by returning to the "house" that stands for his childhood and by confronting the various powers, forces, and desires that lurk in that otherwise distant, closed realm. And this theme, of course, is essential to great epics and the most banal of children's tales both. There is, further, the imagery of the haunted house, again susceptible to psychoanalytic interpretation: the boy's task is ultimately to battle the satanic majorettes, half-human (half-woman) and half-machine, who simultaneously seduce him and turn him into an object. Finally, the underlying magical effect is that the boy creates not only the fantastic worlds within these mundane objects, but even "reality" itself, out of a few colored blocks; but although he has brought them into being, they assume lives of their own, beyond his control.

You the Better (1983) uses a 16mm format to expand on the themes and effects of Beckman's earlier work. Not only are the special effects more complex, including insets, superimpositions, and animation, but also Beckman uses dialogue for the first time. The use of the technologically slicker gauge fits the content of the film, for although Beckman's preferred structure remains that of the game (rather than the narrative), the film is about game strategies in realms that are far removed from the homemade tone of the 8mm films: gambling and capitalist expansion. Yet, in keeping with the style of her oeuvre so far, Beckman uses play in every sense to shape her message—using one thing to stand for its opposite; using one meaning of a word to stand for another meaning; constructing verbal images that function like puns to reverberate with meanings that are simultaneously linguistic and visual, literal and figurative; and mixing types of games to create hybrids with new rules. The result is a satisfying, even delightful slipperiness of meaning, a mental vertigo induced by the changefulness of contexts and rules in regard to a given word or object. For instance, the film opens with a song and animation sequence about subdivisions. As in certain TV ads, a matter with serious implications is made to look like fun in its mock-childish way: we see houses spreading—finally, marching—to cover every inch of space, until there is no space left, to the tune of a perky song with youthful voices urging "Subdivide!" At one point, as the houses revolve in what looks like an intoxicating dance, the subdivision's crossroads become a body, topped by a large house that becomes a face, and given hands that gesticulate to illustrate the song, which we now perceive as emanating from the house-man-construction. "The house" as commodity, as community, as home base, as a body or face, as the management of a casino, as the audience in a theater, and as a disco[9] is central to the gyrating meaning of the film. So is the act of spinning, as if the film itself, making use of various images of turntables, roulettes, and other circular motions, were a giant wheel.

Another instance where meaning pivots takes place at the end of the subdivision song. The voices ask how it is possible to go on subdividing when it seems there is no place else to expand, then suggest an answer. "Points! in the distance. Points! on the land. Points! make it possible / To expand." We see an endless row of yellow dots stretching out from the little houses that form a grid over the black ground. But then the song shifts to another meaning of the word "points," observing that playing games creates these points. The rest of the film shows two different games played by two teams in blue uniforms. They use a bright yellow ball, recalling the yellow points expanding the subdivision. The yellow circles are repeated on their backs, where three black circles on top of the yellow circle make the insignia look like a cross between a bowling ball and the ubiquitous smiling face from the logo "Have a nice day!" As the first team begins to play on a huge roulette wheel, coins tumble onto either a red or a green outline of a house, recalling the houses and hotels of the game Monopoly. The game is like a machine, manufacturing points, and shown in juxtaposed shots as equivalent to a man sitting at a turntable dealing cards, and a blue spiral figure, like an incandescent Michelin ad, that spins and seems to generate more yellow balls for the thrower. A roller coaster delivers chips to a house, like a mining chute. Hortatory songs suggesting teams of cheerleaders urge the players to "Get to the top! Don't stop!" One player breaks into the center of the wheel. As in the recent movie *Tron,* he is suddenly inside the game and the inanimate object that was the game is anthropomorphized. He plays a game that is part bowling, part football, part discus throwing. At first his shots hit the red or green houses that revolve around him, but then they go beyond the circle to land in the lighted window of the house in the distance. The other members of the team try to catch the ball and complain that he should stick to the red and green houses as his targets. Finally the game ends because the plays have run out. "Chance makes it so that / Things can't just go back / To where they once came from," the ghostly cheerleaders sing. The song, using "things" in both a specific and a general, idiomatic sense, shifts levels of meaning and also inaugurates a new section of the film. Now a new game begins on a new court, shaped like the familiar house diagram with a yellow hoop like a basketball goal at the peak of its "roof." The players dribble, pass, and throw the ball through the hoop. "Take a shot / Put a house on a lot," the voices chant. The players take turns facing the camera to make testimonials about their style of playing, as though the game were interlarded with interviews or deodorant ads. The game is not exactly a basketball game, however. As each shot is made, a cartoon cowboy and clatter of golden coins appear on the screen, and drawling voices sing "Hands up! Put your hands up! Give me your / Better give me more." We are drawn to interpret the game as partly a one-armed bandit. As each shot is made, the basket moves, pole and all, away from the court and then returns, making the players look as though they are being released from a box deeper into the game. The players take turns cutting capers under the basket. In the final shot of the film, we see a house that magically turns into a cartoon face, and the game board wheel spins out a face.

The ambiguity of the film begins with its title and with the opening lines of the first song heard in the film, "Things can only change for the better." The audience is both bettor—since the implication is that the audience is placing bets on the outcome of the game and taking sides with first one team, then the next—and better, in the sense that the audience sees the game from the outside, from various points on the revolving circle, from the vantage point with the most information, and also in the sense that "things will get better"—the false optimism gambling propagandizes. Beckman makes fun of this superior notion of the audience at the same time that she pokes fun at complacency in general, for at the same time that the lyrics of the song seem optimistic, they can be read equally as a bitter submission to fate: "Things can only change—for the bettor [and not for the team]."

I have already referred to the multiple, contradictory meanings of the house in *You the Better*, as well as to the ways in which Beckman makes metaphors by letting one thing stand for its opposite or for something close to, but not identical to it. In *The Broken Rule* work and play were poetically conflated. In *You the Better* Beckman makes syntheses not only of game forms, but also of game functions, creating a delightfully nonsensical situation in which one class of games is explained in terms of another class. For example, Roger Callois has divided games into four categories: competition, chance, simulation, and vertigo. (Within these categories, the form ranges along a spectrum from joyful improvisation [*paidia*] to a "taste for gratuitous difficulty" [*ludus*].) Brian Sutton-Smith, however, has made a different classification system, according to social function and whether the outcome of the game depends on skill, strategy, or chance. Both of these systems, as well as other recent theories of play, are useful in thinking about Beckman's films.[10] In *You the Better* Beckman begins with a situation that has nothing to do with play—the construction of houses. In fact, this situation is normally considered a typical work situation. Beckman transforms work into a game, but a game that shifts between competition, chance, strategy, mimicry, and vertigo, as each type of game becomes yet another representation of the original situation, in an interlocking chain of metaphors. The result, in this film as well as in Beckman's earlier films—all of which are shaped by play and game structures—is an oxymoronic vision of the very workings of the mind, in which the most profound issues of thought and experience are made concrete and comprehensible once they are cast into the exuberant, antic terms of child's play.

NOTES

1. Interview with Ericka Beckman, New York City, June 22, 1982, and subsequent conversations.

2. Interview with Beckman.

3. For an explication of verbal images, see Noël Carroll, "Language and

Cinema: Preliminary Notes for a Theory of Verbal Images," *Millennium Film Journal* 7/8/9 (Fall/Winter 1980–81): 186–217.

4. On children's word play, see Barbara Kirshenblatt-Gimblett, ed., *Speech Play* (Philadelphia: University of Pennsylvania Press, 1976), and the many works cited in its extensive bibliography.

5. See Jean Piaget, *Dreams and Imitation in Childhood*, trans. C. Gattegno and F. M. Hodgson (New York: W. W. Norton, 1962).

6. Ernestine H. Thompson and Tanya F. Johnson discuss the cultural functions of the "Imaginary Other" in "The Imaginary Playmate and Other Imaginary Figures of Childhood," in *Studies in the Anthropology of Play: Papers in Memory of B. Allan Tindall*, ed. Phillips Stevens Jr. (West Point, New York: Leisure Press, 1977), 210–22.

7. Conversation with Beckman, June 13, 1983.

8. David Hume, *A Treatise of Human Nature*, 2nd ed., ed. L. A. Selby-Bigge and P. H. Nidditch (New York: Oxford University Press, 1978).

9. "The house" has been used recently in disco music and rapping music to refer both to discotheques and to the community dancing together at a party or disco. "Rock the house" is a favorite rap expression. This domesticization of the public dance space is a key element of urban teenage culture. See, for instance, Sally Banes, "A House Is Not a Home," *Village Voice*, April 13, 1983, 77. Beckman's music is related both rhythmically and imagistically to rap music and punk music and her visual style is also related (but not, I would argue, derived from or identical) to the two streams of youth culture associated with these two kinds of music—the world of wild style graffiti and the punk or new wave style—which have recently begun to fuse.

10. See Roger Callois, *Man, Play, and Games*, trans. Meyer Barash (New York: Schocken Books, 1979; reprint of 1961 Free Press edition); various works by Brian Sutton-Smith, especially *The Folkgames of Children* (Austin: University of Texas Press; American Folklore Society Bibliographical and Special Series, vol. 24, 1972); and the essays in Stevens, ed., *Studies in the Anthropology of Play*.

The Last Conversation
Eisenstein's Carmen *Ballet*

In 1947 Sergei Eisenstein choreographed a miniature ballet. Since Eisenstein was a man of the theater and a visual artist as well as a filmmaker, it should not surprise us that he also ventured into the world of dance, although he had no formal dance training. That he should do so, however, while suffering from acute heart disease, about a year before his death, is rather surprising.

This miniature ballet was a duet created for and with the Bolshoi dancers Susana Zviagina and Konstantin Rikhter (Rikhter had appeared in the *Dance of the Oprichniki* in the film *Ivan the Terrible, Part Two*). Entitled *The Last Conversation*, the dance was set to a musical pastiche (apparently created by Eisenstein himself) and was based on the final scene of the Bizet-Mérimée opera *Carmen*.

The Last Conversation was a ballet in the general sense—that is, a theatrical dance. A brief variety show duet—what dance people call a "concert number"—rather than a full-scale ballet, it made use of typical

SOURCE: Paper presented at the "Eisenstein: Texts and Contexts" conference, Oxford, England, 1998

Spanish-style character dancing from the ballet repertory, but removed from the usual three-act ballet framework in which those steps are usually embedded as a contrast to the classical ballet dancing. The dance embodies Eisenstein's abiding interest both in Spanish culture and in popular entertainments as a source for movement in both theater and film.

According to Zviagina, who described her work with Eisenstein in a 1979 article in *Sovietskaya Musika,* during the shooting of the *Dance of the Oprichniki* in *Ivan,* "[Rikhter] . . . began to catch [Eisenstein's] attention."[1] She tells us that after Eisenstein had a heart attack in February 1946, she and Rikhter visited him often at the Kremlin Hospital, and he began to plan a dance for them.

During the summer of 1946, when Eisenstein moved to his dacha in Barvikha, Zviagina and Rikhter called on him regularly. They spoke often about art, and Zviagina recalls that "[he] made us look around with more perceptive eyes and find something new everywhere. He made us understand people and events differently." By the fall, Eisenstein was back in Moscow, where he often went to the Bolshoi Theatre (at which theater he had, in 1940, directed a production of Wagner's *The Valkyrie*). Apparently Eisenstein was an avid ballet spectator. According to Zviagina, he considered Lavrovsky's *Romeo and Juliet,* to music by Prokofiev, with Galina Ulanova as Juliet, a work of genius. When Zviagina danced the role of the Basque heroine Thérèse in Vainonen's *Flames of Paris,* about the French revolution, Eisenstein summoned the dancer to his apartment, criticized everything about her performance, and then coached her on her makeup, hairstyle, costume, and onstage behavior.

It was at the Bolshoi Theatre, seeing his two young friends in a Spanish gypsy dance in the ballet *Don Quixote,* that the idea for *The Last Conversation* began to germinate. The ballet *Don Quixote* is a staple of the Russian ballet repertory. A nineteenth-century classic based on an episode in Cervantes's novel, set to music by Minkus, it had been rechoreographed by Rostislav Zakharov in 1940. (It was Zakharov who worked on the dances and movements in *Ivan the Terrible.*) After seeing *Don Quixote,* Eisenstein was inspired to make his own Spanish ballet, based on *Carmen.*

Rehearsals for *The Last Conversation* began. The dancers borrowed a ballet studio at the Moscow Choreographic Institute, working at midnight (after official Bolshoi rehearsals ended) with Eisenstein and the musical director Solomon Bricker. Eisenstein's film students came to observe. At the first rehearsal, Zviagina remembers, Eisenstein sat down at the piano and "began shredding the score to pieces."

Though Zviagina claims that the musical director was horrified by this sacrilege, in fact what Eisenstein created was a *Carmen* pastiche. A pastiche, also known as *pasticcio*, is a technical term in music that refers to a medley, especially of operatic themes. *Carmen* pastiches were an extremely popular musical trend in the mid-twentieth century; indeed, the tradition of pastiches of this opera date all the way back to the nineteenth century, to Bizet's own *Carmen Suite*. Eisenstein had, in fact, created a musical montage, according to his own principles of contrast and counterpoint in film montage.

As Zviagina describes the rehearsals, she and Rikhter danced to the music and also to Eisenstein's directions, which focused on both the physical encounters and the emotional content of each moment. He directed them as if they were actors, rather than dancers, and *they* supplied the movements. What emerges from her account (and the other documentation) is that the steps were relatively unimportant; it was the acting, and the action, that mattered. This might seem strange to those who only know Western-style ballet, where the face is relatively inexpressive, but in the Russian ballet tradition, character dancing supplies a rich arena for not only "exotic" dancing of other cultures but for emotionally rich, expressive acting—very similar to the silent film acting that Eisenstein knew so intimately.

Zviagina gives an example of their working method:

"She runs toward Escamillo," [Eisenstein said,] "but you don't let her, you walk down the diagonal, and she walks up it."

"But how should I walk?"

"Ah-ha, you don't know? Let's try it." And we rushed to meet one another. Sergei Mikhailovich frenziedly stamped his feet: "Listen to the music!!" We began to listen to the music, and Sergei Mikhailovich set before each of us, one after another, completely detailed, concrete tasks. "Stop her; turn her toward you; look in her eyes; ask her, 'What does this mean?'"

Limited by strict semantic "frames," we tried various movements, until Sergei Mikhailovich recorded which among them were the most expressive and at the same time the most laconic. The precision of his directorial imagination in its essence opened up to us as performers previously unknown possibilities for creating choreography.

It was created and rehearsed in Moscow, but the dance was never performed there. It was performed at least once in Tblisi, perhaps on a variety program while Zviagina and Rikhter were on tour with the Bolshoi company. And it may have been performed elsewhere. It was never filmed, or if it was, the film has been lost.

Although, like most ballets, *The Last Conversation* was not systematically notated, during rehearsals the artist V. Levin (who perhaps was one of Eisenstein's students) made drawings of Eisenstein energetically demonstrating movements and, crucially, of thirty-three poses from the dance in sequence.

In his essay "Eisenstein's Graphic Work," Naum Kleiman, Eisenstein's archivist, notes that Eisenstein also hoped to create a dance based on Chekhov's comic play *The Wedding* for the same dancers and, further, that Eisenstein planned a ciné-dance, "not merely to film an existing ballet production on stage, but create a real filmed dance using all the resources of choreography and cinema."[2]

Marie Seton notes that in 1947 Eisenstein had requested and received (and presumably read) Paul Magriel's monograph on Nijinsky from his (Eisenstein's) former film student Jay Leyda, who was living in New York at the time and was married to a dancer—Si-Lan Chen, whom he'd met in Moscow.[3] Perhaps the Nijinsky book was part of Eisenstein's research for the film version, mentioned by Kleiman, of *L'après-midi d'un faune*. In any case, it's clear that at this time Eisenstein had become extremely interested in theatrical dancing, and that his *Carmen* ballet was not an isolated project, but rather, was only one step in a sequence of dances and choreographic plans that burst forth from the frames of *Ivan*.

The Reconstruction Process

I began work on this project in 1995 in Moscow, when Kleiman showed me Levin's drawings and encouraged me to contact the original dancers, who in fact are still alive. Having worked on reconstructions and film documentations of American avant-garde dances of the 1960s, I immediately became interested in the possibility of recreating the dance.

I should point out that dance reconstruction is an important component of the dance world today. Recent reconstructions of ballets like Vaslav Nijinsky's *The Rite of Spring*, Bronislava Nijinska's *Les Noces*, and Balanchine's *Cotillon* have been major landmark events, as has the recent reconstruction in Moscow of Lavrovsky's *Romeo and Juliet*, and several international conferences have been held to discuss and debate issues of reconstruction (an important one was held in London in November 1997 and another in Stockholm in June 1998). Reconstructions are, in a sense, attempts to learn dance history through embodiment and to swim against the tide of dance's vaunted transience and ephemerality.

Unlike paintings, dances can be quite fugitive temporally. Unlike music (at least in the West), dance has no universally accepted notation system. So dance reconstruction works against the odds—the odds of time. Making and watching dance reconstructions is an important part of my work as a dance historian.

In using the term "reconstruction," I refer to Ann Hutchinson Guest's terminology. She distinguishes between various ways in which earlier dances may be preserved and brought back to life. For her, reconstruction (one of the six terms she defines) means "constructing a work anew from all available sources of information; aiming for the result to be as close as possible to the original. . . . The term 'reconstitution' might also be appropriate here."[4]

Kleiman generously made a Xerox for me of these drawings, and I called Zviagina, by then in her late seventies, to set up an interview on the day before my departure for the United States, hoping she would also put me in touch with Rikhter and that the two of them would help me reconstruct the dance, teaching it to younger dancers. But over the course of three years' attempts to set up interviews during various visits to Moscow, it became clear to me that Zviagina didn't want to participate in the project, whether because she didn't remember the dance or for other reasons.

I worked on digging up other materials relating to the dance over those three years—the musical score, director's notes, costume notes, and some of Eisenstein's own drawings at the Russian State Archives of Literature and Art (RGALI), photographs at the Bakhrushin Theatre Museum and the Bolshoi Archives, and documentary film footage of other ballet dancing of the period at the Russian Documentary Film Archive—and I finally decided to reconstruct the dance in the United States, with dancers Galina Zakrutkina and James Sutton, and with pianist Jeffrey Sykes. We recreated the dance using a variety of sources: the drawings, the musical score, Eisenstein's director's and costume notes and drawings, Zviagina's article, photographs of Zviagina and Rikhter, and, importantly, the repertoire of the Russian character dancing tradition.

Working in Madison, Wisconsin, with Galina Zakrutkina, who for over twenty years worked as a character dancer in the renowned Maryinsky (formerly Kirov) Ballet, I had a source of movement and memory as reliable (if not more reliable) than Zviagina's. Zakrutkina has performed what the choreographer Ben Harkarvy calls "Russian-Spanish" dances in such classical and modern ballets as *The Nutcracker, Swan Lake, Don Quixote,* and *Laurencia*—in other words, she had the same specialty as Zviagina and danced many of the same roles, including the Spanish roles. Zakrutkina was able to supply the steps from the Russian-Spanish repertoire in what I expect was almost exactly the same manner Zviagina and Rikhter had, because she knows the same preserved tradition.

Let me clarify and restate my point here a bit. The documentation strongly suggests that Eisenstein did not design the choreography at the level of creating individual steps. It's highly unlikely that he could have, since he lacked the requisite ballet training. Where, then, did the steps come from? From the dancers, who would have most likely used the vocabulary available in their Russian character-dancing tradition for Spanish dances. By enlisting Zakrutkina, a character dancer with a nearly identical professional background to Zviagina's, and by using Eisenstein's director's notes, in my reconstruction I adopted the same strategy Eisenstein originally used to create the dance. I directed the action and encouraged the dancers to link their poses with the most likely steps in the repertoire.

This method doesn't guarantee that the dance we produced looks exactly like the one created in 1947. But I still consider it a reconstruction of the same dance, since, in fact, having the same exact steps is not so important for the identity of this dance, given the way it was originally constructed. We definitely could approximate the feel of the dance, since we had Eisenstein's notes and scores. And in any case, our production is in accord with what appear to be the author's intentions, which is always the bottom line in historical reconstruction.

Significance for Soviet Ballet

In 1947 socialist realism ruled the Bolshoi Ballet. Its repertory was a treasure-house of classic ballets from the days of the Imperial Ballet—such as *Swan Lake* and *Giselle*—as well as new Soviet ballets with positive heroes, such as *Laurencia* and *Romeo and Juliet*. Of course, *The Last Conversation*, although it made use of Bolshoi dancers, was not at all part of the Bolshoi repertory, nor was it performed on the Bolshoi stage. But one needs to take into account what Eisenstein's miniature, unofficial version of *Carmen* meant in the context of these monumental official works, framed as social dramas. Indeed, given that Lavrovsky's *Romeo and Juliet* was revived for the Bolshoi Ballet in December 1946, one wonders whether Eisenstein's much more abstract and individualistic dance, using bodily poses and movements rarely, if ever, seen on the ballet stage, but along the same themes of lust, love, and violent death, was a direct and immediate response not only to *Don Quixote* but also to Lavrovsky's well-known ballet, which he so admired.

In a typically Eisensteinian mode, the themes of *Romeo and Juliet* were distilled into a condensed, miniature form, using cinematic devices like flashbacks and expressive dancing that advanced a narrative without words, and thus closely resembled silent-film acting, with a nearly film-frame sense of composition. Passions were deepened and heated up, so to speak, by using the character dancing genre, in particular the Spanish mode, rather than the cooler classical ballet style. In this sense, Eisenstein's ballet is unconventional artistically. But since Eisenstein was working with ballet dancers used to performing in a particular character-dancing style, the dance is also somewhat conservative artistically, since it departs from the often grotesque movement style he had used in his theater and film works since the 1920s.

And, at the same time, the dance has a socially conservative bent. After the explosive, closed male homosocial world of *Ivan*, *The Last Conversation* returns expressiveness to a conventional, heterosexual world, and it is notably free of political themes. The musical choices for the pastiche stress the individuality and love themes in the opera, isolating Carmen and Don José from their social milieu, though it is the passionate and sexual, rather than romantic aspects of love that the musical themes underscore.

Significance as an Adaptation of *Carmen*

It's very interesting to note that several ballet choreographers had essayed *Carmen* before Eisenstein. These include the French choreographer Marius Petipa (who later, transplanted to Russia, became the great ballet master of the nineteenth-century Russian Imperial Ballet). He choreographed *Carmen* during his youth, in Spain in 1845—the very year Prosper Mérimée's story was first published. And, in 1931 (shortly before his "reassignment" to the provinces) Kasian Goleizovsky choreographed a constructivist *Carmen*. Goleizovsky, an experimental Soviet choreographer who worked on the Bolshoi stage and also had his own small ballet company during the 1920s, often working in the miniature genre, was criticized during the Socialist Realist period for his overly erotic and "formalist" compositions.[5] In fact, Si-Lan Chen Leyda was a dancer in Goleizovsky's company in the late 1920s and early 1930s, and one of the pieces he made for her in 1929 was a Spanish dance. It's possible—though I don't yet have evidence for this—that Eisenstein's *Carmen* duet may have been a tribute to Goleizovsky's version—and to Goleizovsky's ill-fated experimentalism. Perhaps Eisenstein saw in Goleizovsky someone who suffered a similar fate to his own and created *Carmen* as a gesture of respect and sympathy.

Significance for Eisenstein's Theory and Practice

In 1947, of course, Socialist Realism was at its pinnacle in all the arts, including film, in the Soviet Union. In August 1946 the Communist Party condemned *Ivan the Terrible, Part Two*. Eisenstein's image of Ivan was too uncomfortably close to that of Stalin. So Eisenstein's retreat from film may not have been only for reasons of physical health. And in an economy such as that of the Soviet Union, it would have been impossible for Eisenstein to raise the massive amounts of capital filmmaking requires outside of the official, state-run film industry.

But as he turned to dance, to writing, and to drawing, Eisenstein did not entirely turn his back on cinema. In fact, he saw those three arts as closely connected to cinema—or at least to his view of cinema as dynamic, rhythmic, metaphoric montage. Moreover, dancing for

Eisenstein was a mysterious event that called up both pleasurable sensations of vitality and anxiety-ridden psychosexual memories from his
childhood. In the section of his autobiography entitled "How I Learned
to Draw: A Chapter About Dancing Lessons," Eisenstein writes that
"drawing and dance are, of course, the fruits of the same loins: they are
merely two different embodiments of the same impulse."[6] Constrained
by "the aridity of inviolable formulae and canons," Eisenstein never
could draw or dance according to the rigid standards of his education,
but his self-taught techniques in both arts were lively, graceful, eccentric, and sensual.

"While I was learning the foxtrot," he wrote, "I realised something
very important: unlike the dances of my youth with their strictly pre-
scribed pattern and sequence of movements, this was a 'free dance,'
governed only by the strict rhythm within the confines of which you
could embroider any freely improvised movement. . . . Here I found
once more the free run of line that captivated me [in drawing], allowing
the hand a free run, subject only to the inner law of rhythm."[7] Later in
the essay, Eisenstein compares this sense of liberation with that of writing itself—of his style of writing, that is, with its free-associative flour-
ishes and digressions.

In *The Last Conversation* Eisenstein almost seems to be making a live
film. Indeed, Levin's drawings—which in their low-angle perspective so
resemble Eisenstein's own drawings—not only serve as a choreographic
score, but also resemble a film storyboard; they suggest not only theatrical blocking, but also long shots and closeups. Thus Eisenstein seems to
test on the dance stage many of the cinematic theories he was working
on at the time. These include his mature refinements of the concept of
montage, as he sought a more organic filmic unity and explored the expressive possibilities as well as the kinesthetic foundations of what he
called "vertical montage"—the complex rhythmic, melodic, and tonal
synchronization of the visual and auditory tracks of the film.[8]

Eisenstein used the term "vertical montage" to denote a type of
audiovisual unity or synthesis that incorporated not only the shot-to-
shot, or horizontal, montage of silent film, but also the relationship between that visual temporal progression and another layer of horizontal
composition—the sound score. Vertical montage, then, encompasses
three compositional processes: the two sets of horizontal relationships as
well as their interweaving or stacking together at any given moment. For
Eisenstein, vertical montage was closely akin to musical composition

itself, to the complex polyphonic orchestration of the separate instrumental lines, for instance, in a symphony.

Several aspects of Eisenstein's thinking about vertical montage are relevant to this dance project of Eisenstein's and our reconstruction of it. First, I think Eisenstein may have been interested in working with dancers, and in particular with Spanish character dancers, partly because the richness and complexity of the flamenco rhythms in the dancing gave him an opportunity to test his theories about the primacy of rhythm, first in creating a "generalized image" about a theme and second in generalizing "the appropriate emotion." Dance is a very good medium for generalizing emotion—and this scene of *Carmen* is packed with several, often conflicting, intense emotions. For Eisenstein, movement provides the link between sound and vision. Movement is the means, and emotional expressivity is the end. And dance is, above all, an art of movement.[9]

Second, in our reconstruction we took into consideration Eisenstein's insistence that the synchronization of sound and image should not always be strict or consonant, but should vary. There is plenty of dancing to the music, but sometimes the relationship is one of syncopation, and sometimes the music and movement are in counterpoint or even direct conflict, as when Carmen dies slowly to the upbeat toreador theme. The repeated gestures we used—like Carmen's backbend or the upheld curved arms of the dancers—supply a series of visual rhythms.

In his essay on rhythm, Eisenstein almost seems to lay out a Brechtian idea of *gestus* when he writes:

> The very concept of montage has been raised up from the crude notion of "cutting up and gluing together" to a very advanced conception of it as breaking down a phenomenon "as such" and recombining it into something qualitatively new, into a view of an attitude towards a phenomenon that is a *socially interpreted generalization* about it. (emphasis added)[10]

Third, Eisenstein even refers to *gesture* as the basis of both musical and graphic structures. When watching *The Last Conversation*, one can see the relationship between the two "tracks" by doing the exercise Eisenstein did with his students while analyzing a shot sequence in his film *Alexander Nevsky*. He suggests describing in the air, with one's hand, the line of movement dictated by the movement of the music—not just the melodic line, but also the rhythm, tonality, and even the emotional coloring.[11] I think that dancing allowed him to explore fully the embodiment of that gesture, since so much dancing *is* visualization of music, which may in part explain why he worked on this project and planned future dance projects.

The theme of *Carmen*, especially the last scene—in which a quickly shifting compound of love, rage, jealousy, and misery reaches a crescendo of passion, exploding in a violent murder—was particularly apt for Eisenstein's inquiry into emotional affect and spectatorial absorption. Eisenstein's concepts of pathos (or artistic exaltation) and ecstasy (the outcome of pathos—a sense of transcendence) thread throughout *The Last Conversation*, reaching a tragic, rapturous climax in Don José's penultimate gesture, when he lifts his arms heavenward, acknowledging his own damnation, before collapsing on Carmen's lifeless body.[12]

NOTES

1. This and all of the following quotations from Zviagina are taken from Susana Zviagina, "Poslednii razgovor" (The Last Conversation), *Sovietskaya Musika*, no. 9 (1979): 91–95.

2. Naum Kleiman, "Eisenstein's Graphic Work," in *Eisenstein at Ninety*, ed. Ian Christie and David Elliott (Oxford: Museum of Modern Art, 1988), 11–17.

3. Marie Seton, *Sergei M. Eisenstein* (New York: Grove Press, 1960), 469.

4. Ann Hutchinson Guest, "Is Authenticity to Be Had?" Conference on Preservation Politics, Roehampton Institute, London, November 1997.

5. Not only was the Moscow art world small enough for Eisenstein and Goleizovsky to be acquainted, but also Si-Lan Chen, Jay Leyda's wife, danced with Goleizovsky in 1931. See Si-Lan Chen Leyda, *Footnote to History*, ed. Sally Banes (New York: Dance Horizons, 1983).

6. Sergei M. Eisenstein, "Kak ya uchilsya risovat, Glava ob urokakh tantsa," *Izbrannye proizvedeniya*, Tom 1 (Moscow: Iskusstvo, 1964). I have used Richard Taylor's translation, which may be found in *Eisenstein at Ninety*, 53.

7. Ibid., 58–59.

8. Eisenstein lays out his theory in his long essay "Vertical Montage," in *S. M. Eisenstein: Selected Works, Volume 2: Towards a Theory of Montage*, ed. Michael Glenny and Richard Taylor, trans. Michael Glenny (London: British Film Institute, 1991), 327–99. For an excellent discussion of vertical montage, see David Bordwell, *The Cinema of Eisenstein* (Cambridge, Mass.: Harvard University Press, 1993), 184–90.

9. See Sergei M. Eisenstein, "Rhythm," in *Towards a Theory of Montage*, 227–48.

10. Eisenstein, "Rhythm," 246–47.
11. Eisenstein describes this exercise in "Vertical Montage," 378–99.
12. See Bordwell, 190–95.

Homage, Plagiarism, Allusion, Comment, Quotation

Negotiating Choreographic Appropriation

Although choreographers have complained regularly about plagiarism at least since the early nineteenth century, until the Copyright Act of 1976 choreography per se was not protected under U.S. federal statute. But in the twenty years since that law has been in effect, there has been only one federal court decision regarding infringement of choreographic copyright.[1] Indeed, it has been remarked that the number of law review articles on choreography and copyright by far exceeds the number of court cases.[2]

SOURCE: Lecture, "Performance and the Law" seminar, American Society for Theatre Research conference, Washington, D.C., 1998

It seems that although ballet and modern dance choreographers are and have been extremely sensitive to issues of intellectual property and its infringements, they are not rushing in great numbers to the courts in order to pursue redress, either under the recent revision of the U.S. copyright law or under other intellectual property laws, such as those covering trademarks.[3] In fact, my research shows that most are moving slowly to take the simplest steps to protect their copyright, and that many choreographers are ignorant about what the copyright law requires as well as what, precisely, falls under the purview of the law. I have also found that some choreographers question whether copyright and other legal intellectual property protections are necessary, artistically sound, or even morally just, given long-standing custom and standard practices and ethos of the dance world. But at the same time, this seems to be a threshold moment when the actions of a few major choreographers and their heirs are beginning to set the stage for new dance world attitudes and practices.

The purpose of this paper, which is preliminary to a larger work-in-progress, is several-fold: to review briefly the protection afforded a choreographer under the current U.S. Copyright Law, to explore dance world custom concerning the redress of perceived plagiarism and copyright infringements, to offer an explanation for the dance world's apparent reluctance so far to take advantage of the legal system for intellectual property protection, and to consider recent shifts toward institutionalized protection under the law. Although many choreographers, dance administrators, and legal commentators have assumed that the 1976 Act was an unqualified victory for the dance world, I want to end by asking whether choreographers in particular and the dance world in general are well served by current intellectual property laws. This is a complex question that is not easily resolved.

Choreography and Copyright

Prior to January 1, 1978, when the Copyright Act of 1976 went into effect, choreography was not specifically protected by federal copyright statute except as part of a dramatic or "dramatico-musical" work.[4] In 1892 the modern dance pioneer Loïe Fuller sued for copyright infringement but was denied protection because, the court ruled, her dance was not "a dramatic composition." The court found that the dance simply consisted of "a series of graceful movements, combined with an attractive arrangement of drapery, lights, and shadow, telling no story, portraying no character, depicting no emotion."[5] This set a precedent for refusing copyright to abstract choreography. In 1952 Hanya Holm's choreography for the musical *Kiss Me, Kate*, fixed in Labanotation, was accepted by the U.S. Copyright Office.[6] This was the first time the office accepted a copyright registration for choreography, although it is not clear whether the dances were considered dramatic in themselves or were accepted as part of a larger musical theater work.[7]

The Copyright Act of 1976 included the words "choreographic work" in the federal statute's list of the categories of works protected by copyright for the first time.[8] Most importantly, whereas prior to 1978 a work had to be registered to be protected, the Copyright Act of 1976 provides that copyright protection begins as soon as the work is "fixed" in a tangible copy (for choreography, this would be either by written notation, film, videotape, or other means).[9] Beyond fixation, the law requires that the work be original.[10] The law protects five rights of authors: to reproduce the work (i.e., to make copies), to distribute copies to the public (i.e., to sell copies), to perform the work, to display the work (i.e., to broadcast it or in other ways show copies), and to make derivative works based on the copyrighted work (i.e., adaptations). These rights endure for the life of the author plus fifty years.

Copyright law exists to secure these rights of authors (the right to perform, reproduce, distribute, and display the work, as well as to make derivative works) against unlawful copying, whether in the case of unlicensed performances or videotaping or broadcasting or in the case of plagiarism. Thus, potential copyright infringement would cover a situation in which my dance company performs José Limón's *Moor's Pavane* without a license from the Limón Institute, or in which my television station broadcasts a video of the dance without permission, as well as one in which my dance company performs Limón's dance—or something very similar to it, perhaps under a different title—and attributes the choreography to me. However, in the latter case, it is still entirely unclear how much similarity between the two works would constitute true copyright infringement, because whether the standard for "substantial similarity" is quantitative or qualitative has not been definitively established; in the other arts, courts have interpreted this both ways.[11] At issue, too, is the ontological question of what constitutes the choreographic composition itself. These questions remain to be tested in the courts. As Julie Van Camp points out in her comprehensive essay "Copyright of Choreographic Works," since we lack both a history of court interpretations to provide precedents and a history of full theoretical discussion about choreography, not only the questions of similarity and the identity of the dance work, but also such fundamental copyright issues as originality, fixation, and derivative works with regard to choreography remain a source of confusion in the dance world.[12] That the copyright law covers only choreography and not performance (of dance or any other art) also presents a challenge, since if most of the fixations take the form of videotape or film recording, it will be hard to detach the choreographic "text" from its performance, the "dancer from the dance."[13]

Immediately after the new law took effect, several leading American choreographers, including George Balanchine, Martha Graham, and Alwin Nikolais, as well as the heirs of Michel Fokine, assiduously began registering their works; Graham even began putting copyright notices in her program notes.[14] But of the many choreographers and administrators I spoke to about copyright while doing research for this article, some did not even know that they could copyright (and probably already had copyrighted) their choreographic works simply by videotaping them, and very few seemed familiar with the rights and requirements set out in the 1976 Act. Several articles had appeared in the dance and public press shortly after the Act went into effect, but that was twenty years ago; younger generations of choreographers simply weren't reading *Dance Magazine* or the *New York Times* in the late 1970s and early 1980s, and they have never learned about copyright or other intellectual property laws as part of their professional training.

Even several older choreographers and their administrators evinced uncertainty when I asked them what steps, if any, they were taking to protect their intellectual property. Of the individuals I interviewed, most did not know that all it takes is to copyright a work is to fix the choreography in some tangible, nontransient form—that is, to notate, videotape, or film it. Several thought that although they had videotaped the work, it wasn't really copyrighted yet, since they hadn't included any copyright notice or registered the work with the U.S. Copyright office. And, in our discussions of copyright, some choreographers expressed the erroneous belief that if another choreographer had made a work based on the same or a similar idea, that might be a copyright violation.[15] However, many of the individuals I spoke to said that they now felt the need to educate themselves about copyright and other intellectual property rights in order to protect their work, and that they were beginning to take steps to do so.

Dance World Custom

In the many years before the law covered choreographic copyright, the dance world used other methods to protect choreography as intellectual property and to seek redress for what was perceived as artistic theft. These included formal or informal contracts as well as informal preventative measures and informal sanctions after the fact. Of the informal means, an example of prevention is an instance in which New York City Ballet dancers refused to allow Jerome Robbins to set a section of a new dance on them in rehearsal, objecting that the passage he demonstrated already existed in the repertoire of another choreographer. Thus, the dancers—who recognized the similarity between the two passages and enforced the moral rights of the first choreographer—prevented Robbins from doing something that they perceived as plagiarizing the earlier work. The second informal method—sanctions after the fact—takes place when producers, curators, funding panels, adjudication panels, artists' representatives, colleagues, critics, and even knowledgeable audiences identify a work as a copy or partial copy, or simply as what they perceive as overly derivative of another choreographer's work.

Legal commentator Barbara Singer thoroughly examined the procedure of licensing dance works through contracts, arguing that this customary dance world practice works efficiently in ensuring artistic control and "[offers] equal, if not superior, protection for choreographic works," because it protects the moral, as well as economic, rights of the artist. And she remarks, "Breaches of these contracts are . . . rare." When they do occur, according to Singer, "community sanction or the philosophy of the risk of the trade [i.e., balancing the benefit of free publicity against loss suffered] resolves most . . . violations."[16]

For the most part, it seems that choreographers or their heirs complain privately to friends and colleagues when incidents of perceived plagiarism or copyright infringement take place. In some cases they may apply peer pressure behind the scenes. But they rarely threaten legal action. In fact, it is newsworthy when they do.

Singer offers several reasons for choreographers' avoidance of legal remedies for copyright infringement. These include a preference for negotiation (a practice to which I will return in the next section); the high costs of litigation; the low stakes (in the dance world, there are few blockbusters, so in most cases only a small amount of money would be in dispute and perhaps not worth the effort of recovering); the lack of bargaining power on the part of all but the most famous choreographers; and what she calls "the philosophy of the risk of the trade," that is, reconceiving the "theft" as free publicity.[17]

In talking to choreographers and studying the literature, I find that reconception (whether conscious or unconscious, generous or grudging) is a common refrain, both among choreographers who appropriate from others and among those whose work has been appropriated. However, most choreographers do not reconceive "theft" or copying as free publicity. Rather, they see it as homage, allusion, comment, or quotation. Mark Morris has declared, "I like to think that I've built on what's gone before me. . . . I certainly refer to it. And I don't know if that's homage or plagiarism. But I use things I like. And I often like things that have been done before."[18] While Paul Taylor has complained privately that David Parsons, a former dancer with the Taylor company whose work is now all the rage, "stole" his entire career, Taylor himself has boasted publicly that "I steal from everyone—and if you're going to steal, you might as well steal from the best."[19] Several choreographers repeated to me the old adage, "Imitation is the sincerest form of flattery." And some reported that although they initially felt angry or outraged that another choreographer seemed to be plagiarizing their work, eventually they decided to "move on," to "let go," to "stop being too possessive." Anna Halprin, who creates community-based works, sees herself as part of a dance tradition of generosity, of giving her work to others.

Dance World Resistance to Legal Redress

Why have so few choreographers availed themselves of the redress promised by the copyright law?[20] Beyond the practicalities of cost, lack of evidence, difficulty of enforcement, and even ignorance of the law, more fundamental, it seems to me, are the long-standing, deeply entrenched misgivings about official legal institutions, in particular but not exclusively intellectual property laws, in the dance world.[21]

Both social and economic aspects of the dance world have traditionally made copyright, trademark, service marks, and other intellectual property protections alien practices, militating against redress through legal means. (By social, I mean the way dancers are trained and socialized into the profession.) These aspects have to do not only with issues of training, but also the nature of choreographic composition and the nature of the dance world itself.

In many ways, dance is an almost medieval, artisanal profession, an "oral" tradition in which knowledge is passed down from one person to another; there is a strong tradition of teacher-student training, even in those areas where innovation is highly valued, and students standardly serve apprenticeships with masters. Dancers receive instruction in choreography even as they learn dance technique, since what they practice daily in their lessons are the building blocks of either academic or personal dance techniques, including not only individual steps (which are not copyrightable) but also phrases (which may be copyrightable) from old and new choreographic compositions. In composition classes, as well, students train as choreographers by copying their teachers and the masters of the craft; it's not unusual to see entire generations of choreographers who are epigones of this or that choreographer's technique or choreography—that of Martha Graham, George Balanchine, Merce Cunningham, Alvin Ailey, and so on. In other words, dance students learn the classics, whether those of ballet or modern dance, by imitating them, much as visual artists once routinely copied the paintings of the masters.[22]

But also, choreography itself (even more so than orchestral music, but perhaps not unlike the improvising musical group) is a collaborative, cumulative enterprise both historically and at the time of its making. Historically, especially in ballet, choreographers build on the body of dance tradition that came before them. And choreographers usually make dances directly on their dancers' bodies, so the dancers contribute to the creative process, sometimes to a very great extent, in both ballet and modern dance. Despite the often hierarchical nature of dance companies, the communal process of making dances contributes to the widely shared attitude that the dance world is a family (or at least that dance companies are families), and that to assert intellectual property rights or workers' rights is to value *gesellschaft* over *gemeinschaft,* to violate a treasured system of shared trust and intimacy gained through person- alistic but closely connected informal networks in favor of individual- istic but bureaucratic, selfish business interests. To assert these rights is sometimes even seen as sacrificing one's noble dedication to art for base financial motives. Contracts are seen as only a mild way of asserting ownership, while copyright, perhaps because it is seen as mediated by a faceless, bureaucratic federal agency, is seen as stringent.

It is sometimes implied that this kind of action is uncollegial and even un-American, a holdover from alien, rapacious European or Rus- sian émigré business practices. In 1989 Barbara O'Dair reported that the U.S. premiere of a reconstruction by the Oakland Ballet of the 1924 ballet *Le Train Bleu* (choreographed by Bronislava Nijinska, to a libretto by Jean Cocteau, with music by Darius Milhaud, costumes by Coco Chanel, and a curtain by Pablo Picasso), would take place shortly, "un- less the efforts of Irina Nijinska, daughter of . . . the dance's first choreographer, derail it."[23] As her article demonstrates, in public dis- course there is a high level of resistance to the control of choreographic ownership through official legal means.

More recently, a British dance critic wrote of the Royal Ballet's withdrawal of a Balanchine work in 1997 in the face of the Balanchine Trust's now-notorious tight control over every aspect of licensing:

> Balanchine detector vans patrol the globe making quite sure that any ballet company planning to perform one of the master's works has a valid license to do so. Anthony Dowell had allowed the Royal Ballet's rights to *Apollo* to lapse last year but planned to revive the work this spring regardless. Oh no you don't, said the Balanchine Trust. Not only does it safeguard the steps, costumes and staging of the productions in its care, it also exercises strict quality control over casting. Although more than happy with Darcey Bussell and Jonathan Cope—not to mention NYCB's Igor Zelensky, who was scheduled to guest in the ballet—the Americans were uncertain about Irek Mukhamedov. Maybe if he slimmed down?[24]

The almost feudal nature of the dance field, its suspicion of "profes- sionalism" and formal institutions, including legal institutions, and its preference for operating within either informal, egalitarian friendship networks or patron/client relations, leads to a preference for finding redress within the community rather than resorting to official means such as litigation. Moreover, there is a gender issue here, in that the

American dance world is dominated by women who in the past have preferred to negotiate within informal networks, rather than formal bureaucratic institutional structures.

Too, there are different subworlds in dance where borrowings, re-workings, or other aspects of reusing another person's choreography take on different meanings and values. Since nineteenth-century European ballets are all in the public domain, ballet choreographers have long felt free to rework them regularly (as they were in their own time constantly reworked, revised, and adapted). So in the ballet world, at least, choreographers may have gotten used to seeing choreographic material (whether a phrase or an entire ballet) as freely available for reuse. And it may be that, given the oral tradition of the art form, the nature of a classic ballet "text" is an extremely malleable one, compared to other art forms or even other dance forms. More like folklore—for instance, jokes that are reinvented with each telling—than like "signed" and static works of art, the classic ballets belong to no one and to everyone. Every dancer potentially contributes something new to the choreography, and every choreographer may create his or her own version.[25]

Also, ballet has an established, codified technical vocabulary that has always been in the public domain. Just as there are stock phrases in epic poems and blues songs, there are stock movements and phrases in ballets. Although the Copyright Act of 1976 says neither individual steps nor social dances are copyrightable, it would be extremely difficult to prove that not only the individual steps in a ballet, but certain familiar combinations of steps or even entire variations are the original creations of any single individual's hand (or foot), rather than an accretion of many different individuals' versions over the years.

The twentieth century wrought new changes in the notion of innovation and thus intellectual property in ballet choreography, and it also saw the birth of a new dance form, modern dance, that prized artistic invention. In those worlds, not only individual steps and phrases, but even ideas (which, of course, are not protected by any copyright legislation) are guarded jealously. Yet, oddly enough, so many modern dances look alike, in particular those emanating from a single school of technique, such as Martha Graham's.

In postmodern dance, sometimes the choreography itself may consist only of an idea: a dance generated from instructions, for instance, in which the look of the movement would not be central to the identity of the dance. The challenges postmodern dance has posed for the issues of a dance's identity and the blurring of the line between idea and expression complicate the issue of copyright. If this year a choreographer set a man walking down the side of a building quite differently from the man in Trisha Brown's 1969 dance *Man Walking Down the Side of a Building*, would the new work infringe the copyright in the older one?[26]

Some postmodern choreographers, such as Karole Armitage, Mark Morris, Doug Elkins, and Stephen Petronio, in fact view choreography entirely as recycling; rejecting the very concept of originality, they blatantly appropriate movements, phrases, and dance styles from anywhere and everywhere, radically challenging notions of plagiarism and intellectual property and raising the question of how one marks quotations or allusions in a dance or other performing art. In fact, shortly after the 1976 Act went into effect, several postmodern choreographers created dances that satirized copyright and anxieties about intellectual property.[27]

There is another extremely powerful reason for the dance community's resistance to redress through the federal copyright law. Historically, not only was much dance excluded from protection by the Copyright Act before 1976, but that same law imposed enormous financial hardships on choreographers and dance teachers for the use of music in the dance studio as well as in public performances. Thus dancers and choreographers, who view their compulsory fees to ASCAP and BMI as an unfair and oppressive form of taxation, have come to view copyright law with deep suspicion.[28]

Recent Shifts

Despite these factors, increasingly choreographers and their heirs are moving toward taking steps to ensure protection. During the dance boom of the 1970s and 1980s, the same pressures that led to the naming of choreography in the Copyright Act led to an increased institutionalization and professionalization of the dance field. Growth entailed new financial concerns and responsibilities; funders insisted on administrative accountability; newly hired company administrators recommended enlisting an array of other services and experts, including booking agents, accountants, and lawyers.

Further, while dance had long suffered from a lack of visibility and mass distribution, since 1978 when the Copyright Act took effect there

has been exponentially increased reproduction, first through the avail-
ability of inexpensive videotape technology, and second through television broadcast and (more recently) the Internet. So choreographers
are only now being faced with challenges regarding reproduction and
distribution that have been discussed at length in the courts regarding
the music industry, for instance, continually since 1909. After the death
of George Balanchine in 1983, his heirs formed the Balanchine Trust,
which not only protects the copyrights in the choreographer's ballets,
but also has trademarked his style, technique, and even his name.[29]
Other choreographers' heirs have followed suit. Beyond the artistic control of individual dance works offered by the Copyright Act, other cre-
ators of dance techniques have turned to trademark and service mark
law to protect their financial interests.[30]

Conclusion

In 1938 the British philosopher R.G. Collingwood argued convincingly
against artistic ownership, pointing out:

> We need to try to secure a livelihood for our artists (and God knows
> they need it) by copyright laws protecting them against plagiarism; but
> the reason why our artists are in such a poor way is because of that very
> individualism which these laws enforce. If an artist may say nothing ex-
> cept what he has invented by his own sole efforts, it stands to reason he
> will be poor in ideas.[31]

While one suspects that Collingwood exaggerated the extent of the
copyright law for rhetorical effect, his point about the value of artists'
feeling free to elaborate on what came before them—not only in terms
of ideas, but also in terms of expression—is well taken. More recently
the dance critic Jack Anderson speculated that Americans have come to
fetishize originality. "Perhaps," he wrote, "we should worry not because
a few student choreographers happen to be influenced by [Laura]
Dean's spinning movements but because not enough of them are: they
may be missing the opportunity to master a striking way of dancing."[32]

   At one level, it seems only fair that choreographers and other authors
be protected from unauthorized copying and artistic theft, whether by
contract, copyright law, or the law of moral rights.[33] And in a modern

free-market economy, to refuse one's rights to one's intellectual property is in some measure to live in a dream world.[34] And yet, the outlaw musical sampling once favored by contemporary hip-hop artists is only the latest instance of a long tradition of artistic borrowing that has served to enrich the various arts while simultaneously raising anxieties about proprietary rights.[35] Copyright laws not only protect individual interests; they are also meant to protect the common good. And this raises questions about the relative benefits of protecting individual property at the potential expense of advancing the art form. Singer states that "American choreographers [eschew statutory protection because they] have their own 'law,' and they, at least for now, choose to be governed by it."[36] But dance world custom has the potential for abuse when unchecked peer pressure or rumor serves to intimidate and obstruct those choreographers who, while merely borrowing ideas or imitating styles (both of which are tolerated under the copyright law), are wrongly accused of outright plagiarism. In cases like these, obviously working within the law is far preferable to vigilante justice. But at the same time, it seems worth wondering whether the increasingly diligent legal protection of choreography, dance technique, and even dance style through the ensemble of intellectual property laws—from the rather limited copyright law to the extremely broad concept of protecting the "look" or "feel" of a product though trade dress—will have a chilling effect on the art.

As the millennium turns, it seems clear that despite some doubts in the profession about the value and the extent of copyright protection for dance, prevailing pressures as well as the new ease of copyrighting (whether intentionally or unintentionally) will lead to a steady increase in the number of dance works copyrighted. And it seems clear that conditions in the culture generally and in the dance world in particular will lead to more litigation and the use of other legal avenues of control. These conditions include expanded capacities for technological reproduction and distribution, the aforementioned escalating bureaucratization of the dance world, increased preservation efforts in dance, and a higher level of awareness of choreographer's rights. Also, in terms of the gender issue I discussed earlier, a new generation of postfeminist, professionalized women—both choreographers and administrators—who have no nostalgia or preference for quietly doing business "inside the family" will more often assert those rights publicly through official legal channels. Whether this is for good or for ill, only time will tell.[37]

NOTES

1. The Copyright Act of 1976 went into effect on January 1, 1978. The one court decision regarding choreography and copyright since that time has been *Horgan v. Macmillan*. In that case, a Federal Court of Appeals reversed and re-manded a lower court decision that photographs in a book about the New York City Ballet's *Nutcracker* did not infringe the copyright to George Balanchine's choreography.

The District Court had decided that the sixty photographs in the book did not constitute an infringement because they captured the dancers "in various attitudes at specific instants of time"; the judge in that decision pointed out that "choreography has to do with the flow of steps in a ballet," and that "the staged performance could not be recreated" from the photographs (621 F. Supp. 1169 [S.D.N.Y. 1985]). But the Appeals Court found that "even a small amount of the original, if it is qualitatively significant, may be sufficient to be an infringe-ment although the full original could not be recreated from the excerpt," and further, that "a snapshot of a single moment in a dance sequence may commu-nicate a great deal." And the judge pointed out that the question might be that the book constituted a copy or derivative work, in which case the issue was sim-ilarity, not the ability to reconstruct the ballet from the photographs (*Horgan v. Macmillan, Inc.*, 789 F.2d 157 [2nd Cir. 1986]). The Court of Appeals sent the case back to the District Court for reconsideration, but before the case could be decided there, Macmillan settled with the Balanchine Trust. See Julie Van Camp, "Copyright of Choreographic Works," in *1994–95 Entertainment, Publish-ing, and the Arts Handbook*, ed. Stephen F. Breimer, Robert Thorne, and John David Viera (New York: Clark, Boardman, and Callaghan, 1994), 58–92; Ade-line J. Hilgard, "Can Choreography and Copyright Waltz Together in the Wake of *Horgan v. Macmillan, Inc.*?" *University of California, Davis, Law Review* 27 (1994): 757–89. Philip Auslander discusses the role of memory in copyright in-fringement cases and in particular in *Horgan*, in "Legally Live," *The Drama Re-view* 41, no. 2 (T-154) (Summer 1997): 17–18.

In 1992 a suit charging copyright infringement and unfair competition over the infringement of Gower Champion's 1961 choreography for *Bye Bye Birdie*, which had been specifically excluded from the licensing agreement for the mu-sical, was settled out of court, thus not setting any legal precedent, although the plaintiff's lawyer stated that the settlement "enhances the rights of choreogra-phers" (*Champion Five Inc. v. National Artists Management Co. Inc.*, 91 8503, filed in a Manhattan federal court in December 1991, was reported in Stan Soocher, with Richard L. Curtis and Amiana Pytel, "Bit Parts," *Entertainment Law & Fi-nance* 8, no. 4 [July 1992]: 8).

2. See Laura Mansnerus, "The Dance Is Made and Danced: Now, Whose Property Is It?" *New York Times*, May 14, 1990, C13.

3. Space prevents me from discussing other aspects of intellectual property law beyond copyright here. But it is worth noting that the only court case I have found concerning dance and trademark law was one in which Les Ballets Trockadero de Monte Carlo, a satirical, all-male ballet troupe based in New York, successfully sued a rival troupe under the Lanham Act. The Trocks (as they are known) had registered the name of their troupe as a service mark. When the group's own Japanese producer hired a former member of the company to start a similar troupe, named "Les Ballets Torokka de Russia," and advertised that company's upcoming Japanese tour at the Trocks' performances in Japan in 1996, the Trocks sued and won an injunction that barred the new group from using the similar name. *Les Ballets Trockadero de Monte Carlo, Inc. v. Trevino*, 945 F. Supp. 563 (S.D.N.Y. 1996). See Robert Gurrola, "New York's 'Les Ballets Trockadero' Wins Injunction Against Copycat Competitor," *The Legal Intelligencer* (November 13, 1996), 11.

4. Colleen McMahon points out that choreography was protected by state common law prior to the 1976 Act and does an excellent cost-benefits analysis of both copyright and common law for dance in "Choreography and Copyright," *Art and the Law* 3, no. 8 (January 1978): 1–4.

5. *Fuller v. Bemis*, 50 F. 926, 929 (C.C.S.D.N.Y. 1892). See Heather Doughty, "The Choreographer in the Courtroom: Loie Fuller and Leonide Massine," *Proceedings, Fifth Annual Conference, Dance History Scholars* (1982): 35–39.

6. See "Copyright by Hanya Holm," *Dance Magazine* (July 1965): 44; also Lucy Wilder, "U.S. Government Grants First Dance Copyright," *Dance Observer* 19, no. 4 (May 1952): 69.

7. Regarding the history of copyrighting choreography, see Nicholas Arcomano, "Choreography and Copyright, Part One," *Dance Magazine* (April 1980): 58–59.

8. U.S.C. 102(a)(4). See Nicholas Arcomano, "Choreography and Copyright, Part Two," *Dance Magazine* (May 1980): 70, 119; and Nicholas Arcomano, "Choreography and Copyright, Part Three," *Dance Magazine* (June 1980): 62–63 for a summary of the new law and its application.

9. Although neither a copyright notice nor registration are now required for copyright protection, as they were in the past, both greatly enhance the rights of the author if a case of copyright infringement goes to court.

10. Many commentators have pointed out that "originality" has a different meaning under the law than in common usage. To be original only means that the work originated in the work of the author, not that it is necessarily particularly innovative. In *Feist Publications, Inc. v. Rural Telephone Services*, for instance, the Supreme Court stated, "Assume that two poets, each ignorant of the other, compose identical poems. Neither work is novel, yet both are original and, hence, copyrightable" (499 U.S. 340, 346 [1991]). In *Alfred Bell & Co. v. Catalda Fine Arts*, the court considered mezzotints based on sources in the public domain

copyrightable because the works in question were new "versions," which "'originated' with those who made them" (191 F.2d 99, 102 [2nd Cir. 1951]).

11. Recall that the *Horgan* court found that "even a small amount of the original, if it is qualitatively significant, may be sufficient to be an infringement." In February 1998, the renowned French choreographer Maurice Béjart was found guilty of plagiarizing a section of Frédéric Flamand's ballet *La Chute d'Icare* (The Fall of Icarus) (Jean-Pierre Borloo, "Maurice Béjart a bien plagié Frédéric Flamand dans 'Le Presbytère . . . ,'" *Le Soir*, February 28, 1998, 9). In his ballet *Le Presbytère . . .* , the court found, Béjart copied a one-minute, forty-three-second movement sequence. Béjart's office stated that he would appeal the case because the court "abusively protects" an author's rights to a point that impinges on other artists' creative freedom (Karyn Bauer, "Béjart Sued for Plagiarism," *Dance Magazine* [May 1998]: 22, 24). However, this would not serve as a precedent for violations of American copyright law, since the European concept of "author's rights" or "moral rights" is far more comprehensive protection than that of copyright. The judge in the Béjart case specifically stated that the plaintiff's "patrimonial rights," a crucial part of the concept of moral rights, had been violated.

12. See Van Camp for an excellent, thorough assessment of the challenges still facing the interpretation of the Copyright Act of 1976 in regard to choreography in light of the *Horgan* court's statements. Also see Hilgard; Martha M. Traylor, "Choreography, Pantomime and the Copyright Revision Act of 1976," *New England Law Review* 16, no. 2 (1981): 227–55; and Leslie Erin Wallis, "The Different Art: Choreography and Copyright," *UCLA Law Review* 33 (1986): 1442–71 for considerations of the application of the 1976 Act to choreography.

13. Van Camp, 68, discusses the problem posed by the difficulty of separating the dance from the performance. This might be an argument in favor of notation, rather than audiovisual recordings of a single rehearsal or performance, as a fixation method. However, notation is expensive and has its own limitations. And practically speaking, more choreographers videotape their work, whether for copyright or other reasons, than have it notated. See Auslander, 9–18, for a discussion of the relationship between copyright and performance.

14. Nicholas Arcomano, "The Copyright Law and Dance," *New York Times,* January 11, 1981, sec. 2, 8.

15. Section 102(b) of the Copyright Act states: "In no case does copyright protection for an original work of authorship extend to any idea, procedure, process, system, method of operation, concept, principle, or discovery, regardless of the form in which it is described, explained, illustrated, or embodied in such work." Since there can be many, if not infinite, expressions of a single idea, the dichotomy between idea and expression is a basic principle of copyright. In principle, the law does not protect the ideas or facts underlying a work; it protects particular expressions of ideas. However, in practice, this dichotomy

may not always be entirely distinct. See Van Camp, 66–67, for a discussion of the problematic application of the idea-expression dichotomy in regard to choreography.

16. Barbara A. Singer, "In Search of Adequate Protection for Choreographic Works: Legislative and Judicial Alternatives vs. The Custom of the Dance Community," *University of Miami Law Review* 38 (1984): 290, 295–96.

17. Singer, 296.

18. *Mark Morris Dance Group*, dir. Thomas Grimm, prod. Judy Kinberg and Thomas Grimm, co-prod. WNET and Danmarks Radio, 1986.

19. Paul Taylor in public discussion at the American Dance Festival, Durham, N.C. This was reported to me by Douglas Rosenberg.

20. I should stress that not all choreographers mistrust the protection afforded them by copyright. George Balanchine, Martha Graham, Alwin Nikolais, and Ruth Page, among others, welcomed that protection, and Agnes de Mille worked tirelessly to lobby for it, partly because she felt that since she did not receive royalties, she was never properly compensated for her choreography for the musical *Oklahoma!* (However, Julie Van Camp notes that de Mille "*could* have gotten royalties, even without a new copyright law, if she had had a better contract" [Personal communication, September 24, 1998]).

21. Space does not permit me to analyze another aspect of dance world resistance—the rhetoric of evanescence as an essential feature of dance. Barbara Kibbee offers this as a reason for dance world resistance to copyright protection in "Copyright Protection for Choreography," *Art and the Law* 2, no. 2 (January 1976): 1. Also, see Auslander for a criticism of this position in performance theory generally.

22. While this type of training (working with master teachers, learning the classics, and so on) exists in other fields, such as theater and music, I would argue that the difficulty of separating the dance "text" from performance is an important difference. While it's true that some theater companies create pieces without a preexisting dramatic script, and some musical ensembles makes pieces without a preexisting score, there is a tradition in Western culture of the separability of dramatic script and musical score from their performances and a recognition that the script and the score may be copyrighted. Were theatrical performance to become copyrightable, it would be interesting to study whether theater companies who operate more like dance companies in creating the whole work from scratch also for the most part resisted copyright.

23. Barbara O'Dair, "Copyright Question Kicks Up a Storm Over 'Train' at UCI," *Orange County Register*, February 1, 1989, L1.

24. Louise Levene, "Dance/Royal Ballet triple bill ROH, London," *The Independent* (London), May 5, 1997, Arts Section, 12.

25. So, in ballet, for instance, we have Peter Martins's 1991 *Sleeping Beauty*, modeled after the original Petipa *Sleeping Beauty* of 1890, a direct descendant

(separated by only two generations) of the original. And this isn't just a parallel case, for instance, to the many painters over generations who paint crucifixion scenes (although it may have been for Petipa in his day), but rather is more in the nature of a reworking of a specific classic under the new choreographer's name. (As, in fact, Balanchine's *Nutcracker* was a reworking of the Ivanov original of 1892.) When Rudolf Nureyev fought bitterly with the Paris Opera Ballet over control of his stagings of *Swan Lake*, *The Sleeping Beauty*, *Giselle*, and *Cinderella*, the chairman of the Opera simply declared, "If he refuses to come to an agreement, we will perform these ballets with a new choreography" ("Nureyev and Paris Opera Ballet Choreograph Ugly Legal Battle," *Los Angeles Times*, February 8, 1990, P8).

26. See Sally Banes, *Terpsichore in Sneakers: Post-Modern Dance* (Boston: Houghton Mifflin, 1980; rev. ed. Middletown, Conn.: Wesleyan University Press, 1987) for a description of Brown's work and that of other postmodern choreographers of her generation.

27. Daniel McCusker took the notion of plagiarism to the point of absurdity when, according to Jack Anderson, he copied his own choreography in *Reviews, Redactions, Plagiarisms* ("Daniel McCusker," *New York Times*, March 28, 1981, sec. 1, 12). This is absurd because, of course, it is impossible to plagiarize one's own work. And in *Copyright* Nina Martin satirized the quest for originality in modern dance (Jack Anderson, "Nina Martin Presents 'Copyright,'" *New York Times*, November 26, 1984, C16).

28. See Gerald E. Deakin, "Watch That 'Rhapsody to a Fig Leaf,'" *Dance Magazine* (November 1963): 48–49; Julie Wheelock, "Dance and Exercise Studios Paying the Piper," *Los Angeles Times*, September 17, 1989, 56; Marian Horosko, "Classroom Music License Fees, Why?" *Dance Magazine* (April 1997): 58–59.

29. Bernard Taper, "Choreographing the Future," *Ballet Review* 23, no. 3 (Fall 1995): 27.

30. See, for instance, Rod Riggs, "Jazzercise Classes Started for Fun, But Passion Pays Off in Millions," *San Diego Union Tribune*, September 20, 1995, C1.

31. R. G. Collingwood, *The Principles of Art* (Oxford: Oxford University Press, 1938; paperback ed., 1958), 325.

32. Anderson continues:

> In the 1830s, the ballerina Marie Taglioni amazed audiences with her ethereal dancing on point. . . . Other ballerinas immediately tried to equal or surpass her achievements.
>
> Those ballerinas could have done something else. They could have said, "If we danced on point we wouldn't be original. So let's leave toe steps to the Taglionis." But, conceivably, toe steps might then have been regarded as only a stunt and their possibilities would have been neglected. As a result, today we might not have the intricate and beautiful passages of toe steps in the ballets of

George Balanchine, Antony Tudor, or Sir Frederick Ashton. The late nine-teenth century might not even have seen such ballets as "Swan Lake" or "The Sleeping Beauty." Toe steps were not merely invented. They were steadily developed. (Jack Anderson, "Critic's Notebook: Dance and the Influence of Others," *New York Times,* April 18, 1989, C15.)

33. American intellectual property laws do not currently protect the moral rights of artists to the extent that the Berne Convention (of which the United States is a party) guarantees. Moral rights include the author's right to proclaim or disclaim the authorship of the work and to dispute any changes in the work that would damage the author's reputation. Singer discusses moral rights in re-gard to choreographic works (307–17).

34. Singer suggests that it might be better for choreographers not to copy-right their works at all (that is, to perform but not record them), since then their common-law rights could last indefinitely, beyond the life of the author plus fifty years (303–4). This idea, however, seems utterly unrealistic, though more so perhaps in the late 1990s, when nearly every choreographer videotapes his or her dances, than in the early 1980s when Singer wrote her article, and video technology was less widely available. For to videotape a dance, under the 1976 Act, is to copyright it. See Auslander for a criticism of the position that views "performance as a discourse that escapes and resists the terms of [a capitalist representational] economy" (16).

35. While it is now standard within the music industry that those who use the samples pay for the right to do so, sampling began as a defiant act of artistic piracy and was part of an underground hip-hop culture, including subway graffiti (artistic defacing of public property) and break dancing (artistic recla-mation of public space), that challenged official rules of various kinds.

36. Singer, 319.

37. I would like to thank Phil Auslander, Gigi Bennahum, Noël Carroll, Neil Donahue, Lynn Garafola, Beth Genné, Sandi Kurtz, Cecilia Olsson, Marcia B. Siegel, and especially Julie Van Camp for their help with this essay.

Institutionalizing Avant-Garde Performance

A Hidden History of University Patronage in the United States

The performance avant-garde has historically positioned itself as an oppositional, anti-institutional movement. The usual narrative of the birth of avant-garde performance locates its nineteenth-century roots both in the little-theater movement in France and England (which protested against the commercial practices of mainstream theaters) and in various *salons des refusés* (which protested against the entrenched conventions of visual arts museums and galleries) and avant-garde visual art movements. Eschewing (or having been rejected from) mainstream theater and art world institutions, avant-gardists founded a terrain of their own in unofficial spaces like garrets, basements, cabarets, lofts, and private apartments.[1]

Yet, like most myths, the romantic legend of the anti-institutional nature of the avant-garde is both true and false. Avant-garde performance *has* often operated in an alternative arena. But in stressing the ingenuity, nonconformism, and agonism of advanced experiments in performance,

SOURCE: In James M. Harding, ed., *Contours of the Theatrical Avant-Garde: Performance and Textuality* (Ann Arbor: University of Michigan Press, 2000)

this narrative fails to acknowledge two key points. One is that the avant-garde has regularly formed its own alternative institutions, which in turn have been co-opted by the mainstream to become establishment schools and venues. The second is that, particularly in post-World War II America, intellectual and religious organizations—in particular, colleges, universities, and churches—have played a central role in the development of avant-garde performance, serving as research and development centers, venues, catalysts, and patrons.[2]

There are other sources for American postwar avant-garde performance (broadly defined), including not only government funding and private funding by individuals, corporations, and foundations, but also trust funds from wealthy parents, more modest support by middle-class parents, and even real-estate speculation.[3] To analyze the entire complex financial underwriting that supported the blossoming of American avant-garde performance in the second half of the twentieth century would be a significant chapter in the history of American performance, but it is far beyond the scope of this essay. The present essay focuses on support for avant-garde performance by American colleges and universities.

I should note that in discussions of postmodernism in recent years, the question has been raised as to whether, in the 1990s, one can still speak of a living avant-garde tradition of innovation and insurgency. Certainly in an era when college students are as likely to study Karen Finley's and Annie Sprinkle's performances as Duchamp's *L.H.O.O.Q.*—not to mention the *Mona Lisa*—the issue of whether anything can now shock or surprise the bourgeois sensibility (Jesse Helms and Donald Wildmon notwithstanding) may be moot. And indeed, some may argue that if my claim in this essay—that support for the avant-garde is by now an established part of our American academic economy—is true, to call these arts activities avant-garde is simply an oxymoron. But I want to propose an alternative reading of university patronage of avant-garde performance, a reading that sees arts funding as a result of the dynamic interplay of forces. Avant-garde expressions of opposition and resistance (especially at present) are always the product of negotiations and compromises. And the avant-garde's peculiar historical relation to the university exemplifies this process. I want to argue

that there remains a variegated arena of art activity we can still identify
as avant-garde, despite its changing political and cultural functions and
contexts, as well as its present recirculation of traditional forms. It is
avant-garde partly because it identifies itself as breaking with hegemonic artistic, cultural, and/or political discourses, and partly because
it remains (whether by choice or not) largely marginal to the established
mainstream presenting institutions (other than universities)—for example, Broadway theaters and established art museums.

As American academia becomes distanced from mainstream society, some (though certainly not all) of its cultural events develop in what
anthropologist Victor Turner calls a "liminoid" space, where "anti-
structural" activity and "ludic" invention can take place outside of nor-
mative social constraints. Turner argues that "universities, institutes,
colleges, etc., are 'liminoid' settings for all kinds of freewheeling, experimental cognitive behavior as well as forms of symbolic action," from
theoretical science to fraternity initiations.[4] Still, as I will show, avant-
garde performance has not entirely stepped outside of the culture or the
economy, for the backing the academy provides is still (relatively) mainstream compared to the bohemias of Paris and Greenwich Village.

I should also note that one can (and should) raise crucial questions
about the ways in which until very recently definitions and histories of
the avant-garde have been based on biases of class, race, and ethnicity,
but that is a very complex story beyond the scope of this essay.

Patronage and the Performing Arts in the United States

In looking at the issue of patronage for avant-garde performance in the
United States, it might be useful first to sort out briefly the differences
between various kinds of financial support for the arts in general. Judith
Huggins Balfe points out that patronage—which she defines as "the deliberate sponsorship of the creation, production, preservation, and dissemination of the so-called 'fine arts'"—is just one category of (and
therefore not identical to) the broader class of support for the arts. Support also includes earned income, or the direct financial contributions
of arts consumers (i.e., audience members, museum-goers, and so on).
As Balfe points out, patrons are traditionally active on the "supply side"
(that is, they work with the artist, commissioning and often influencing
the making of the artwork), while audience members occupy the

"demand side" of art (they are the artwork's consumers after it is finished—as is, of course, the patron, too). In recent debates about public arts funding, Balfe observes, problems have arisen partly because many seem to assume that the consumer should exercise the patron's traditional right to control the artistic product.[5]

But, one might ask, why would patrons choose to sponsor avant-garde art in the first place, since either as an activity or product, avant-garde art often—in principle—resists control by both patron and consumer? Avant-garde arts, especially avant-garde performance, seem to call for a special kind of patronage, one that endorses experimentation and artistic risk for its own sake (or for some other purpose or interest, such as the educational value of art making), one that tolerates or even encourages social and political resistance, and one that is willing to forgo artistic control over the final product. For numerous reasons the university fits this description.

It is often said that the performing arts in general (implicitly, those associated with "high" or elite culture) require intensive financial support by the patrons exactly because they are so expensive to produce; if theater, dance, and music groups had to rely on box-office sales for support, they would have to sacrifice much of their vision and quality. This was the argument often advanced to advocate federal funding for the arts in the early 1960s, prior to the establishment of the National Endowment for the Arts. The government, advocates of federal funding asserted, should become an active patron of the arts because they are vital to a democratic culture.

The statistics published by the Ford Foundation in 1986 indicate that the need for subsidy has not diminished since the 1960s. Experimental theaters, the foundation discovered, earn only 35 to 45 percent of their operating income through ticket sales (as opposed to the 65 to 70 percent earned by large nonprofit theaters)—in keeping with various assessments of the labor- and capital-intensive nature of the performing arts.[6]

Just in order to proceed without the need for wealthy patrons, state support, or large audiences—in order to be beholden to no one—avant-garde performers have often adopted a low-technology, antispecialist modus operandi. A case in point is the well-known story that the early realist director André Antoine borrowed his mother's furniture for the set of Zola's *Jacques Damour,* given by his Théâtre Libre in Paris in 1887. (In 1887, of course, theatrical realism itself was avant-garde.)

Another is the birth of the Living Theatre, whose first performances the codirectors, Julian Beck and Judith Malina, presented in their New York City apartment in 1951.

My first example above comes from France and the second from the United States, but it is important to keep in mind the drastically different systems of patronage for the arts in the United States and Europe and, therefore, the different role and status of both mainstream and avant-garde arts in the two cultures. In Europe the model may vary from one country to another according to whether state support for the arts is centralized or decentralized. But in general, from the Renaissance to the present, both church and state (whether royal, democratic, or totalitarian) have sponsored the arts financially. In the United States, by contrast, we have had direct federal support for the arts for approximately thirty-five years (with the notable exception of the arts projects of the Works Progress Administration from 1935 to 1939, which were, in effect, relief programs to put people back to work, rather than arts subsidies). The National Foundation for the Arts, established by President Kennedy in 1963, eventually grew into the now-embattled National Endowment for the Arts in 1965. In 1964 arts councils were established in thirteen U.S. states. Prior to 1963 arts patronage flowed primarily from private individuals, foundations, and corporations (although prior to 1963 the U.S. government did promote American art abroad, but not domestically, as a form of Cold War propaganda,[7] and local governments helped to support some arts projects, such as the municipally assisted City Center of Music and Drama in New York City).

In establishing the National Endowment for the Arts, the U.S. federal government did take on the role of a patron, but only to a limited extent, especially compared to the extensive government arts patronage in Europe, Canada, and Latin America. The limited state-funding situation in the United States places other types of patronage (that is, non-state patronage) under different kinds of stresses and demands.

The Value of Art as Pedagogy

In arguing not only for federal funding for the arts, but for a national appreciation of the arts that would match Europe's, early advocates of the National Endowment for the Arts had to join battle with an old quarrel against state patronage: centuries of American rhetoric against federal patronage as an emblem of royalist regimes and a symptom of the elitist luxury and decadence of both church and state in Europe.

As cultural historian Neil Harris has remarked, the entrenched American attitude of anxiety not only toward patronage but toward art making itself has roots in the very beginnings of American culture—not, as one might expect, as the result of Puritan moralizing, but rather as the product of a utilitarian political agenda. Art in the early days of the American republic was seen as a frivolous luxury—much as it is seen now, in an era of downsizing and budget cutting. And, since art, like other forms of luxury, required money, it was seen as a superfluous extravagance, as well as an unhealthy link to the aristocratic cultures of the Old World. Moreover, art was seen as capable of stirring up the emotions and supporting tyrannical regimes, both secular and religious, of all kinds.[8]

Eventually, Americans began to value art for its utilitarian purposes and to create hierarchies of types of art according to their relative usefulness. Alexis de Tocqueville noticed, on his trip to America in 1831–32, that in the United States

> the general moderate standard of wealth, the absence of superfluity, and the universal desire for comfort, with the constant efforts made by all to procure it, encouraged a taste for the useful more than the love of beauty. Naturally, therefore, democratic peoples with all these characteristics cultivate those arts that help to make life comfortable rather than those that adorn it. They habitually put use before beauty, and they want beauty itself to be useful.[9]

Besides comfort and advertising, utilitarianism in regard to the appreciation of art came to include art's functioning to provide moral uplift, and in particular, art's relation to education as a form of moral elevation. Crucially for the history of arts patronage in the United States (and for the story I want to tell here), as early as the late eighteenth century the rhetoric of pedagogy became the most effective means for advancing the establishment of arts institutions for exhibition and training.[10] American arts patronage, that is, has historically harnessed itself to what is seen as the higher political and moral good of education.

But avant-garde work seems to forsake, indeed to criticize radically (and often actually to fulminate against), traditional American views of art as well as traditional views of society. As I implied earlier, it is certainly not in the utilitarian interest of the state (or of the wealthy) to support art that criticizes it and threatens the status quo. Nor does avant-garde work generally command mass commercial audiences. Thus one needs to ask what institutions or individuals are likely to support or commission antiestablishment, avant-garde work, and for what reasons. In a capitalist marketplace, where the special financing of the avant-garde may in fact be a political contradiction, for whom is it a necessity (or at least a strong attraction)?

It may not be directly in the university's interest to teach and sponsor avant-garde art—and much of its sponsorship may be ad hoc and even unwitting—but it is nevertheless in the interest of many people involved with the university, for a variety of reasons, ranging from the noble to the pragmatic to the parsimonious. Some students want to learn how to enter their chosen arts professions as cutting-edge innovators of the upcoming generation; besides, they are of an age when they like to rebel in general, which is part of forging their own identities, even as professionals. Their parents, who are willing to sponsor arts training as long as it comes earmarked with a college degree, support them in this demand; teachers whose research and teaching areas include the avant-garde want to show their colleagues and students how developments even in the mainstream arts came from avant-garde inquiries in and among the disciplines; administrators uphold the teachers' and students' avant-garde proclivities because it shows they tolerate free expression. The innovative avant-garde telos fits with the research university's mission to create new knowledge, and the avant-garde's critique of the status quo suits the liberal arts college's mandate to foster critical thinking. And, in a crude economic sense, to hire marginalized avant-gardists as faculty or guest artists (whether because that's what they really are by choice or because they haven't yet succeeded in joining the mainstream) is much cheaper for the university administration than to hire established artists.

Perhaps there is even a certain cachet attached to avant-garde performance from which university administrators derive various benefits. Just as avant-garde artists sometimes serve as a catalyst for the gentrification of neighborhoods, so they can also function as honeypots to sweeten the university administration's fundraising efforts or even its glamour quotient.

Certainly not all universities or colleges are hotbeds of avant-garde activity. But if there is an interest in this activity by faculty, staff, or students, participation of various kinds can take place surprisingly easily.

And this is not, as Michael Mooney paranoiacally suggested in 1980, because there is a secret alliance among Congress, the White House, business, and the academic "knowledge industry" to foist a radical left-wing, avant-garde cultural policy on an unsuspecting nation.[11] At the beginning of the twenty-first century, when Congress and the White House are at loggerheads and both corporate and federal arts patronage are shrinking, the university still supports the avant-garde; indeed, it has taken on an increasing burden of avant-garde support as other sources dwindle. Rather than a conspiracy by a unified "ministry of culture," university patronage survives because it is one of the few places in an increasingly conservative American culture where the avant-garde can still flourish and find protection from the demands of the commercial marketplace—where insurgency and both social and artistic criticism may be protected by the principle of academic freedom.[12]

In terms of performance art, Laurie Anderson may earn income on hit records, and Spalding Gray, Eric Bogosian, Willem Dafoe, John Leguizamo, and Steve Buscemi may find work in Hollywood films and on television. But for every Laurie Anderson or Spalding Gray there are scores of performance artists who either shun the capitalist marketplace and showbiz, or find their work shunned by popular and mass-media venues. Teaching jobs and guest residencies in the university system can sustain those noncommercial avant-gardists with both money and research time.

However, rarely is the avant-garde patronage function of the university, even the part that flows from economic self-interest, acknowledged in the literature about arts patronage, either journalistic or scholarly. (Two important exceptions to this lack of recognition are *The Arts at Black Mountain College*, by Mary Emma Harris, and *Off Limits: Rutgers University and the Avant-Garde, 1957–1963*, edited by Joan Marter.)[13] For instance, Gideon Chagy's 1972 book *The New Patrons of the Arts* emphasizes the increased patronage of the arts by corporations in the late 1960s. His historical survey of traditional patronage in Europe and the United States encompasses not only merchants and corporations but also the church, the state, wealthy individuals, and foundations. But, except for one mention of courses offered in arts administration, Chagy refers to universities only as examples of recipients of corporate giving for arts buildings and other capital projects.[14]

More recently, a 1986 Ford Foundation working paper lists the sources of support for the arts as individuals, corporations, government,

the marketplace, and foundations. It traces the history of arts funding in
the United States and of the Ford Foundation's generous patronage of
the performing and visual arts since the mid-1950s, with its major grants
to key institutions in the early 1960s and, its support, since the late
1980s, of both experimental work and ethnic diversity in the arts. Yet it
never mentions the important role universities have played in furthering
the Foundation's priorities. In fact, the word *university* shows up only
three times in this publication—two of them in a citation of a study on
foundation support of the arts, only because the work cited, *Non-Profit
Enterprise in the Arts*, was written by Paul DiMaggio of the Program on
Non-Profit Organizations at Yale University's Institution for Social and
Policy Studies and was published by Oxford University Press.[15]

However, it is worth noting that even this small citation, so easily
overlooked, illuminates two different ways in which universities more
and more play key roles in advancing the arts: by studying (and making
recommendations for) arts-funding policies, and by publishing books
(through university presses) about the arts.

Even major foundation grants for innovative work are now frequently funneled through universities, and thus become coproductions
with universities, which supply the overhead. For instance, as I noted
above, the Ford Foundation has long supported avant-garde performance. But in 1981 for the first time it linked its Arts Culture program to
its Education program.[16] Beginning in 1994 the Ford Foundation's mission in funding the arts shifted to support a new area: "cultural institutions in the United States that are trying to 'internationalize' their
multidisciplinary performing arts programs . . . involving collaborations
between artists from the United States and artists in the developing
world." As the 1995 Ford Foundation annual report states, "this program builds on the Foundation's continuing interest in new interdisciplinary performing arts activities but broadens that work to involve regional cultural institutions and universities that have strong program
interests in the arts and cultures of Asia, Latin America, and Africa."[17]

In 1996 the Lila Wallace-Reader's Digest Arts Partners Program
gave implementation grants to proposed projects involving Arizona
State University, University of Colorado–Boulder, Stanford University,
and Lafayette College for avant-garde projects. It gave planning grants
to projects involving California State University, Los Angeles; St.
Mary's University; Miami Dade Community College; University of
California Extension; University of Arizona; University of Kentucky;
and University of Wisconsin. And it gave a $750,000 grant to National

Performance Network, a thirteen-year-old touring organization for avant-garde performance; approximately one-fourth of NPN's tours include residencies for artists of at least one week's duration through university partners.[18]

Finally, the National Endowment for the Arts itself increasingly funnels its funds for artists through universities and colleges. The fiscal year 1998 NEA application guidelines state specifically that "independent components that meet [criteria for eligible applicants] often will be part of a university/university system or part of a cultural/community complex." The guidelines give as examples of these independent components (i.e., eligible to apply separately, even though the NEA accepts only one application per organization) "a presenter, literary magazine or press, museum, radio station, theater, etc., within a university campus or larger university system." Although "academic departments of colleges and universities will not qualify as independent components," conceivably (given the guidelines quoted above) five or more units within a university could receive NEA funding in a single year.[19]

The ways in which foundation and government funds are currently funneled through universities (which provide the necessary institutional home and overhead for large, complex projects, as well as for smaller-scale residencies) and the ways in which university personnel currently work with foundations and the government both testify to the increasing role universities play in supporting the arts, and the avant-garde arts in particular.

Perhaps the universities remain invisible in public and scholarly discourse about arts patronage because their support often comes in forms that are indirect, rather than direct grants and contributions to individual artists. But there are still myriad ways in which universities and colleges support the arts. And, given the changing support system for the arts since the 1960s, as well as the changing nature of the university since the 1960s, avant-garde performance has been one of the beneficiaries of this hidden underground stream of arts patronage.

Two Early Models
of American Avant-Garde Patronage

Two early, unique models of artistic nurture in American academe in this century exemplify the stress on pedagogy that links fostering artistic freedom with upholding academic freedom. Neither the New School for Social Research, founded in New York City in 1918, nor Black Mountain College, established near Asheville, North Carolina in 1933 originally envisioned the fostering of avant-garde art and performance as part of its mission, but for complex reasons, both created congenial grounds for artistic experimentation.

The foundings of both were prompted by faculty outrage at encroachments on academic freedom at other universities. Further, both the New School's and Black Mountain's pedagogical principles were inspired by John Dewey and, generally, the progressive movement in education. This movement led to the founding of such schools as Bennington College and Sarah Lawrence College, as well as to changes in curriculum at established colleges like Bryn Mawr, Swarthmore, Reed, Antioch, and Columbia. For Dewey, the arts served as a practical, exploratory, experiential model for creativity in general, and therefore they were intimately linked to the democratization of education, because they could form students with inquisitive, critical minds.

In furthering these goals that yoked the practice of art with liberal democratic humanism, both schools hired modern artists; sponsored innovative projects in the arts by faculty, students, and visiting artists; and attracted creative students who eventually came to populate the avant-garde movements of the 1950s and 1960s. A most important influence on postwar avant-garde performance activities at both schools, leading to a broader avant-garde influence in American performance in the 1960s, was the presence of the composer John Cage.

The New School for Social Research, established by historians and political scientists, grew out of ideas regarding academic freedom and democratic education that reached a crisis in 1917, when two Columbia University faculty members were fired and several others subsequently resigned because they disagreed with the university administration's support of President Wilson's war policies. The funding for the school originally came from philanthropist Dorothy Straight, heir to the Whitney fortune. Influenced not only by Dewey's ideas about progressive, democratic education, but also by Thorstein Veblen's writings on the institutional reform of universities, the founding group opened an anti-hierarchical school for adult education—as its name suggests, focusing on research carried out by teachers and students—that initially stressed graduate and professional education. But over the course of the school's existence, its emphasis has oscillated several times between the social-science orientation of its graduate faculty and the cultural-enrichment aspect of its adult education division.[20]

Although in the early years of the school very few courses in the arts were offered, beginning in 1923 (when Alvin Johnson assumed administrative leadership of the school and it moved to Greenwich Village) the New School became a center for both innovative artistic and intellectual life in downtown New York. Johnson saw the appreciation of and participation in the arts, and in particular, the new modernist movements in the arts, as instrumental to social change. Not only were young artists and critics hired to teach courses and to give occasional lectures, but also Johnson commissioned a new building in the modernist International style to house the school, which included an auditorium shaped like an ancient Greek amphitheater, symbolizing the school's commitment to liberal democratic values as well as providing a venue for its arts events.

By hiring artists as teachers, Johnson in effect was also buying them time for "research," or artistic creativity. In the 1920s, and especially during the depression years in the 1930s, Johnson attracted a diverse group of modern composers, including Aaron Copland, Henry Cowell, and Hans Eisler. He also hired choreographer Doris Humphrey, the leading modern dance critic John Martin, visual artists Stuart Davis, Seymour Lipton, and Berenice Abbott, and the art critic Meyer Schapiro to teach at the school.

Also, importantly, Johnson hired the German avant-garde political theater director Erwin Piscator, who had earlier influenced Bertolt Brecht's notions of the epic theater. Piscator established the Dramatic Workshop at the New School in 1939; it not only offered an academic curriculum, but also sponsored three semiprofessional off-Broadway theaters, a repertory theater, a children's theater, and other performance activities. Piscator's Dramatic Workshop lasted at the New School until 1949, when it became an independent entity in New York for two years, continuing until the director returned to Germany in 1951. Among other students of the Dramatic Workshop (many of whose acting and directing remained in a more mainstream mode), Judith Malina studied with Piscator from 1945 to 1947 and was partly inspired by him to start the Living Theatre.[21]

In the late 1950s the liberal arts components of the adult education division of the New School flourished, although music and dance thrived less than literature and the visual arts.[22] Still, John Cage (who had himself studied briefly with Henry Cowell at the New School in the 1930s and occasionally substituted for Cowell in the 1940s) began in 1956 to teach a course in "Composition of Experimental Music" at the

New School that had an enormous impact on the development of
Happenings, Fluxus, and performance art, as well as music and poetry,
in the 1960s and after.[23] According to Cage, when he decided to teach
in a formal way in the 1950s, "It never entered my mind to teach in
any other place in New York City than the New School. Nor is it likely
that any other school would have accepted me, since my work and ideas
are controversial."[24] Cage's students included composer Toshi Ichiya-
nagi, poet Jackson Mac Low, Happenings makers Allan Kaprow and
Al Hansen, and Fluxus members Dick Higgins and George Brecht.[25]
Also among his students was Robert Dunn, a composer whose own
dance composition course at Merce Cunningham's studio, modeled
after Cage's music composition course, was the seedbed for postmodern
dance.[26] Thus the lively avant-garde performance scene of the 1960s
may be traced back in large part to the New School, although in the late
1950s there was another university outpost of avant-garde activity in the
New York City area at Rutgers University, involving other Happenings-
and Events-makers, who included faculty member Allan Kaprow, students Lucas Samaras and Robert Whitman, and neighbor George
Segal.[27]

 Black Mountain College was founded by faculty members from Rol-
lins College who had either resigned or been dismissed over issues of
academic freedom. Its initial funding came primarily from Mr. and
Mrs. J. Malcom Forbes and was raised by one of the founding faculty,
Theodore Dreier, whose wealthy family in New York was active in promoting social reform, women's rights, poverty programs, and the arts;
Dreier's aunt Katherine had been (with Marcel Duchamp and Man
Ray) a founding member of the Société Anonyme, a private collection
of modern art. From the start, Black Mountain was an alternative educational establishment with a radically democratic structure. And also
from the beginning, the school included visual art and theater as an integral part of its liberal studies instructional curriculum.[28]

 For a variety of reasons, including the interdisciplinary, democratic,
and participatory theory of education it espoused, Black Mountain always stressed (even more than did the New School) practical studies in
art as a core aspect of the curriculum. In this it also differed from most
other undergraduate colleges, where, as historian Mary Emma Harris
notes, the arts were often relegated to noncredit or extracurricular
status. At Black Mountain the arts were seen as foundational, not in
order to train students as professional artists, but because, following

Dewey's ideas in *Art and Education* and *Democracy and Education*, the college's founders saw in the arts a means of stimulating creativity and independent thought in all realms of life.[29]

Black Mountain was also deeply influenced by the Bauhaus in Germany, which was closed down by the Nazi government in 1933, the same year that Black Mountain was founded. The Bauhaus influence was both indirect, in the college's adherence to a utopian communal ethos based on practical work in the arts, and direct, in that Josef Albers (one of the Bauhaus master teachers) and his wife Anni Albers (a weaver who also taught at the Bauhaus) were immediately invited to join the Black Mountain faculty, and other Bauhaus teachers later followed. Josef Albers became one of the Black Mountain faculty's most influential members.

During the depression and war years, Black Mountain became known as a center for experimental, modernist art, especially the abstraction espoused by Albers. And, although it was an institution of higher learning, the college staked out an antiacademic position regarding both the study of the artistic canon and the practice of art.[30] On the Bauhaus model, the students learned art, design, and craft in a practical, functional way—including weaving, photography, graphic design, typography, bookbinding, music, drama, dance, and creative writing. Xanti Schawinsky, who had been a student at the Bauhaus and had collaborated with Oskar Schlemmer on several productions in the 1920s, joined the Black Mountain faculty in 1936 and for two years worked with the students to create a nonnarrative, nonmatrixed theater of "total experience," based on music, light, movement, and masks.[31] In the early 1940s Eric Bentley taught history, literature, and drama, and he directed the student theater group, most notably in readings from Bertolt Brecht's *The Private Life of the Master Race*, which Bentley was then translating.

In addition to its core curriculum, Black Mountain College sponsored many artistic residencies and collaborations from the time of its founding. Special summer institutes in the arts, initially meant to educate teachers, began at the college in 1944. Guest teachers included Walter Gropius, Robert Motherwell, Lyonel Feininger, and Charles Olson. Olson eventually joined the regular faculty and became rector of the college. After World War II more and more arts students were attracted to study at the college. According to Harris, "by 1945 the college had become 'a natural gravitational force' for those interested in the arts," eventually drawing students like Ray Johnson, Ruth Asawa, Robert Rauschenberg, Sue Weil, Kenneth Noland, Arthur Penn, and Joel Oppenheimer.[32] And by 1948, when John Cage, Merce Cunningham, Willem de Kooning, Buckminster Fuller, and Richard Lippold were on the summer faculty, Black Mountain fostered the emergence of a specifically American avant-garde art, no longer beholden to European models, especially the functional modernism of the Bauhaus. Importantly, these American teachers were not yet established artists. According to Harris, "In 1948 these people, most of whom had been living a hand-to-mouth existence in city apartments, were all thankful for room and board for the summer, a modest salary, and an opportunity to work in a sympathetic community of artists and friends."[33]

Two crucial events happened during the 1952 summer session. One was the beginning of a long collaboration and a meeting of like minds in the encounter of Cage and Rauschenberg. The second was a groundbreaking postwar performance event: John Cage's untitled chance-composed event, which, on the one hand, was inspired by futurist and Dada events and, on the other, was a precursor of Happenings.[34] Also at around this time, Black Mountain faculty member M. C. Richards was translating into English several essays by Antonin Artaud, which were eventually published as *The Theater and Its Double*.[35] John Cage showed those essays before they were published to Malina and Beck. The influence of those essays on the avant-garde and experimental theater of the 1950s, 1960s, and after, is incalculable.

The New School and Black Mountain were founded as alternative institutions. Thus, like other schools including Bennington, Antioch, and Mills Colleges, they created a framework in which avant-garde arts activities were supported and encouraged as part and parcel of the institutional raison d'être. But for a variety of reasons, by the 1960s even mainstream universities offered a home for the avant-garde.

The University as Patron since the 1960s

In the late 1940s and the 1950s, returning servicemen, under the GI Bill, had entered college in large numbers and forced certain changes in arts education. The mission of the university in regard to the arts altered in the postwar years as well. A 1965 Rockefeller Panel report shows that the function of the university in relation to the art world shifted after

World War II from training students in appreciation of the arts to a complex, multifunctional support, training, and patronage system.[36] The report explains that by the early 1960s institutions of higher learning were increasingly taking on the role of training performing artists. This was because the costs of conservatory and independent arts schools had risen and ideas about higher education had changed, while an expanding broad economic base of public and private support at universities slowed for more experimentation. Of course, in order to do this, universities hired professional artists to train students, thereby setting up another layer of patronage: they provided salaries and other benefits (including space, materials, and time for research/creative work) to their full-time and part-time faculty.

A change took place during the 1960s in regard to the expansion of performing arts programs in universities. As universities, with the help of foundations, were building up their theater programs, the lack of innovative work in the academy—in contrast to the lively performance scene, for instance, off-off-Broadway—was much commented upon in the mid-1960s. However, shortly after these reports were issued, university campuses underwent drastic transformations, not only politically but also artistically.

In the late 1960s a generation of baby boomers entered college in large numbers and swelled the ranks of students enrolling in arts and humanities programs. More theater departments were formed, sometimes by splitting off from speech or communications departments. The political upheavals taking place at many universities in 1968 (and after) swept both radical political theater and artistically experimental theater onto American college campuses. Not only were there national tours by the Living Theatre, the San Francisco Mime Troupe, the Open Theater, and other groups, but also those troupes left in their wake students who were galvanized to form local guerrilla theater groups that used theater for political agit-prop and local artistic collectives that used performance for artistic exploration. Although both the tours and the local activities, sponsored either by student organizations or political groups, often simply bypassed the official theater departments, many theater departments also were deeply influenced by political experimental work in the 1960s and 1970s.

In the 1980s and 1990s, however, the focus of many theater departments is on faculty-student productions, and many are forced, either by the necessity of relying on earned income or by the training requirements for students, to cater to middlebrow taste. Thus, small-scale or imported performances may more easily happen in formats more familiar to dance and art departments. College and university dance departments have since the 1930s sponsored tours and hired artists in residence. Art departments invite visiting artists, including performance artists, to teach and critique student work.

In 1957 what is now known as the Association of Performing Arts Presenters was founded, primarily to present classical music and dance concerts. Those presenters eventually added avant-garde events, such as performance art and postmodern dance, to their classical music series. Of the fifteen hundred presenters belonging to that association in 1997, 38 percent were affiliated with universities.[37]

In summary, although avant-garde arts were supported in academia in various ways before the 1960s, since the late 1960s universities and colleges have dramatically increased their patronage of the performing arts, including avant-garde performance. These include hiring artists, critics, and scholars to serve on departmental faculties—as either full-time or part-time employees—where they may receive both salaries and grants to do their creative work, as well as having access to in-kind contributions of space, materials, and staff support. University patronage also includes hiring nonacademic artists, critics, historians, and theorists to do lectures, performances, workshops, and master classes, as well as to do guest residencies of various lengths, from a week to a semester or a year. And universities sponsor museum exhibitions and installations, university press publications by artists and scholars, conferences, appointments to research institutes, and the preservation of artists' archives. As well as financial and in-kind support, universities provide symbolic capital to avant-garde artists in the form of prestigious honorary degrees.

Since the 1970s, arts administration programs have been established at major universities; these programs train those individuals who will eventually serve as fundraisers and company managers for performing artists. Finally, since the 1980s, the outreach components of many university performing arts programs have mushroomed. While many of these practices and programs may originally have centered on educating audiences for mainstream high art—in outreach, bringing classical music to schoolchildren, for instance—to a large degree, the same infrastructures are now being used to support innovative and avant-garde work in the arts, including performance.

The Academic Mainstreaming of Avant-Garde Performance

As universities expanded with the influx of baby boomers and simultaneously underwent radical political and institutional changes in the late 1960s, many of their arts programs gravitated toward supporting innovative work by faculty, students, and guest artists. By the early 1970s students and faculty from these academic milieux were moved to found alternative galleries and artists' spaces, where avant-garde performance took place outside of the academic or museum setting. But what may have looked at the time like a gesture *against* academia, in favor of small-scale alternative institutions, in time took on the shape of a lively interchange, as the two situations fed one another and activists in alternative galleries and performance spaces eventually rejoined the academy.

By the mid-1970s the loose confederation A Bunch of Experimental Theaters facilitated tours of avant-garde groups to campuses. For instance, at the University of Pittsburgh a program called the Pittsburgh 99 Cent Floating Theatre sponsored performances in the 1970s by many visiting companies from A Bunch, including Charles Ludlam's Ridiculous Theatrical Company, Meredith Monk and the House, Mabou Mines, the Iowa Theatre Lab, the Medicine Show, and others.[38]

But also, in the 1970s and 1980s many avant-garde artists of the 1960s and slightly younger baby boomers joined the cohort of faculty populating the visual and performing arts departments. There, themselves formed by the experiments of the 1960s, they began to institutionalize avant-garde history and practice through teaching, research, and publication, producing new generations of avant-garde practitioners as well as a new level of scholarly and public discourse about the avant-garde. For instance, the Experimental Theater Wing in the New York University Department of Undergraduate Drama was formed by Ron Argelander in 1976 to create a situation in which students could work directly with avant-garde artists; Anne Bogart, Richard Foreman, and Robert Wilson have directed student productions, and ETW graduates include Kate Valk and Jeff Webster of the Wooster Group and performance artist Gayle Tufts.

As the economy shrank in the late 1980s and early 1990s, many avant-garde artists who had not previously been affiliated with academia began to seek the economic security—including not only salaries, but health insurance and retirement plans—of university teaching positions, while still carrying on their experimental and avant-garde theater activities. Antioch College's theater department, for instance, which is part of the American Theater Festival Campus Diversity/Cultural Research Initiative, is chaired by Louise Smith, a solo performer who has appeared with Otrabanda and Ping Chong, and it regularly sponsors guest artists and experimental productions by students and faculty.[39] The Barnard College Theater Department faculty includes Amy Trompeter, formerly of Bread and Puppet Theater, and Deni Partridge, formerly of the San Francisco Mime Troupe. John Bell, another Bread and Puppet Theater alumnus, teaches at New York University.

Yet the myth of the natural antagonism between the avant-garde and academe persisted into the 1990s, despite overwhelming evidence that, at least since the 1950s, much of the radical activity in American avant-garde performance has been sponsored and supported by universities and colleges, whether those (like Black Mountain or more recently the Naropa Institute) that were or are committed to experiment or those (like Rutgers University or Kutztown University) that simply have allowed pockets of radical artistic activity to occur among interested faculty and students.

Avant-garde chronicler Richard Kostelanetz, for instance, upholds the myth by staking out a pure antiacademic stance. In his 1993 *Dictionary of the Avant-Gardes*, under the entry "Academic Critics," he writes:

> When professors discuss avant-garde art, particularly literature, they tend to focus upon the more conservative, more accessible dimensions of an artist's work, in part to make their criticism more digestible to the ignorant (e.g. students and colleagues), rather than pursuing radical implications to their critical extremes. . . . Academics tend as well to reveal incomplete familiarity with new developments (especially if they would be unknown to their fellow professors). . . . When a professor writes three words about an avant-garde subject, one of them is likely to be superficial and a second to reveal ignorance.

And, he concludes, "Genuinely innovative art measures itself as avant-garde by a healthy distance from the academy."[40] Kostelanetz may disparage academic criticism. But he himself, willy-nilly, acknowledges the myriad important ways in which the university supports the avant-garde when he records, for example, Cage's important work carried out during various university residencies.[41] *HPSCHD* (1969), one of Cage's "most abundant pieces" according to Kostelanetz—a collaboration with Lejaren Hiller that took place at Assembly Hall, a sports arena, at the University of Illinois, Urbana—probably could not have taken place anywhere in the United States but a university setting, because of the resources available there both for the performance itself and for the preparation of the sound tapes. *HPSCHD* involved enormous projection screens, film projections, fifty-two slide projectors, fifty-two tape recorders playing computer-generated tapes, and seven live harpsichordists. A later performance at the Brooklyn Academy of Music (under nonuniversity auspices) had to be drastically reduced.[42]

The university can provide the kind of time needed for the long incubation of artistic creation. In her article on the New World Performance Laboratory, a joint project of the University of Akron and the Cleveland Public Theatre founded by two actors who have worked with the late Jerzy Grotowski, Lisa Wolford explains that "within university theatre departments Grotowski sees a possible site of resistance against the superficiality and slapdash craft dictated by the culture industry." Since university theater departments "enjoy a basic level of funding, access to work space, and a relatively stable population of unpaid student actors," they "provide a structure which allows for long-term, systematic work; and, [Grotowski] argues, are relatively free to negotiate the constraints which plague commercial theaters." Under these auspices, "would it not be possible to spend months or even a year preparing a single performance?"[43]

The Wexner Center, a major presenter of avant-garde performance, is a part of the Ohio State University; the Walker Art Center, long an avant-garde venue but most recently infamous for its controversial hosting of Ron Athey's performances in 1994, is independent but closely connected to the University of Minnesota at Minneapolis. The Haggerty Museum, part of Marquette University, has presented performances by Adrian Piper, Rachel Rosenthal, Ping Chong, and others. National Performance Network brings groups like the Five Lesbian Brothers, Spiderwoman Theater, Eiko and Koma, and the Hittite Empire to many campuses.

By the mid-1980s it was clear that much work in performance art and its documentation and criticism was underwritten by both long-range and short-term academic support. It was also evident that much training for performance artists was taking place in academia or art schools that offer college degrees.[44]

But of course it's not only short- or long-term residencies by artists, or faculty and student support that constitute patronage for the avant-garde. Sustenance also includes university-sponsored publications, including preeminent journals covering avant-garde performance like the long-lived *Drama Review,* edited by Richard Schechner and published by MIT Press, but housed and staffed at New York University's Department of Performance Studies, and the newer *TheaterForum,* edited by Theodore Shank and housed and staffed at the University of California, San Diego. Patronage in the form of publication includes, as well, books on avant-garde performance increasingly published by university presses, as changes in commercial publishing over the past decade or so have made small print runs of books nearly impossible without subventions from large institutions like universities. Wesleyan University Press has long produced books on avant-garde performance, from John Cage's *Silence* to C. Carr's *On Edge: Performance at the End of the Twentieth Century.* Other publishers of books on the avant-garde include the University of Michigan Press, Duke University Press, MIT Press, and Indiana University Press.

Academic conferences about avant-garde performance, too, are a form of patronage. Since 1995 the Performance Studies conferences hosted by New York University, Northwestern University, the Georgia Institute of Technology, City University of New York, and the University of Wales have featured not only scholarly presentations but also performances by both academic and non-academically based performance artists. The Performance Art, Culture, Pedagogy Symposium held at Pennsylvania State University in November 1996 showed just how entrenched avant-garde performance in academe has become. Indeed, the theme of the conference was performance art pedagogy "as an emerging form of arts education," and the majority of the presenters were academics.[45]

Conclusion

The question arises as to whether the funding of avant-garde performance by academic institutions is good or bad, and further, whether, if this activity is being funded by a mainstream institution, it may still be considered avant-garde. According to antiacademic critics like Kostelanetz, the university is inimical to avant-garde activity by definition. Surely one result of the institutionalization of avant-garde performance by the mainstream university is that much postmodern performance of the 1980s and 1990s has been driven by criticism and theory—that of poststructuralism and identity politics—rather than, as was predominantly the case previously, serving to spark criticism and new theories. Insofar as one way of defining the avant-garde since its emergence in the nineteenth century might be that it contests academic critical discourse, this new turn suggests that sustenance by the mainstream university has co-opted, if not killed off, much avant-garde performance. However, here it should be noted that some of the most exciting avant-garde performance of the last fifty years has emerged partly as a result of artists' exploring the histories and theories of their practice. So to embrace Kostelanetz's position seems to be to endorse a naïve romanticism that flies in the face of historical reality.

There is another way of looking at the university patronage system, one that I, as a historian, curator, reconstructor, and sometime participant in avant-garde performances, as well as a university professor and author of university press books, must take seriously. We *do* live in a capitalist marketplace, where—especially since recent NEA cuts and the discontinuation of NEA grants to individual artists—the bulk of what scanty arts funding there is in the federal budget goes to support mainstream institutions like symphonies, art museums, regional theaters, and major dance companies (which may occasionally present an avant-garde work but are not dedicated to the avant-garde project). In the pre-NEA early 1960s a lively avant-garde performance scene flourished without any federal support and only sporadic university support. Although presently our economy is booming, the costs of both living and making art have risen astronomically in the 1980s and 1990s. That the university now provides a protected haven—however random or small-scale—for experiments in performance; that it animates in the next generation of young artists ideas—however embattled—about innovation and originality; that it literally feeds those who make iconoclastic, deviant, or alternative art; and that it supplies dissident voices within the university system itself, all these aspects are crucial politically as well as culturally—not to mention pedagogically.[46]

NOTES

1. See Noël Carroll, "Performance," *Formations* 3, no. 1 (1986): 63–79, for an account of performance art and art performance since the 1970s as two interrelated and intertwined strands of activity with separate roots in avant-garde theater and visual art.

2. I should note that I am consciously using the word "America" here interchangeably with "United States." I recognize that the arts practices and funding situations in Canada and Mexico, not to mention Central and South America, differ from those of the United States. But in the interests of an efficient prose style, references to American art, American institutions, and American society should be understood to mean those of the United States.

3. I am grateful to Philip Auslander for suggesting that a "real-estate theory" would partly explain the economic base for postwar avant-garde performance activities in New York (personal communication). In this context George Maciunas, in particular, was instrumental in buying and establishing several low-cost artists' cooperative loft buildings in the SoHo district, which included living, working, and performance spaces. Maciunas was a key figure in setting precedents for the legal exemptions and rent controls that allowed for an explosion of artists' living and working lofts in SoHo in the 1960s and 1970s. See my *Greenwich Village, 1963: Avant-Garde Performance and the Effervescent Body* (Durham, N.C.: Duke University Press, 1993), 64–65, for a discussion of Maciuna's real estate activities, which he modeled on ideas inspired by early Soviet arts cooperatives as well as Soviet collective farms. Also see the various Fluxnewsletters and other documents reprinted in Jon Hendricks, *Fluxus Etc.: The Gilbert and Lila Silverman Collection, Addenda I* (New York: Ink &, 1983), 170–228.

4. Victor Turner, "Liminal to Liminoid in Play, Flow, Ritual: An Essay in Comparative Symbology," in *From Ritual to Theatre: The Human Seriousness of Play* (New York: Performing Arts Journal Publications, 1982), 33.

5. Judith Huggins Balfe, ed., *Paying the Piper: Causes and Consequences of Art Patronage* (Urbana: University of Illinois Press, 1993), 1.

6. *Ford Foundation Support for the Arts in the United States: A Discussion of New Emphases in the Foundation's Arts Program* (New York: Ford Foundation, 1986), 10.

7. See, for instance, Naima Prevots, *Dance for Export: Cultural Diplomacy and the Cold War* (Hanover, N.H.: Wesleyan University Press/University Press of New England, 1998); and Robert Haddow, *Pavilions of Plenty: Establishing American Culture Abroad in the 1950s* (Washington, D.C.: Smithsonian Institution Press, 1997).

8. Neil Harris, *The Artist in American Society: The Formative Years, 1790–1860* (1966; New York: Simon and Schuster, 1970), 28, 34–36.

9. Alexis de Tocqueville, *Democracy in America*, trans. George Lawrence, ed. J. P. Mayer (New York: HarperCollins, 1988), 465.

10. Harris, *The Artist in American Society*, 90–91, 94.

11. Michael Macdonald Mooney, *The Ministry of Culture: Connections among Art, Money, and Politics* (New York: Wyndham, 1980).

12. In response to NEA cuts, in 1999 the Creative Capital Foundation was formed by over twenty foundations and individual philanthropists "to support artists who challenge convention" (Judith H. Dobrzynski, "Private Donors

Unite to Support Art Spurned by the Government," *New York Times*, May 3, 1999, E1).

13. Mary Emma Harris, *The Arts at Black Mountain College* (Cambridge, Mass.: MIT Press, 1987); Joan Marter, ed., *Off Limits: Rutgers University and the Avant-Garde, 1957–1963* (New Brunswick, N.J.: Rutgers University Press, 1999).

14. Gideon Chagy, *The New Patrons of the Arts* (New York: Harry N. Abrams, 1972). Chagy mentions arts administration courses on p. 67.

15. *Ford Foundation Support*, 6–7.

16. The rationale for this change is given in ibid., 18.

17. Ford Foundation, *Annual Report, 1993*, http://www.fordfound.org/AR.93/AR9311.html; Ford Foundation, *Annual Report, 1994*, http://www.fordfound.org/AR.94/AR9413.html; Ford Foundation, *Annual Report, 1995*, http://www.fordfound.org/AR.95/AR9513.html.

18. Lila Wallace-Reader's Digest Fund, "1996 Grants," http://www.lilawallace.org/ 96grant.htm#writer; telephone interview, Cathy Edwards, managing director, National Performance Network, February 21, 1997.

19. National Endowment for the Arts, FY '98 Application Guidelines, 7.

20. Peter M. Rutkoff and William B. Scott, *New School: A History of the New School for Social Research* (New York: Free Press, 1986).

21. *The Diaries of Judith Malina, 1947–1957* (New York: Grove Press, 1984), 463.

22. Rutkoff and Scott, *New School*, 229.

23. See John Cage, "[The New School]," in *John Cage*, ed. Richard Kostelanetz (New York: Praeger, 1970), 118–20; Ellsworth Snyder, "Chronological Table of John Cage's Life," in Kostelanetz, 39. On the influence of John Cage's class on Fluxus, see Philip Auslander's essay in James M. Harding, ed., *Contours of the Theatrical Avant-Garde: Performance and Textuality* (Ann Arbor: University of Michigan Press, 2000), 110–29.

24. Cage, "[The New School]," 119.

25. See ibid,; and also Al Hansen and Dick Higgins, "[On Cage's Classes]," in Kostelanetz, *John Cage*, 120–24.

26. On Dunn's class, see my *Democracy's Body: Judson Dance Theater, 1962–1964* (Ann Arbor, Mich.: UMI Research Press, 1983; rpt. Durham, N.C.: Duke University Press, 1993), 1–33.

27. See Phyllis Tuchman, *George Segal*, Modern Masters (New York: Abbeville Press, 1983), 13–15; Michael Kirby, *Happenings* (New York: E. P. Dutton, 1965), 53; Barbara Haskell, *Blam! The Explosion of Pop, Minimalism, and Performance, 1958–1964* (New York: Whitney Museum of Art and W. W. Norton, 1984), 41.

28. My information about Black Mountain College relies on two important sources: Martin Duberman, *Black Mountain College: An Exploration in Community* (New York: E. P. Dutton, 1972); and Harris, *Arts at Black Mountain College*.

29. Harris, *Arts at Black Mountain College*, xix, xx, 7.

30. For instance, John Rice, one of the founders of Black Mountain, trained as a classicist, wrote a spirited response to Robert Maynard Hutchins's experiments in general education at the University of Chicago, in which Hutchins posited "a common stock of fundamental ideas" that would make "education everywhere the same," teaching "correctness in thinking as a means to . . . intelligent action," but "leav[ing] experience to life." Rice argued against "a common stock of fundamental ideas" and claimed that other modes than the written word (such as the arts) could contribute to education. Further, he expostulated that the classics should be seen as products of their times, not as eternal truths, and that "Gertrude Stein's *Lectures in America* is headier than Aristotle's *Poetics* or Horace's *Ars Poetica*" (Harris, *Arts at Black Mountain College*, 15).

31. Ibid., 40; see also Xanti Schawinski, "From the Bauhaus to Black Mountain," *Drama Review* 15, no. 3a (1971): 30–44. On nonmatrixed performance, see Michael Kirby, "The New Theater," in *The Art of Time: Essays on the Avant-Garde* (New York: E. P. Dutton, 1969), 78–80.

32. Harris, *Arts at Black Mountain College*, 122.

33. Ibid., 151.

34. For several, often conflicting, descriptions of this event, see Duberman, *Black Mountain College*, 370–78.

35. Antonin Artaud, *The Theater and Its Double*, trans. Mary Caroline Richards (New York: Grove Press, 1958).

36. *The Performing Arts: Problems and Prospects*, Rockefeller Report on the future of theater, dance, and music in America (New York: McGraw-Hill, 1965).

37. I am grateful to Michael Goldberg for these statistics.

38. Attilio Favorini, personal communication.

39. John Fleming, personal communication.

40. Richard Kostelanetz, *The Dictionary of the Avant-Gardes* (Pennington, N.J.: A Cappella, 1993), s.v. "Academic Critics." Despite my disagreement with Kostelanetz on the antipathy of academia toward the avant-garde, I do appreciate the fact that he singles me out, along with some other full-time academics— Gerald Janecek, Roger Shattuck, Michael Kirby, Mark Ensign Cory, Jack Burnham, Hugh Kenner, Laszlo Moholy-Nagy, Jo-Anna Isaak, and the classicist Donald Sutherland—as having written intelligent books on avant-garde art.

41. Ibid., s.v. "Cage"; Snyder, "Chronological Table," 36–41.

42. Kostelanetz, *Dictionary of Avant-Gardes*, s.v. "*HPSCHD.*"

43. Lisa Wolford, "Re/membering Home and Heritage: The New World Performance Laboratory," *Drama Review* 38, no. 3 (1994): 128–29. I thank Claudia Nascimento for referring me to this article.

44. In *The Amazing Decade*, Moira Roth documents the work of fifty-three women performance artists active from 1970 to 1980, including Laurie Anderson, Eleanor Antin, Judy Chicago, Leslie Labowitz, Linda Montano, Pauline

Oliveros, Adrian Piper, Yvonne Rainer, Faith Wilding, and Martha Wilson. Of those fifty-three, twenty noted in the biographies published with their documentation that they either had teaching positions in or graduate degrees from universities and colleges. One can assume the number was in fact higher, since several artists mentioned neither their graduate education nor whether they earned money through college teaching.

45. Guest speakers at the Performance Art, Culture, Pedagogy Symposium included not only active performance artists working for the most part outside of the university, like Tim Miller and Guillermo Gómez-Peña (although they, of course, often teach and perform at universities), and curators of museums and performance spaces, but several historians and theorists of performance, including Kristine Stiles (Duke University), Peggy Phelan (New York University), Henry Sayre (Oregon State University), and Moira Roth (Mills College). Perhaps most significantly, the symposium roster also included a number of performance artists who are tenured professors at a wide variety of institutions, including the conference organizer, Charles Garoian (Pennsylvania State University), as well as Suzanne Lacy (California College of Arts and Crafts), Joanna Frueh (University of Nevada, Reno), William Pope (Bates College), Jacki Apple (Art Center College of Design and University of California, San Diego), Lin Hixon (School of the Art Institute of Chicago), John White (University of California, Irvine), Roger Shimomura (University of Kansas), and Daniel Collins (Arizona State University). Allan Kaprow (professor emeritus, University of California, San Diego), the eminent creator of Happenings and performance art since the late 1950s, was the conference's opening speaker. At the time I wrote this article, the webpage for the symposium could be viewed at http://iso4.ce.psu.edu/c&i/PACP.html/.

46. In addition to those individuals who either corresponded with or spoke to me, already acknowledged in notes above, I would like to thank all those who responded to my email survey regarding university support for avant-garde performance. I am also indebted to Agatino Balio, David Bordwell, Laurie Beth Clark, Kevin Kuhlke, Meredith Monk, Michael Peterson, Stan Pressner, Mark Russell, Arthur Sabatini, and Dan Wikler, who spoke with me in illuminating ways about, and provided factual data for, many of these issues during the writing of this essay. Finally, I would like to thank my editor, James Harding, for suggesting this topic; Phil Auslander and Lynn Garafola for their careful readings of an earlier draft; and, especially, Noël Carroll, without whose insights, questions, and criticisms this essay could not have been written.

Olfactory Performances

The smells of Western culture attenuated for much of the twentieth century; modern sanitation reduced "bad" odors in daily life, while changing values diminished the rich use of scents for special occasions, such as religious rituals and theatrical events (see Classen et al. 1994). The beginnings of Western theater in ancient Greek festivals like the Eleusinian mysteries (in modern times considered the prototype of the modern *gesamtkunstwerk*) were suffused with intense aromas of all kinds—including fruit, floral, grain, and animal offerings; blood and burning animal flesh; wine, honey, and oil libations; and the burning of incense and other materials in sacred fires (see Burkert 1985). In our times, the use of incense in Catholic churches constitutes a diminished survival of the ritual use of smell in religious performances. Scented theater programs and perfume fountains were only two of the nineteenth-century olfactory devices in Western theaters (see Haill 1987), but during most of the twentieth century, the "fourth wall" conventions of realism generally divided the

SOURCE: *The Drama Review* 45, no. 1 (Spring 2001): 68–76

spectator from the mainstream stage and permitted only sight and sound to cross its divide.[1]

Historically, the cultural uses of aromas in the West diminished with the hygiene campaigns of the late nineteenth and early twentieth centuries, since the spread of disease was linked to foul odors. Perhaps the deodorization of the theater was in some ways connected to the scientific ambitions of naturalism, to an idea of the theater as a sanitized laboratory (whereas odor could be precisely described in the pages of a naturalistic novel, safely distanced from the body of the reader).[2] The deodorization of the modern theater may also be one facet of a conscious move away from—even an antagonism toward—religious ritual. In that context, it's not surprising that the Symbolists, hostile to naturalism and fascinated by religious mysteries, restored aroma to performance in the late nineteenth century.

Over the course of the twentieth century, various artists (both mainstream and avant-garde) repeatedly attempted to renew the sense of smell as part of the theatrical experience (including plays, dances, operas, and performance art)—using aroma both to challenge and to expand the realist aesthetic. In the 1990s, olfactory effects in performance became particularly pronounced. And yet, the use of aroma onstage has received surprisingly little critical or scholarly attention; there is no published history of olfactory performances, nor have most theater semioticians included smells in their analyses of theatrical signs. Thus there exists a largely unexplored rhetoric of what I will call *the olfactory effect* in theatrical events—that is, the deliberate use of "aroma design" to create meaning in performance.[3] Perhaps this is because so often the use of smell seems merely iconic and illustrative, a weak link in a chain of redundancy across sensory channels that does nothing more than repeat what is already available visually and aurally. However, I contend that smell has been used and may be used in a wide variety of ways; that on closer analysis even the seemingly elementary use of smell as illustration proves more complex than at first glance; and that it is useful to the history and criticism of both theater and aroma to anatomize these distinctions. (Although throughout the history of Western performance there have been all sorts of accidental and/or unintended smells in the theater, from the food spectators eat to the odor emanating from urine troughs, in this article I am concerned only with olfactory effects through aroma design.)

Jim Drobnick has noted the "ambiguous semiological status" of smell—the way it is situated, as Alfred Gell puts it, "somewhere in between the stimulus and the sign" (Drobnick 1998, 14). Perhaps this ambiguity (and also the technical difficulty of controlling scent in the theater) has served as a deterrent to the elaboration of aroma design. Yet despite its low aesthetic status,[4] aroma is not simply part of nature, but does carry cultural meaning, and certainly the conscious use of aroma design in the theater—a place characterized, as Roland Barthes has put it, by a "density of signs" (Barthes 1972, 262)—is a mode of communication that, like any other element in the mise-en-scène, can be used for artistic effects and thus analyzed and interpreted.

In his 1964 essay "Rhetoric of the Image" Barthes analyzes how visual images (like advertisements) communicate meaning (Barthes 1977). I find Barthes's "spectral analysis" of the visual image useful for my project for a number of reasons, in particular because he separates out the various components of images, according to their communicative channels (linguistic as well as visual). This can be useful by analogy for separating out and then reassembling the various components of the theatrical mise-en-scène, including the olfactory.

My project of anatomizing a rhetoric of aroma in theatrical representations begins from the premise that there is a total, integrated sensory image (or flow of images) created in the theater, of which the olfactory effect may be one component. Thus in analyzing meanings conveyed by aroma design in the theater, one needs to discuss the use of odors in relation to the dominant sensory channels of theater—the visual and the aural—and not simply as isolated sensory events. The aroma may work in concert with the other sensory channels to reinforce meaning, or it may complement or conflict with the other channels. Moreover, keeping in mind C. S. Peirce's semiotic triad, icon-index-symbol (1991), will be useful in distinguishing among various representational strategies, especially in understanding how aroma either enhances or departs from realism.

I begin my poetics of theatrical aroma design with a taxonomy that is structured according to the representational function the odors in the performance are intended to discharge. I should point out that my categories in this taxonomy are not mutually exclusive, since these olfactory effects may perform more than one function (and the functions are not all parallel in nature). There are six categories so far: to illustrate words, characters, places, and actions; to evoke a mood or ambience; to complement or contrast with aural/visual signs; to summon specific memories; to frame the performance as ritual: and to serve as a distancing device. (There is also a seventh category, that of unrecognizable smells, which remains to be explored further.)

The most common use of aroma onstage is *to illustrate words, characters, places, or actions*. For instance, in *The Governor's Lady* (1912) director David Belasco enhanced the realistic effect by creating an onstage replica of Childs' Restaurant, complete with the aroma of actual pancakes, which were cooking during the play; in *Tiger Rose* (1917) he scattered pine needles on the floor to create the proper scent for the forest setting; and in *The First Born* (1897), set in San Francisco's Chinatown, he burned Chinese incense (Marker 1974, 61–63). Often (but not always), the mode of technological dissemination of odor in this category of illustration involves cooking food, either onstage or offstage—for instance (in various recent productions): bread, toast, bacon and eggs, hamburgers, soup, spaghetti sauce, omelettes, popcorn, onions, garlic, artichokes, mushrooms, panela (carmelized cane sugar), hazelnut cookies, risotto, jasmine-scented rice, fish and chips, curry, sausages, sauerkraut and kielbasa, kidneys, boiled beef, Cajun shrimp, and Australian barbequed meats of all kinds.[5]

But there are many other illustrative aromas besides those derived from food—for example, the smells of manure, diesel, and citronella in Ivo van Hove's 1999 production of *India Song* (Wilson 1999, 8); of rose perfume in the Persian Garden scene of the 1952 Paris Opera revival of Rameau's opera-ballet *Les Indes Galantes* (Guest 1976, 201); of various eighteenth-century "unhygienic" smells in Mark Wing-Davey's 1995 production of *The Beaux' Stratagem* (Winn 1995, 35); of marijuana in various productions of *Hair;* and of cigarette smoke in countless performances.

Related to the illustrative function, but operating more generally, is the use of olfactory effects *to evoke a mood or ambience*, as in Vsevolod Meyerhold's 1910 production of *Don Juan*, when "proscenium servants" sprayed perfume to create an aura of luxury (Leach 1989, 89–90). Similarly, but more recently, Graeme Murphy's ballet *Shéhérazade* for the Sydney Dance Company (1979) incorporated perfume smells wafting from the silken canopies of the set (Cargher 1979, 47). In Valentine de St.-Point's *métachorie* dance performances in Paris in 1913, the dancer burned large

pots of incense, according to her theory of correspondences—no doubt
derived from Baudelaire and also the Symbolist staging of *The Song of
Songs* at the Théâtre D'Art in 1891[6]—governing the scent, predominant
color, musical environment, and central poetic idea for each dance
(Moore 1997). In Le Théâtre La Rubrique's 1993 production of *Cendres
de Cailloux* by Daniel Danis, "the audience was put in darkness during
most of the two hours' performance. During the course of the play, the
actors used . . . natural essences to recreate, through smell, the feeling of
being in the forest of Northern Quebec" (Lavoie 1999). A 1996 New
York production of Joe Orton's *Entertaining Mr. Sloane,* directed by David
Esbjornson, used strawberry-scented room spray to create a tacky ambience (Brantley 1996).

By far the most frequent use of aroma design, where it does occur,
seems to fall in these first two categories: to illustrate the dramatic or visual text specifically or, more generally, to create a mood. But it is significant to note that, more rarely but perhaps more pointedly, directors,
choreographers, and performance artists sometimes engage the use of
odors for exactly the opposite function than illustration: *to complement or
contrast with* what is happening in the rest of the performance. That is,
rather than creating redundancy along all the channels of the message,
in this category of our taxonomy, the odor introduces new or even conflicting information.

A striking example of the contrastive use of aroma took place during the British performance artist Cosey Fanni Tutti's performance
Women's Roll (1976), in which Tutti slashed her clothing and created
artificial wounds using both stage makeup and crushed berries. Tutti
has remarked that she wanted the spectators to get "an unpleasant visual stimulus but a pleasant olfactory stimulus" (MacGregor e-mail), thus
perhaps unsettling their views of how to interpret this display of a
woman's body (see also MacGregor 1999; Goldberg 1998, 118). In another mode entirely, Shaun Lynch's *Clean Smell Opera* (1980) used so
many cleaning products—as the performer showered, washed her hair,
cleaned dishes, and laundered and bleached clothes—that their smells
became overpowering and repugnant, thus commenting punningly as
well as ironically on the soap opera and the advertisements being
broadcast by the television that was present onstage during the performance (see Carroll 1980).

Several theater artists have used aroma design to focus particularly
on what is often said to be a unique, or at least striking, quality of the

sense of smell—its power vividly *to summon up memories*. The contemporary magician/performance artist Aladin has discussed the way he "[uses] his 'magic' abilities to create a very localized scent of jasmine in various parts of the audience, using this device to conjure some sense of remembrance" (Hewitt 1999). In *El Hilo de Ariadna* (Ariadne's Thread) (1992), by the group Imagen (Taller de Investigación de La Imagen Dramática de la Universidad Nacional de Colombia), participants were led blindfolded through a labyrinth, entering rooms with distinctive scents (such as those associated with a schoolroom or a child's nursery) that were meant to evoke distant memories (Nascimento 1999). And in Theresa May's site-specific performance *Dragon Island* (1993, produced by Theater in the Wild), a priestess instructed the spectators to crush herbs she passed to them. The scent of the potpourri was meant to take them back in time; they were invited to narrate their memories, casting a "magic spell" that brought them into the play's events to help Arthur find the dragon (May 1999).

Finally, my last two categories have to do less with aroma design as part of the work's representational strategies than with the framing and contextualization of those representations. First is the use of aroma *to frame the performance as a ritual*. Here odor functions not strictly as a representation itself, but as a contextualizing condition for appreciating the other representations the performance creates. The constant burning of incense throughout Peter Brook's *Mahabharata* (1985) may on the one hand fall into the illustrative category as an olfactory icon of Indian culture, but on the other hand, it shapes the ways in which the audience understands and experiences the performance: it suggests that this is a sacred, not a secular event, and not only because it is based on a sacred Hindu text.

In the final category the olfactory effect *serves as a distancing device* (or, in Russian formalist terms, as a mode of defamiliarization) by calling attention to itself as a theatrical effect, thus foregrounding its own operation as a semiotic system.[7] For instance, in the Irish troupe Barrabas's production of *The Whiteheaded Boy* (1997), aroma calls attention to the artifice of theater (and perhaps of representation altogether) when an actor holds a piece of bread up to a patently fake fireplace and suddenly, magically, the smell of toast wafts through the theater (see Marks 1999).

If in some sense the use of odors onstage, even as a mode of enhancing realism, always calls attention to itself in Western theater as unusual, even a gimmick, several other productions have also used aroma design for this function of distantiation, not only foregrounding the olfactory effect, but further, underscoring its use as always potentially excessive and therefore bordering on camp. These productions flamboyantly exploit what might be called AromaRama or Smell-O-Vision (to borrow the terms from the short-lived cinematic experiments with smell in the late 1950s). And as in *The Whiteheaded Boy*, olfactory effects here, while illustrative on one level, function deliberately to undermine, not enhance, realism. A notable example of this combination of illustration and distantiation—which I call ostentatious illustration—is Richard Jones's staging of Prokofiev's opera *The Love for Three Oranges* (for the English National Opera in 1989), which used scratch-and-sniff cards (like those used at screenings of John Waters's 1981 film *Polyester*). The cards could, when scratched, release one of six different smells at specific points in the performance, ranging from (according to one writer) "oranges, [. . .] 'an exotic perfume,' [. . .] and 'a cross between bad eggs and body odour' for the entrance of Farfarello, a demon noted for his bad breath and wind" (Reynolds 1989, 3).[8] Through aroma design, directors, choreographers, and performance artists use different representational strategies that may also be categorized not according to this taxonomy of function, but along another grid—that of Peirce's semiotic triad of icon-index-symbol—taking into account the relation of the signifier (in this case smell) to the signified. Recall that in Peirce's system, an icon *resembles* that which it signifies; an index has a natural relation to it, such as *cause or effect;* and a symbol has no natural relation to its signifier but represents it through *social* (or here, we can also say *artistic*) *convention* (Peirce 1991). Adding this semiotic system to the taxonomy of functional analysis I have just sketched gives us deeper insight into the poetics of aroma onstage.

Aroma was an important part of the 1999 New York production of Ayub Khan-Din's play *East Is East,* a bittersweet comedy about an Anglo-Pakistani working-class family in England in the 1970s; both of the published reviews of the play's production start by discussing the smell of fish and chips that pervades the theater even before the play begins (see Kuchwara 1999, D3; Brantley 1999, C13).[9] It is the smell of the family business, a chips shop owned by the Pakistani father, in which his English wife and most of their kids work. Taken purely as a separate component, the smell operates indexically, as an "effect" or natural sign of cooking fish and chips (in the way that smell will always serve indexically to "point to" its source and therefore signify *it*, first and foremost).

But taken as part of the total representation, here the aroma operates iconically, as one element in a gestalt or ensemble of theatrical means that creates a realistic representation of a particular, localized setting through principles of resemblance.

It's interesting to note in the case of this particular play that the smell effect creates an ironic aspect. The aroma of fish and chips is strongly associated with a particular ethnicity—that is, British (Anglo) ethnicity. Yet in *East Is East* this aroma works incongruously and ironically along several dimensions, for on the one hand, the olfactory effect connotes (through the strong cultural meaning of the fish-and-chips odor) that the former colonial (the Pakistani patriarch) has appropriated the smells of the colonizer, while on the other hand, in the play's action the father refuses to assimilate into British culture, even while his business smells like he has.

As I've noted, the most frequent use of aroma design is iconic and illustrative. But there are cases that fall into Peirce's second category, the indexical, where the olfactory effect, as part of the theatrical ensemble, either foreshadows what is to come (as in the case of another scene in May's site-specific *Dragon Island*, when the spectators passed a smelly stream that alerted them they were about to reach the lair of the "odorous dragon") or, more poetically, sets conceptual categories of association in motion through metaphor and other literary tropes. In Jenny Strauss's twenty-four-hour ritual performance piece *Idio/Passage: Private Vernacular, Public Catharsis* (1996), the smell of rotting meat mixed with other items (including honey, urine, and dirt) in order, according to the artist, to create a "provocative/nauseating smell" and to "mark time in a non-linear way" as the odors intensified during the course of the performance (Strauss 1999). The sweet smell of honey and the fresh smell of dirt (indices of nonhuman nature) mixed with the putrescence of meat (working metaphorically here to stand for human flesh) and acrid urine (an index of the human body), suggesting a view of human substance as both repulsive and yet part of an attractive natural world.

There are also uses of aroma that are purely symbolic and conventional—that is, not linked in any natural way, whether analogous or causal, to what they represent. For instance, Michael Dempsey, in his 1999 production of Thomas Kilroy's *Talbot's Box*, burned laudate incense to suggest the obsession of the main character, a recovering alcoholic, with religion and prayer. In what is probably the best-known use of aroma in performance, the Symbolist production of *The Song of Songs*, the author/director Paul Roinard posited a mystical correspondence among speech, music, color, and scent. For instance, in one section, the vowels *i-e*, illuminated with *o*, corresponded to music in D, the color pale orange, and the scent of white violets (Roinard 1976, 131).

The symbolic use of olfactory effects often suggests (without directly illustrating) liturgical uses of incense and other aromas, but there are symbolic uses that fall into other cultural categories than the religious. For instance, Bobby Baker's *Cook Dems* (1992)—in which the perform-ance artist made a pizza-dough breastplate, antlers, and a bread-ball skirt—used the smell of baking dough as a metaphor for the female body. In Robbie McCauley's *Food Show* (1992, with Laurie Carlos and Jessica Hagedorn), the performers made and served to the spectators various foods with particular ethnic resonances and associations.

Two aspects of the use of olfactory effects in recent performances are noteworthy. One is that aromas are often effectively used to telegraph a stereotype of class or nationality or ethnicity—as in McCauley's work, Tim Miller's grilling hamburgers in *Postwar* (1982), the use of incense in *India Song*, or the real spaghetti dinner eaten by the Italian family in var-ious productions of Eduardo de Filippo's *Saturday, Sunday, Monday* (such as Franco Zeffirelli's production at the National Theatre in 1973). To re-turn to Barthes's rhetorical analysis of images, one could say that what is being strongly indicated associatively by the aroma in these cases is not suburbia, India or Italy, but suburbanicity, or Indianicity, and so on—that is, the aroma contributes not to an illustration of those specific geographical sites but to a condensed, culturally embedded association of those cultural sites instantly recognizable to that particular audience (Barthes 1977, 48).

The second striking aspect, related to the first, is that often the ethnicity or nationality invoked by the olfactory effect is an exotic "Other"—that is, the exotic "Other" is represented precisely as possess-ing a smelly (or fragrant) identity. The intense use of aromas in van Hove's *India Song;* in the Tamasha company's London production of Sudha Bhuchar and Shaheen Khan's *Balti Kings* (2000) (see Marsh 2000; Nightingale 2000); in a recent Toronto adaptation of *The Arabian Nights* (1995), directed by William Lane (see Wagner 1995); in Kai Tai Chan's dance *One Man's Rice* (1982), performed by his One Extra Dance Com-pany in Sydney (see Lester 2000); in the French equestrian theater com-pany Zingaro's production *Chimère* (see Holden 1996); and in so many other productions in the West that make use of non-Western themes, implies that the East (or subaltern culture in the West) is suffused with aromas, both pleasant and unpleasant, but in doing so creates an ideological representation of the West as odorless and therefore neutral and the norm.

The question arises as to why smell has returned to the theater with a vengeance at the turn of the twenty-first century. I'd like to advance two possible answers. One is that in recent years mainstream Western culture has in fact turned away from its prior deodorizing trajectory; indeed, our culture has become obsessed with experiencing smells intensely, from incense to herbal potpourris to perfume and aromatherapy. And surely the current fascination with olfactory effects in the theater is itself part of this Western renascence of scent. But also, it may well be that the recent rash of olfactory performances in the West is yet another plot turn in the continuing narrative of the theater's anxiety toward the mass media—of its reaction first to movies and then to television, which ironically can produce realism even better than live theater. Perhaps the olfactory effect in performance is a way to engender an impression of authenticity—a way to supply the spectator with a vivid slice of "the real," whether or not the theatrical style is realistic—and thus a way to carve out a niche for theater where "liveness" makes a difference.

NOTES

1. This article is an expanded version of a paper delivered at the "Uncommon Senses" conference, Montreal, April 27–29, 2000.

2. André Antoine used sides of beef that must have exuded a strong odor in his 1888 production of Fernand Icres's *The Butchers*. But for the most part, by the twentieth century, realism opted for a deodorized stage.

3. A recent exception, pointing to a new scholarly interest in aroma design onstage, is Shepherd-Barr (1999). Also see Zgutowicz (1980).

4. See Drobnick (1998, 10–14) for an overview of philosophical views about smell in relation to art.

5. For the various examples in this essay, I have collected anecdotal information about theatrical aroma design from a large number of people who either responded to my e-mail queries on various theater, performance, and dance studies Listservs or corresponded (or spoke) with me privately. I will not cite those unpublished sources here unless quoting directly from them (although I am extremely grateful to all those individuals). Where available, I will supply citations for published documentary references to the performances.

6. On *The Song of Songs*, see Roinard (1976) and Deák (1976).

7. Keir Elam discusses this aspect of foregrounding in terms of what the Prague structuralists called *aktualisace*, which as he points out, is closely related to the Russian formalist idea of *ostranenie* (defamiliarization, making things strange) and also to Brecht's *Verfremdungseffekt* (1980, 16–19).

8. The scratch-and-sniff cards were created by Givenchy, a renowned perfume house (Greenfield 1989). When the opera was broadcast on television by BBC on Boxing Day 1989, *The Listener* (circulation 60,000) distributed the cards in its Christmas issue for viewers to use at home (Henry 1989).

9. *East is East* was originally commissioned by the Anglo-Asian theater company Tamasha, which produced it in London in 1996. The 1999 New York production, directed by Scott Elliott, was coproduced by the Manhattan Theatre Club and the New Group. A film based on the play and directed by Damien O'Donnell was released in 1999.

REFERENCES

Barthes, Roland. "Literature and Signification." In *Critical Essays,* translated by Richard Howard, 261–67. Evanston, Ill.: Northwestern University Press, 1972 [1964].

———. *Image-Music-Text.* Translated by Stephen Heath. New York: Hill and Wang, 1977 [1964].

Brantley, Ben. "A House Guest Inspires Not So Maternal Feelings." *New York Times,* February 22, 1996, C13.

———."Pungent Life with Father, Serving Love and Chips." *New York Times,* May 26, 1999, E1.

Burkert, Walter. *Greek Religion: Archaic and Classical.* Translated by John Raffan. Cambridge, Mass.: Harvard University Press, 1985.

Cargher, John. "Reports: Foreign, Sydney." *Ballet News* 1, no. 6 (1979): 47.

Carroll, Noël. "Cleaning Up Her Act." *SoHo Weekly News,* July 27, 1980.

Classen, Constance, David Howes, and Anthony Synnott. *Aroma: The Cultural History of Smell.* London: Routledge, 1994.

Deák, František. "Symbolist Staging at the Théâtre d'Art." *The Drama Review* 20, 3 (T71, 1976): 120–22.

Drobnick, Jim. "Reveries, Assaults, and Evaporating Presences: Olfactory Dimensions in Contemporary Art." *Parachute* 89 (1998): 10–19.

Elam, Keir. *The Semiotics of Theatre and Drama.* London: Methuen, 1980.

Goldberg, RoseLee. *Performance: Live Art Since 1960.* New York: Harry N. Abrams, 1998.

Greenfield, Edward. "Arts: Review of 'Love for Three Oranges' at the Coliseum." *The Guardian* (London), December 8, 1989.

Guest, Ivor. *Le Ballet de l'Opéra de Paris.* Paris: Gallimard, 1976.

Haill, Cathy. "'Buy a Bill of the Play!'" *Apollo* 126 (1987) (New Series 302): 284.

Henry, Georgina. "Media File." *The Guardian* (London), December 18, 1989.

Hewitt, Christopher. E-mail correspondence. November 9, 1999.

Holden, Stephen. "Magical World of Man and Beast." *New York Times*, September 19, 1996, C13.

Kuchwara, Michael. "'East Is East' Might Play Better on TV." *Washington Times*, May 29, 1999, D3.

Lavoie, Bernard. E-mail correspondence. November 9, 1999.

Leach, Robert. *Vsevolod Meyerhold*. Cambridge: Cambridge University Press, 1989.

Lester, Garry. "Kai Tai Chan: A Different Path." Ph.D. diss., Deakin University, 2000.

MacGregor, Catherine. "Abject Speculation: Refiguring the Female Body in the Performance Work of Cosey Fanni Tutti." Paper delivered at Performance Studies International 5, Aberystwyth, April 10, 1999.

———. E-mail correspondence. November 23, 1999.

Marker, Lise-Lone. *David Belasco: Naturalism in the American Theatre*. Princeton, N.J.: Princeton University Press, 1974.

Marks, Peter. "An Irish Classic Given Cartoon Form." *New York Times*, October 8, 1999, E3.

Marsh, Tim. "Hot Ticket." *The Times* (London), January 15, 2000.

May, Theresa. E-mail correspondence. November 9, 1999.

Moore, Nancy. "Valentine de St.-Point: 'La Femme Intégrale' and Her Quest for a Modern Tragic Theatre in *L'Agonie de Messaline* (1907) and *La Métachorie* (1913)." Ph.D. diss., Northwestern University, 1997.

Nascimento, Claudia. Interview with author. Madison, Wis., November 18, 1999.

Nightingale, Benedict. "*Balti Kings*." *The Times* (London), January 17, 2000.

Peirce, Charles S. *Peirce on Signs: Writings on Semiotic*. Edited by James Hoopes. Chapel Hill: University of North Carolina Press, 1991.

Reynolds, Nigel. "Opera Lovers Smell After Scratching Through Prokofiev." *The Daily Telegraph*, December 7, 1989, 3.

Roinard, P. N. "*The Song of Songs of Solomon* (script)." [1891]. Translated by Leonora Champagne and Norma Jean Deák. *The Drama Review* 20, 3 (T71, 1976): 129–35.

Shepherd-Barr, Kirsten. "Mise en Scent: The Théâtre d'Art's 'Cantique des cantiques' and the Use of Smell as a Theatrical Device." *Theatre Research International* 24, 2 (1999): 152–59.

Strauss, Jenny. E-mail correspondence. November 7, 1999.

Wagner, Vit. "Arabian Nights Weaves Together Ancient Tales." *Toronto Star*, September 14, 1995, H5.

Wilson, Sue. "Tales of Passion, Obsession and Tragic Isolation." *The Independent*, September 4, 1999, 8.

Winn, Steven. "Smells Like Old Times." *San Francisco Chronicle*, September 10, 1995, Sunday Datebook, 35.

Zgutowicz, Monica. "A Study of the Use of Odor in Western Performance." M.A. thesis, New York University, 1980.

Beyond the Millennium
Recent Dance Writings

Our Hybrid Tradition

Although we regularly categorize theatrical dance traditions as "Eastern" or "Western," and we often speak of cultural hybridity or fusion now as if it were a brand-new phenomenon—in dance, as in world music, an outgrowth of multiculturalism and a utopian view of a completely racially and ethnically integrated, harmonious world to come—in fact theatrical dancing in Europe and America has long been a hybrid tradition, borrowing freely from non-European (that is, Asian and African) ritual, folk, and classical theater forms.

The syncretism of African dances with European dances in the new world since the transatlantic slave trade began—leading to tap dance and jazz dance especially in the United States, but also in Europe—has been widely acknowledged, as have Ruth Saint Denis's borrowings of Asian dances. But these are not isolated examples. As Martin Bernal has shown in *Black Athena* in regard to ancient Greek civilization, what we call "the Western tradition" in dance has always been a cultural mélange.[1] It

SOURCE: In Chantal Pontbriand, ed., *Danse: langage propre et métissage culturel / Dance: Distinct Language and Cross-Cultural Influences* (Montreal: Parachute, 2001)

257

has never been purely Western (that is, European or Euro-American), and thus its hybrid quality is not at all recent. Further, as the examples I mentioned above show, hybridity comes in many forms. It can arise out of different kinds of cultural contacts—some forced, some voluntary, and some actively sought out. And yet, although not all political circumstances leading to the synthesis of dance traditions are happy ones, cultural fusion can have positive results, even if created in unfortunate or repressive circumstances. Dance hybridity has sometimes served as a route of resistance to imposed cultural systems—for example, the American cakewalk.

In thinking about artistic hybridity, it is worth remembering that there are different kinds of fusions and syntheses, depending on the cultural identities of the choreographer(s), the relative proportions of what goes into the mix, the means of mixing, and the implications for the audience that views the hybrid form.

One could trace the history of Western theatrical dancing in the twentieth century as a continuing story of infusions with "non-Western" styles and ideas—not only from African and Asian traditions, but from Native American dance that, although located in the Western hemisphere, is not considered part of the "Western," that is, Euro-American cultural matrix. In both ballet and modern dance, as well as in popular entertainments like musical theater and screen musicals, twentieth-century Western choreographers have regularly borrowed themes, images, and movement motifs from the non-European Other. As a result of the modernist imperative to "make it new," avant-garde choreographers in the twentieth century have always looked to non-Western cultures (as well as to the folk forms of Western nations) to find a different way of moving from what they have been taught (even if what they were taught was once itself a hybrid form, now institutionalized and therefore naturalized as always already Western). Paradoxically, the traditions of ancient cultures look new on the Western stage once they've been transplanted to a different context. Moreover, dance as a commodity is also under pressure to "make it new." So there has been a permanent drive in professional choreography in the West, especially during the twentieth century, to find fresh sources for movement inspiration. And not only the avant-garde, but mainstream dance as well has perennially sought energy, exoticism, and difference in the vernacular dances of other cultures through appropriation.

But also, identity politics have throughout the twentieth century led, for a different set of reasons, to the use in the West of non-European traditional dance forms. For instance, in the late 1960s the rediscovery of African dance roots in the work of African American concert choreographers like Chuck Davis, during a period of intense black nationalism in the United States, was a seemingly new intervention, but it had a history, one that repeatedly arose in opposition to a mix of dance traditions that was politically unsatisfactory to black nationalists. Popular dancing, both black and white, in the United States since the mid-nineteenth century had been formed from a synthesis of European and African forms. Tap dancing, which mixed percussive Irish step dancing with African-derived ground-hugging footwork and flexible-torso body movement, was born in bars and street corners in the poorest ethnic urban neighborhoods, and it flourished in the racist milieu of the minstrel show. Cakewalking, to which I've already alluded, was a different kind of hybrid form arising from forced contact between blacks and whites; it emerged when African American slaves parodied the European social dances regularly danced by aristocratic plantation owners.[2]

But from the time of the black nationalist movements of the 1920s calling for blacks to acknowledge proudly their African roots, African American choreographers have sought out a different kind of hybridity than the one that gave rise to tap dancing and cakewalking, one that arises from artistic research, rather than forced contact. They have shifted the balance of the proportions between African and European elements by bringing authentic African dancing (as opposed to the concocted fantasies of Africa in many popular entertainments, as well as ethnographic exhibitions[3]) to the foreground, but still located in concert dance contexts in an American setting. Charles Williams and the Creative Dance Group at the Hampton Institute, with their program of African-inspired dances performed publicly in the late 1920s, and Asadata Dafora, with his *Kyunkor*, a spectacle with a witch-doctor theme enacted through African dancing, singing, and drumming, pioneered what Lynne Emery calls the "African heritage" genre of American dance.[4] This genre also includes work by the dancer-anthropologist Pearl Primus beginning in the 1950s, and an increasing number of African American choreographers from the 1960s to the present. Though the African heritage dance-spectacle as a serious concert-dance form is in one sense a search for authenticity, for purity, for the stripping away of European elements in order to reveal the West African substratum of African American dance, nevertheless it is itself a hybrid event, since West African dancing is traditionally done not in a European-style concert setting, but as a community occasion.[5]

Contemporary with the "rediscovery" of African dance by black dancers during the 1960s and 1970s, American postmodern dancers, who were predominantly Euro-American, explored both African American dance and music structures and Asian movement forms. A number of choreographers were inspired by jazz traditions of improvisation and by the energy and various forms of black social dancing. Yvonne Rainer used the imagery of Indian erotic sculpture in the early 1960s and later was inspired by Indian dance-dramas to inaugurate her emotion-packed narratives of the early 1970s; Deborah Hay used Tai Chi Chuan in her circle dances; and Steve Paxton built Contact Improvisation on principles of Aikido.[6] As with the interest in African dance in the 1960s and 1970s, these movement investigations may have seemed new and surprising, but they also were innovations with a legacy. Modern dance itself was born, at the turn of the last century, in a crucible of hybridity, for the three forerunners of modern dance—Loïe Fuller, Isadora Duncan, and Ruth Saint Denis—were all present at the International Paris Exhibition of 1900, which offered up, especially at its colonial pavilions, a broad variety of cultures, both Western and non-Western; Near Eastern, and Asian.[7]

The kaleidoscope of world dance and music in Paris in 1900, inspiring to a number of artists, both European and North American, who visited the Exhibition (and undoubtedly to the performers at the colonial pavilions themselves, though this has not been documented) was a small-scale model of a Western world that had fully become, in the height of the colonial era, a cultural mosaic. The events at these pavilions, and Sadda Yacco's Japanese dances at the exhibition and at similar fairground performances at Coney Island in New York City, inspired Saint Denis to create her repertoire of exotic, Orientalist dances.[8] These non-Western influences may be obvious, but there are other, more subtle hybrid relationships evident in early modern dance. For instance, Loïe Fuller's own sinuous Art-Nouveau dancing line was itself partly a product of the *Japonisme* that had animated Western European art at the turn of the century.[9]

In the next generation of modern dance, Mary Wigman's early work was clearly inspired by Asian dance-theater forms and Asian music; her

Witch Dance, for instance, samples different Japanese traditions, including percussion music that is very similar to the Japanese Noh ensemble, and the use of the frozen stylized pose *(mie)* of Kabuki.[10] Martha Graham's technique and choreography drew widely and eclectically on Asian, African American, and Native American sources, from the pelvic contractions of *Lamentation* to the quotations of Southwest Indian rituals in *Primitive Mysteries* to what she called the "Bali turns" and "Javanese foot movement" in *Night Journey*.[11] Zen Buddhist and Confucian philosophies underlie Merce Cunningham's choreography, including his use of stillness and of chance techniques and his cool approach to emotional content; his first dance made with chance operations, *Sixteen Dances for Soloist and Company of Three*, was built on ideas about the nine permanent emotions taken from classical Indian aesthetics.[12]

It seems that in their aspiration to differentiate their art from ballet, which was often castigated (especially by Americans) as an expression of European elitism and decadence, modern and postmodern dancers promiscuously incorporated images and dances of the Other in their choreography. Different from the Africanist version of hybridity as a search for ethnic heritage, this was nevertheless, like the Africanist model, another form of hybridity through the assertion of artistic choice. Rather than a quest for the genealogy of the self that led black dancers back to their roots in Africa, this turn to the exotic Other was a reaction by Europeans and Euro-Americans against a European cultural heritage. (However, I want to stress that I am not assuming an essentialist, mystical connection between ethnicity and dance traditions; it should be acknowledged that to many black American dancers of the 1960s or of the 1920s, African dance forms were as much Other as Asian dance forms were to Saint Denis or Paxton.)

Although modern dance, that quintessentially twentieth-century dance form, rejected the Europeanness of ballet, ironically, both European and American ballet in the twentieth century have also repeatedly turned to the cultural Other for theme and movement, from the Orientalism of Diaghilev's productions like *Schéhérazade* and *Le Dieu Bleu*, to the African inspiration of the Ballet Suédois's *La Création du Monde*, to the balletic translation of Native American ceremony in the San Francisco Ballet's *To the Stamping Ground*, and beyond.[13]

George Balanchine's entire choreographic career was marked by a continuing fascination with black dance forms, which he was already exposed to in Russia and which he then learned directly from African

American collaborators (including Josephine Baker, Buddy Bradley, the Nicholas Brothers, and Katherine Dunham) in both Europe and the United States. In dances such as *The Four Temperaments* and *Agon*, Balanchine's use of angular arms, flexed feet, turned-in legs, pelvic thrusts, and syncopated rhythms—derived from African American jazz dancing—become building blocks for a distinctive modernist abstraction that still remains within the ballet idiom. That is, Balanchine's hybrid mixes African elements, already synthesized with European folkdance elements to form an African American social-dance idiom, together with another mode of European theatrical dance.[14]

So far, I have been tracking some of the recurring threads of non-European influences on Western dance in the twentieth century. Some of these fusions have been hailed as brilliant artistic creations; some have been criticized as cultural theft. But it is worth remarking that cultural borrowing in dance is not a one-way street; both Asian dance and African dance, contemporary and traditional, have been influenced in a variety of ways by "Western" dance. Sometimes this has been the result of colonialist repression, but it has also come about through voluntary, even enthusiastic cultural exploration, by non-Western artists, of the West as Other.

For example, I have already mentioned a fascination with Indian dance in Western choreography. But various forms of Indian dance have also repeatedly incorporated aspects of Western methods. Ironically, if colonialist anxiety about unfamiliar uses of the body led to the suppression of Indian dancing, especially temple dancing, during the British Raj, both political and cultural resistance to British cultural imperialism were informed by Western models. In dance, both Anna Pavlova (who worked closely with Indian choreographer Uday Shankar) and Ruth Saint Denis (whose school, Denishawn, may well have served as a model for Shankar's pan-Indian dance academy) have been credited by Indians with having helped to spark the nationalist revival of Indian dancing in the 1920s and 1930s, as the movement for independence built momentum and temple dancing was reclaimed and re-imagined as an ancient classical tradition.[15]

While the renascence of traditional dance in India, beginning in the 1920s but especially with the establishment of state-supported dance academies after independence, has been a major cultural movement and may look relatively unhybridised to an outsider (though it was partly inspired by the above-mentioned Western dancers and by Western notions of nationalism), since independence there has also been a modern dance movement, as Western choreographers visited India and as Indian dancers came to Europe and the United States to perform and to study dance. The constant traffic between the Indian diaspora and the subcontinent has led to a fluid dance culture moving in and out of India, which includes fusions of classical Indian forms with American and German modern dance, kathak and tap dance, devotional Bharata Natyam on Christian themes, Bollywood films that incorporate jazz moves, and hip-hop-inflected bhangra.[16] And these intercultural fusions do not only take place on an axis connecting India to Western nations; for instance, Mallika Sarabhai, who has worked in the West and experimented in many directions, has collaborated with African dancers and actors and with Japanese composer Toshi Tsuchitori as well.[17]

As early as the 1910s and 1920s, both Western ballet and Western modern dance found their way to East Asia. White Russian émigrés fleeing the Bolshevik revolution landed in China and Japan and opened dance studios that trained a generation of dancers who went on to found dance companies. (In fact, the British ballerina Margot Fonteyn had her earliest ballet training as a child in Shanghai in the early 1930s from former Bolshoi Ballet dancer George Gontcharov.[18]) Tours by Isadora Duncan's students and by Denishawn inspired movements in modern dance in China and Japan. In the 1920s and 1930s, Japanese dancers traveled to Europe and studied German expressionist dance, which they brought home and which Chinese dance students in Japan then took home to China. Thus both Russian-style ballet and modern dance became entrenched in China and Japan (and there took on Japanese and Chinese characteristics) at approximately the same time these forms became established in North America. (After World War II, as political alliances shifted, Japanese dancers brought modern and postmodern dance back home from the United States rather than Germany; butoh is a complex fusion of traditional Japanese dance-theater forms, Japanese avant-garde performance, German expressionist modern dance, and American modern dance and happenings. But this is a thickly layered version of multiple hybridization, since both German and American modern dance had themselves been influenced by Asian dance.)[19]

Perhaps one of the great ironies of dance hybridization is the way in which classical ballet, born and refined in the courts of the European aristocracy, became the dominant mass entertainment dance form in China during the Cultural Revolution and an important medium for communist Chinese propaganda. A distinctively Chinese ballet idiom emerged, one that used toe dancing to create images of female strength transmuting into militancy.[20]

That Chinese ballet developed as a mode of socialist realist art in the 1950s and 1960s is not surprising when one remembers that it emerged from a political alliance between Communist China and the Soviet Union that was at first marked by Soviet cultural dominance over China. This alliance and this legacy bring us back to one of the dark sides of dance hybridization—its long history as an imperialist dynamic. For Soviet ballet is a direct descendant of the czarist Imperial Russian Ballet, whose institutions persisted under the new political regime. The images of empire in nineteenth-century Russian ballet (which, after all, is the paradigm of Western dance classicism)—all those dances of tribute from foreign nations, like *The Nutcracker*'s Coffee (Arabian dancing) and Tea (Chinese dancing), in the onstage representation of imaginary royal courts—express a naked Russian imperial will, couched here in dance terms, to dominate Central Asia and the Far East. This was a political reality that was part of Soviet Russia as well as Imperial Russia, and that had lasting impact on dance culture, both East and West. By criticizing the imperialist politics that gave rise to these dance expressions, however, I don't mean to say that the impact on dance has been entirely negative.

I stated earlier that hybridization in dance is nothing new, but so far I've mainly been discussing cultural borrowings in dance (both Western and non-Western) in the twentieth century. However, one might even go so far as to argue that European theatrical dancing was always culturally hybrid, since its very beginnings. Simultaneously with the birth of ballet itself, early explorations of Asia and Africa by European nations during the Renaissance brought the imprint of other cultures to European dance. If *The Masque of Blackness* (1605), with its Ethiopian nymphs, supplies African imagery in a Western "ballet," and if (as Lincoln Kirstein tells us) a Chinese ballet took place in Europe in 1601, and a Turkish ballet as early as 1596, then non-Western influences, or at least a fascination with non-European dance and spectacle, are manifest almost from the very beginning of European ballet history, which is said to have begun in 1581.[21]

Les Indes Galantes, with its four entrées set in Turkey, Peru, Persia, and North America, is emblematic of the eighteenth-century passion for what Kirstein calls the *ballet géographique*, reveling in Orientalism, *Chinoiserie*, and the *sauvagerie* of the New World, pictured then not at all as coterminous with European culture but as utterly exotic.[22] And then throughout the pre-Romantic and Romantic eras, not only do themes and images of the cultural Other recur regularly in European ballet, but there are even attempts, as in Noverre's *Fêtes Chinoises,* to stage an entire spectacle in imitation of non-European dance-theater and ceremonial forms.[23] That is, choreographers did not just represent the Other, but attempted to incorporate foreign movement motifs in their dances. The character dancing in Romantic ballet also sought to reproduce a variety of ethnographically specific dance forms, like the Egyptian-inspired *pas de l'abeille* in *La Péri* or the variety of ethnic dances—Scottish, Craco-vienne, Spanish, and gypsy dancing in *La Gypsy* (and all of these were considered exotic).[24] The *bayadère,* or Indian temple dancer, is a persistent image in early nineteenth-century ballet, long before Marius Petipa's well-known 1877 ballet of that name (which was based on the play *Shakuntala,* by Kalidasa); and an Indian dancer appears in an early version of *Giselle*'s libretto.[25]

Dance fusions have taken place in both East and West ever since colonial powers (both Eastern and Western) spread their influence abroad and brought home new images of foreign bodies and foreign dances. Dance fusions in both East and West have taken place in the context of hegemonic domination, of resistance to colonial and other forms of repression, of cultural collaboration, and of avant-garde exploration. They have taken place, ironically, in the name of cultural authenticity and purity, as well as in the name of cultural complexity and mixture. The globalization and homogenization of world dance in recent years have surely been accelerated by the spread of Western movies and television, but, as I've argued, dance hybridity is a very old phenomenon. It has a long history. Why, then, do we hear claims that hybridity in dance is something new?

Perhaps it is because, like the nectarine, our hybrid dances often appear natural to us; we think of them as our traditions, coming to us already packaged; we don't recognize them as mixtures. But maybe now, in an era of mulitculturalism, we have become sensitized to diverse traditions and are more readily able to notice the hybridity of, say, a Balanchine ballet, whereas in the past, a different aesthetic led us to attend to other aspects of the same work, which we thought was "pure dance." Indeed, Western demographics are now so mixed that to speak of "our" traditions in the West is always to speak of a global mosaic; the Other has become "us."

Perhaps, in the face of increasing ethnic conflict worldwide, we would like to believe that miscegenation on the dance floor will fulfill the myth that dance is "a universal language" that can bind the world into one happy family. And yet these bitter ethnic conflicts take place in a postmodern world that global capitalism has increasingly universalized and homogenized, to the point where anyone can take any elements from virtually any culture and recombine them as they please. Paradoxical as it may seem, as cultural differences erode, the notion of hybridity may itself be a way of hanging on to identity in a postidentity world—a way of claiming that there are still separate traditions available to be mixed.

NOTES

1. In *Black Athena: The Afroasiatic Roots of Classical Civilization* (New Brunswick, N.J.: Rutgers University Press, 1987), Martin Bernal argues that ancient Greek civilization, in the standard view seen as the beginnings of Euro-American Western traditions, was already a melting pot of peoples and therefore of various cultural hybrids and fusions.

2. On the history of African American dance, see Richard A. Long, *The Black Tradition in American Dance*, photographs selected and annotated by Joe Nash (New York: Rizzoli, 1989); and Lynne Fauley Emery, *Black Dance in the United States from 1619 to 1970* (Palo Alto, Calif.: National Press Books, 1972).

3. See Bernth Lindfors, ed., *Africans on Stage: Studies in Ethnological Show Business* (Bloomington: Indiana University Press, 1999).

4. Emery, 244.

5. Yasmina Porter discusses the ways in which African dancing has been reshaped for the Western stage in "Ghanaian Dance on the U.S. Stage: Thirty Years of Cross Cultural (Mis)communication, 1969–1999," M.A. thesis, University of Wisconsin–Madison, 2000.

6. See Sally Banes, *Terpsichore in Sneakers: Post-Modern Dance* (1980), 2nd edition (Middletown, Conn.: Wesleyan University Press, 1987); and Sally Banes, *Greenwich Village 1963: Avant-Garde Performance and the Effervescent Body* (Durham, N.C.: Duke University Press, 1993).

7. See "Exposition Universelle Internationale de 1900," *Record of the Paris Exhibition, 1900, Engineering Times* 4, no. 2 (London: P. S. King, 1900); and Philippe Jullian, *The Triumph of Art Nouveau: Paris Exhibition 1900* (London: Phaidon, 1974).

8. On Sada Yacco, see Shelley C. Berg, "Sada Yacco in London and Paris, 1990: Le Rêve Réalisé," *Dance Chronicle* 18, no. 3 (1995), 343–404; and Shelley C. Berg, "Sada Yacco: The American Tour, 1899–1900," *Dance Chronicle* 16, no. 2 (1993), 147–96.

9. See Gabriel P. Weisberg et al., *Japonisme: Japanese Influence on French Art, 1854–1910* (Cleveland: Cleveland Museum of Art, n.d. [1975]).

10. See Sally Banes, *Dancing Women: Female Bodies on Stage* (London: Routledge, 1998), 129.

11. Martha Graham, *The Notebooks of Martha Graham*, introduction by Nancy Wilson Ross (New York: Harcourt Brace Jovanovich, 1973), 158.

12. Merce Cunningham, *Changes: Notes on Choreography*, Frances Starr, ed. (New York: Something Else Press, n.d. [1968]), n.p. Also, for a thorough analysis of Cunningham's influences and intentions, see David Vaughan, *Merce Cunningham: Fifty Years / Chronicle and Commentary*, Melissa Harris, ed. (New York: Aperture, 1997).

13. See Shirada Narghis, "India's Dance in America," *Dance Magazine* (August 1915): 10–11; Milton Epstein, "Terpsichorean Acculturation," *Dance Observer* 13, no. 10 (December 1946): 120–21; and Ram Gopal, "Eastern Dances for Western Dancers," *The Dancing Times* (October 1962): 16, for early commentaries on the influence of Asian and African dance on both ballet and modern dance in the West.

14. See Sally Banes, "Balanchine and Black Dance," *Choreography and Dance* 3, no. 3 (1993): 59–77, reprinted in Sally Banes, *Writing Dancing in the Age of Postmodernism* (Hanover, N.H.: Wesleyan University Press / University Press of New England, 1994), 53–69.

15. Sunil Kothari, *Bharata Natyam* (1979), revised edition (Mumbar: Marg, 1997), 31–35. On Shankar, see Joan L. Erdman, "Performance as Translation: Uday Shankar in the West," *The Drama Review* 31, no. 1 (T113; Spring 1987): 64–88; and Mohan Khokar, *His Dance, His Life: A Portrait of Uday Shankar* (New Delhi: Himalayan Books, 1983).

16. I have seen some of these forms, both live and on film or TV, in India and have learned about others in conversation with Sunil Kothari. On bhangra, see Sarah Kaufman, "Hip-Hopping to a Hindi Beat: Bhangra Dance Showcase Joins Cultures, Generations," *Washington Post*, March 30, 1998, C1.

17. Darpana Academy of Performing Arts, "Ik2—the Myth of Myths," Press Release, http://www.darpana.com/natrani/ik2.htm; John Percival, "Changing Planes, The Place," *The Times*, September 30, 1993.

18. Alastair Macaulay, *Margot Fonteyn* (Stroud: Sutton, 1998), 7.

19. On ballet and modern dance influences in China, Japan, and other Asian cultures, see Ruth Solomon and John Solomon, eds., *East Meets West in Dance: Voices in the Cross-Cultural Dialogue* (Chur, Switzerland: Harwood Academic Publishers, 1995). See also *International Encyclopedia of Dance*, s.v.v. "China: Contemporary Theatrical Dance," "Japan: Ballet," and "Japan: Modern Dance."

20. See Gloria B. Strauss, "Dance and Ideology on China, Past and Present: A Study of Ballet in the People's Republic," *Asian and Pacific Dance* (CORD Research Annual VHD), New York: Congress on Research in Dance, 1977, 19–53.

21. Lincoln Kirstein, *Movement and Metaphor: Four Centuries of Ballet* (New York: Praeger, 1970), 110, 114.

22. Lincoln Kirstein, *Dance: A Short History of Classic Theatrical Dancing* (New York: Dance Horizons, 1969), 205.

23. See Kirstein, *Movement*, 111.

24. See Lisa C. Arkin and Marian Smith, "National Dance in the Romantic Ballet," in *Rethinking the Sylph: New Perspectives on Romantic Ballet*, ed. Lynn Garafola (Hanover, N.H.: Wesleyan University Press/University Press of New England, 1997), 11–68.

25. Preface to *Giselle*, in Théophile Gautier, *Théâtre, Mystère, Comédies et Ballets* (Paris: Charpentier, 1872), 366, quoted in Ivor Guest, *The Romantic Ballet in Paris* (1966), 2nd revised edition (London: Dance Books, 1980), 205.

The Scent of a Dance

One of Banes's latest and most intriguing research interests is the use of scent on stage. In "Olfactory Performances," published in The Drama Review *and reprinted in this volume, Banes examined scent in theater. In the following paper Banes begins a history of aroma in dance.*

—m—

Recently, Western culture has been distinctly undergoing a reinvigoration of the senses, including that of smell. (Whether our more fragrant world is a physical fact or a discursive formation—whether, as Foucault pointed out in terms of sex, it's not that we're *doing* it more [smelling, in this case] than in the past, but that we're *talking* and thinking about it in a heightened way—is not clear.) After a century in which the smells of Western culture seemingly attenuated—as the result of modern sanitation that reduced "bad" odors in daily life and changing values that

SOURCE: Paper presented at Society of Dance History Scholars conference, Towson, Maryland, 2001

diminished the rich use of scents for special occasions, such as religious rituals and theatrical events—the pleasures of the body, including those specifically of the nose, are everywhere celebrated and marketed. We are surrounded by fragrant products and practices, from make-your-own colognes, soaps, and hair products at The Body Shop and Aveda boutiques to wine tastings to aromatherapy spas. As well, we are more highly attuned to unpleasant smells, and to potential unpleasant effects of both good and bad smells; a backlash against the public use of perfumes and other scented products is part and parcel of the new olfactory sensibility. (The Seattle English Country Ball, for instance, advertises itself as a fragrance-free event and posts on its website a list of truly fragrance-free products, including deodorants, hair gels, and shaving creams.) This refreshed millennial fascination with the olfactory, both discursively and experientially, extends to the arts, as well. Patrick Süsskind's novel *Perfume* is a striking example, but in the performing arts the use of smell is also on the rise.

The beginnings of Western theatrical dancing in ancient Greek festivals like the Eleusinian mysteries (considered the prototype of the modern *gesamtkunstwerk*) were suffused with intense aromas of all kinds. The use of incense in Catholic and Eastern Orthodox churches constitutes a diminished survival of the long-standing ritual use of smell in Western religious performances, while diasporic traditions from Asia and Africa have in our postcolonial era introduced new (that is, old) fragrant ritual and religious practices into Western culture, including danced devotions. Scented theater programs and perfume fountains were two of the nineteenth-century olfactory devices in European féerie-spectacles, but during most of the twentieth century, only sight and sound were usually permitted to cross the divide that generally divided the spectator from the mainstream stage. For the most part, we'd forgotten that in previous centuries and in other cultures, dance had been part of a performance that was not just a spectacle for visual consumption but also an embodied multisensorial event.

Yet over the course of the twentieth century, various artists (both mainstream and avant-garde) have repeatedly attempted to renew the sense of smell in dance. Experiments with smell in Western art dance, as in the other arts, increased significantly in the 1990s, I would argue, as one component of the broader trend towards the corporealization of culture, fueled partly by an increasingly multicultural demography in the West, partly by a decade of economic growth that has stimulated conspicuous consumption (which always involves indulging the body and all its senses), and partly by the mainstreaming, in America, Europe, and Australia, of the body-conscious counterculture of the 1960s and 1970s.

As in theater studies generally, aroma design in dance has received little critical or scholarly attention. There is no published history of aromatic dance performances, nor have most dance critics or scholars included an analysis of smells in their documentation and investigation of dances either past or present. In recent times, although the use of scent in individual dance events has been striking enough to garner notice from critics, smells are usually simply noted in dance reviews, rather than described and interpreted. There is no systematic way of notating aromas in dance (or in other artistic activities). Moreover, a persistent romantic myth that regards the senses other than sight and sound as impervious to rational discourse leads to vagueness, bordering on mystification, in discussions of olfaction, including its descriptions and meanings. Thus there exists a largely unexplored rhetoric and history of what I call the "olfactory effect, or aroma design, in the theater, including dance events—that is, the deliberate use of fragrance, pleasant or unpleasant, to create meaning in performance. I'm not claiming here that the use of aroma design is a major historical thread or current trend in dance. However, it is a neglected and yet striking aspect of the art that deserves consideration.

My ongoing study of aroma design in dance has several parts, including research into rehearsal and other pre-performance practices that make use of scent, as well as a consideration of the strong cultural and gendered association, especially within the dance world itself, of dance (in particular ballet) and its critical language with perfume.

Today I will focus on historical and theoretical aspects of olfactory effects in Western theatrical events and offer a poetics of aroma design in dance, examining how olfactory effects operate in terms of representation, expression, exemplification, and other artistic functions. Along the way I'll mention various technologies of disseminating scent in performance. These include (but are not limited to): incense burners; perfume fountains, atomizers, and other dispensers; and cooking food on- or off-stage.

Unlike the histories of costume, set and lighting design, and other aspects of dance's mise-en-scène, the history of aroma in dance may simply be lost to us, due to a lack of documentation. There is a specular orientation in the historiography of dance that frames choreography primarily as a visual form and secondarily as a musical form of art. And

while it may largely be true that these have been the dominant values of
Western theatrical dancing, that specular orientation has led to a loss of
information about other facets of performance that can now only be
considered on the basis of a few clues and scanty evidence. We know,
for instance, that in the earliest Greek festivals, prior to the development
of classical theater, dance was part of a larger ritual practice closely associated with bacchic rites. These dances were definitely fragrant occasions; their aromas included those of fruit and animal offerings; wine,
honey, and oil libations; and sacred fires. There is also some evidence
(though it is derived from fiction and therefore not hard proof) that
scent may have been used in Roman pantomimes. In his *Metamorphoses*,
Apuleius describes how, during the climax of a pantomime on the
theme of the Judgment of Paris, the entire theater at Corinth became
"sweet with the scent" of saffron-infused wine, which spouted forth
from a wooden mountaintop to express all the captivating qualities of
Venus, the winner, as well as the joy of her triumph.

The event that is usually considered the first ballet—*Le Ballet Comique de la Reine* (1581)—was well documented by its choreographer and
metteur-en-scène, Balthasar de Beaujoyeulx. His description of the performance provides evidence that the very first ballet used at least one olfactory effect: the fountain of the naiads in the scene immediately following Circe's first appearance flowed with scented water, emitting a
sweet smell easily perceptible to the audience as the mobile car supporting the structure moved around the room. Here the quality of sweet-
ness, associated with Queen Louise and her ladies (in the role of the
naiads), seems to have stood not only for beauty but also for moral harmony, in contrast to Circe's evil chaos (and her artificial, scentless garden). That Beaujoyeulx does not single out this particular olfactory effect as a remarkable feat of theater engineering leads me to think that
the naiads' perfume fountain (along with the ballet's other fantastic mechanical devices) was not unique to this event. The perfume fountain
was just one of the entire panoply of fantastic machines created by Italian and then French theater designers during the Renaissance era of
court entertainments. The perfume industry flourished in the Medicean
culture of Florence, inspired by practices and substances imported from
the East, and Catherine de Medici brought master perfumers, along
with chefs, choreographers, composers, poets, and festival masters, with
her to Paris. So the emphasis on dramatized and choreographed flavors
and fragrances in Italian Renaissance feasts made their way into the
French *ballet de cour*.

As theaters became more public and grew in size, as the use of the proscenium theater for dance events increasingly separated the spectator from the dance spectacle, and as dancers, choreographers, and theorists struggled to make dance an autonomous art, the use of the intimate senses of taste and smell seems to have diminished from dance performance. This was a matter of aesthetic focus as well as practicality. In the late eighteenth century the system of the fine arts was crystallizing in Western Europe, in both theory and practice. In this new hierarchy, the fine arts were now becoming distinct—and valued differently—from the crafts and the sciences. Perhaps for this reason, aroma design was devalued, in order to set the work of the choreographer apart from that of the perfumer and the chef (since perfume and cooking were now considered only minor arts, or merely crafts). As well, Gotthold Lessing's idea of medium specificity—the idea that each art form specializes in a particular function and is thereby distinct from the other arts—began to take hold. The concept arose of dance as a separate art form, rather than as one of many components of a fusion of all the arts (as in *Ballet Comique*). Also, the perfumer's "art" was perhaps seen as ornamental, rather than imitative, falling into a lower realm (along with jewelry, fabric, and other decorative arts), according to those who advocated imitative theories of the fine arts. Finally, philosophers (most notably, Immanuel Kant) proposed a hierarchy of the senses in which smell inhabited the lowest, most animalistic rung—not, it seemed, a suitable sense to engage in art.

Noverre wanted dance to gain the status of the other fine arts—like drama, painting, and sculpture—by imitating nature, as Aristotle recommended for tragedy. And yet, he also wanted dance to differ from those other arts—to distinguish itself from drama, for example, by finding nonverbal, rather than verbal, means of representing action. Yet these nonverbal means, for Noverre, were still visual and auditory or visual-kinetic, involving gesture, posture, and movement. Despite his wish to restore ancient practices, the classical and Renaissance fusion of the arts was precisely what Noverre wished to dismantle.

By the nineteenth century, the greatest concern regarding smell in the theater seems to have been not how to create olfactory effects as part of the performance onstage, but how to remove or at least mask undesirable odors in the auditorium. These were the by-products of smoky candles and later, gaslight, as well as the stench of the urine troughs running outside theaters and the general miasma of urban life—of sewers, garbage, and other detritus. For much of the eighteenth and nineteenth centuries, malodor itself was considered a dangerous bearer of infection. So a preponderance of patents throughout the nineteenth century shows that engineers and architects grappled with the problem of the smells any congregation of people creates, diligently searching for methods to deodorize and thus, in their view, to sanitize theaters. They invented systems of pipes and other methods for removing stale air, pumping in fresh air, and even (for instance, in W. E. Newton's patent of 1867) pumping in perfume, certainly a more attractive substance than the so-called fresh air from the street. However, this precursor to what today we would call room fragrance differs from the meaningful effect Eugène Rimmel—historian as well as maker of perfumes—sought when he sprayed the audience with perfume during the Alhambra Theatre's 1868 production of *The Fairy Acorn Tree*. Here the scent functioned semiotically—as it had in Roman pantomime and Renaissance festivals—to create meaning in the artwork itself. Rimmel's vaporizers may have been a novelty effect, a case of product placement, meant to advertise his wares—just as his perfumed programs did—and yet, aesthetically it operated perfectly in concert with the fantastic scenography of the late nineteenth-century spectacle-ballet.

Although the historical evidence of the scenographic use of olfactory effects in Western dance is scanty, it does give us a broad aesthetic explanatory framework. It shows us a general movement from a Renaissance model of total theater—imaginatively inherited from classical models and fortified with aspects (like spices and perfume) imported from the East—to an Enlightenment model of diversified theater as primarily visual and aural culture.

There seems to be no direct evidence that Wagner, in his challenge to that Enlightenment model, used fragrance in his stagings of his operas at Bayreuth. But his vision of a new *gesamtkunstwerk* did inspire others to experiment with the long-neglected "minor" senses, including smell, on stage at the end of the nineteenth century and the beginning of the twentieth—or at least to envision, if not realize, multisensorial performances. These included works staged in the French Symbolist theater and Alexander Scriabin's plan for a synesthetic organ of sound, light, and aroma, controlled by keyboard. These uses of smell were connected with a utopian desire to escape what is and to construct a consummate Other. The use of perfume and incense became a significant marker of a new, modern sensibility that was intimate as well as holistic—and that was enabled, in part, by an international colonialist culture. Artists searching for new models now often turned to the old traditions, new and revelatory to them, of aromatic performance traditions in Asia and Africa, not only in dance-theater and religious ritual, but in daily life as well.

Both Ruth St. Denis in *The Incense* (1906) and Valentine de St.-Point in her *métachories* of the 1910s burned incense, setting their dance stages for a mystical exploration of the senses. Their performances may have had something to do with the sacred sensuality of Catholic worship, but they primarily evoked an Orientalist Other, a yearning, utopian vision of a full-bodied South Asian and North African spirituality. Both of these dancers used a particular form of fragrance with non-Western cultural and mystical associations to delve into a corporeal spirituality that seemed to offer an escape from, or an attractive alternative to, an increasingly industrialized and secularized West.

The nostalgic or utopian attempt to reinvigorate and integrate Western culture, specifically the culture of the body, through infusions of scents—whether exotic or familiar—is a recurring thread again on the cusp between the late twentieth and early twenty-first centuries. But the use of aroma design in dance serves a number of other functions as well. I want now to examine the poetics of those functions, expanding on a taxonomy that I have already established for olfactory effects in performance generally. I have found ten functions for aroma design in performance: (1) representation, or reference to people, places, objects, events, or actions; (2) exemplification, or the presentation of qualities; (3) expression, a subcategory of exemplification in which the quality presented is a mood, emotion, or other anthropomorphic property; (4) association, or summoning up memories; (5) defamiliarization or distantiation; (6) refamiliarization, or the insertion of the real; (7) temporalization, or marking the passage of time; (8) ritualization, or framing the event itself as a ritual performance; (9) identification, or marking cultural and/or personal identity; and (10) innovation, or creating a new aroma. I need to qualify this rough, provisional taxonomy of significant functions, however, by pointing out that these categories are not only not mutually exclusive but are subject to further refinement.

Unlike dramatic theater, which often trades in unconditional representation (or innately recognizable imitation), dance tends to create either more conditional representations (that is, our recognition of the person, place, or action depends on the condition that we already know what is represented) or more lexical ones (that is, encoded—as in ballet pantomime). Moreover, dance's representational strategies are frequently generic and inferential, rather than specific and strictly imitative. (We need to know the play *Othello*, for instance, in order to understand what is going on in José Limón's *Moor's Pavane*, and we need to know the stories of the Ramayana to understand much Balinese dance.) Increasing conditionality in representation nudges drama toward dance; increasing specificity and unconditionality in representation nudges dance toward drama.[1] And so, unlike dramatic theater, in which directly illustrative olfactory effects abound, there are not many examples of aroma design contributing to unconditional representations in dance. One of the few I have discovered took place during the 1952 Paris Opera revival of Rameau's opera-ballet *Les Indes Galantes,* during which, Ivor Guest tells us, rose scent was released into the auditorium when Micheline Bardin, in the role of the rose, appeared in the Persian Garden scene. In a more parodic vein, in Les Grands Ballets de Loony's *Nutcracker* (c. 1992), the Flowers diffused a rose scent (perhaps with an atomizer) as they waltzed down the aisle of the auditorium. (In fact, I would argue that the use of aromas in representation, especially in unconditional representation, can easily slip into excessive redundancy and become parodic.) In *Morning Song* (1999), a dance-theater piece by the Belgian group Needcompany, among other activities in the life of a boisterous extended family, a dinner is cooked and served. Though this is no ordinary family, the act—and smell—enhances the recognizable scene of domestic life.

Again in contrast to much dramatic theater, dance frequently traffics in exemplification, the presentation or sampling of qualities. For instance, Graeme Murphy's recent version of *Shéhérazade* (1979) created an exotic essence of Arabian splendor with perfumes and silken canopies. In this dance, the perfume stood for and intensified an idea of Orientalism, of a fairy-tale Arabianness.

One subcategory of exemplification is expression, whether of specific moods, feelings, or emotions or of other anthropomorphic qualities. Critic Lewis Segal suggested that the baking bread in Liat Dror and Nir Ben Gal's *Dance of Nothing* (1998) expressed generosity.[2] Nancy Moore has observed that St.-Point's *métachories* used various aromas of incense to correspond to a series of specific emotions, in the manner of Baudelaire's *Corréspondances*. In both these cases, the use of aroma design heightened dance's expressive means.

Another subcategory of exemplification involves the summoning up of specific memories—one of the most remarkable capabilities of our human sense of smell. In a Proustian manner, as Judith Bennahum notes, Antony Tudor called up the heady fragrance of spring and of sexual passion when he sprayed lilac cologne in the auditorium at the premiere of *Jardin aux Lilas* (1936). More than contributing to a representation of a place, the scent conjured up all the associations that constitute "lilacness." Moses Pendleton of Momix attempted to trigger memories of stadium hot dogs with the smell of fried onions in *Baseball* (1996).

While redundant uses of aroma can function representationally, expressively, or through exemplification, a dissociation of olfactory effects from other components of a dance can work to jar the spectator's expectations or understanding—to defamiliarize either the image or the aroma. This was the case in Pina Bausch's *Nelken* (1982), in which the ten thousand carnations promised by the title were plastic and scentless, but the spectators were sprayed with artificial carnation scent in the form of air freshener, perhaps underscoring our contemporary culture's artificiality. Talking about his Jewish roots as well as about his struggle with being overweight, Lawrence Goldhuber cooked up a bacon, lettuce, and tomato sandwich and ate it in *When the World Smells Like Bacon*—just the thing an overweight Jewish person should not be eating, but also a shocking evocation of the smell of burnt Jewish flesh in Nazi concentration camps.

Cooking onstage, with its associated fragrances, may often serve a representational function, as in *Morning Song*, but in other contexts, cooking has a way of anchoring performance in the real—as if to challenge the frame of representation and to attempt to break down boundaries between art and life. This function of aroma design is the reverse of *trompe l'oeil*, for it is not as easy to *trompe le nez*. Thus in a piece like Anna Halprin's *Apartment 6* (1965)—in which the choreographer cooked pancakes, among other tasks—or Ken Pierce's *Cooking at the Dance* (c. 1980)—in which in an intimate loft setting the dancers danced while cookies were being made, and then when the cookies were done the dancers sat down and ate them—the boundaries between art and life, backstage and onstage behavior, were breached. Conventional performance etiquette has it that eating (for real) is a disruption of onstage public behavior, so these performances constituted an intrusion of post-performance private behavior into the performance. But the real can intrude in other ways, as well, as with Tedd Robinson's fragrant grapefruits, a load of which he balanced on his head in *Anti-Social Studies, No. 1 through 21* (1992). The smell of the fruit here brings the real world into the dance—not to illustrate or evoke anything, but to be there, in all its materiality.

A related function, certainly present in Pierce's *Cooking,* and appropriate for a time-based art like dance, is the use of a fragrant activity like cooking or baking to mark the passage of time. In various dances, like the piece by Motion (Joya Cory, Suzanne Hellmuth, Nina Wise) in which they baked an apple pie, or *Vera's Body* (1999) by Troika Ranch (Mark Coniglio and Dawn Stoppiello), in which they bake bread, the activity of baking, apparent to the audience through aroma, makes concrete the process of time's passing.

I suggested earlier that Western choreographers have, at least since the early twentieth century, tried to lend an aura of sanctity (and consequently, perhaps, seriousness and status) to their dances by marking them as sacred rituals—often as rituals of exotic, non-Western cultures. Ruth St. Denis did this in her *Incense.* More recently, Donald McKayle also turned to the myths of India and their associated culture of fragrant rituals in *Mysteries and Raptures* (1993), a piece that synthesized modern dance with Indian classical and folk dance forms. In McKayle's choreography, scenes from a cycle of life and death, including encounters with goddesses of Creation, Preservation, and Destruction, are punctuated by transitions in which a "purifier" crosses the stage with a censer—each time burning a different incense, including patchouli, jasmine, and amber. In Mimi Chen's 1998 dance for her father, she burned incense in a ritual to honor the dead transplanted from her native Taiwan.

Both McKayle and Chen use aromatic cultural markers, specifically for religious rituals, in their dances. A striking number of dances that use smell do so to mark cultural identity—either one's own (as in Chen's case) or that of an Other (in McKayle's case)—and, I need to note, sometimes in ways that, when taken out of the context of the culture, may prove offensive, and not only when "outsiders" appropriate them. Food smells are particularly strong signifiers of ethnic and national affiliation, as are food-connected substances like herbs and spices, especially when used for bodily regimens, such as eating, bathing, medication, or massage. Kai Tai Chan, a Chinese Malay chef and choreographer in Sydney, Australia, often cooked food during his dances; in *One Man's Rice* (1982) he made jasmine rice specifically to assert his own ethnic identity. André Lepecki has written about the insistent national and class implications of strong smells—of fresh sardines, kerosene, and melting wax in *Perhaps she could dance first and think afterwards* (1991) by Portuguese choreographer Vera Mantero. In *Nana's Wedding Suit* (1999) Kimberli Boyd evoked various uses, both positive and negative, of ancient African American "herbal magic" as she told a story about the clothing, poisoned with herbs, that was thought to have killed her grandmother, and later she took a ceremonial herbal bath.

Though it is too complex an issue to analyze here, there is a salient relation between how smell on the one hand mobilizes personal memory and on the other hand constructs or invokes cultural, ethnic, and national identity, both on stage and in daily life. Thus several of my functions may at times be conflated, as association (summoning up personal memories) is often tightly linked to identification (invoking political and cultural identities).

My tenth and final category is innovation—the creation of new or unrecognizable aromas. In 1996 Michel Roudnitska (son of the famous perfumer Edmond Roudnitska) served as the *metteur en scène d'odeurs* as well as dramaturge for a ballet, *Quintessence,* choreographed by Jacques Fabre for the Avignon Festival. In it, the final scene involves the creation of an entirely new perfume.

Fabre and Roudnitska's ballet traces the history of perfume (including its technical manufacture) and the history and geography of Provence, the French capital of perfume production, through various metaphors and symbols—including the elements fire, earth, water, air, and light; symbolic color schemes; and generic images of heterosexual love. Each scene has a corresponding fragrance: spices, the aromatic plants of Provence, green herbs, jasmine, and a new composite perfume. For the production, Roudnitska worked with José Martin of Sigmacom to create a special technology for disseminating scent in large spaces, including outdoor venues. This ballet, with its multiple functions, including representation, exemplification, expression, identification, and innovation, and with its deliberate use of a complex aroma design—what Roudnitska calls an olfactory score—underlines the fact that the ten functions I have sketched here are not necessarily mutually exclusive but may be compounded in various ways. Now that I've isolated these categories, the next step in my research will be to explore how the functions of aroma design can be combined as well as to refine and extend this taxonomy. I invite your help.

NOTES

1. See Noël Carroll and Sally Banes, "Dance, Imitation and Representation," in *Dance Education and Philosophy*, ed. Graham McFee (Oxford: Meyer & Meyer Sport, 1999).

2. Lewis Segal, "Israel's Liat Dror/Nir Ben Gal Cooks up a Hot Performance," *Los Angeles Times*, November 4, 1999, F55.

Choreographing Community
Dancing in The Kitchen

When I lived in the SoHo area of New York City, working as a dance and performance art critic in the late 1970s and early 1980s, I was a frequent visitor to The Kitchen Center for Video, Music, and Dance. Recently, while in New York to dig through The Kitchen's archives in preparation for this article, I saw their production of Ann Carlson's *Night Light*. This site-specific performance was a social archeology of a neighborhood in the form of an artful walking tour through the streets of the Chelsea area between Greenwich Village and midtown, where The Kitchen has been located since 1985, punctuated by a series of frozen tableaux recreating historic photographs of Chelsea incidents. Afterwards, we all reconvened at The Kitchen, to drink beer and chat with the tour guides and performers in the downstairs performance space.

One of the many projects commissioned by Elise Bernhardt, the current executive director of The Kitchen Center for Video, Music, Dance, Performance, Film, and Literature (as it is now called), *Night Light* was a performance about community pride and preservation that

SOURCE: *Dance Chronicle: Studies in Dance and the Related Arts* 25, no. 1 (2002): 143–61

created intimate, interactive relationships between the tour-guide performers and spectators. It set me thinking about the history of The
Kitchen as an institution in relation to changing ideas of community in
the arts.

When Bernhardt was invited to run The Kitchen in 1998, she told
Deborah Jowitt in a *Village Voice* interview that her vision for this well-
established "alternative space" had to do with balancing neighborhood
engagement and support for experimentation by artists—not always an
easy task for an institution committed to avant-garde arts. The neighborhood, she pointed out, was extremely diverse in terms of class, culture, and commerce, embracing "Chelsea Piers [a new sports center],
the women's prison, thirty-eight art galleries, the [Episcopal] seminary,
the housing projects [for low-income families], four public schools,
Chelsea Market [an upscale food market], and the Roxy [nightclub]. . . .
If you could figure out a way to embrace all those worlds—not all at
once necessarily, but in strategic partnerships—you'd create sort of a
model of how a cultural center should function."[1] She told Jennifer
Dunning of the *New York Times*, "There are rich and poor people here, a
strong gay community, middle-class people with kids, sports, arts, fruits
and vegetables. It's about as diverse as you can get. The first thing I did
was to send staff out to let people know they worked at The Kitchen,
and invite them to something. The Kitchen is a base, not a space. A cultural center."[2]

Bernhardt's vision of The Kitchen as a local cultural center with
programming targeted to various audience strata (including families
with kids) and with an emphasis on outreach and education to draw in
diverse Chelsea neighborhood residents not only differentiates its presenting program from two other dance spaces in Chelsea—the Joyce
Theater and Dance Theater Workshop—but also dovetails neatly with
state, federal, and private funding criteria since the mid-1990s; her ap-
pointment was a strategic move by The Kitchen's board of directors,
and it was good for dance as well, for Bernhardt had for fifteen years
run the organization Dancing in the Streets, which she founded to
present modern and postmodern dance for free in public spaces like
parks, streets, swimming pools, and train stations.

As well, Bernhardt's view of art's agenda as community-building
verging on social services and her insistence on bringing people together
with art over meals, on one hand, returns full-circle to an ethos of com-
munalism and commensalism embraced by the founders of The Kitchen

(who were rooted in a utopian, collectivist 1960s alternative culture[3]), but on the other hand conceptualizes that community in a very different key, one that suits our own era of multiculturalism, of targeting the needs and rights of special interest groups, of esteem-building, and of anti-elitism in the arts. The community the early Kitchen fostered was a community of avant-garde artist-participants, whereas Bernhardt's Kitchen seeks to make art accessible to a flourishing neighborhood community. This article explores how, since the founding of The Kitchen and especially since it became an institution in the late 1970s and early 1980s, the organization's notion of community has changed several times and how its relationship to different perceived communities has affected its dance program.

During the period 1976–84 The Kitchen, then located in SoHo, metamorphosed from an informal artists' space to a major arts presenting institution. At the same time, significant shifts took place in postmodern dance; it changed from a purist, reductive, analytic style to a more theatrical, expressive, even flamboyant idiom.[4] Although dance had been presented at The Kitchen sporadically as part of its regular video presentations and music performances since shortly after its founding in 1971, during this period in the mid-1970s and early 1980s, increasing numbers of dance events took place, systematic dance programming was added to the organization's mission, and a dance director (Eric Bogosian) was listed on staff for the first time. The dance program received regular financial support from government funding agencies. And even the organization's name changed to recognize this, as The Kitchen Center for Video and Music became The Kitchen Center for Video, Music, and Dance. All of these developments took place in the context of The Kitchen's growing institutionalization, and also in terms of changing notions of community in the arts. Although in this article I trace the history of dance at The Kitchen and its relation to community from the time of the organization's founding to the present, I focus particularly on that crucial period when The Kitchen's dance programming officially began and when Dancing in The Kitchen helped to shape a pivotal change in American postmodern dance.

The Kitchen was ready for growth, especially by the late 1970s, with the arrival in 1978 of a new executive director, Mary MacArthur, who came from the public funding sector with an expanded budget and with a more ambitious and diversified performance program. MacArthur had previously worked for Creative Artists Public Service (CAPS), a federal program administered by individual states that funded artists to do local outreach work. And while the original Kitchen budget, in 1971–72, was $7,000,[5] from 1977–78 to 1981–82 alone, The Kitchen's total expenses grew from approximately $200,000 to $1,269,309.[6] By 1981 The Kitchen was not only involved in exhibiting videos (in a newly constructed video viewing room) and visual art (in a newly constructed gallery) and presenting music, dance, and performance, but also distributed videotapes and audiotapes made by Kitchen artists; produced international tours by composers, dancers, and performance artists; and produced local television programs. The Kitchen received between five hundred and eight hundred applications annually from artists seeking presentation at the space or through its other presentation programs.[7]

In the late 1970s SoHo itself was becoming the highly visible, affluent international center of the avant-garde art world, and many of its residents were beginning to trade their bohemian, countercultural values for aspirations toward professionalization and recognition. These were the years of the American "dance boom," when audiences for concert dance grew, every genre of dance flourished, and dance companies, schools, and artists proliferated. During this period public funding for the arts also expanded exponentially, with the proviso that informal institutions be strengthened administratively.[8]

I would argue that the institutionalization of downtown dance at The Kitchen and the organization's increasing importance in the New York and international dance worlds were the result of vigorous curatorship that was itself partly a consequence of pressures and influences from funding agencies (including the presence, expertise, and goals of MacArthur herself[9]) to fortify the center's administrative infrastructure. But despite critics who charged that MacArthur had utterly bureaucratized The Kitchen and had betrayed the anarchic spirit of The Kitchen's original founders, this institutionalization should not be seen as a negative process. On the contrary, increased staffing, funding, and stability sustained more ambitious as well as more visible programs. Through a consolidated dance series, Dancing in The Kitchen, the organization's dance curators (as they came to be called by the early 1980s) profoundly influenced shifts in postmodern dance by identifying, producing, and promoting a second generation of postmodern choreographers and by building community in the downtown dance world.

This second generation of postmodern dancers emerging in the late
1970s and early 1980s inherited the adventurous iconoclasm of the Judson dancers of the 1960s, but forsook the minimalist values that had become dominant in what was called "downtown" dance by the early and
mid-1970s. They turned, in a mode more frequently associated with
postmodern gallery art and the newly emerging genre of performance
art than with first-generation postmodern dance, to entertainment, appropriation, and pastiche. These choreographers also began to take serious avant-garde dance out of the museums and galleries, where the
minimalists had performed in the late 1960s and early 1970s in programs at various sites like the Walker Art Center in Minneapolis and
the Whitney Museum in New York,[10] and into the music clubs—that is,
out of the art world and into the popular music world. That the music
presented at The Kitchen was also changing, borrowing from punk and
other forms of "avant-fringe" popular music, allied these younger choreographers with developments in both avant-garde and popular music.
Like many younger composers, they sought wider audiences for their
work; turning to popular culture and collaborating with artists in other
media were stylistic choices but were also, in part, ways to find broader
appeal.

I do not mean to say here that The Kitchen's dance series created
this new generation of choreographers *ex nihilo*, or that The Kitchen was
the only place they appeared; there was also Dance Theater Workshop,
Danspace at St. Marks Church, and P.S. 122, and, for the most successful experimentalists, the Brooklyn Academy of Music's Next Wave Festival. However, the way The Kitchen packaged its programming, its location in SoHo, and its European touring program gave these young
choreographers visibility, income, and cachet.

Founded by video artists Steina and Woody Vasulka in the summer of
1971, The Kitchen got its name from its location in the former kitchen of
the old Broadway Central Hotel in Greenwich Village, a building that
housed the short-lived Mercer Arts Center, which was a conglomeration of boutiques, theaters, and cabarets. This original Kitchen had a
casual, "cozy"[11] setting (a large room, 1,500 square feet, seating between
50 and 150 on folding chairs), and it trafficked in the hippie, countercultural, McLuhanesque rhetoric of the times.

From the very beginning, The Kitchen's leadership defined the
organization as a laboratory where experimental work could be

pursued—in particular, interarts work in electronic media and a mixture of live and recorded sounds and images. In its first year The Kitchen offered seminars on cybernetics and perception as well as video showings and live and electronic music concerts. But it was also, from the outset, partly a commercial venture, offering various video recording and editing services. Nevertheless, it adhered to a modernist, avant-garde, anti-commodity ethic that sharply bifurcated art and entertainment.

That its earliest public communications promised "food and related gastronomic events, beginning with a fund raising dinner," signaled The Kitchen's paradoxical strivings: on the one hand, to serve a warm, utopian community-building function by offering a ritual communion of shared meals, in a McLuhanesque tribalist spirit, and on the other hand, to cope fully with the cold fiscal realities of the art-market world.[12] In terms of definitions of community and relations between community and organization, in its early years The Kitchen was a bohemian, collectivist, informal gathering place that offered services and spiritual comfort to artists—as makers, presenters, and consumers of art—who were united by their shared artistic medium (first video, and soon after, electronic music), by their interest in technological experimentation and intermedia, and by their self-appointed marginalization from mainstream formations. In this latter respect, the early Kitchen was a community by and for artists dedicated to hermetic aesthetic research.

In this context, it is interesting to note that what seems to be the very first dance performance at The Kitchen, in February 1972, was given by Morocco, a belly dancer who claimed to offer a countercultural feminist recuperation of a dance form that was wrongly understood to be, as she put it, "synonymous with seamy sex and strippers"—in other words, with female degradation and perhaps even prostitution. In attempting to offer a positive, nonsexist perspective on belly dancing, Morocco stressed the rhetoric of organic, originary, edenic community, stating that "originally . . . the whole community, men and women, [belly] danced to assure a successful harvest and acknowledge women as the source of all life."[13] But live dance concerts were rare in the Mercer Street Kitchen; there were several mixed-media videodance collaborations between choreographer Judith Scott and videographer Elsa Tambellini involving televised and live action, but most of the dancing seen there was in occasional dance videos by videomakers such as the Vasulkas themselves.[14]

In the summer of 1973 the Broadway Central Hotel collapsed, just a few weeks after The Kitchen had moved to an elegant, spacious renovated loft space in a stately Italianate building at the corner of Wooster and Broome Streets in SoHo, a neighborhood that was fast becoming an artists' enclave but that was not yet the internationally commodified art world center it would become by the late 1970s. The Kitchen's new location made it a neighborhood gathering place in a very specific arts neighborhood; now video artists and new music composers mingled with the visual artists, performance artists, and postmodern dancers who lived and worked in SoHo lofts and who also became regular Kitchen audience members.

Along with this pivotal change of location, significant transformations also took place in The Kitchen's administration. For a few months in 1973, the old Kitchen had been run by a collective of seven directors, undifferentiated by genre or rank, including the Vasulkas—the very model of a 1960s-style countercultural alternative institution. But with the move to the SoHo space, the Vasulkas left and the collective shrank to three people.[15] Robert Stearns, who had joined the staff as a music producer in 1973 (just before the collective formed), emerged out of the new, smaller collective to serve first as administrative, then executive, director of The Kitchen from 1974 to 1977. Although Stearns was not himself an artist as the Vasulkas had been (he has gone on to work as an administrator at several museums, including the Walker Art Center and the Wexner Center for the Arts), he was an ambitious leader who brought the organization out of its funky, in-crowd, countercultural mold and created a professionalized template, with a new staff of specialist artist-directors and funding from a variety of private and public sources, that nevertheless preserved the alternative temper of the space.[16] This was in keeping with the artist-activist ethos of SoHo during that period, when various artists' organizations were formed to legalize loft-space living and to improve artists' working lives in other ways.

A board of directors, including artists (like Philip Glass) and gallery owners (like Paula Cooper), was appointed in the 1975–76 season. Contracts were written and signed, and artists were now paid fees and/or part of the gate, with TDF vouchers (subsidized tickets issued by the Theater Development Fund) being accepted in lieu of the $3.50 admission charge for certain events. A membership campaign enlarged the audience base, as well as the institutional coffers. The calendar took on a more sophisticated graphic design look, and glossy catalogues were published for the 1974–75 and 1975–76 seasons. In 1980 the organization bought the loft space it had previously rented.[17] It was in this milieu of professionalization and institutionalization, as well as in the context of the growing dance "boom" in all areas of dance in the 1970s, that the Dancing in The Kitchen series consolidated, in a way that was both efficient and energizing, what had until then been a largely ad hoc activity.

Although at first there was no special programming for dance in the new SoHo space, between 1973 and 1977 dance events (either live or on video) by such first-generation postmodern choreographers as Trisha Brown, Joan Jonas, Batya Zamir, the group Grand Union, Barbara Dilley, Tina Girouard, Simone Forti, Nancy Lewis, Laura Dean, Elaine Summers, Steve Paxton, and other Contact Improvisers were presented at a regular pace. In the 1976–77 season seven dance or dance-related events took place, a number that approached a respectable dance season once the dance series officially got underway, the following year.[18]

At this point, The Kitchen had only two programming directors, one for video and one for music, but by 1976, publicity noted that its programming could be divided into exhibitions (primarily of video art), performances, and contemporary music concerts. However, in the monthly calendars these separate categories were subsumed under the all-inclusive term "performance," which also included dance. Thus an event like the music and dance performance by Peter Van Riper and Simone Forti in December 1976 was simply listed in the monthly calendar as "a performance," along with music concerts, video screenings, and a "situational slide performance reading."[19] That is, until 1977, despite its regular presentation of dance performances, The Kitchen had neither a dance programming mission nor a separate dance director.

The first dance director, Eric Bogosian, had a background in theater, not dance. A recent Oberlin College graduate, in 1977 he was working at The Kitchen as Stearns's assistant, and he was also friendly with an emerging circle of gallery visual-art postmodernists, including Robert Longo and Cindy Sherman, whose polished, figurative, media-scavenging aesthetic challenged that of the previous generation of modernist minimalists.

According to Bogosian, the dance program he established at The Kitchen got started almost by accident, when in 1977 "some friends I knew from my dance class came by [The Kitchen] to visit. They were amazed by the large shiny space. . . . They asked if they could do a 'contact improv' concert there."[20] This was not the first dance concert at The Kitchen by any means; nor was it the first Contact Improvisation concert there. (In fact, one wonders why Bogosian's friends had not yet seen a dance concert in the space.) Although the space *was* large (7,500 square feet) and shiny, with a varnished floor, high ceilings, and enormous windows, it was always problematic for dance performance, since it was dotted with columns that, for structural reasons, could not be removed.

The success of that first Bogosian-produced concert, joined with The Kitchen's new professionalizing predilections, led in 1978 to the creation of a formal series, "Dancing in The Kitchen," supported by a $995 New York State Council on the Arts (NYSCA) grant, and then to more than twenty years of subsequent dance seasons and increased funding. In late 1977 Stearns had left The Kitchen to take another position, and the older staff members left as well.[21] For a few months, as Bogosian recalls, at the age of twenty-three he suddenly found himself, along with some other very young artists, running a major avant-garde arts center in the world capital of art. Even when MacArthur assumed the directorship of The Kitchen in early 1978, she saw her job as primarily administrative and left the artistic choices up to the curators.[22]

What this next generation programmed was a very different kind of avant-garde art from what The Kitchen audiences of the early 1970s were accustomed to. It was "post-avant-garde," postmodern art—music, video, photography, and performance (including dance) that forsook formalism and embraced content. It alluded to, even appropriated from, popular culture genres and styles, shocking members of an older generation of artists and critics, many of whom, mired in a purist brand of modernism, could not at that time see this new art that looked so flamboyant, expressive, and entertaining on the surface as distinct from mainstream commercial culture. Of course they knew about Pop Art. But this work seemed far less engaged in art-world reflection than Pop Art had been.

Ironically, exactly the same thing had happened earlier with Pop Art. Critics initially (in the early 1960s) could not see Pop as anything other than nonreflexive mass culture, and it took quite a few years before Pop's "art-world reflection" became apparent. Critics' blindness to the possibility that the work was reflecting in some way on the things it represented (rather than just presenting them) was a key characteristic of the early reception of Pop, just as it was of the early reception of postmodern performance. The work no longer even seemed like *work*— the watchword of the minimalist and conceptualist avant-garde.[23] Audiences laughed; they had fun. Could this really, then, be art? Or, if audiences and critics were disturbed and their emotions were stirred, could this really be the sort of serious avant-garde art that had long since distanced itself from expressionism? Long before Pina Bausch brought her German brand of Tanztheater to New York, Bogosian introduced a new generation of more theatrical and expressive choreographers to the public, including Molissa Fenley, Johanna Boyce, and Karole Armitage.

In 1977 Robert Mapplethorpe showed photographs at The Kitchen, David Salle showed paintings, the Talking Heads and Laurie Anderson gave musical performances. Already the new sensibility was apparent in the other arts programs, and in 1978 curator RoseLee Goldberg began to program a group of performance artists she dubbed "the media generation."[24] Bogosian's programming choices began to dovetail with the new direction in the arts The Kitchen sponsored across all its disciplines, as well as with his own trajectory as a performance artist. Discussing his own work, Bogosian later identified his interests with those of postmodern visual artists such as Robert Longo and Cindy Sherman: "We're making a media world in which there is a vibration between the self and the roles one plays. . . . The point is . . . the identity thing, the transformation." Not only the format of the mass media, with their "short bursts of information," but also media content and style, as well as a broader postmodern theory of identity, were crucial influences on this group of artists.[25]

The first dance season Bogosian produced, in the spring of 1978, consisted of six monthly concerts (three performances each) by the following choreographers: David Woodberry, Dana Reitz, Satoru Shimazaki, Nancy Lewis, and Mary Overlie. Each concert cost approximately $1,000, the bulk of which was the choreographer's fee of $200 plus 50 percent of the box office receipts after expenses were deducted. The Kitchen offered to each choreographer the opportunity to have the performance videotaped and photographed (at a cost to The Kitchen of $20 for the videotape and $40 for the photos) and ran an advertisement in the *Village Voice* (at a cost to The Kitchen of $50). The outlay for programs and posters averaged less than $150. Ticket sales (averaging $1,000) and the NYSCA grant covered the costs, and usually The Kitchen cleared a few hundred dollars per concert, although overhead costs were not factored into this first budget.[26] In addition to the fully produced Dancing in The Kitchen series, dancers appeared on The Kitchen's Sunday Series of music and performance art as well as dance, which provided space and limited technical assistance but no other services to artists for a charge of 25 percent of the gate, but not exceeding $150. In the spring of 1978 choreographers Victoria Larrain and Ellen Webb participated in the Sunday Series.

The second season, presented in the fall of 1978 and the spring of 1979, included works by Andy deGroat, Lucinda Childs, William Dunas, Kenneth King, Bill T. Jones and Arnie Zane, Margaret Fisher, and Grethe Holby. By now, the artist's fee for each choreographer had risen to $400 plus 50 percent of box office receipts, and the contract now stipulated that the work must be a New York premiere, "as advertised," and that "no other concerts may be given within a 50-mile radius within 90 days before and after without approval."[27]

When Bogosian presented his third season, highlighting a new group of young choreographers in 1979–80, it was clear that The Kitchen was doing something other than expanding the A-list of "regulars" in the downtown dance scene. Rather, this season of new choreographers, including Molissa Fenley, Johanna Boyce, Min Tanaka, Cesc Gelabert, and Karole Armitage, truly seemed to herald a stunning change of the guard in postmodern dance, from minimalism to an electrifying maximalism dealing in narrative and emotion. "A Walk on the Wild Side" was what I titled my *SoHo Weekly News* review of a number of Bogosian's new discoveries, presented in what he called the Dance Now series of 1979–80, and clearly a second generation of postmodern dancers.[28]

At that time, the first generation of postmodern dancers had entered the dance canon: my book *Terpsichore in Sneakers: Post-Modern Dance* was published in January 1980; Merrill Brockway's television documentary *Beyond the Mainstream* was broadcast by the Public Broadcasting System's (PBS) Dance in America series in May 1980; and Michael Blackwood's 1980 film *Making Dances: Seven Post-Modern Choreographers* was screened at The Kitchen in April 1981. Nearly twenty years after the Judson Dance Theater had electrified the downtown scene, it was time for a change of the artistic guard, and Bogosian seemed to have his finger on the pulse of the next generation.

Bogosian was pleased when some of the first-generation postmodern dancers, who had their choice of pr esenters, agreed to appear on his series, but he saw his primary mission as presenting "a new breed" of "lesser known choreographers" who were "new and interesting," "energetic," "idiosyncratic," even "young and awkward."[29] Yet despite his eye for innovation, Bogosian did not only program newcomers. In the four years he ran the dance program, before he left to launch his own career as a high-energy performance art monologist, The Kitchen presented the work of over forty choreographers, as well as work about dance by several filmmakers. Ultimately, Bogosian's roster ranged from Merce Cunningham (represented by a videotape) to Karole Armitage to Frank Conversano. By 1981 The Kitchen's dance program was garnering NEA grants of $15,000 and, in addition to concerts and videotape documentation, it provided international touring opportunities for dancers.

What is striking about this period is that both Bogosian and the downtown dance world saw The Kitchen's mission as providing a service to a new, expanding experimental dance community, what could be defined as the artists (now labeled a community because it was more than a handful of Judson dancers[30]) and the conditions of their making and showing work. Although this was not necessarily a warm and fuzzy communal, commensal, or collective 1960s-style group—certainly there were professional rivalries and conflicting artistic styles among its members—it was nevertheless a community both in the geographical sense (many of the choreographers, dancers, and critics lived or worked in SoHo or nearby, though some were from other parts of the country or abroad) and the professional sense. The Kitchen offered a performance space, which was crucial. It also provided rehearsal space, photo and video documentation, a video viewing room (so choreographers could review rehearsal and performance tapes in those days before home video), professional seminars and workshops (on such topics as health, publicity, and fundraising), visibility not only in individual concerts but in the marathon Dance Days (and later, Dance Weeks), and by 1980, for several of the dancers and their companies, it offered touring engagements in Europe.

From the beginning, Bogosian stressed The Kitchen's role in community-building. "We are not Lincoln Center," he wrote to NYSCA, "but we are an important part of the younger dance community." And he pointed out that The Kitchen provided important services to bolster the dance community, including its video viewing room and its practice of providing low-cost rehearsal space rentals.[31]

Bogosian organized several day-long festivals of dance, including performances and panel discussions. A letter sent to potential participants in the first Dance Day states, "We hope the day will act as a sign of solidarity for the downtown dance community."[32] Although this statement was partly meant euphemistically to encourage participants to perform free of charge to benefit The Kitchen's dance program, the fact that so many dancers responded positively and volunteered to perform indicates that this spirit of community Bogosian invoked was genuine. The dancers themselves felt they were part of a community that willingly gave to an institution like The Kitchen, which they saw as acting in their interest, as well as receiving from it. The Kitchen staff consciously worked not only to provide services for individual artists but, especially for the younger choreographers, to function as a service and networking center for an emergent professional community of artists— to help form, as well as to serve, that community.

If in Bogosian's view Dancing in The Kitchen served a community of rising young experimental artists by helping them produce, publicize, and document their work, during the time Jamie Avins was curator, from 1981 to 1985, the focus began to shift to audience-building, as the recession and thus anxieties about the bottom line hit The Kitchen, along with so many other arts institutions. The Kitchen had expanded during a time when, in a recession economy, it could operate on a shoestring. During the early 1980s the economy grew in some sectors (increasing expenses) but not others (reducing income). The Kitchen's NEA grants began to shrink and, as building maintenance costs rose, building code problems emerged, residents of the building complained about the noise, and the limitations of the SoHo loft space for a lively performing arts program made themselves felt, the organization began looking for a new space, a move that had been discussed since the late 1970s, but that had now become more pressing.

Partly for aesthetic reasons, but certainly to build audiences, Avins (like the curators of other art forms at The Kitchen during her term) took an even more extreme position than Bogosian had in presenting artists who blurred the lines between "high" and "low" art. She programmed break dancing and other forms of vernacular dance at The Kitchen along with the latest avant-garde experiments. But even those avant-garde experiments themselves were no longer esoteric; in their dances, people like Pooh Kaye, Yoshiko Chuma, Timothy Buckley, Bebe Miller, Barbara Allen, Yves Musard, and Elizabeth Streb presented high-energy events that may have appropriated or commented on entertainment and popular culture but were also meant to be pleasurable in themselves. Dancers like Jim Self, Eric Barsness, Ishmael Houston-Jones, and Hope Gillerman reveled in danced storytelling. Avins also presented reconstructions of significant avant-garde dances of the past, including Bauhaus dances by Oskar Schlemmer and Russian Constructivist dances by Nikolai Foregger. Indeed, the aura of a postmodern historical sensibility the dance program fostered in those years included looking back at an even more recent avant-garde: the history of dance presenting at The Kitchen itself.[33] As well, Avins collaborated with the other Kitchen curators to produce interarts festivals of dance and film, dance and music, and dance and performance art.

All of these directions served the artists' choices, but they were also useful in another way: since funding agencies were now, for political reasons, making audience development a priority, art that was accessible and that expanded audiences, in terms of both numbers and heterogeneity, was favored over the previous funding criteria of individual artistic exploration and innovation. Moreover, as the Next Wave Festival collaborations at the Brooklyn Academy of Music during these years proved, festivals across artistic genres—such as dance and film or dance and performance art or dance and music plus visual art—brought aficionados from each of the genres to performances, doubling (and sometimes even tripling) potential audience appeal. And pop culture appropriation, or presenting pop culture itself (in the form of break dancing, rapping, and MTV) could certainly bring in more spectators. Thus the community The Kitchen perceived as its constituency shifted in the early and mid-1980s from the world of artists to the world of art consumers. And in order to attract more heterogeneous audiences, including the international audiences to which its programs toured, it stressed the presentation of more democratic art, that is, art that was accessible to broader audiences.

After a striking period of growth, including administrative expansion, in the 1970s and early 1980s, like so many arts organizations, in the late 1980s and 1990s The Kitchen underwent a period of retrenchment and reassessment. In some ways, its success had led to overextension, given new cutbacks in public funding, and, some even charged, to mismanagement.[34] In 1984 MacArthur stepped down from the directorship of The Kitchen and was eventually replaced, in 1985, by Stuart Hodes, a former dancer with the Martha Graham Company and chair of New York University's Department of Dance, who served for less than a year. While Hodes did not program dance at The Kitchen, and admittedly was not an insider to the avant-garde world the organization stood for, he had to trim drastically and reshape its administrative structure. Under Hodes's directorship, The Kitchen sold its SoHo loft and moved into a large multistory building, a former film studio owned then by the Dia Foundation, where artist Robert Whitman had for several years been presenting his theater of images. It was located in Chelsea, which at that time, with its location north and west of Greenwich Village, seemed far from both SoHo and the lively, newer East Village club and art scene. Although two important dance venues, Dance Theater Workshop and the Joyce Theater, were also located in Chelsea, The Kitchen's new building, two long blocks west of those stages, felt far more remote. Yet ten years after The Kitchen moved to west Chelsea, the neighborhood had become the new arts center of New York and a thriving, diverse neighborhood. The black box performance space at the remodeled Kitchen, measuring forty-five by ninety feet, with a twenty-three foot high ceiling and a state-of-the art dance floor, was widely acknowledged as one of the best in the city.[35]

Hodes left by the end of 1985, and in 1986 Barbara (Bobbi) Tsumagari, a former program specialist with the Interarts Program of the National Endowment for the Arts, became director. As she pointed out, The Kitchen by then was rather awkwardly situated in an artistic middle, somewhere between more mainstream places like the Brooklyn Academy of Music and the newer upstart spaces, like P.S. 122 on the Lower East Side. Its uncertain identity, along with financial and administrative instability, had nearly forced The Kitchen to close. *New York Times* music critic John Rockwell noted that the new director was only twenty-nine years old, implying that (in contrast to Hodes, who was sixty years old when he became director) her youthful energy and vision would provide a much-needed shot in the organization's arm. Tsumagari wanted to pull back on The Kitchen's predilection for what Rockwell called "rather giddy, pop-flavored performance art and music" and to present serious avant-garde art that looked to a future she saw as "increasingly ethnically oriented," art that would provide "a sense of other."[36] Indeed, issues of multicultural identity politics were coming to the fore in the content of much experimental dance and performance art at that time, and while Tsumagari was sincerely committed to this agenda, she also knew well from her term at the NEA that this had become a priority for federal funding.

Cynthia Hedstrom, dance curator from 1985 to 1990, broadened the notion of community by diversifying further the roster of postmodern dancers The Kitchen presented. More choreographers of color, including Jawole Willa Jo Zollar of Urban Bush Women, Nelson Zayas, Eiko and Koma, and Kumiko Kimoto, appeared at The Kitchen for the first time, and Bill T. Jones, Ishmael Houston-Jones, and Fred Holland returned. Hedstrom also presented dancers with a "bad-girl," punk-feminist edge, like Cydney Wilkes and the groups Kinematic and Dancenoise, along with new discoveries from Europe, such as Wim Vandekeybus, mixed with names familiar to spectators from The Kitchen's SoHo days, among them Steve Paxton, Wendy Perron, Susan Rethorst, and Molissa Fenley. Thus her vision of community included a more diverse roster of artists, both in terms of American multiculturalism and in terms of an international exchange; although the touring program of The Kitchen had been discontinued by 1986, its video documentations of American choreographers went abroad and European and Asian choreographers came to The Kitchen.

By the time of its twentieth anniversary, The Kitchen had a new director, Lauren Amazeen, and it owned the building (and a large mortgage) in Chelsea. With an MBA in arts management from Columbia University, Amazeen took over in 1991 during a time when The Kitchen was under direct attack from powerful right-wing governmental opponents of NEA funding, such as Jesse Helms, singled out for work they found objectionable due to political and sexual content. According to C. Carr, The Kitchen's risky programming of the 1980s and early 1990s—including, for instance, the performance artists Annie Sprinkle and Karen Finley—was "a casualty of the censorship wars." In a 1994 *Village Voice* article deploring what she saw as Amazeen's mismanagement (and strikingly reminiscent of William Harris's article, nearly a decade earlier, making similar charges against MacArthur), Carr objected to Amazeen's emphasis on high technology and repeatedly mourned The Kitchen's loss of community and cutting-edge, risky work as a result of its new administration.[37]

Whether or not the "fortress mentality" and anti-artist attitude some artists and curators told Carr they found at The Kitchen in the early 1990s were real, and whether or not, as Carr implied, the board of directors deliberately took a more conservative approach to programming to avoid more scandal, The Kitchen underwent administrative and fiscal turmoil while trying to present new art in a world of rapidly changing technology. If The Kitchen was to survive, it had to find funding; as in the early 1970s, when it was born, funds for technological experiment were growing exponentially in the early and mid-1990s. So, while Amazeen's managerial skills may have been problematic, her focus on technology was fiscally apt for the times.

And during this turmoil, the Dance Program continued. Steve Gross, curator from 1990 to 1992, had since 1987 been director of The Field, a SoHo dance studio and service organization that provided a place for concerts, structured feedback sessions, and legal and business advice, as well as camaraderie, for dancers and choreographers. For many, The Field seemed to offer a combination of what the Judson Dance Theater had been in the 1960s and Dancing in The Kitchen had been in the 1970s and early 1980s. Gross, who continued to direct The Field while working at The Kitchen, introduced a new dance program that, inspired by his work at The Field, emphasized in-progress feedback and support for emerging choreographers. This was Working in The Kitchen, a program in which four choreographers met weekly for two months to show work in progress for "peer review," then presented their dances to the public. Re-titled Dance in Progress, this program is still a Kitchen staple in 2001.[38]

For JoAnn Jansen (dance curator from 1992 to 1994) and Neil Greenberg (dance curator from 1995 to 1999), a major challenge was to simply keep the Dance Program afloat during this period of deep retrenchment in the arts, when many alternative spaces closed altogether. Harking back to the earliest days of The Kitchen, Greenberg emphasized multimedia presentation, bringing in choreographers like Cathy Weis, who worked with video while still "preserving dance values" in their performances.[39] He also brought in artists who had not previously appeared at The Kitchen, including the new improvisers of the 1990s, like Jennifer Monson. By the mid-1990s, bereft of outside funding, the Dance Program's budget had become nonexistent; the fiscal arrangement had reverted back to that of the early 1970s, when the choreographers received 50 percent of the box office proceeds.

In 1999 Dean Moss was appointed curator of performance, which as in the 1970s includes dance. During his tenure, a separate budget for performance and dance was restored (it was $50,000 for the 2000–2001 performance season), and artists receive fees. In many ways, although it has changed to suit the times, the current vitality of dance programming at The Kitchen is reminiscent of the late 1970s, with a variety of events and even more diversified funding. The widespread contemporary concern on the part of producers and funders, in the wake of the culture wars of the 1990s, that artists explain their work to the public is reflected in several Kitchen programs, most notably Open Kitchen, which features open rehearsals, talk-backs, and interactive workshops, with an emphasis on family events (perhaps reappropriating the right-wing idea of family values).[40] For the first time, there is an education and outreach director (Treva Offutt) on staff.

The dance events also reflect this sensibility. The work may still be artistically or politically radical or technologically sophisticated, and the mix of artists is more multicultural and international than ever, but performances are regularly presented in situations engineered to defuse shock value and unfamiliarity through education. Like Bogosian and other dance curators since the late 1970s, Moss looks for "experimental work" and for "young, upcoming artists," whom he balances with older choreographers like Molissa Fenley, who twenty years ago was produced at The Kitchen as one of those upcoming artists.[41] But, given The Kitchen's current mission, more than any of his predecessors, Moss has emphasized public access to dance, looking for community ties not only among artists but also between artist and spectator. Besides the aforementioned Dance in Progress, Two on Two [2/2] is an ongoing project for two "seasoned" choreographers, who work for two weeks and then present their dances in the second-floor theater. MIST— movement, image, sound, and text—is a multimedia performance program in which, again working for two weeks, artists receive feedback from a number of Kitchen curators. The regularly scheduled TV Dinner: Dance@The Kitchen presents a lesson in dance history, as restored dance videotapes from The Kitchen's archives are screened. In the series Talking Dance, Moss presented, both live and on film, several generations of choreographers who combine spoken text with dance, from Yvonne Rainer, Trisha Brown, and David Gordon to Foufwa d'Imobilité and Cynthia Oliver, thus teaching the history and future of the form simultaneously. Other projects have included international collaboration over the Internet as well as collaborations across artistic genres. Most of these programs are framed with preperformance and/or postperformance discussions with artists, critics, historians, journalists, and/or political activists, sometimes over a meal.

Since its founding in 1971, The Kitchen's notions of community, and with it the dance series' notions of community, changed from a constituency of artists to a constituency of audiences, leading to its current focus on prospective audiences. And the organization's relationship to that perceived community shifted from presenting new art to audience development, leading to its current aim to demystify art—clearly a response, in part, to the 1990s funding backlash against what was perceived as elitism and obscurity in experimental art. If at present we are in the midst of yet another redefinition of the notion at The Kitchen, one that conceptualizes its community-building goals in terms of outreach and education, then the significance and historical specificity of the present moment can be fully appreciated only by situating it in a continuous process of transformation that has gone through several stages and that is linked, though not necessarily in a cynical way, to transformations both in the priorities of funding agencies and in the relations between art and society. It has moved from an esoteric community of artists, first conceived as bohemian artists but then as professional artists, whose quest for broader audiences put them on the pathway of community-building and ultimately to aesthetic public service.[42]

NOTES

1. Deborah Jowitt, "Cooking in Chelsea," *Village Voice*, September 22, 1998.

2. Jennifer Dunning, "Dance Notes: Redefining the Kitchen," *New York Times*, June 3, 1998.

3. See Sally Banes, *Greenwich Village 1963: Avant-Garde Performance and the Effervescent Body* (Durham, N.C.: Duke University Press, 1993).

4. See the Introduction to Sally Banes, *Terpsichore in Sneakers: Post-Modern Dance*, 2nd ed. (Middletown, Conn.: Wesleyan University Press, 1987), xiii–xxxix, for a discussion of analytic postmodern dance and the various generations and phases of postmodern dance from the 1960s to the mid-1980s.

5. John Rockwell, "Something's Always Cooking at the Kitchen," *New York Times*, April 29, 1977.

6. Mary MacArthur, Executive Director's Report to the October 5, 1978 Board of Directors Meeting; Haleakala, Inc./The Kitchen, Grant Application for Fiscal Year 1980, National Endowment for the Arts, Dance Program; Budget Sheets, Kitchen archives.

7. See David Sterritt, "'The Kitchen': An Arts Experiment Aimed at the World, " *Christian Science Monitor*, July 29, 1981.

8. However, already by the early 1980s, Reaganomics had begun to threaten the National Endowment for the Arts with budget cuts.

9. In her Executive Director's Report to the October 5, 1978 Board of Directors Meeting, MacArthur identified as one of her top priorities for her first full year as Executive Director "to expand the administrative support system."

10. See Sally Banes, "Dancing in the Museum: The Impure Art," in *Art Performs Life: Merce Cunningham, Meredith Monk, Bill T. Jones* (Minneapolis: Walker Art Center, 1998), 10–15.

11. Peter Frank, "New Music: Cookin' in the Kitchen," *SoHo Weekly News*, February 5, 1976; also see Tom Johnson, "Someone's in the Kitchen—With Music," *New York Times*, October 8, 1972.

12. A Proposal for Continued Funding: The Kitchen for Electronic Media, n.d, Kitchen archives; Newsletter no. 1: From The Kitchen, April 29, 1971, Kitchen archives.

13. "Scenes," *Village Voice*, February 24, 1972.

14. Judy Kahn, Rev. of *Cycles*, July 6, 1972, *Dance Magazine* 46, no. 9 (1972): 70; Ellen Stodolsky, Rev. of mixed media dance event, November 18, 1972, *Dance Magazine* 47, no. 1 (1973): 80; Jack Anderson, Rev. of Judith Scott and Elsa Tambellini, February 16, 1973, *Dance Magazine* 47, no. 4 (1973): 92, 94; Kitchen calendars.

15. Kitchen calendar, November 1973. They were Shridhar Bapat, Jim Burton, and Robert Sterns.

16. Kitchen catalogue, 1975–76, 3. For instance, the 1975–76 Kitchen catalogue lists the numerous sources of financial support. In the public sector, these included the New York State Council on the Arts and the National Endowment for the Arts; in the private sector, the Walter Foundation, the Martha Baird Rockefeller Fund for Music, the CBS Foundation, and Christophe de Menil. Also, grants to individual artists from various funding programs helped to underwrite those individuals' performances at The Kitchen; these included the Creative Artists Public Service Program (CAPS), Meet the Composer, and the Media Equipment Resource Center (MERC) of the Young Filmmakers Foundation.

17. William Harris, "Slouching Toward Broome Street: Can the Kitchen Survive?" *Village Voice*, March 5, 1985.

18. The seven dance (or dance-related) events presented at The Kitchen from October 1976 to May 1977 included two Contact Improvisation concerts and work by Sylvia Whitman, Simone Forti (two events), Sheryl Sutton, and Elaine Summers.

19. Kitchen calendar, December 1976.

20. Eric Bogosian, "That Large, Shiny Space," in *The Kitchen Turns Twenty: A Retrospective Anthology*, ed. Lee Morrissey (New York: The Kitchen Center for Video, Music, Dance, Performance, Film, and Literature, 1992), 54.

21. Stearns's new position was at the Contemporary Arts Center in Cincinnati, which ten years later gained notoriety for its Robert Mapplethorpe show, and a related obscenity lawsuit; ironically, Mapplethorpe had had an exhibition of photographs at The Kitchen in 1977.

22. Bogosian, "That Large, Shiny Space," 53–54; Eric Bogosian, telephone interview, February 27, 2000.

23. See Stephen Koch, "Where the Avant-Gardest Work the Hardest," *Esquire* 83, no. 4 (1975): 116–17.

24. RoseLee Goldberg, *Performance Art: From Futurism to the Present*, rev. and enlarged ed. of *Performance: Live Art 1909 to the Present* (New York: Harry N. Abrams, 1988), 190–95.

25. Sally Banes, "Bits and Pieces of Bogosian, " *Village Voice*, July 19, 1983; reprinted in Sally Banes, *Subversive Expectations: Performance Art and Paratheater in New York, 1976–85* (Ann Arbor: University of Michigan Press, 1998), 184–85.

26. Dance Program 1977–78 folder, Kitchen archives.

27. Dancing in The Kitchen Performance Contract, Dance 1978–79, contract folder, Kitchen archives.

28. Sally Banes, "A Walk on the Wild Side," *SoHo Weekly News*, October 25, 1979.

29. Eric Bogosian, draft of Press Release, winter 1978; Eric Bogosian, letter to Shelbe Freeman-Bullock, Dance Program, New York State Council on the Arts, September 9, 1977; Eric Bogosian, letter to Mary Lear, Dance Program, New York State Council on the Arts, November 22, 1977; Eric Bogosian, draft of letter to Nancy Vanden Berg, The Beard's Fund, fall 1977 or winter 1978; Eric Bogosian, memo, fall 1977 or winter 1978; Eric Bogosian, Dance in The Kitchen, Executive Director's Report to the Board of Directors, October 5, 1978.

30. In their article "Space and Support," Cynthia Hedstrom and Judy Padow wrote, "In the last fifteen years, since the experimental work of the Judson Dance Theater, a whole new dance community has evolved creating a boom of activity, which is now in urgent need of money and space to sustain and support it. It is not a question of the success of isolated individuals, but the body of work of a large and growing community of artists which has blossomed since Judson" (*Dance Scope* 14, no. 4 [1980]: 8).

31. Eric Bogosian, letter to Mary Lear; Eric Bogosian, letter to Shelbe Freeman-Bullock.

32. Eric Bogosian, letter to multiple artists, December 14, 1979, Kitchen archives.

33. Jennifer Dunning, "After Modernism," *New York Times*, June 9, 1982.

34. Harris, "Slouching Toward Broome Street."

35. See Stephen Greco, "Beating the Real Estate Crunch: The Kitchen's New Space Opens in New York," *Dance Magazine* 60, no. 4 (1986): 4.

36. John Rockwell, "Under New Chief, the Kitchen Has Regained Some of Its Zip," *New York Times*, September 17, 1987.

37. C. Carr, "Will the Kitchen Sink?" *Village Voice*, October 11, 1994.

38. Dean Moss, telephone interview, July 11, 2001; Diane Vivona, "Courage at the Kitchen: Dance in Progress," *Dance Insider*, January 3, 2001, http://www.danceinsider.com/f2001/f103_2.html.

39. Neil Greenberg, telephone interview, August 13, 2001.

40. For a similar assessment of alternative visual art galleries' recent turn to public awareness programming, see Linda Yablonsky, "When the Mainstream Takes Over Outsiders' Turf," *New York Times*, July 22, 2001.

41. Moss, interview.

42. I would like to thank Jamie Avins, Eric Bogosian, Neil Greenberg, Cynthia Hedstrom, Dean Moss, and Wendy Perron for their conversations with me about their work at The Kitchen as I was preparing this article, as well as the staff members of The Kitchen who gave me access to archives and other information.

"A New Kind of Beauty"

From Classicism to Karole Armitage's Early Ballets

The Ideal of Beauty in Ballet

Following Kant, the Russian-French ballet critic André Levinson states in his 1922 essay "Some Commonplaces on the Dance" that "it [is] difficult to define beauty."[1] A few years later, in his seminal 1925 essay "The Spirit of the Classic Dance," Levinson remarks that "the dancer is a machine . . . for manufacturing beauty," suggesting that it is in the dancer's body, rather than the choreographer's composition, that the beauty of ballet may be found.[2] Although Levinson refers to ballet's "logic" of "creating beauty by *organized dynamism*" and its "spirit of order and discipline," implying that both the dance composition and the dancer's technical prowess might provide grounds for discovering beauty, in neither essay does he establish specific criteria for defining or gauging beauty in ballet—in performance or composition.[3] He seems, like Kant, to think of beauty as subject to no prescriptive formula but

SOURCE: In Peg Zeglin Brand, ed., *Beauty Matters* (Bloomington: Indiana University Press, 2000)

rather as particular to each object. One can recognize free beauty when one sees it, but one can't conceptualize it.

And yet, in his attempt for the first time "to formulate specifically the laws of this art on its own ground, . . . to portray the intrinsic beauty of a dance step, its innate quality, its esthetic reason for being," Levinson does lay down the basic principles of ballet, or classic dancing, that many historians, theorists, and critics since his time have used repeatedly as a framework for discussing how ballet as an art form generates its own kinds of beauty in specific works.[4]

According to Levinson, the three basic principles governing ballet are verticality, the five positions of the feet, and the turnout of the body (especially the legs). These are the constraints that define and limit classic dancing. By verticality, Levinson means not only the upright carriage of the individual ballet dancer, but also the very "configuration of motion in space" oriented along the vertical frontal plane of the proscenium arch.[5]

Turnout, or the rotation of the legs outward from the hips, was also a result of the move to the picture-frame proscenium stage. Dance historian and theorist Lincoln Kirstein calls turnout "the bedrock of ballet style and practice," and he explains that it is the means through which the human body achieves theatrical legibility — it allows "the frontal plane of the dancer's body [to face] his audience in its maximum silhouette."[6] Turnout also permits the dancer total freedom of lateral, forward, backward, and diagonal movement while still facing front; Levinson observes that "instead of being restricted to a simple backward and forward motion . . . many motions otherwise impossible are thereby facilitated."[7] And turnout creates a perspectival, rather than foreshortened, view of the dancer's body within the proscenium picture frame.[8] This constraint, Levinson argues, proves to be the exact opposite of a restriction, for it leads to a state in which "the dancer is freed from the usual limitations upon human motion."[9]

The five positions of the feet are, in a sense, a logical extension of turnout, since they constitute the various relationships between the legs as, rotated, they line up (first position), cross (fifth and third positions), or separate (second and fourth positions). The five positions allow the feet to navigate without collision, arranging themselves parallel to one another as the legs move in a variety of directions.[10]

Added to these three principles or constraints are the generative possibilities facilitated by elevation (including aerial work like jumps and leaps) and pointe work, or dancing on the tips of the toes (for women).[11] And resulting from these restrictions and possibilities are the qualities of equilibrium, symmetry, harmony, and unity of line, made all the more arresting because of their contingency—because in ballet, unlike in static art forms such as sculpture and architecture, they are achieved, disturbed, and found again in the flow of motion.

The presence of the three principles adumbrated by Levinson does not, in itself, constitute beauty; most experts would agree with Levinson that all ballet dancing, beautiful or not, is grounded at least in these principles. But it is widely believed among dance critics that the perfect achievement of these principles of the dancer's technique typically contributes to the beauty of the work. Levinson states that the difference between the athlete or the mechanical doll and the dancer is that "the technique of a dancer . . . is physical effort constantly informed by beauty."[12]

Critics look for another quality when they judge ballet beauty: a perfect line. Kirstein refers to beauty in ballet in compositional terms as deriving from eighteenth-century principles of naturalness in art, making reference to William Hogarth's analysis of the serpentine "line of beauty," which supplies "composed variety," rather than the monotony of simple straight lines.[13] But, perhaps because in a temporal art (where composition is constantly shifting) it is difficult to pinpoint formal aspects of visual pleasure, far more often beauty in ballet is associated with the body of the dancer—with technique and its perfect achievement. Most dance critics use the term "line" quite differently than Hogarth did, to speak of the harmonious, dynamic alignment of the dancer's body, rather than the shape of the dance's overall composition. Echoing Levinson's difficulty in delimiting beauty in dance, dance critic Robert Greskovic observes that "line is something you come to recognize, even when you can't quite define it." He approaches a definition, however, calling line "an internal dimension, a sublime inner connection of all the physical aspects that make up a dancer's physique . . . something far greater than a mathematical whole." And, he continues, "line is able to ground external surfaces with inner understanding. Great dancers with impeccable line . . . [show] themselves to us in a supremely internalized, unending harmony."[14]

Beauty and Morality

The beauty of ballet is not based only on formal principles, however. For many it has an added moral dimension. Stéphane Mallarmé called ballet "that catalyst and paradise of all spirituality."[15] Ballet is, first of all, derived from Renaissance court entertainments in which every posture, gesture, and movement had its emblematic political and metaphysical meaning. The stress on vertical carriage that characterizes ballet technique is rooted in the noble deportment required of Renaissance and Baroque courtiers, and that postural verticality itself has deepseated moral associations that reach back to classical Greece. In his discussion of slavery in the ancient world, Bernard Williams points out that Aristotle tried to justify slavery by claiming that "nature aims to make the bodies of free men differ from those of slaves, the latter adapted in strength to necessary employment, the former upright and not suited to such work."[16] Thus ballet's verticality has an ethical dimension whose origins are sociopolitical. Associated with the elite ruling classes of Europe from the Renaissance to our day, it is based on political hierarchies and moral traditions that equate beauty of outward or physical form with both nobility and inner goodness.

But beyond the ancient Greek idea of nobility manifested in the upright posture that was invoked in early modern times, it is easy to see how, in the Christian (and more specifically Catholic) French and Italian cultures in which ballet was born and initially flowered, verticality could take on religious as well as moral connotations. One looks upward to find God, and the vertical body aspires heavenward. Verticality suggests spirituality as well as nobility, for in Christian cosmology spirits rise to join God and the angels, who dwell in the upper regions of space, in heaven. Verticality may, in fact, be seen as a form of grace. By the late nineteenth century, evolutionary concepts about "man's" upright posture, separating humans from animals, added another layer of meaning to vertical carriage.

For the Russian dance and art theorist Akim Volynsky, the vertical is the basic principle of ballet. In *The Book of Exultation* he explores the social and moral meaning of the vertical orientation of human bodies, though—understandably, for a dance theorist writing in Soviet Russia in 1925—he stresses the socially and politically ethical over the religious aspects of the erect body. He notes that Kant "emphatically asserted standing upright as an act of the spirit that overcomes the natural state and raises man above nature." He points out that to the ancient Greeks, "to see straight, to speak straight—all this is at once pictorially sensible and heroic. An upright city is a city of good and high morals that rests firmly on its foundation in a state of political and economic welfare."

And he tells us that "the Romans demanded that the heart burn as a flame, high and heavenward." He concludes that "only in ballet do we possess all aspects of the vertical in its exact mathematically formed, universally perceptible expression. Everything in ballet is straight, up-right, as a taut string that sounds a high note."[17]

Just as the postural and pictorial principle of verticality has profound moral and even spiritual meanings for many interpreters of dance, so too has the balletic principle of turnout taken on ethical implications. For Volynsky, the openness of the turned-out body is analogous to the "in-creased intimacy, warmth, and meaningfulness" of the open palm of the hand, and even more crucially, to the very act of seeing, of observation, that occurs when we open our eyes. When the eyes are truly open, "the act of will, set in motion, tears the veil from the eyes and makes possible the observation of beauty. Beauty demands of us a certain enrapture, a stubbornness of observation, eyes turned outward to the light and real-ity." Thus, Volynsky claims, when in ballet "insofar as the body turns in every direction and opens 'outward,' it becomes susceptible to radia-tions of the spirit and an instrument of ardor." The turned-out leg "re-veals closed surfaces that had been hidden in darkness. And everything appears pure, harmonious, and exultantly bright." But this exposure is not, for Volynsky, erotic or pornographic. "This glowing transport is . . . of a higher nature. . . . Only he can experience it . . . who opens wide all the gates, windows, and vistas of his soul, turning them 'outward.'"[18]

The British dance critic Adrian Stokes expands Levinson's formal scrutiny of turnout into the moral realm. For Stokes, it is turnout that is "the essence of ballet," and not only for the sake of the technique that allows the dancer to show "as much of himself as possible to the specta-tor." In Stokes's view, this is not simply a matter of aesthetic form, for it implies a salutary, almost religious disclosure. When the ballerina's cav-alier turns her as she stands on pointe, he writes, "she is shown to the world with the utmost love and grace."[19]

Stokes also extends Levinson's contrast between the inward turning of Asian dance and the turnout of Western ballet into the moral realm, arguing that turnout serves metaphorically to symbolize the openness and outwardness that he sees as embodying European values. If the dances of Indian, Javanese, and other non-Western cultures express, for Stokes, "the absorption of strength, the building up of a reserve of vital-ity, a kind of inner recreation" in which "the dancer is drawing to himself the strength of the outside world," European dances "show a dissolution of mystery." Like European visual art, Stokes claims, ballet projects outward from the body. "The same fixity without distortion and without sternness, the same outwardness, is the hall-mark of our art, a steady revelation that calls to mind the open face of the rose or smooth mountains in unbroken sunlight. . . . We like to have the mystery cleared, to see our feelings laid out as something concrete and defined."[20] He explains: "In ballet the human passions are expressed by the gradual uncontorted curves and straight lines of the extended human body. There is no residuum, no veil. The human body is purged of atmosphere. All is shown."[21] The British critic Alastair Macaulay further elaborates Stokes's argument when he writes:

> The classicism that we recognize in ballet seems to have originated in twin principles: the idea we find in Homer that embedded in the human is something divine and that the gods are active in human warfare and human love and human conduct; and the idea we find in Genesis that God created humankind in God's own image. Is that so when we look at the different classicism of Javanese culture? What I don't see is that outwardness of impulse, that openness, the sense that the body radiates into infinity. There is a more inward concentration that has different moral suggestions for all of us.[22]

The moral significance of the human body's geometry, exemplified by the Vetruvian man, is the classical image that rules this conception of ballet. Even when the limbs move in opposition or the shoulders tilt away from the hips in contrapposto, the dancing body in ballet is fundamentally open and symmetrical. And although its turned-out posture may be unnatural in relation to our movement in everyday life, the classical dancing body makes turnout look easy, graceful, and natural.

Finally, the special balletic terrain of pointe work by women dancers also lends itself to moral metaphors. Levinson devotes only a few sentences to pointe work, but he clearly suggests that it conjures a spiritual meaning closely related to verticality: "[W]hen a dancer rises on her points, she breaks away from the exigencies of everyday life, and enters into an enchanted country—that she may thereby lose herself in the ideal."[23] The near-impossibility of walking, running, and balancing on the very tips of the toes makes the ease with which the ballet dancer moves seem miraculous, even magical; standing on pointe effects in the spectator an extraordinary awareness of an equilibrium that seems superhuman, buoyed by grace. And moving quickly on pointe creates the impression of an ethereal, immaterial body in flight, calling up images of angels and other holy spirits (though of course pointe work has also been used in the service of unholy spirits, such as the vampire-like Wilis in *Giselle*).

The Grotesque Tradition

Although the theorists and critics I have cited so far have been at pains to describe and account for the beautiful and the classical in ballet, most of them acknowledge that there has always been a place for classical values to coexist with anti-classical, or grotesque, elements within the art form itself. In thinking about the relationship between the balletic bodily canon[24] of beauty and its opposite, I find the Russian literary critic Mikhail Bakhtin's study of the grotesque body in *Rabelais and His World* suggestive. Bakhtin contrasts Renaissance values of beauty in the human form (derived from classical ideals) with the medieval, folkloric, "grotesque" (and, one might add, peasant) body. For Bakhtin, the classical body is smooth, finished, closed, and complete, in contrast to the grotesque body, which is rough, uneven, unfinished, open, and full of apertures—and therefore, in the classical view, "hideous and formless."[25] In ballet up to the twentieth century, the conflict between these two sets of values held up the classical body as the political and moral ideal and the grotesque body, though at times formally more interesting, as a threat to the classical norm.

Ever since the birth of ballet during the Renaissance, sinister mythological characters, witches, wizards, furies, evil fairies, madmen and madwomen, and humans transformed into animals, as well as exotic (non-Western) characters and peasants, have provided dramatic tensions in the story lines. These tensions were formally embodied in the contrast of "inappropriate," grotesque bodily canons—often angular and asymmetrical—to the symmetrically balanced, classical form. Dramatically speaking, evil made incarnate in the form of physical monstrosity (the grotesque body) posed a threat to the reign of virtue in the form of the classical body; as the classical body triumphed, virtue's dominion was ultimately strengthened or restored. For instance, in *The Sleeping Beauty*, the evil fairy Carabosse, danced by a man in travesty, violates classical lines in multiple ways, from her overly large scale to her asymmetrical, bent-over, turned-in posture. Even in Romantic ballets that seemed to end in the tragic defeat of the virtuous—like *La Sylphide*, in which Madge the witch destroys the hero James—the classical body remained the ideal.

Thus in ballet, deliberately breaking the classical bodily canon has traditionally signaled social or moral malignancy first and foremost. It has also served to express negative emotions such as anger and jealousy, or to signal situations of chaos and disorder. Finally, it has marked the exotic or picturesque, in the form of character dancing (or balleticized folk dances) by the lower classes. In character dancing, angular shapes and turned-in body postures may not have stood for evil, but they nevertheless hinted at Otherness: either Oriental mysteries or rustic crudities. Even when bucolic life was idealized as robust, as in the Romantic ballet, its earthiness was expressed in grotesque terms, breaching the decorum, elegance, and grace of the noble classical ballet line. Until the end of the nineteenth century, these various forms of grotesque embodiment derived their meaning in the context of and in contrast to the classical norm that regulated definitions of beauty in the human form, whether in painting, sculpture, or dance.

The history of ballet in the twentieth century, however, has been punctuated with calculated infractions of the classical bodily canon for other purposes, especially that of expression. Perhaps inspired, or perhaps challenged, by modern dancers' rejection of the balletic principles of verticality and turnout, choreographers like Michel Fokine and Alexander Gorsky at the turn of the century sought a greater range of expressivity, while still remaining within the domain of ballet, through the use of turned-in stances and a variety of steps and gestures previously excluded by the strict ballet vocabulary. For Fokine, fascinated by unclassical notions of beauty culled from non-Western and modern art, the first principle of "the new ballet" should be "to create in each case a new form corresponding to the subject, the most expressive form possible for the representation," without following preordained rules.[26]

Vaslav Nijinsky went even further, introducing extremely awkward bodily shapes and contorted movements into his ballets. The ballerina Tamara Karsavina writes that in *L'Après-midi d'un faune* and *Le Sacre du printemps*, "Nijinsky declared his feud against Romanticism and bid adieu to the 'beautiful.'" She describes the posture Nijinsky asked her to achieve in *Jeux*, a ballet of modern life based on a tennis game and a sexual triangle, as follows: "I had to keep my head screwed on one side, both hands curled in as one maimed from birth." Although she records her irritation at and incomprehension of Nijinsky's demands at the time, reflecting later on Nijinsky's work in her autobiography Karsavina suggests that the choreographer, however inarticulate about his own aesthetic program, was surely influenced in *Jeux* by Italian Futurism and by Filippo Marinetti's vehement rejection of beauty and of the masterpieces of past art.[27]

George Balanchine, schooled in Imperial Russia but thoroughly American in his taste, tampered differently with the rules of ballet. Balanchine opened ballet up to a spectrum of steps and movements alien to the pure classical style (including modern dance and African American jazz dancing[28]), departing in surprising ways from the traditional vocabulary, from canonical body shapes, and even from the tempi of classical ballet. Yet dance critic Edwin Denby observed that Balanchine had developed "a largeness of expression" in his dancers that showed "the kind of beauty classic ballet is by nature about." In his 1953 essay "Some Thoughts about Classicism and George Balanchine," Denby writes, "Classic ballet . . . tries to be as wonderful as possible in its own beautiful and voluntarily limited way, just as does any other art. What correct style exists for, what it hopes for, is a singular, unforeseen, and out-of-this-world beauty of expression." Balanchine's attention to "continuity in motion," Denby argues,

> develops in his dancers a gift for coherent, vigorous, positive, unsimpering movement, and a gift too for a powerful, spontaneous rhythmic pulse in action. . . .
>
> Clear, sure-footed dancing travels through space easy and large, either in its instantaneous collective surges or in its slow and solitary paths. So space spreads in calm power from the center of the stage and from the moving dancer and gives a sense of human grandeur and of destiny to her action.[29]

The image of the female dancer, especially, that Balanchine created—slim, long-legged, with a jutting hip and elegantly angled wrists—was that of a runway model. His distortions were anything but ugly. Rather, even during the prefeminist era of the 1940s and 1950s, they defined a contemporary vision of glamorous and assertive female beauty.

A New Kind of Beauty for Our Time

Unlike Fokine, Nijinsky, or Balanchine, Karole Armitage was not necessarily fated to work only in the arena of ballet. When she began her

career as a choreographer, she was a member of the Merce Cunningham Dance Company, one of the major modern dance companies in
the United States. Although trained in her youth by a New York City
Ballet dancer and a veteran of several years spent performing a
Balanchine-dominated repertory in the Geneva Ballet, by 1978—when
she created her first piece, *Ne*—she had been dancing with Cunningham for two years and was equally immersed in downtown New York
avant-garde culture and the art-punk-music scene.

Armitage's early pieces—*Ne* (1978), *Do We Could* (1979), *Objectstacle*
(1980), and *Vertige* (1980)—took off from a recognizably Cunningham-
esque technique, using a foundation of classical principles—verticality,
turnout, and the five positions—in the lower body and a flexible upper
torso and freely mobile arms. But her dances also toyed with extremely
unclassical possibilities. In *Ne* the stiff-legged, knock-kneed, pigeon-toed
stance nearly brought all movement to a halt. The reckless aggression of
Vertige, a duet for Armitage and guitarist-composer Rhys Chatham, ve-
hemently threatened verticality as Armitage repeatedly lurched danger-
ously off balance and scrambled all around the musician, worrying him
like a mosquito and disrupting his performance by reaching over to un-
tune his guitar as she flippantly turned the pegs. Armitage says that at
the time, inspired by punk music, she "went into the studio and started
making distorted and dissonant raw movement to correspond to that
sound and those ideas." She describes her movement as "[retaining] a
regal center from classicism," but adds that "basically, I was taking all
the rules from the classical canon and breaking them. If they said keep
your shoulder down, I would bring it up. And if the hand was supposed
to be elegant, I was taking it into angular types of shapes and adding
extra planes and angles to the whole body." And she explains, "The
reason I did this is because I thought it was a new kind of beauty, one
that demanded a kind of passion, because it had a troubled spot at the
center."[30]

In *Drastic Classicism* (1981) Armitage seriously began her systematic
critique of classical movement. Still working in the idiom of a Cunning-
hamesque technique that, while based on the classical principles of verticality and turnout, does not make use of pointe technique, she opened
up a frontline attack on the matter of line. Armitage's publicity materials describe *Drastic Classicism* as "a strictly choreographed violation—
and amplification—of virtuosic dance technique, with a rock rhythmic
structure in which constant tension between restraint and clarity vied
with drastic, passionate impulses."[31]

Through a variety of strategies, Armitage conspicuously framed her distortions and deformations of the elegant classical line. As the dancers calmly executed straightforward, rhythmically precise classroom exercises (i.e., the building blocks of ballet and of Cunningham's technique, in which the control over the body necessary to achieve perfect line is practiced daily), wild, out-of-control movements suddenly seemed to take over their bodies. It was not so much as if they were possessed, but as if they had been repressed, and now were throwing off the shackles of that stifling regime. High-voltage, unbridled social dancing moves straight from the Mudd Club seemed to have invaded the ballet studio. Arms flailed, legs crossed over in the extreme; dancers lunged off balance, ran at full speed, made fighting gestures, and jumped on the musicians with whom they shared the stage. There was a general spirit of willful, bratty (mis)behavior threading through dance images of incredible speed, power, and extreme beauty. And that defiant misconduct was not just expressed by, but was also on a deep moral level constituted by, the drama of the imperiled vertical and the tortured line. While the classical core of the dance seemed to survive a battering in ways that spoke metaphorically of human dignity in the face of a daily assault on the senses in contemporary life, its ferocious tone and rebellious energy implied that no principle is fixed or can be taken for granted but must be tested for its merits.

The punk style of the loud, dissonant music (by Rhys Chatham) as well as of the childlike costumes and dark lighting (both by Charles Atlas) drenched the dancing as well. It underscored metaphorically the theme of a youthful revolution against all self-styled "civilized" values. And yet, as dance critic Arlene Croce put it: in *Drastic Classicism,* "classical values that were flayed alive stayed alive."[32] As in Fred Astaire's drunk dances, it was clear that despite the frenzied pacing and the nihilistic gestures, nothing here was chaotic or unplanned. Without exquisite technique, the dancers would fall down instead of balancing off-kilter; their feet would tangle instead of nimbly crisscrossing at lighting speed.

The painter David Salle, who would later become Armitage's fiancé and collaborator, has said of seeing her dance at this time, "It wasn't simply the fact that Karole's dancing was extreme, which it was, that made it interesting. She is very long-limbed and had amazing extensions and the ability to appear as though all four limbs were working in contradictory ways, but also with complete visual harmony. The fact that it was wild and extreme was simply a condition, one of its conditions." In other words, Salle noticed that Armitage achieved perfect line (that is, visual harmony) despite the extreme tests to which she put the classical bodily canon. Echoing Denby's remarks on Balanchine, Salle observes another aspect of Armitage's classicism when he says what he saw in her work of this period was "an image of a woman who was look-ing at fate unafraid. This image was not created with acting . . . but with a controlled *barrage* of steps."[33]

One year after the Paris Opera Ballet commissioned her to create *GV-10,* in which she worked with both the Opera's modern dance group and its ballet troupe, Armitage moved squarely into the arena of ballet in terms of technique, if not in terms of institutional affiliations, with *The Watteau Duets* (originally titled $-p = \partial H / \partial q$, 1985). With this dance, she introduced extended pointe work into her choreography, although she continued to present her work at various downtown New York venues known for postmodern choreography (as well as at clubs, galleries, and rock festivals). Above all *The Watteau Duets* was a concentrated explora-tion of two important ballet conventions: the pas de deux (or duet form), and pointe work.

The dance has six sections. In each, Armitage and her partner (origi-nally Joseph Lennon) wear unusual, even fantastic costumes. They range from a black leotard and tights under a breastplate in one section and boxer shorts and undershirt in another for him to a diaphanous apricot negligee with satin toe shoes dyed to match in one section and a white T-shirt, black tights, white anklets, and black patent leather shoes with five-inch stiletto heels for her. The dance is performed to live music by David Linton—primarily percussion, it seems based on military marches with Scottish bagpipes—and intermittent taped musical quotations from Stravinsky, Handel, Verdi, and Wagner. The partners, in black leotards and tights trimmed with leather cuffs, headbands, and boots, greet each other in a formal ritualistic moment like two medieval joust-ing opponents and then begin about an hour's worth of intense interac-tion. Always erotic and intense, each section of the dance varies partly because the dancers change costumes, but also because of affective tone: formal, haughty, tender, playful.

Croce, though enthusiastic about the piece, remarks that the danc-ers "didn't contribute . . . to the lore of the pas de deux—their 'erotic' number was essentially a variation on Nijinsky's *Faune,* and later they added variations on the *Agon* pas de deux."[34] What Croce seems to have missed, however, is the deliberateness of the reflexive allusions to ballet history, especially to Balanchine. The allusions to *Agon,* especially, are not derivative, but rather are obviously quite conscious quotations.[35] (In 1982 Armitage choreographed *Slaughter on MacDougal Street,* an homage to Balanchine's jazz ballet *Slaughter on Tenth Avenue.* She had never seen the Balanchine ballet but was inspired by seeing photographs of a recent revival.) In *The Watteau Duets* Armitage invokes a history in order to interrogate and elaborate it. Armitage assertively takes the leading role in the pas de deux even more than Balanchine's ballerinas do, in a way that is conspicuously marked. If in *Agon* the man manipulates the ballerina, here the ballerina (man)handles her partner, directing the action, calling the shots, pushing him away, and pulling him into position. Thus she makes manifest and calls into question the relations of the sexes in the tradition of the ballet pas de deux as well as in society.

It is no secret that the standard ballet pas de deux, however chastely danced, is about the sex act. But in *The Watteau Duets* the slightly sadomasochistic aspects of the *Agon* pas de duex (and so many other ballet pas de deux) are heightened, brought to the surface, and made explicit by the leather accessories in the first section and by the tortuous, contortionist methods the dancers use to maneuver one another. Too, there are many other overtly sexual elements: Armitage's spread legs and grinding hips; a moment when she climbs onto and straddles her partner's back; another moment when, as she stands over him and he reclines on the floor (one of the allusions to *Agon*), he raises and lowers his leg repeatedly as his foot flexes, comically indicating a phallus becoming erect; not to mention her patent leather high heels (purchased in the red light district of Paris). All these details unmistakably signal a frank carnality that most earlier ballets, even those considered shocking in their time, only gestured toward. But these signs, verging on the pornographic, are mixed with icons of ravishing, transcendent beauty recognizable from the ballet canon—the perfect plumb line of verticality repeatedly achieved in the face of off-balance jeopardy as Armitage stands suspended upright, balancing on one pointe; a hand held outward with palm open in a gesture of greeting; the familiar and beloved supported arabesque, reminiscent of *The Sleeping Beauty,* in the first section; the slow lifts of the leg in *grande battements* that show off Armitage's elegantly long, turned-out limbs and exquisite equilibrium as she stands steady in one high-heeled shoe; her arms circling her head like rose petals. This iconography of balletic beauty exalts the often-shocking sexual imagery, moving it into the realm of the spiritual and the moral. Armitage has spoken about the influence of Hindu temple sculpture and tantric yoga, which merge the erotic and the holy, on her choreography in one of the sections of *The Watteau Duets*.[36] But certainly the dance conjures up modern as well as archaic passions, especially in its contemporary look and its unflinching postfeminist exploration of conflicts, competition, and desire between men and women.

Although Armitage does not wear pointe shoes in every section of *The Watteau Duets*, it is a dance that celebrates and investigates pointe work, whether done in toe shoes, high heels, or the strange combination of stilts and cothurni, attached to two semicircular frames that form the shape of a large skirt, which Armitage wears in the final section. Armitage's pointe work is descended from the "steely toe" of the nineteenth-century Italian ballet, later absorbed into the Russian tradition, and also perhaps from the stabbing steps of Bronislava Nijinska in her 1923 feminist ballet *Les Noces*, rather than from the soft, ethereal tradition of the French Romantic ballet. She seems, as well, to move on pointe precariously, like a tightrope walker—not through lack of technique but as a result of the daring, extreme positions of her legs and torso. Armitage has stated that she sees pointe shoes "as weapons."[37] That implies both technical prowess and erotic frisson.

Judging her pointe technique "a mite tense" and yet, because of her work with Cunningham, connected to a wider range of leg movements, Greskovic writes that, nevertheless,

> the lack of complete ease in her pointes works *for* the drama of her choreography, not against it. Simultaneous to occupying her place in the very real present of longstanding ballerinadom, Armitage also shows us something from the other end of that lineage—the early stages in the long-gone past, where pointe work was experimental, raw, rare. Armitage reveals something of the actual struggle necessary to keep all the figure's weight on the toetip of the foot.[38]

In her utter contemporaneity—her chic style, her use of art-rock music, her explicit sexuality, and her strenuous postmodern inspection of previous techniques—Armitage seemed in *The Watteau Duets* to invent ballet utterly anew, to locate and reframe ballet's beauty for a jaded era when it seemed nothing could be novel or surprising.

Croce had earlier written that "in its over-all effect, 'Drastic Classicism' was . . . a retrieval of classical dance values from their irrelevant mold of decorum." She also explains:

Decorous music, decorous costumes, decorous body positions and shapes were thrown out, together with the notion that all these should be decorously related. Relations were expressed . . . but not decorously . . . [There was] something that we could identify as Armitage's own discovery—the annihilative fury of rock music as a scourge analogous to the flaying of the systematic and the habitual in the dance.[39]

In 1986 Armitage took up the question of ballet decorum even more directly in *The Mollino Room*, a thirty-minute work commissioned by the American Ballet Theatre under the direction of Mikhail Baryshnikov. The ballet featured Baryshnikov, a lead couple, and an ensemble; Baryshnikov, always dancing alone, often brooding, seemed to be marginalized by the group, although—given his star status—one could also see the ballet as literalizing the adage "It's lonely at the top." Indeed, Armitage intended the ballet to be a portrait of the multiple aspects of Baryshnikov's public persona: "as our greatest male dancer; as a classicist in search of contemporary style; as a movie star; as head of ABT, with all the responsibilities that fall on him; and as a performer who's reached the age of thirty-eight, and can't help but wonder about his artistic future."[40] Salle (who had recently entered the realm of theater design with his set for Kathy Acker's play *Birth of a Poet*, directed by Richard Foreman with music by Peter Gordon) designed the décor for *The Mollino Room*—a series of backdrops both abstract and figurative, depicting large-scale objects: men's shoes, a tea service, and a fishing reel—and the costumes.

The use of the dancers—Baryshnikov as soloist, then a lead couple, then four ensemble couples—was so academic that it almost seemed Armitage was drawing attention to and commenting on ballet's institutional hierarchy with dry irony. And, for the most part, the movement vocabulary was classical. Greskovic comments, "The travels and in-place posings of the soloists are always distinguished by some definition of limb or appendage that acknowledges the special geometry of academic dancing (and this includes the eccentric angles and twists that Armitage intermittently imposes in her plainly classical inventions)."[41]

At the time she was working on *The Mollino Room*, Armitage had declared that "my own interest now is almost exclusively in ballet."[42] She remarked that the ballet vocabulary "was figured out over three hundred years by some very intelligent people, and I think it is wise to use all those years of thinking, rather than to start in the poverty-stricken position of zero." She explained that whereas in her earlier work she had wanted to break the rules, now she was interested in "[making] a classicism about our time."[43] In this she seemed to share a twin path with Salle, whose complex, disjunct paintings are monumental in scale and clearly rooted in classical forms, but are also suffused with eroticism (often centering on the female body) and with references to art history, popular culture, and contemporary everyday life.

But if *The Mollino Room* was classical in movement terms, Armitage slyly breached opera-house decorum in other ways. The program note stated that the ballet took its title from the twentieth-century Italian architect and designer Carlo Mollino, who celebrated "bad taste," suggesting that this champion of kitsch was a precursor to the generation of postmodernist painters, musicians, performance artists, and choreographers who came of age in the 1980s. *New York Times* critic Jack Anderson declared, "For an example of bad taste, one need go no further than the ballet's own accompaniment." Although the first and third movement were set to difficult music by Paul Hindemith, the second movement was danced to a 1960 comedy routine by Elaine May and Mike Nichols—"My Son, the Nurse"—in a recording in which one can hear the comedians losing control, giggling, and trying to reestablish their composure to resume the routine with their usual deadpan wit. Clearly, in the routine May and Nichols intend to ridicule the stereotypical Jewish mother's notorious desire that her son become a doctor. But Anderson points out that "the dialogue's mockery of the honorable profession of male nursing and the self-satisfied sniggering of its performers might well draw the wrath of sexual liberation groups if this sketch were to turn up in a club today."[44]

Salle has commented that what he understood the May and Nichols routine to be about was "improvisation, the making of humor—that is, *meaning*, before an audience in an unexpected way. . . . [I]t created a metaphor for creativity," and, moreover, he remarks "that Nichols and May, with their sheer creative brilliance, could have been reduced to a sign for *gender roles* makes me want to laugh and cry."[45] However, given the homage to Mollino that frames the ballet, this apparent gaffe could also be read as deliberate in its politically incorrect outrageousness, as indeed signaling gender roles, not in the way that Anderson and other critics thought offensive, but rather by laughing rudely at those who uphold traditional gender stereotypes. Among the dancers' three changes of costume were 1950s-style Bermuda shorts for the men and cartoon-like false breasts for the women—costumes that comically underscored the heterosexual imperative and the strong gender divisions underlying every aspect of ballet, from its choreography to its social institutions. On the one hand, Armitage choreographed a lusciously erotic duet for the lead couple. On the other hand, she simultaneously poked fun at the "ballet boys and girls" who always populate the ballet stage—both the characters in the ballets and the dancers who portray them docilely, never questioning the stereotypical gender roles they enact.

Seen in this light, in a post-Stonewall, postfeminist era, Armitage herself seems to be engaged in ironizing "My Son, the Nurse" as a comic success, and thus in criticizing the sexist and homophobic culture of the 1950s and early 1960s that would find male nurses hilarious. That is, by showing in a vulgar way—one that contrasts shockingly with the refinement of the dancing—how the comedy routine (and in general ballet) subscribes to unenlightened values regarding sex and gender, she unmasks ballet's hypocrisy, even while loving its ways of moving. She seems to say bluntly to the opera-house audience, "Yes, it's beautiful, elegant, and satisfying to watch. But don't you also see that ballet is about sex but doesn't admit it? Don't you see that ballet costumes salaciously reveal the body's erogenous zones even as ballet calls itself high art, not pornography? Don't you see that ballet 'boys' and 'girls' are stuck in impossibly old-fashioned, false gender codes?"

The Morality and Politics of the New Beauty

Armitage has stated, "Manners, style, morality, point of view—one leads to the other through musicality. As someone else has said, dance is not only entertainment, it is truly a spiritual question."[46] Since ballet's beauty, as I have indicated, is deeply connected with the body and the issues of morality surrounding the body, it's not surprising that Armitage's ballets, which feature the bodies of unruly women, have often been criticized on moral grounds. Dance and art critic Jill Johnston wrote of *The Mollino Room* that it brought "a certain traditional, and reactionary, trend in the culture of the 1980s into focus. With their considerable skills [Armitage and Salle] service a prefeminist world view, profiting sharply demarcated sex differences which are rooted in the male gaze and the female as object. This is a world view preeminently represented by the classical ballet." Johnston chastised Armitage for her

"exhibitionism and female posturing," suggesting that this inappropriate behavior called into question the choreographer's lineage as a
postmodern choreographer and speculating that, since modern dance is
matriarchal, perhaps Armitage's "partnering and posing and deference
to the male" locate her squarely in the patriarchal ballet tradition.[47]
Performance art critic Jacki Apple wrote of *The Tarnished Angels* and *The
Elizabethan Phrasing of the Late Albert Ayler* (both 1987), "Armitage claims to
be a feminist, liberating the female image in ballet. A pretentious con-
ceit on her part! . . . Armitage's women are still sexual cartoons. . . .
Gender definition in Armitage's scheme of things is both regressive and
oppressive."[48]

And yet, seen from the vantage point of the 1990s, Armitage's cartoon representations of gender codes mark her as a harbinger of what is
now identified as postfeminist, "bad girl" art. In the exhibition catalogue essay for the sister shows *Bad Girls* and *Bad Girls West* held, respectively, in New York and Los Angeles in 1994, curator Marcia Tanner
writes that bad girls are "truly unruly women who threaten to turn the
social order upside down," and she characterizes their art work as "[se-
ducing] the viewer via humor, the bracing shock of freedom unleashed
by its unexpected, often subtle subversion of accepted rules, and its projection of countervailing versions of experience." Unlike the program-
matic, often humorless politically correct work of an earlier generation
of feminist artists, bad girls "invite the viewer to see and think beyond
stereotypes and simple either/or oppositions, to imagine a more inclusive, various, and funny world." Unlike good girls, who "don't rock the
boat . . . don't talk openly about their own sexual proclivities and erotic
fantasies . . . don't invent their own jokes, don't mock truths held to be
self-evident," bad girls "flout all these precepts. As Cyndi Lauper sings,
these 'girls just wanna have fun.'"[49] Bad girls make transgressive art that
revels in taboo content, that trades in stereotypes precisely in order to
turn them on their heads, that uses the shock of impropriety and the
politically incorrect to make its points, and that rejects the puritanism
of early feminism to embrace all sorts of pleasures—bodily, visual, and
intellectual—and to fashion a new kind of beauty.

Outrageous and beautiful in their way, Armitage's reworkings of the
ballet choreography of a long line of male predecessors function simultaneously as tongue-in-cheek parody, serious critique, and loving homage. Johnston disparages Armitage as somehow betraying feminism as

well as her own identity as a woman in choosing to work in the male world of ballet choreography rather than the female domain of modern dance. But it seems to me that Armitage made that choice expressly to bring a postfeminist sensibility to a world in which images of women predominate and yet are usually made by men. Like Madonna's videos of the same period, Armitage's dances of the 1980s show contemporary young women who are figuring out their lives; they're angry or hostile or just generally in charge. If the dances show conflicts between men and women, it is also true that the women often best the men. Lynn Garafola is one of the few dance critics who has written directly about Armitage's feminism:

> Gutsy, sexy, streetwise, [Karole Armitage's women are] big-city teens who go to seamy discos and pick up boys their mothers would never approve of and have sex for the fun of it. When the going gets rough, they know how to call it quits. With a shrug that seems to say, chalk that one up to experience, these brave new girls pick themselves up and move on. . . . When it comes to sex Armitage's women are as independent as Amazons, even if they happen to like men. . . . Again and again, they show us their spunkiness.[50]

Armitage recalls that "the real reason that I became attracted to dance was seeing photos in *Life* magazine of the New York City Ballet. There were these gorgeous dancers who looked like a garden of tropical flowers, both very artificial, daring to be that beautiful, controlled, and warm at the same time."[51] For the generation of feminists who emerged in the 1960s and 1970s, female beauty was suspect, for it simply pandered to male desire. And for the modernist artists of that period, beauty in art had long since been banished. But for Armitage's generation, already empowered by the political gains of feminism on the one hand, and engaged in a postmodernist challenge to the values of artistic modernism on the other, beauty in art and the female body could once again be appreciated. If Armitage was drawn, as a child, to the beauty and glamour of ballet, her own interventions into the history of the art form have given that beauty a new, more complex face. Her unabashed love of ballet's beauty (especially its female beauty) and its erotic display, combined with her intelligent interrogation of the grounds for that beauty, her historical references, and her witty irreverence, wickedly and triumphantly reclaim the art form for our postfeminist times.[52]

NOTES

1. André Levinson, "Some Commonplaces on the Dance," *Broom* (December 1922), reprinted in *André Levinson on Dance: Writings from Paris in the Twenties,* ed. Joan Acocella and Lynn Garafola (Hanover, N.H.: Weslyan University Press/University Press of New England, 1991), 32. Noël Carroll argues for Kant's influence on Levinson in "Theater and Dance: A Philosophical Narrative," *Dance Chronicle* 15, no. 3 (1992): 317–31.

2. André Levinson, "The Spirit of the Classic Dance," *Theatre Arts Monthly* (March 1925), reprinted in Acocella and Garafola, *Levinson*, 48.

3. Levinson, "Some Commonplaces," 32, 34.

4. Levinson, "Spirit," 43.

5. This Levinson sees as a break from a "'horizontal' conception of the dance, based on outlines and figures marked by the feet of the dancer on the floor—what you might call his itinerary" (Levinson, "Spirit," 45).

The vocabulary and technique of academic ballet were born in the Renaissance courts and retain the courtly, vertical carriage they inherited from noble deportment and such other physical techniques as fencing. But the visual interest of horizontally oriented, geometric floor patterns of court entertainments, designed to be seen—as if from a bird's-eye view—by spectators seated in balconies, came to be replaced in the seventeenth century by a composition more suited to the picture-frame shape and frontal orientation upon which the proscenium was based. It is as if the plane on which the dance activity took place was raised perpendicularly from the horizontal flatness of the floor to the vertical flatness of the window; it is as if dancing had been a carpet, full of interesting figures, that was suddenly hung on the wall like a tapestry, for better viewing.

6. Lincoln Kirstein, *Movement and Metaphor: Four Centuries of Ballet* (New York: Praeger, 1970), 5; Lincoln Kirstein, *Dance: A Short History of Classic Theatrical Dancing* (New York: Dance Horizons, 1969), 187.

7. Levinson, "Spirit," 46.

8. Levinson remarks that "the turning outward of the body increases [the dancer's] space to an extraordinary degree, . . . multiplying to an infinite degree the direction of the movement as well as its various conformations. It surrounds the vertical of the body's equilibrium by a vortex of curves, segments of circles, arcs; it projects the body of the dancer into magnificent parabolas, curves it into a living spiral; it creates a whole world of animated forms that awake in us a throng of active sensations" ("Spirit," 46–47).

9. Levinson, "Spirit," 46.

10. Ibid.

11. Ibid., 47.

12. Ibid., 44.

13. Kirstein, *Movement and Metaphor*, 11.

14. Robert Greskovic, *Ballet 101: A Complete Guide to Learning and Loving the Ballet* (New York: Hyperion, 1998), 151–52.

15. Stéphane Mallarmé, "Ballets," in *Mallarmé: Selected Prose Poems, Essays and Letters*, trans. Bradford Cook (Baltimore: Johns Hopkins University Press, 1956), reprinted in *What Is Dance?: Readings in Theory and Criticism*, ed. Roger Copeland and Marshall Cohen (Oxford: Oxford University Press, 1983), 113.

16. Bernard Williams, "Necessary Identities," in *Subjugation and Bondage: Critical Essays on Slavery and Social Philosophy*, ed. Tommy L. Lot (Lanham, Md.: Rowman and Littlefield, 1998), 10–11. Williams cites Aristotle, *Politics* 1254b27 seq. He points out that Aristotle cannot fully justify his claim, since, Aristotle admits, "the opposite often happens, and some people have the bodies of free men and others the souls."

17. A. K. Volynsky, "The Book of Exultation," trans. Seymour Barofsky, *Dance Scope* 5, no. 2 (spring 1971): 18–20.

18. Ibid., 24, 26–28.

19. Adrian Stokes, "The Classical Ballet," in *To-night the Ballet* (London: Faber and Faber, 1935), reprinted in Copeland and Cohen, *What Is Dance?* 244–45.

20. Ibid., 245–47.

21. Ibid., 247.

22. Alastair Macaulay, "What is Classicism? International Critics Look at Javanese Bedhaya," in *Looking Out: Perspectives on Dance and Criticism in a Multicultural World*, ed. David Gere (New York: Schirmer Books, 1995), 147.

23. Levinson, "Spirit," 47.

24. I use the term "bodily canon" to denote a set of standards for approved images of the body, as well as for authorized behaviors, stances, shapes, postures, and gestures.

25. See Mikhail Bakhtin, *Rabelais and His World*, trans. Helene Iswolsky (Bloomington: Indiana University Press, 1984), 19–30.

26. Michel Fokine, "Letter to *The Times*, July 6, 1914," reprinted in Cyril W. Beaumont, *Michel Fokine and His Ballets* (New York: Dance Horizons, 1981), 146.

27. Tamara Karsavina, *Theatre Street* (New York: E. P. Dutton, 1961), 236–37.

28. See my articles "Balanchine and Black Dance," *Choreography and Dance* 3, no. 3 (1993), reprinted in my *Writing Dancing in the Age of Postmodernism* (Hanover, N.H.: Wesleyan University Press/University Press of New England, 1994), 53–69; and "Sibling Rivalry: The New York City Ballet and Modern Dance," in *Dance for a City: Fifty Years of the New York City Ballet*, ed. Lynn Garafola and Eric Foner (New York: Columbia University Press, 1999), 73–98.

29. Edwin Denby, "Some Thoughts about Classicism and George Balanchine," *Dance Magazine* (February 1953), reprinted in Edwin Denby, *Dance Writings*, ed. Robert Cornfield and William MacKay (New York: Knopf, 1986), 440, 433, 438–39.

30. *South Bank Show: Karole Armitage,* London Weekend Television, producer and director David Hinton, 1985.

31. Performing Artservices, "Karole Armitage: Narrative Biography," Press Kit, 1985.

32. Arlene Croce, "Closed Circuits," *New Yorker,* January 30, 1984, reprinted in Arlene Croce, *Sight Lines* (New York: Knopf, 1987), 165.

33. *Salle: An Interview with David Salle by Peter Schjeldahl* (New York: Vintage Books/Random House, 1987), 44.

34. Arlene Croce, "Modern Love," *New Yorker,* April 29, 1985, reprinted in Croce, *Sight Lines,* 255.

35. On *Agon,* see my extended analysis in Sally Banes, *Dancing Women: Female Bodies on Stage* (London: Routledge, 1998), 194–211.

36. *South Bank Show.*

37. Quoted in Robert Greskovic, "Armitagean Physics, or the Shoes of the Ballerina," *Ballet Review* 13, no. 2 (Summer 1985): 79.

38. Ibid., 79–80.

39. Arlene Croce, "Think Punk," *New Yorker,* March 9, 1981, reprinted in Arlene Croce, *Going to the Dance* (New York: Knopf, 1982), 351.

40. Quoted in Alan M. Kriegsman, "A Dancer's Circle: Karole Armitage and ABT's 'Mollino Room,'" *Washington Post,* April 10, 1986, C4.

41. Robert Greskovic, "The Past, the Present, and the Future: American Ballet Theatre and the Kirov," *Ballet Review* 14, no. 2 (Summer 1986): 68.

42. John Mueller and Don McDonagh, "Making Musical Dance: Robert Irving, Richard Colton, Kate Johnson, Karole Armitage," *Ballet Review* 13, no. 4 (Winter 1986): 39.

43. *South Bank Show.*

44. Jack Anderson, "Dance: Baryshnikov in 'The Mollino Room.'" *New York Times,* May 18, 1986, sec. 1, pt. 2, 68.

45. Quoted in *Salle,* 55.

46. John Mueller and Don McDonagh, "Making Musical Dance," 44.

47. Jill Johnston, "The Punk Princess and the Postmodern Prince," *Art in America* 74, no. 10 (October 1986): 24–25.

48. Jacki Apple, "The Los Angeles Festival: The Armitage Ballet," *High Performance,* issue 39, vol. 10, no. 3 (1987): 32–33.

49. Marcia Tanner, "Mother Laughed: The Bad Girls' Avant-Garde," in *Bad Girls* (Cambridge, Mass.: MIT Press, 1994), 48, 51. Tanner cites the Lauper song as follows: *Girls Just Want to Have Fun,* music and lyrics by Robert Hazard, New York, Sony Tunes, Inc., 1982. Recorded by Cyndi Lauper, 1983.

50. Lynn Garafola, "The Armitage Ballet," *Dance Magazine* 62, no. 11 (November 1988): 80.

51. *South Bank Show.*

52. Thanks to Noël Carroll, Neil Donahue, and Robert Greskovic for their help with this essay.

TV-Dancing Women
Music Videos,
Camera-Choreography, and
Feminist Theory

Although a great deal of scholarly attention has been paid to representations of women in music videos, very little work has been done on how television-dancing creates gendered images and how women are represented through dancing for the TV camera on music videos. For example, Ann Kaplan (1987), and the articles in Cathy Schwichtenberg (1993) discuss representations of women in video but with scant attention to how choreography for the TV camera contributes to those representations. But perhaps this is not surprising, since there is a paucity of in-depth general analysis of dancing in music videos—what might be called "camera-choreography" (in terms of structure) and "video-dancing" (in terms of performance)—because in cinema and television, dancing is never autonomous, but always functions together with (and cannot be separated from) camerawork and editing. Theresa J. Buckland with Elizabeth Stewart (1993, 51–79) offers a welcome examination of the dance element of music videos. While providing useful observations

source: In Ruth Lorand, ed., *Television: Aesthetic Reflections* (New York: Peter Lang, 2002)

on women, their work does not specifically focus on gender, because it takes a broader view of the phenomenon of MTV-dancing.

Analyzing "videos that explore the possibilities of a female gaze," Dan Rubey often mentions the expressive potential of dancing as a symbol of pleasure. But usually he simply mentions the fact *that* people dance in this or that video clip, rather than describing the video-dancing or analyzing in detail *how* the camera-choreography creates gendered or sexual meaning. The few times Rubey turns his attention to choreographic description and interpretation he renders only a single phrase. For example, "they move precisely in unison," he writes of Janet Jackson's RHYTHM NATION, "with robotic, stiffly angular arm movements" (Rubey 1991, 895). (In this chapter, I follow Andrew Goodwin's orthographic style, putting the titles of music videos entirely in capital letters to distinguish them from the artist's song with the same title, which would appear in quotation marks. Italics are thus reserved for album, film, and television program titles [see Goodwin 1992, xiii].) Similarly, in looking at representations of masculinity, Gareth Palmer notes *that* Bruce Springsteen dances in the music video DANCIN' IN THE DARK, but never describes or analyzes the camera-choreography (Palmer 1997, 111).

While, again discussing masculinity, Paul McDonald vividly describes the more casual social-dancing and acrobatic "party dancing" moves in Take That videos, when it comes to discussing more formal camera-choreography in the section of his analysis devoted to what he calls "dance mode," oddly enough there is no description or analysis whatsoever of concrete instances of video-dancing. Lisa Lewis's (1990) otherwise thorough analysis of female gender and MTV barely touches on dance. Finally, Andrew Goodwin, whose book on music video is metaphorically entitled *Dancing in the Distraction Factory*, surprisingly devotes only two pages to the videos' camera-choreography. Goodwin, however, tantalizingly acknowledges that it is dancing that often provides the crucial "link between sound and image" in MTV, and his brief suggestions for possible movement analysis are quite discriminating, providing categories and guidelines for future analysis of the kind he himself does not undertake (Goodwin, 68).

Goodwin, Simon Frith, Susan McClary, Sheila Whiteley, and others have pointed out that commentators on music videos often forget that they are forms of *music*, treating the clips merely as visual works (Goodwin 1992, 3–7; Frith 1988, 205–25; McClary 1991, 148; Whiteley

1997, 259). Since popular music is very often made expressly to dance to, it also seems particularly appropriate to pay attention to the camera-choreography in many video clips, especially those made in the early days of MTV in the 1980s, when dance-pop emerged as a dominant form of popular music.

Goodwin, following Frith, argues that part of the pleasure of music video is that, rather than supplying a "sound track" supporting a series of visual images (as in cinema), music video actually does the opposite, making television musical (Goodwin 1992, 70). It seems to me that in many music video clips, through the conjunction of choreography with camerawork and editing—that is, through camera-choreography—music video also makes television *dance*. The paucity of kinetic analysis in the literature on music videos is a particularly striking gap during a period of intellectual obsession with the body. Thus I hope that my brief examination of gendered meaning in the camera-choreography of music videos here will contribute to the ongoing conversation about this recent and extremely popular form of television entertainment.

The question of how the popular music industry in the United States creates video images of women's *dancing* bodies for mass consumption and what those images mean in terms of female sexuality as well as women's roles and status in American society is an important and controversial one. While critics of dance and cultural studies vociferously disagree about gendered meanings in both choreography and music videos, nevertheless many rely on Laura Mulvey's oft-cited essay on the male gaze, "Visual Pleasure and Narrative Cinema," to structure their conversations about representations of women (Mulvey 1975, 6–18, reprinted in Mulvey 1989, 14–26). Even Goodwin, who criticizes the psychoanalytic approach that Mulvey adopts and argues that TV (especially MTV) differs so drastically from narrative cinema that it must be analyzed altogether differently, cites Mulvey in proposing male "scopophilia" (visual pleasure) as a crucial strategy in most music videos. Mulvey's "male gaze" theory posits a dichotomy between the woman as static object-to-be-looked-at versus the man as looker and doer.

But this contrast makes no sense when it comes to dance, because the distinction between looking and doing disappears into the choreography, which is rarely static. Where the exhibition of dancing bodies is concerned, the distinction between *doing* versus *being looked at* is a category error, since with dance *doing* and *being the object of the gaze* are not opposites. The dancer, whether male or female, *does* in order to be looked at and *is looked at* because he/she *does* (i.e., dances). When characters (male or female) in any dance-fiction are "being looked at," they are seldom passive objects of the gaze—male or female—but rather, it is precisely their *doing* that is the active subject of the gaze (see Banes 1999, 117–22).

As a critical model, the notion of the woman as motionless object of the male look was popularized by John Berger with respect to painting before it was psychoanalyzed by Mulvey (see Berger, Blomberg, Fox, Dibb, and Hollis 1972, a book based on Berger's BBC television series of the same title). And perhaps with respect to painting, a little more sense can be made of the notion of the woman as the static object of a male gaze. But with reference to dance, the concept is not feasible. Thus we need to find other models for understanding representations of women not only in live dance performance but also in the camera-choreography of music videos. This is not to say that dancing women, whether live, on film, or in videos, cannot be looked at as erotic objects by men. Clearly, they often are. However, the psychoanalytic approach is not an adequate comprehensive analytic tool for understanding female representations, especially when it comes to dancing representations. In this essay, the "male gaze" theory is challenged by providing an in-depth analysis of a music video, an analysis that offers an alternative interpretation of how video dancing creates a female image.

One could trace the representations of dancing women in music videos back to various precursors of MTV: the "soundies" of the 1940s—short films that were made for jukeboxes with projection screens—as well as television and film appearances by rock and pop groups from the 1950s to the present. Since the early 1980s the popular music industry in the United States has been creating short videos meant for mass TV broadcast to advertise a single rock or pop song—usually in a highly edited format that features extremely rapid cutting and that often switches between live performance footage and fictional narratives (or quasi-narratives). These clips, which are widely distributed to a mass audience but which regularly make use of avant-garde film techniques—including surrealistic dream or fantasy imagery and disjunctive montage—constitute what are now commonly referred to as music videos.

My topic provides many possible threads of inquiry. For instance, one could look at the sexist or misogynistic images of women in many popular music videos that feature male music groups (and therefore are seen by viewers to be male-authored). It should be noted, however, that music videos are not authored solely by the music groups they feature, but by a team that includes a producer, a director, public relations personnel, editors, and so on, as well as the musical artists. Thus, music videos featuring female musicians may well include male "authors" in practice, even though the end result is often received by viewers as being female-authored. By far the majority of video clips in the early days of MTV featured predominantly male (as well as predominantly white) rock groups. Much has been written about the gendered spectatorship of MTV, particularly among both male and female adolescents who, suffering the throes of sexual maturation and identity formation, actively look for role models (or anti-role models) in mass culture, especially in the popular music industry (see Lewis 1990; Fiske 1989, chaps. 5a and 5b). The charge continues to be made that MTV broadcasts mostly male rock groups and, not only in its video clips but also in other programming, appeals primarily to young male viewers. As recently as 1996, Lifetime Television, "the women's channel," announced that it would start a new entertainment channel for younger women, partly because (perhaps unconsciously echoing Lewis's 1990 objection), Lifetime's then-President Doug McCormick asserted, "The 'M' in MTV is for men" (Robichaux 1996, 7E). The title of one section of Lewis's chapter "The Making of a Preferred Address" in her book on MTV is "The 'M' stands for Male" (Lewis 1990, 38).

However, rather than analyzing what most viewers can agree are predominantly negative images of women in male-dominated and male-oriented music videos, I focus here on images—whether negative, positive, or ambiguous—of female popular music stars in music videos. Since the early 1980s, more women rock and pop stars have appeared on MTV and other music television programs and some have created careers through MTV appearances. Film and TV performances by earlier singers such as Janis Joplin, Nancy Sinatra, and Tina Turner set the stage for video performances by female stars of the 1980s and 1990s like Cyndi Lauper, Pat Benatar, Madonna, and Janet Jackson, who not only crashed through the glass ceiling of music television, but also put a frank outpouring of women's dreams, desires, and frustrations on television though popular music. Madonna's rise to stardom had as much to do with MTV airplay of her visual iconography as a postfeminist "bad girl," including her sexual subject matter, as with her music. Her notoriety also increased when MTV refused to air one particularly sexually controversial clip, JUSTIFY MY LOVE, in 1990.

Madonna's video images, especially her video-dancing images, in which dancing itself is a mode and expressive symbol of defying gender stereotypes and expectations, were cultural icons of the 1980s and 1990s, and they also laid a foundation for the next generation of postfeminist pop musicians of the 1990s. Madonna was a precursor of the Riot Grrls, a feminist popular music movement of the early 1990s that included bands like Bikini Kill and Pop Smear and that sang openly and angrily of feminist themes like violence against women and patriarchal oppression. Their extreme stance and marginal relation to the popular music industry tended to exclude them from music television broadcasts. By the mid-1990s, a new generation of postfeminist pop-musicians, including Courtney Love, Alanis Morissette, Salt-N-Pepa, and Tracy Bonham, emerged in the music video mainstream—a generation that no longer has to fight for its rights to female or even feminist expression but confidently assumes that women can take a bold, in-your-face stand on women's political and personal issues. In considering video clips made for TV broadcast, however, we cannot separate the dancing image from the camera's contribution. Surprisingly, despite the enormous literature on Madonna, so far her dancing for the camera has rarely been discussed, and certainly not analyzed in depth. LUCKY STAR, the video clip I analyze here, is particularly striking because it is a nonnarrative work built entirely on video dancing. For the purposes of analysis, I will consider Madonna the author of this video (she was its artistic auteur, even though the director was a man), and therefore I will consider this video to be female-authored.

LUCKY STAR (1984; directed by Arthur Pierson), made early in Madonna's career, is at first glance simple—even rudimentary—both musically and televisually. And, given its nursery rhyme theme, its apparent simplicity and childlike singsong quality is appropriate. Yet on closer viewing/listening, it becomes evident that, despite its rudimentary surface, LUCKY STAR is a complexly layered work that gives rise to multiple interpretations. As Robert Walser points out, "From Stephen Foster to Madonna (not to mention Aaron Copland), many musicians have used great skill to craft musical texts that communicate great simplicity. The musical construction of simplicity plays an important part in many kinds of ideological representations, from the depiction of pastoral refuges from modernity to constructions of race and gender" (Walser 1993, 128). Walser's point, made about popular music, applies to music video as well. In fact, LUCKY STAR constructs a complicated representation of female gender, layering images of eroticism, playfulness, assertiveness, kittenishness, and even boyishness.

LUCKY STAR simultaneously asserts two different aspects of female behavior that have come to mark Madonna's image during her "Boy Toy" period: innocence and experience. Despite her defiant "bad girl" presentation of self-as-persona, it is the virgin/whore dialectic—the tension between innocence and experience—that makes Madonna's work from this early period striking. Although the virgin/whore dialectic has often been discussed, I would argue that in LUCKY STAR and other clips of this early period, precisely through video, and often through video-dancing, Madonna adds additional layers of meaning beyond those two binary, starkly opposed, and stereotyped conceptions of femininity. First, combined here with childlike qualities, that dialectic creates a Lolitaesque image, and second, combined with boyish qualities, it creates the look and moves of a gamin, a street urchin.

The male street urchin is a figure of innocence who shows up in several of Madonna's video clips of this period, including BORDERLINE, in which Madonna plays the role of a young girl who hangs out with adolescent boys, and OPEN YOUR HEART, in which she plays the role of a peep-show dancer who runs away with a boy-child, dressed identically to him. In parts of LUCKY STAR, Madonna herself seems to take on the role of an adolescent male street urchin. This sexually ambiguous facet of her performing image—projecting male adolescent aspects—is rarely noted, but has important ramifications for my discussion both of camera-choreography and of feminist theory. For it complicates, undermines, and subverts any static categorization of female identity and female sexuality.

In *Gender Advertisements* Erving Goffman discusses the focused creation of what he calls "gender commercials" in print-media advertising through specific, common semiotic markers. One is "relative size": women are pictured as smaller than men. Another is "the feminine touch": women are often shown touching faces and hands, and self-touching is a particularly feminine sign. Goffman also discusses "the ritualization of subordination," including the physical prostration of women before men, the higher location of men in space, all sorts of diminutive or mollifying gestures and expressions by women (for example, bending the knee to signify vulnerability, canting the head or body, smiling, "puckish" or childlike dress, clowning, and mock assault). Finally, there is "licensed withdrawal": turning the gaze away, "flooding out" emotionally (often represented by covering a face deluged with feelings), drifting mentally while in physical contact with a man, luxuriating in situations like talking on the telephone, being transported by happiness, snuggling, nuzzling, and so on (Goffman 1979).

LUCKY STAR mobilizes several of these Goffmanian "gender commercials." It is built of two separate video-dances rhythmically interwoven by rapid editing. In the first video-dance, which I will call Dance 1, close and medium shots show Madonna dancing solo in an intimate, abstract white space. This sequence is intercut with predominantly long shots of three dancers in what looks like a larger abstract white space, in Dance 2. The two video-dances are low-contrast, at first seeming like different shots of the same dance. Sometimes it is hard to tell whether a close up of Madonna's face comes from one or the other, since she wears the same outfit in both (her signature "trashy" outfit, with lace gloves, bracelets, mismatched earrings, a short black top that at times reveals her navel, black skirt, leggings, and short boots, and a big black bow in her obviously bleached hair). But upon closer examination, it becomes clear that these two video-dances—the solo and the group dance—take place in different times and spaces. More importantly, they create contrasting images and meanings, which interweave to create a complex representation, through camera-choreography, of a multi-layered female figure who cannot easily be pigeonholed and who, though sensual, is never simply the passive object of a male gaze.

Alone in Dance 1, Madonna reclines, but the evenly lit, undifferentiated white background makes her seem to float in space. She languorously raises herself up, rolling her head slowly, stretching her neck, and looking upward. She seems as if drawn to listen to the celestial-sounding arpeggiated synthesized music, but she also seems like a young animal—or a new astral star in the galaxy, perhaps?—being born, or waking up. Here Madonna indulges in stereotypically feminine behavior, as coded by Goffman: she moves into submissive postures and engages in self-touching, indirect glances, licensed withdrawal, and so on. She often seems to prostrate herself before the camera, but at times she actively moves toward the camera, as if it were a prone lover she is about to perform sexual acts upon. That no man is present to perform an executive role or tower over her, but that the camera sometimes does so instead (with slightly high-angle shots), seems to increase the slightly voyeuristic, soft-porn aspect of her performance.

In the intimate shallow space of Dance 1, Madonna uses the vocabulary of sexy, even lascivious dancing, and the camera's proximity in close shots adds to the sense of privacy as well as to the heat. The camera moves around to frame her body closely, accentuating her movements and suggesting a partner's embrace. When Madonna tilts her head back in the intimate solo space, the camera pans gently upward, as if licking her neck. The more intimate the camera becomes with her body, the more sexually alluring her video-dancing seems to become. She moves at a low level relative to the camera, as if the white background were the sheets of a bed she cavorts upon. She crouches or kneels, moves her torso, belly, and hips, or stretches her arms up luxuriously to lift her hair off her neck—revealing hidden places like her inner arms, the underside of her chin, and her armpits. She rolls her head, or looks over her shoulder, or, on hands and knees, lowers her chin to look up at the camera with a come-hither expression. The combination of her floor-bound, indirect, twining body movements, the closeness of the camera, and the abstract space in Dance 1 is often disorienting, creating confusion as to whether the camera is overhead and looking down on her, or recording her head-on from the usual vertical plane. And this disorientation serves as a metaphor not only for floating weightless in outer space, but for the giddiness of being in love. But if in some sense in Dance 1 Madonna makes love with the camera, she is clearly an active partner: she even crawls on hands and knees toward the camera and lowers her head, mouth open, as if the camera were a supine, passive lover. This is an image of a sexually assured woman, acting on her desires, not an image of a passive or submissive sex object.

Yet this image of intimate, inviting (though sometimes slightly aggressive) feminine sensuality—which is elaborated in the majority of the shots (in fact, fully three-quarters of the shots) in LUCKY STAR—is consistently tempered by regular accents of the androgynous, more ambiguously sexy street-dancing style of the group video-dancing. In most of Dance 2, defined by predominantly long shots, the video-dancing is more "public"—it involves three people—and, furthermore, it is gender-ambiguous. Indeed, so androgynous is the group video-dancing that one writer describes the dancing "chorus" (a white man and a black woman) as two men (Lloyd 1993, 36). The dancers are energetic and high-spirited, yet coolly controlled in their rhythmic stepping and kicking. Rather than isolating the intimate areas of torso, belly, hips,

shoulders, head, and throat, the camera-choreography in Dance 2 usually engages the trunk of the body in an unarticulated, vertical position
while emphasizing the extremities primarily—legs and feet, arms and
hands. The camera's long shots and the choreography function together to distance and desexualize the body relative to Dance 1. Although there is a puckish aspect to the street-kid-style dance behavior,
because it is consciously and deliberately framed by the camera-
choreography as gender-ambiguous, it does not function as a diminutive or mollifying feminine expression. On the contrary, it "corrects"
that representation. The camera's distance, associated with the group
video-dancing, allows all three dancers, but especially Madonna, to
cover space—visually coding her as claiming male territory—and the
shot compositions, in which the dancers form a triangle with Madonna
at the front apex and the other two flanking her to the rear, make her
(through perspective) loom larger than both the man and the woman in
the dancing chorus. Her larger size, too, codes her as taking up space
like a male.

As a hip-hop-flavored musical phrase pounds out its rhythmic $\frac{4}{4}$
percussive beat, long shots of the three dancers turning, lunging, and
stepping are intercut with two close shots of Madonna's face and upper
torso, in the same time and space as the long shots. She is doing a version of break dancing, at first cutting fast, intricate footwork and then
moving down to the floor to strike a pose or, in hip-hop rhetoric, a
"freeze" (on the structure and vocabulary of break dancing, see Banes
1981; reprinted in Banes 1994, 121–25). Thus she mobilizes what Lisa
Lewis calls an "access sign"—a moment when, as Lewis writes, "female
musicians appearing in the videos textually enact entrance into a male
domain of activity and signification. Symbolically, they execute take-
overs of male space, effect the erasure of sex roles, and make demands
for parity with male-adolescent privilege" (Lewis 1990, 109). While one
could argue that many of the adolescents who break-dance are not privileged males, but rather, are part of a marginalized male subculture,
nevertheless in this shot Madonna certainly does take over male space.
She not only enters the all-male adolescent arena of break dancing, but
takes center stage while the other two dancers form a background and
frame her—another claiming of space and dominance that is often socially coded as assertive and male.

Whereas alone Madonna luxuriates in her movements—stretching
out her arms, touching her face or hair, or slowly rolling her head—and

restlessly, constantly turns and writhes, while the camera creates an intimate frame that suggests both narcissistic femininity and sexual heat, the group moves crisply and directly on a straight path, either in unison or counterpoint, evincing the cool control, youthful spirit, and group cohesion of street dancing, while the camera's long shot adds more detachment—"chilling out," in hip-hop rhetoric—through physical/visual distance. The sharp juxtaposition of these two qualities—sexual warmth and asexual cool—suggests a complicated, changeful view of women's sexuality.

In the first closeup in Dance 2, we witness Madonna's vigorous hip-hop dancing. The camera emphasizes her momentum by recording her out of focus, suggesting that there is so much lively energy that the mechanism can't absorb it. In the second closeup, during the freeze, the camerawork and editing emphasize a different quality—a ludic aspect. The camera tightly frames Madonna's face as she rests her chin on her fist and first looks directly into the camera with a sultry expression, then glances offscreen, grins, and winks twice, in time to the irresistible beat, marking the end of the musical phrase. When the musical phrase repeats for a fourth time, it cuts from Madonna lying on her back, stretching and arching, revealing her bare midriff and navel in a lazy, hedonistic mode, in Dance 1, to a closeup of her midriff, but now in the vertical stance of Dance 2. She crisply swings her hips twice to clinch the musical phrase, kinetically rhyming her hip-swings with her earlier winks (as well as with the rhythm of the music and the editing). All this sexiness, she seems to say in this sequence—with her wink, her grin, her off-camera glance, and her highly rhythmic body-snapping accents—is delightful, but partly just a joke. The camera's changing frame and the snappy editing are crucial to that message, which strongly implies that Madonna is involved in parodying, even as she presents, the image of herself as a seductive, sexy woman.

In Dance 1, Madonna lies back, turns over, lounges, crawls, twists around, and arches her back, all on the floor, in close proximity to the camera. Her movements flow together, connoting a compound of not necessarily congruent expressive qualities: alluring, narcissistic, cuddly, restless, and sexually assertive. She moves toward and away from the camera, suggesting sexual aggression as well as flirtation. In Dance 2, Madonna and her two-dancer "chorus" move more abruptly, in what in Labanalysis is called a "bound" manner, keeping energy contained within the body's boundaries. They stand, step, run, and jump in a larger-scale space, usually at a distance from the camera. The space, though abstract, symbolically becomes "the street" since something resembling street dancing takes place in it (Goodwin [1992, 115–16] discusses the importance of "the street" as an emblem of authenticity and experience, but also of male bonding, in popular music). The entirely different mix of (at times oxymoronic) expressive qualities here are precise, relaxed, exuberant, poised, assertive in a relatively nonsexual way. That they move laterally in space, rather than frontally toward and away from the camera, creates a social and sexual gap between the dancers and the camera.

In Dance 1, Madonna fetchingly snuggles into a space that the camera-choreography marks as warm, supple, close, and inviting; in Dance 2, she authoritatively but buoyantly marks off and claims a space that is coded by the camera-choreography as cool, fixed, open, and detached—a space of public appearances and formal identities. In terms of gender advertisements, as the video-dances alternate, she constantly moves in and out of feminine style and behavior, suggesting that female identity is fluid—changeable and multifaceted, reserved and sensual, playful and assertive, innocent and experienced.

The winks and the group video-dancing prevent LUCKY STAR from purely reveling in erotic performance. The street-kid style and the wink—aimed not at the camera (that is, the viewer), but off camera, as if at a friend who is in on the joke—provide an ironic edge that allows the viewer to see even the stereotypically erotic moves as tongue-in-cheek. That is, in LUCKY STAR, through video-dancing, Madonna creates the persona of a "bad girl," but leavens it with playfulness. It is precisely the camera-choreography, especially in creating the gamin qualities of Dance 2, that marks her "bad girl" mystique as all taking place in the ludic realm, framing her as still "just a girl"—not a femme fatale. Thus when in the extreme closeups of Dance 2 Madonna swings her hips, bites her lip, opens her mouth, licks her lips, and puts her finger in her mouth, these sexy moves look playful, like a put-on, because they are associated with the ludic "street dance," rather than the "bedroom dance." Those who speak of the *female* gaze or the *female* address to spectators might argue that it is in the group video-dancing where Madonna shows her energetic power and autonomy, positively contrasting it with the apparently conventional "male gaze"-oriented, seductive behavior of the solo part.

I say "apparently" here, because adding to the multiple meanings as well as to the irony of LUCKY STAR is the suggestion in the camera-choreography that Madonna is both subject and object of the look—and of the song. In the silent black-and-white closeup opening shot of LUCKY STAR, we see Madonna's hands and face as she slides her sunglasses down her nose (invoking both Lolita as portrayed by Sue Lyon in Stanley Kubrick's 1962 film and Audrey Hepburn as Holly Golightly in *Breakfast at Tiffany's*). The image fades to white, suggesting that what she sees, with her sunglasses off, is a dazzling light—perhaps that of the celestial star in the video's title—and then video resumes in color. At the end of the song, as the music fades out, the very first black-and-white image clip repeats, but in retrograde: in the same black-and-white close shot, in silence, Madonna puts her sunglasses back on. The taking down and putting up of those sunglasses provide a frame to contain the song, functioning like a curtain that opens and closes to mark the beginning and end of a stage performance.

But also, rich with connotations, the opening and closing shots suggest simultaneously that Madonna (or at least, the character portrayed by Madonna) herself is a movie star, the object of her fans' regard—because she wears sunglasses and appears in a black-and-white motion picture—*and* that she is taking off her sunglasses to look at a star (in the astronomical sense) whose light is blindingly bright, *and* that she is playing a character who opens the performance of the song by removing her glasses to look at a "star" as a celebrity in the music entertainment world—Madonna herself. Thus the theme of ambiguity regarding the Madonna character (and more generally regarding women) as both subject and object of the look—a reflexive as well as narcissistic theme that the clip engages throughout—is immediately introduced in the brief first framing shot.

Goodwin (1992, 75) points out that in narrative popular songs, the singer-narrator plays all the roles: "he or she is simultaneously both the character in the song and the storyteller," creating a situation of "double address" that often confuses the audience. Although LUCKY STAR is neither a narrative song nor a narrative video, in the clip Madonna plays at least four characters: the person in sunglasses looking, it seems, at the performance in the color section of the video; a break-dancing boy; an androgynous social dancer; a sultry temptress. The conflation of all those characters into one singing and dancing body creates a striking impression of narcissistic self-love, since it makes Madonna seem to be addressing the lyrics of the song to herself. Moreover, in this context, when she looks directly at the camera Madonna seems more to be looking at herself in the mirror and making love to herself than gazing out at an imaginary spectator. When she sings "Shine your heavenly body tonight," and the camera moves in to frame her in a cheesecake pose, it marks her own body as the same heavenly one she is singing about. Is Madonna addressing a lover or herself in this song? The image of narcissistic self-love hinted at in the camera-choreography is complex, because it is both ironized (by the winks and the shot in which Madonna literally puts her tongue-in-cheek), and also creates a strong, positive implication of feminist self-sufficiency that belies any representation of the eroticized woman as sex object. In this interpretation, Madonna is eroticized for her own pleasure, not for a man's. Perhaps it is this interpretation of LUCKY STAR that has led one young Madonna fan to say, "She's sexy but she doesn't need men . . . she's kind of there all by herself" (*Time*, May 27, 1985, 47, quoted in Fiske 1989, 100).

A number of factors create the aural impression that the song is open-ended and ongoing. Musically and in terms of the lyrics, the song has an ABAB CBCB structure; after a bridge when the music heats up, there is no return to the original stanza structure or lyrics, though the chorus continually returns. This sense of forward propulsion, combined with the steady $\frac{4}{4}$ beat of the drum machine underlying the changes of lyric, instrumentation, melody, and rhythm across both halves of the song, as well as the musical fadeout at the end, contributes to the sense of ongoingness. In fact, during the early 1980s popular songs began to be structured this way (and continue to be structured this way) in order to provide a format that DJs at dance clubs could easily mix and remix. So, appropriately enough for a song with a disco flavor, but also a song that deals thematically with outer space, one has the sense that one could "dance all night long" to this music that—though repetitive in many ways and providing the pleasure and comfort of a recurring, familiar chorus—without the closure of a neat musical return to the beginning seems absolutely infinite.

Televisually, the configurations of shot chains keep shifting, never appearing in the exact same relationships even when the music and lyrics repeat. Also, the fact that the singing bridges several cuts from one video-dance to the other yields a complex impression of ongoingness as well as change, the comfort of familiarity as well as the adventure of the unexpected. So the editing also creates a feeling of infinite televisual variety and accelerating energy, anchored to the pleasure of musical repetition.

This creates a sense that the televisual track is an analogue for social dancing in its relation to the music: just as one improvises on the dance floor from a small gamut of set moves, not necessarily repeating the same moves to the same musical phrase or the same lyric in the dance music, so the linkages between image and music in LUCKY STAR are repeatable, yet indeterminate. Indeed, repeatability and duration seem to be the clip's most salient formal qualities, and the imagery of both dances—wallowing in bed, in Dance 1, and hanging out on the street, in Dance 2—serves as a metaphor for those qualities. But also, the feeling created by the music and visual editing—of endless waves of pleasure, comfort, and familiarity—serves as an erotic metaphor. That erotic mood is paradoxically both tempered and heightened by the various little-girl signs; Madonna's voice is both breathy and high-pitched, and her bare navel looks part belly dancer and part Coppertone ad.

The changes in the camera-choreography make the clip, with its repetitive song and its driving beat, become televisually complicated. But additionally, they enrich the song by giving it multiple layers of meaning. On the one hand, it is a pleasurably childish, incantatory "wishing on a star" sing-song nursery rhyme ("Star light, star bright / First star I see tonight / Star light, star bright / Make everything all right . . ." the chorus repeatedly wishes), but on the other hand, several kinds of bodily pleasures are suggested by the video-dancing in alternate moments, particularly in the erotic moves in the close shots. The camera-choreography makes the song oscillate back and forth between youthful exuberance and adult knowingness through double entendres (see Fiske 1989, 107–10 for a discussion of Madonna's puns and double entendres). Although the double meaning of "your heavenly body" is already there in the lyrics, the video-dancing makes explicit the sexual as well as the celestial aspect of that term, as Madonna raises her arms behind her head in the aforementioned cheesecake gesture while the camera cuts from a medium shot to a close shot during the lyric "Shine your heavenly body tonight." She seems to be punning with her body, simultaneously inviting and humorously undercutting an erotic male gaze.

The other meaning of star—a celebrity entertainer—is introduced as well, not only in the initial black-and-white shot when Madonna lowers her sunglasses, but during the many shots in which the camera delivers her iconic face in closeup, as if on a magazine cover (Goodwin 1992, 91, 98–130). Goodwin discusses the incessant narratives of stardom in music videos and points out that an important "visual hook" in music videos is "the routine close-ups of pop stars' faces, which are often repeated during a song's chorus or refrain" (Goodwin 1992, 90). Although Madonna was not yet a star when LUCKY STAR was made, the iconography of the video clip frames her, or at least her performing persona, as one. Yet, as in many Madonna videos of this period, she shows a deliberate, tongue-in-cheek ambivalence toward the phenomenon. She seems to pay homage to the notion of stardom while simultaneously parodying it.

Noël Carroll writes that many music videos have a "rebus-like structure," and he notes that "this structure invites the viewer to entertain different interpretations of the images in light of the song and vice versa" (Carroll 1998, 44). And John Fiske argues that "rock videos are quintessential television" because "they embody in condensed form all the characteristics of television that make it such a popular medium — its 'producerliness' and semiotic democracy; its segmentation; its discursive practices of excess, contradictions, metaphor, metonymy, and pun; and its intertextuality" (Fiske 1989, 115). LUCKY STAR not only activates three meanings of the word "star" and its synonym "heavenly body," but through its multiple, often conflicting meanings, it complicates considerably the question of the "male gaze" and even the general issue of spectator/auditor address in both video and song.

In the continuing debate about whether Madonna's blatant sexuality is simply wholesale seduction or simply an ironic pose, David Tetzlaff, among others, argues (against Fiske) that in LUCKY STAR "the idea that Madonna's tongue is intended as a put-on rather than a come-on hardly seems likely" (in Schwichtenberg, 245). In order to see the "true" message, Tetzlaff complains that instead of looking squarely at the "text" (that is, the clip), commentators have allowed their interpretations of Madonna to be formed instead by "the metatextual narrative of her management of her own career quest for fame, fortune, and independence" (Schwichtenberg, 243). But Tetzlaff himself misses the irony of the sexual display in LUCKY STAR and interprets it simply as a come-on because he hasn't paid attention to the contrasts in the video-dancing "track." Indeed, he doesn't even mention the group video-dancing, which seems to have completely passed him by. In assessing sexual meaning, he has neglected scrutinizing the operations of the body in motion through TV.

We are increasingly aware, in dance criticism, of the dangers of boiling choreography down to literary or narrative plots. There is a similar problem with respect to music videos. Tetzlaff is only one example of many commentators who—blind to the camera-choreography and seeing the clips only as a visual narrative—diminish, besides the musical aspect, the kinetic and televisual richness and complexity of meaning in video-dance.

The video LUCKY STAR offers more meanings than either the lyrics or the music (or both together) in the audio recording "Lucky Star." The camera-choreography intriguingly engages controversial issues in feminist debates regarding women's identity, sexual pleasure, and the male gaze. It suggests not only that women can enjoy sexual pleasure without being objectified by men, but that there are many different ways to be female, ranging from being soft and sexy to acting like a male. It also asserts female freedom to move from one role, one identity, to another. And it hints that female empowerment can take many forms, from sexual assertion to self-love to competing with males on their own turf. When Madonna invokes street culture (as she does again, even more explicitly, in BORDERLINE), Lewis observes that the female character she plays "[asserts] her right to participate in male leisure culture" (Lewis 1990, 122).

In a discussion of Madonna's style and visual image in her early video clips, Lewis points out that Madonna has been criticized by some feminists "for making a sexual spectacle of herself." But, she argues, "Madonna's 'slut' affectation is in actuality marred by the indifference she projects toward men and the self-assurance she displays as an image of her own creation" (Lewis 1990, 124). While direct address by singers in video clips is not unique either to LUCKY STAR or to Madonna, in this context the frequent shots in which Madonna stares right at the camera are reminiscent of Manet's *Olympia*. This is the stare of a woman who does not avert her own gaze when gazed upon, but who intently and assertively looks right back at the spectator. Goodwin notes that "the direct address is intended to mirror the codes of live performance, where singers sing directly to the concert hall audience (a look that is displaced, via camera, onto the television viewer)" (Goodwin 1992, 78).

Madonna doesn't create an image of female aggression in her video-dancing in LUCKY STAR (even in her break-dancing moves), the way Taylor Dayne does, for instance, in her video clip TELL IT TO MY HEART. (TELL IT TO MY HEART bears some intriguing resemblances to LUCKY STAR: both utilize abstract white back-grounds, and both involve the singing star dancing with two "backup" dancers. However, there are also striking dissimilarities, including the more straightforward editing of TELL IT TO MY HEART [which in-corporates only one dance, not two] and the more aggressive quality ex-pressed across the music, lyrics, and dancing.) Dayne's martial-arts-based dancing (also meant to invoke break dancing) suggests that she is capable of punching and kicking the recalcitrant lover to whom the song is addressed. In contrast, Madonna is soft and alluring in the solo section and engagingly spirited in the group section.

Madonna may not be a militant feminist. Yet the alternation of duplex female video-dancing images in LUCKY STAR does make feminist statements. While Madonna has not explicitly intervened in academic feminist debates in print about the "male gaze," and may not even be aware of them, certainly at the time she made LUCKY STAR the downtown New York art and entertainment world she lived in was abuzz with discussion of that gaze. That is, these intellectual debates, taking place in the sphere of theory, were simultaneously being played out in the sphere of practice in Madonna's cutting-edge work. In LUCKY STAR, through music video, Madonna does make an inter-vention into feminist theory, commenting, in particular, on female representations—through the camera-choreography's simultaneous evocation of and ironic subversion of the idea of the male gaze.

REFERENCES

Banes, Sally. "To the Beat Y'All: Breaking is Hard to Do." *Village Voice*, April 10, 1981. Reprinted in Sally Banes, *Writing Dancing in the Age of Postmodernism*. Hanover, N.H.: Wesleyan University Press/University Press of New En-gland, 1994, 121–25.
———. "Talking Women: Dance Herstories." *Dance Research Journal* 31, no. 2 (1999): 117–22.
Berger, John, Sven Blomberg, Chris Fox, Michael Dibb, and Rachel Hollis. *Ways of Seeing*. New York: Viking Press, 1972.
Buckland, Theresa Jill, with Elizabeth Stewart. "Dance and Music Video." In *Parallel Lines: Media Representations of Dance*, edited by Stephanie Jordan and Dave Allen. London: John Libbey, 1993.
Carroll, Noël. *A Philosophy of Mass Art*. Oxford: Oxford University Press, 1998.
Fiske, John. *Reading the Popular*. Boston: Unwin Hyman, 1989.
Frith, Simon. "Making Sense of Video; Pop into the Nineties." Afterword to *Music for Pleasure*. London: Routledge, 1998.

Goffman, Erving. *Gender Advertisements*. New York: Harper and Row, 1979.

Goodwin, Andrew. *Dancing in the Distraction Factory: Music Television and Popular Culture*. Minneapolis: University of Minnesota Press, 1992.

Kaplan, E. Ann. *Rocking Around the Clock: Music Television, Postmodernism and Consumer Culture*. New York: Methuen, 1987.

Lewis, Lisa. *Gender Politics and MTV: Voicing the Difference*. Philadelphia: Temple University Press, 1990.

Lloyd, Fran. "The Changing Images of Madonna." In *Deconstructing Madonna*, edited by Fran Lloyd. London: B.T. Batsford, 1993.

McClary, Susan. "Living to Tell: Madonna's Resurrection of the Fleshly." *Genders* 7 (March 1990). Reprinted in *Feminine Endings*, edited by Susan McClary. Minneapolis: University of Minnesota Press, 1991.

Mulvey, Laura. "Visual Pleasure and Narrative Cinema." *Screen* 16, no. 3 (Autumn 1975): 6–18. Reprinted in *Visual and Other Pleasures*, edited by Laura Mulvey. Bloomington: Indiana University Press, 1989.

Palmer, Gareth. "Bruce Springsteen and Masculinity." In Whiteley, *Sexing the Groove*.

Robichaux, Mark. "Lifetime Aims Shows at Young Women." *Wall Street Journal*, July 10, 1996.

Rubey, Dan. "Voguing at the Carnival: Desire and Pleasure on MTV." *South Atlantic Quarterly* 90, no. 4 (Fall 1991): 871–907.

Schwichtenberg, Cathy, ed. *The Madonna Connection: Representational Politics, Subcultural Identities, and Cultural Theory*. Boulder, Colo.: Westview Press, 1993.

Tetzlaff, David. "Metatextual Girl: -> patriarchy -> postmodernism -> power -> money -> Madonna." In Schwichtenberg, *The Madonna Connection*.

Walser, Robert. *Racing with the Devil: Power, Gender, and Madness in Heavy Metal Music*. Hanover, N.H.: Wesleyan University Press/University Press of New England, 1993.

Whiteley, Sheila. "Seduced by the Sign: An Analysis of the Textual Links Between Sound and Image in Pop Videos." In Whiteley, *Sexing the Groove*.

———, ed. *Sexing the Groove: Popular Music and Gender*. London: Routledge, 1997.

Elephants in Tutus

Banes was planning to deliver this talk at a Society of Dance History Scholars confer-
ence in 2002, but was prevented from doing so by her stroke. She gave a different ver-
sion of her work on Balanchine's dancing elephants at the Association for Theatre in
Higher Education annual conference in Chicago in 2001.

In 1942 the Ringling Brothers and Barnum and Bailey Circus commissioned the ballet choreographer George Balanchine and modernist
composer Igor Stravinsky to create *The Ballet of the Elephants* for "fifty
elephants and fifty beautiful girls." The elephants wore tutus and glit-
tering headdresses, and the star of the ballet, the elephant Modoc, was
billed as the "premiere ballerina." (The other performers were not listed
but simply credited, collectively, as the Corps de Ballet and the Corps
des Elephants.[1]) Modoc's partner, at least on opening night at Madison
Square Garden in New York City (which was a benefit performance for

SOURCE: Planned paper, Society of Dance History Scholars conference, 2002

the Army and Navy relief funds and the President's Infantile Paralysis Fund) was Vera Zorina, Balanchine's then-wife and a ballet dancer who had also appeared in musicals on Broadway and in Hollywood films.[2] Later, she was replaced by Princess Vanessa, "a Hindoo dancer," who had appeared with the Ballet Russe and in Hollywood movies.[3] Wartime patriotism, foreign exoticism, escapist entertainment, industrial "streamlining," rural ballyhoo, urban sophistication, and high culture and low culture all collided in that year's edition of the Big Top, entitled "Gayety," which proved to be a crossroads of American culture and which indelibly shaped "the Greatest Show on Earth," creating a style and approach for the circus that set the standard for future editions.

Today I want to focus on some of the cultural implications of *The Ballet of the Elephants*, exploring in particular two issues: boundary-crossing between cultural strata and representations of female bodies. *The Ballet of the Elephants* was a conscious translation of ballet art from old world to new, and from the opera house to the big top—that is, from "high" to "low" culture along multiple strata. At the same time, it's important to note that the ballet's commission was part and parcel of a transformation of the circus genre itself, a deliberate attempt (not always successful with critics and audiences) to make the circus more artistic, more highbrow—as its producers thought befit contemporary, urban audiences. In terms of gender, the pairing of human and animal "ballerinas" on the one hand wrung new meanings out of familiar images of women and animals in popular entertainments, while on the other hand it reinforced standard circus representations of female sexuality at the time.

In the early 1940s the new Ringling Brothers and Barnum and Bailey Circus impresario John Ringling North had decided to modernize America's most popular of live popular entertainments, to streamline it in accordance with contemporary industrial design and artistic taste, and to make it a more unified and sophisticated spectacle. In 1937 North, the nephew of the original Ringling Brothers, had inherited a circus that was the largest and best known in the country, but that was also suffering from the Depression economy as well as from family infighting, management problems, and what North saw as an outmoded aesthetic. A Yale graduate who loved New York culture and nightlife, North began to bring in theater designers and directors to modernize the circus shows and heighten their sense of style. These included Charles Le Maire, costume designer of the *Ziegfeld Follies*, and Max Weldy, designer for *Les Folies Bergère*. North introduced air-conditioning, and he experimented with the use of floral fragrance sprays; a new, more compact and elegant dark blue big top replaced the off-white canvas that often appeared dingy and that let in sunlight during matinees.

In 1940 North hired Norman Bel Geddes, the theater and industrial designer who had created the 1939 New York World's Fair Futurama, to further the streamlining process. Bel Geddes envisioned a futuristic big top, without poles to obscure audience sightlines.[4] In the meantime, he made the visual style of the circus more colorful and more unified: he tinted the sawdust in rings of red, white, and blue, added red sidewalls to the blue big top, and introduced modern lighting designs that decisively guided the spectator's gaze; he gave the sideshow midway a bright, contemporary, poster-art look; he reorganized the menagerie; and he added large-scale production numbers. Albertina Rasch, a Broadway choreographer, joined the team to infuse more dancing into the circus ballet girls' routines. The critics found it all a smart, snappy visual feast.[5]

For the 1942 edition of the circus, as the country entered World War II and began to pull out of the Depression, besides Bel Geddes a whole new team of New York artists came on board to create a show that was meant to be both glamorous entertainment (which people could now afford) and patriotic spectacle (to raise morale as the circus toured the country as well as to justify the fun the show was purveying in wartime). The Broadway theater director John Murray Anderson oversaw the entire series of acts, from the "Holiday" pageant to the Spanish-themed "Fiesta del Torres" to the clown parody of the wedding of Gargantua and M'Toto, two famous gorillas on display in the menagerie. Known for directing musical revues, musical comedies, and extravaganzas, Anderson may have come to North's attention after he directed *Jumbo*, a Rodgers and Hart musical set in a circus. During the production of *Jumbo*, Anderson had worked with Barbette—the transvestite trapeze artist who had taken Europe by storm in the 1920s and inspired Jean Cocteau—and now he recruited Barbette to stage the large, all-girl aerial number for the 1942 circus.

Bel Geddes's assistant, Miles White, who soon gained fame on Broadway designing *Oklahoma!*, was the uncredited costume designer for most of the production numbers. And Peter Arno, North's classmate and a cartoonist for the *New Yorker*, spent months designing the program, which was full of witty cartoons of circus life, as well as drawings of the artists and acts, articles, and the usual photos, program notes, credits, and advertisements.⁶ The cover featured a fanciful Arno cartoon of *The Ballet of the Elephants*, imagining a scene that never really happened: a male elephant in shorts amorously embraces a shy female elephant in a skirt.

And then there were George Balanchine and Igor Stravinsky. Anderson may have called on Balanchine to create *The Ballet of the Elephants* because they had already worked together in the 1936 edition of the *Ziegfeld Follies*.⁷ Balanchine had arrived in the United States eight years before his circus commission, after a peripatetic choreographic career, first in Russia, then in Western Europe. Though classically trained in ballet since childhood (and though he is largely remembered now as a canonically modernist, serious high-art ballet choreographer) Balanchine had already had extensive experience both in the avant-garde and in popular entertainments by the time he arrived in the United States, opened the School of American Ballet, and established, with Lincoln Kirstein, a series of small ballet companies. During the late 1930s and early 1940s, Balanchine worked on both lyric and popular stages in the United States, choreographing dances for the Metropolitan Opera, for his own American Ballet company, on Broadway, and in Hollywood films.

Thus in choosing Balanchine to create *The Ballet of the Elephants*, the circus not only imported a pedigreed alumnus of the elite Russian Imperial Ballet, but also a man who knew and loved American showbiz. In Stravinsky, Balanchine had a long-time collaborator who, in turn, had created a serious, even difficult musical style inspired by jazz and other popular idioms.⁸

According to Balanchine's biographer, the choreographer called Stravinsky in Los Angeles in the fall of 1941 to invite him to compose the music.

> "I wonder if you'd like to do a little ballet with me," Balanchine said, "a polka, perhaps."
> "For whom?"
> "For some elephants," Balanchine said.
> "How old?" asked Stravinsky cautiously.
> "Very young," Balanchine assured him.
> There was a pause. Then Stravinsky said gravely, "All right. If they are very young elephants, I will do it."⁹

The result, later retitled *Circus Polka*, strikingly combines aspects of French ballet music of the 1910s and 1920s with a celebration, in the manner of Charles Ives, of American vernacular musical traditions. (In some ways, *Circus Polka* harks back to *Parade*, that momentous 1917 Cubist ballet about circus performers, collaboratively created by Erik Satie, Jean Cocteau, Pablo Picasso, and Léonide Massine and produced by Serge Diaghilev in Paris for his Ballets Russes. That team, too, made references to American popular culture.) *Circus Polka* is whimsical and witty, lively and full of arch allusions—most notably to Franz Schubert's *Marche Militaire*—as well as sounds imitating elephants trumpeting. Arranged for a circus band and full of lush, open tonalities, but simultaneously dissonant and polyrhythmic, it is utterly unlike anything in the circus music repertoire. (According to Merle Evans, the circus band leader for Ringling at the time, both the elephants and the band members had a hard time with this "Harvard music," as he called it, because it had no solid beat.[10]) Perhaps this tongue-in-cheek *Circus Polka* is not a surprising composition for a composer who had only two years earlier left wartime Paris to find an artistic and personal haven in the United States and who had, earlier that same year, created his own new arrangement of *The Star-Spangled Banner*.

Balanchine said at the time, "Elephants are no harder to teach than ballerinas," but later claimed that he kept the elephants' steps as simple as possible.[11] Yet Zorina reports that when they arrived at the circus' winter quarters in Sarasota to begin work on the project, "George soon found that it did not matter *what* choreographic splendor he had in mind for them, because the elephants were going to do the same routine they had done for years. The only thing that ever changed for them was the music and the costumes. So George ordered fifty pale-blue tutus . . . and jeweled headbands for their foreheads."[12] However, certainly Balanchine created new choreography for *The Ballet of the Elephants*, by building on what the elephants already knew, adding to it the human dancers' ballet steps and formations, reconfiguring the pas de deux (or duet form), and reframing the pachyderms' basic routines as an act of grace as well as might. When elephants stand on two hind legs on a wooden tub, we admire their acute sense of balance.[13] When the elephant is wearing a tutu, suddenly we re-see her as a gigantic version of a ballerina, a creature who balances equally astonishingly on one leg, on the boxy tip of a pointe shoe. She has been anthropomorphized and transformed—she is no longer a trained animal, but, as if through a fairytale transformation, suddenly, she is a smiling ballet dancer.

Though Brooks Atkinson said the elephant ballet was nothing new, skeptically declaring it "still an act of performing elephants,"[14] an anonymous critic for the *New York Times* described the number as "breathtaking," noting:

> They came into the ring in artificial, blue-lighted dusk, first the little pink dancers, then the great beasts. The little dancers pirouetted into the three rings and the elephant herds gravely swayed and nodded rhythmically.
>
> The arc of sway widened and the stomping picked up with the music. In the central ring, Modoc the Elephant danced with amazing grace, and in time to the tune, closing in perfect cadence with the crashing finale.
>
> In the last dance fifty elephants moved in an endless chain around the great ring, trunk to tail with the little pink ballet girls in the blue twilight behind them. The ground shook with the elephants' measured steps.[15]

The story goes that John Ringling North first had the idea for this act after seeing an elephant ballet in Budapest during one of his many trips abroad.[16] Certainly trained elephants had been known in the West, and even in circuses, since Roman times.[17] Some of them even danced on tightropes.[18] And beautiful women—in circus lingo, ballet girls—had definitely appeared in the ring with elephants before.

But what *was* unusual about *The Ballet of the Elephants*—what was different, *pace* Atkinson, from the traditional elephant act—was the semiotics of the choreography, the costuming, the props, and the music. The dancers did ballet poses, including an arabesque on the elephant's head; both elephants *and* dancers wore tutus; the dancers held up garlands; they separated from the elephants to do dance steps on their own; and the music was modern and dissonant.

It all meant something new this time. Adding elements from both classical and modern ballet to the standard circus number created two immediately evident distinctions from the traditional elephant act. First, with their tutus, their garlands, their arabesques (and other ballet steps), and their ports de bras (rounded arm gestures), dancing to serious music, the circus "ballet girls" were elevated to the status of "ballerinas" (that is, from low-culture to elite performers), even though they also did acrobatic show-girl poses. And second, as I've suggested, the elephants also became ballet performers—that is, animal bodies were compared to human bodies and endowed with newfound grace. (American ballet bodies were not yet the stick figures they became in the 1970s, so a plump "elephanterina" would not have connoted obesity to a 1942 spectator, though of course the sheer scale of the elephant stood in stark contrast to the size of a human dancer, now miniaturized by her massive partner; the elephant's lumbering bodies set off the human dancers' agility but also gained their own form of beauty.) Accordingly, the status of the act rose from a circus number to a lyric ballet.

In 1942, ballet was a novelty for American audiences. Though there had been sporadic performances and visiting artists on tour from Europe since the eighteenth century and even a few home-grown companies that took root in the early twentieth century, it was not until the mid-1930s, when Balanchine established his school and began organizing a company, and when the American Ballet Theatre was founded, that ballet began to seem like it could be something more than an exotic, aristocratic, and effete European oddity to many Americans, especially those living in the heartland, far from the urban cultural centers of the Eastern Seaboard.[19] In the early 1940s ballet was still a curious novelty. Although in the late nineteenth century European ballet dancing had often entered American culture through popular entertainments, like *The Black Crook* and *The White Fawn*—extravaganzas not far removed from early burlesque—by the 1930s, when ballet began to take root in the United States, ballet had gained a patina of gentility, of high-art opera-house appeal to the intelligentsia.

Now Balanchine, a recent émigré and an exemplar of the refined imperial Russian tradition, was bringing ballet back down to earth, back into American popular entertainments, in ways that audiences barely remembered from generations before—but now with a difference. The elephants themselves (and the circus ballet girls, too) were uplifted, drawn into a world of cultivated elegance, just as on Broadway and in Hollywood Balanchine's ballets often provided an aura of classicism—a touch of class. Though more than one reviewer assured readers "not to worry" at the prospect of encountering ballet at the circus[20]—that is, not to suffer cultural anxiety when contemplating this display—clearly by 1942 those who viewed *The Ballet of the Elephants* were part and parcel of a struggle being waged between high and low culture in America. Americans were learning, sometimes under duress, how to appreciate high European culture—opera, symphonic music, ballet. And they were trying to find ways to reclaim those forms—to make those forms their own.

Balanchine's own avant-gardism on the ballet stage partly consisted in his negotiating a pact between those two apparently antithetical systems, high and low culture. He appropriated in his serious ballets popular culture, both old and new, American and European—jazz tap dancing and square dancing, Western movies, and the bodily habitus of fashion models and Rockettes, as well as elements from commedia dell'arte and the British music hall. But at the same time, as Balanchine and other ballet choreographers found work on Broadway and in Hollywood, the jazz and tap dancing familiar in these American popular entertainments began to give way to classical ballet sequences. (The battle between high and low culture was ironically embodied in Balanchine's *Romeo and Juliet Ballet* in the film *The Goldwyn Follies* [1938], in which the Montagues were ballet dancers and the Capulets were tap dancers.)

Although no reviewers I've found commented on the similarities between the "Dance of the Hours" section of *Fantasia,* the 1940 Disney animated film set to symphonic music, and *The Ballet of the Elephants,* clearly there is a strong relationship between them.[21] And that relationship is more complex than may appear at first glance. For not only does the "Hours" section of *Fantasia,* with its ostriches in toe shoes, its hippopotami in pink tutus, and its effervescent dancing elephants, display a particular American cultural anxiety about ballet—an anxiety that takes the form of parody and that is answered in part, perhaps, by the dignified *Ballet of the Elephants*—but also, the animal ballet sequence in *Fantasia* itself seems to have been inspired by the *Water Nymph Ballet* Balanchine choreographed two years earlier for Vera Zorina in the film *The Goldwyn Follies.* The *Water Nymph Ballet* featured a surrealistic landscape with classical architecture and a pool out of which Zorina emerged like a latter-day Venus, a model for *Fantasia*'s scene in which Hyacinth Hippo appears.[22]

Thus an intertextual conversation—if not an outright comic duel—seems to have taken place between Balanchine and the Disney artists; *The Ballet of the Elephants* perhaps afforded Balanchine a chance to make a witty retort to the elephantine ballerinas in *Fantasia,* which itself partly spoofed Zorina, Balanchine's ballerina wife. And of course, both *Fantasia* and *The Ballet of the Elephants* featured music by Stravinsky (one section of *Fantasia* is set to *The Rite of Spring*). (Ironically—or perhaps appropriately—later in 1942, when the circus musicians' union went on strike and the entire production relied on recorded music for its accompaniment, since Stravinsky's music for the elephant ballet had not yet been recorded, "The Dance of the Hours" was substituted for it.[23]) However, though clearly Balanchine knew all about *Fantasia* (publicity photos were taken of him and Stravinsky on the set), "The Dance of the Hours" was itself inspired by earlier traditions of depicting dancing animals in drawings and cartoons, such as those by the German graphic artist Heinrich Kley.[24] *The Ballet of the Elephants* may have its own roots in those traditions as well.

Fantasia and *The Ballet of the Elephants* share a similar project: both endeavored, more or less successfully, to make high European culture palatable for American popular audiences.[25] But they did this in diametrically opposed ways. *Fantasia* showed how an imaginative listener could provide visual programs—stories—to give narrative shape to seemingly unfathomable and intimidating symphonic music (thereby undoubtedly prompting formalist music critics like Edward Hanslick to turn over in their graves).[26] (Indeed, only a few years later, Balanchine scoffed in print at this philistine need to make *all* music program music.[27])

But in *The Ballet of the Elephants* Balanchine did just the opposite. Though external narrative frames may sometimes be built around circus acts, they don't have internal stories or fictional characters—they present interesting actions (they are what the Russian filmmaker Sergei Eisenstein called "a montage of attractions"). That is, they are presentational, not representational, performances. In *The Ballet of the Elephants* Balanchine seemed to be saying to American audiences, "Look, you can watch and savor plotless ballets in much the same way you already knew how to enjoy the circus." In a culture where abstract ballet was almost unknown at that time, Balanchine put formal meaning—movement, spatial design, and the grace and skill of bodies (here, both human and animal)—in the foreground of the work and brought it down to earth (or sawdust).

Walt Disney and John Ringling North gained cachet for cartoons and circuses by adding serious high culture to their popular entertainments. But for Balanchine, the opposite was true—coming from a European opera-house tradition, his gravitating to popular entertainment enhanced ballet's accessibility for American audiences. At this time the United States was coming into its own as a center for Western high art—a cultural role that had previously been anchored in Europe. And, for a multiplicity of reasons, the two-way street between high art and low culture became a well-traveled route in the Americanization of high art.

The Ballet of the Elephants was a graphically striking paradigm of this process of building a modern American culture through a dialectic between high and low art. As well, effortlessly educating the American eye to watch ballet as abstract formal design, it helped prepare the way for Balanchine's modernist choreography.

There is another very striking and distinctive aspect of this ballet— besides the obvious fact that animals starred in it—that also makes it unusual as a circus elephant routine. The basic choreographic format of *The Ballet of the Elephants* was a pas de deux for two females, backed up by an ensemble that performed both group (corps de ballet) dances and female-female duets. Although there were male elephant handlers in the ring, semiotically speaking they were invisible to the spectator, in much the same way a Bunraku puppeteer is understood by convention to be outside of the theatrical image. This does not need to be the case in a circus elephant act; the handlers could be costumed and thus brought into the presentational framework of the act. But in this case, the handlers wore clothes that looked like the uniforms of service people, not ballet dancers, thus remaining outside the frame and, effectively, disappearing choreographically. That in itself is interesting, because a pas de trois (dance for three) involving one male and two female dancers— intimating a particular male sexual fantasy of "two girls for every boy," as the sixties singing group Jan & Dean put it—was by 1942 already a standard Balanchine trope. So clearly the creation of a specifically female-female duet, despite the presence of the male handlers, was the effect Balanchine intended in this ballet. It was one he had not (to my knowledge) used previously, though he did return to it three years later in *Symphonie Concertante* (1945).

In the standard classical story ballet pas de deux, a ballerina and her male cavalier perform a highly structured duet that serves as a condensed, embodied metaphor for the unfolding of their heterosexual love relationship, which is the nucleus of the ballet's basic plot. While it is true that there are some exceptions to this rule (in some story ballets, for instance Michel Fokine's modern ballet *The Firebird*, there are pas de deux that involve struggles and that might not even take place between the amorous partners), the tradition is so entrenched that, as Robert Greskovic notes, even "in the non-story-ballet pas de deux, the form has been consistently if not exclusively seen as a love story even if a specific narrative plays no part."[28] The nineteenth-century ballet choreographer August Bournonville (and other Romantic ballet choreographers) made duets for two female dancers, but these were not supported pas de deux, with all the metaphorical implications of sexual and emotional relationships implied by physical partnering. Rather, these operated as a double optic—creating an effect for the spectator of watching a dancer and her reflection in a mirror, or of watching twin sisters.

Although the elephants in *The Ballet of the Elephants* were biologically female (and, according to their trainers, backstage they paired up in long-standing lesbian emotional, if not physically sexual, relationships), there is no particular reason spectators would have known that, since many circus animals are seen as genderless or, as a default, male. Balanchine could have coded these female elephants as male partners to the human ballet girls. Moreover, often in elephant circus routines, the pachyderms, not necessarily coded as either gender, take on a phallic role, especially when the ballet girls sit astride their rising trunks. However, Balanchine chose to put these elephants in tutus, to have them perform femininity. This was not, as I suggested earlier, in order to satirize human ballerinas' bodies and behaviors, as *Fantasia*'s dancing animals so clearly did.[29] Rather, it seems, this decision generated new creative possibilities for Balanchine as a choreographer. How, then, are we to understand this gender coding that gave rise to female-female duets?

One's first response might be to transfer directly to this ballet the assumed narrative and metaphoric meaning of dance partnering—that it stands for sexual partnering, or at least amorous partnering—and to interpret *The Ballet of the Elephants* as a radically modern gay ballet, celebrating lesbian love in the manner of Bronislava Nijinska's piquant *Les Biches* (1928). The famous photo of Vera Zorina with the elephant's trunk between her legs does arouse phallic imagery—and given that both elephant and ballerina are female, it is intriguingly ambiguous just what kind of phallus (and whose) this picture presents.

However, I would argue that, given the other evidence, both pictorial and verbal, of the choreography, ultimately in this ballet the phallic aspects of the elephants were offset by their feminization. But if the elephants were feminized, the ballet girls were infantilized, partly by the design of their tutus, which made them look like little girls in party dresses, and partly because the elephants' gigantic scale made the women look tiny. Critics referred to them as "little dancers," "little ballet girls," "nymphs," and "fairies," recalling the "baby ballerinas" Balanchine worked with in the early 1930s. The ballet girls' appearance of childlike innocence dampened any sexual aspects of the ballet—undermining a lesbian love interpretation (which, in this age of queer theory, is admittedly an attractive interpretation to a contemporary dance historian of any sexual persuasion). So, it seems that the female-female duet is not about the *presence* of sexuality, but its *absence*. It is not about lesbian sexuality; it is about chastity.

Circus historian Janet Davis has pointed out that in earlier periods of American history, the circus was considered a site of salacious, if not downright obscene and illegal, behavior. Not only was it subject to all the anti-theatrical prejudices leveled at dramatic theater, but it also displayed and celebrated the human body in a state of undress that at the time was considered equivalent to nudity.[30] Besides, as one religious newspaper's editorial fulminated, the circus "encourages idleness, intemperate drinking, profanity, a taste for low company [and] boisterous vulgarity."[31] The circus, with its itinerant and ethnically mixed lower-class workforce, was closely linked to gambling, swindling, and prostitution. Even more than actresses on the legitimate stage, circus women's scanty attire, physical exertion, and itinerant lifestyle made them susceptible to lewd reputations, if not directly to charges of prostitution and of degrading the entire female sex. Some circuses, subject to being outlawed for their flagrant displays of human physicality, even advertised that no women appeared in their shows.

But during the early twentieth century, circus owners, attempting to attract new middle-class audiences, and responding to the increasing entry of women into public life as well as to a booming female physical culture movement, began to ballyhoo the "family values" their spectacles purveyed. Their marketing rhetoric emphasized their performers' discipline, industry, and respectability, and both circus advertising and the patter within the show itself underscored (or created the fictional impression of) the domesticizing presence of circus families throughout the spectacle (and hence, backstage as well). Circus publicity stressed (or constructed) the female performer's virtue and domesticity: usually, she was said to be white, upper class, modest, either married or engaged, and often, for an extra lamina of respectability, if not labeled a farm girl, she was called a member of an old European circus family (since European circuses were not itinerant working-class entertainments, but a form of theater that upper-class patrons, including royalty, regularly attended). Newspapers and biographies reported on the conduct rules written into their female employees' contracts to protect their virtue — the single women could not date; traveled with a matron in the "Virgins' Car" of the circus train; had to dress modestly; and even had to bathe, though in the ladies' dressing room, under a robe. The highly publicized "weddings" of circus animals further contributed to this campaign to tout the moral character of the family-oriented American circus. The ballet girls in the circus were meant to be seen as separate from the lascivious cooch dancers in the sideshow, even if they were part of the same corporation.[32]

None of this had changed by 1942. Connie Clausen, who joined the Ringling Brothers and Barnum and Bailey Circus during the 1942 season and danced in *The Ballet of the Elephants*, tells of exactly these same practices and restrictions—and she even, albeit perhaps unconsciously, narrates her own circus adventure according to the rules.[33]

Within the framework of the American circus' self-representation as wholesome family entertainment, *The Ballet of the Elephants* both referred to and contributed to the circus' positioning of its ballet girls as innocent and virtuous, protected by mother figures or female guardians (thus allaying any fears about women's chastity during wartime). Yet at the same time—and somewhat paradoxically—figuring the elephants as ballerinas attributed power, strength, and self-sufficiency to the female dancer—a vision Balanchine returned to in later ballets where women partnered with women, such as *Symphonie Concertante* and *Agon*. I'm not claiming here that Balanchine was part of a Ringling Brothers publicity machine manufacturing images of female propriety for American circus audiences. However, it seems his own interests and choreographic predilections partly fed into that view of innocent American girlhood.

And yet, the story, as I've suggested, is not that simple. The female image in the ballet is complex and multifaceted. In choosing to create both an all-female ensemble and a set of female-female duets in *The Ballet of the Elephants*, Balanchine was probably most interested in the play of formal contrasts he could generate. (For reasons of formal visual design, he had earlier stated that he was interested in building a racially integrated company of black and white dancers—a radical political proposal in the 1930s, but one he posed purely as a design project.) Using only female dancers—the same but different: large and small, or rather, gigantic and miniature, strong and delicate, animal and human—created a striking play of contrasts that was foregrounded by the lack of gender differentiation. And the play of formal contrasts—whether or not Balanchine intended this—also created a multidimensional view of the capacities of female bodies—and, metaphorically, of the range of women's powers—saliently set forth here as a series of extremes.

Thus, as with his mixing of high and low culture, in terms of his choreography for women dancers, for Balanchine *The Ballet of the Elephants* was not simply a bagatelle—an amusing but inconsequential commission that was a break from his "real work" on the lyric stage. Rather, it served as yet another arena for his ongoing experimentation with the rules and meanings—in this case, the gendered rules and meanings—of ballet.[34]

NOTES

1. *Ringling Bros. and Barnum & Bailey Circus Magazine* [Program] (1942): 62.

2. Zorina describes the making of the ballet and her performance in Vera Zorina, *Zorina* (New York: Farrar, Straus, Giroux, 1986), 258–61. On the making of the ballet, see also Connie Clausen, *I Love You, Honey, But the Season's Over* (New York: Holt, Rinehart, and Winston, 1961). Clausen was one of the "North Starlets" who appeared in the ballet. I have also relied on information given to me in an interview with another North Starlet, Mary Lee (a.k.a. Jerul Dean), March 4, 2001, New York City.

3. "Pulses Quicken Everywhere as the Circus Rolls Again," *Toronto Daily Star*, April 4, 1942.

4. "The Big Top of the Future," *Ringling Bros. Magazine*, 26.

5. See David Lewis Hammarstrom, *Big Top Boss: John Ringling North and the Circus* (Urbana: University of Illinois Press, 1992) for biographical information about North, a detailed account of the making of each year's circus edition, and critical responses to performances. On the 1942 circus, see Joseph T. Bradbury, "Ringling Bros. and Barnum & Bailey Circus: The First John Ringling North Era, 1938–1942: Part V–1942 Season," *The White Tops* (July–August 1978): 31–53. For information on North and on the 1942 edition (and earlier editions) of the Ringling Bros. and Barnum & Bailey Circus, I have also relied on the clippings files and scrapbooks at the Robert L. Parkinson Library and Research Center, Circus World Museum, Baraboo, Wisconsin.

6. See Don McCloud, "John Ringling North Engaged Collegemate to Modernize Program," *New York Enquirer*, April 20, 1942.

7. Although, oddly enough, in his autobiography Anderson takes credit for the creation of the ballet and doesn't even mention Balanchine's name in his discussion of it, all the other evidence—the program, the circus publicity, photographs, and the other participants' memories (including Balanchine, Stravinsky, and Zorina, as well as the ballet girls)—proves otherwise. In *Out Without My Rubbers* (as told to and written by Hugh Abercrombie Anderson; New York: Library Publishers, 1954) Anderson writes that he engaged Stravinsky to write

the music for the ballet (212), while Balanchine's biographer reports that Balanchine called Stravinsky to ask for the music (see Bernard Taper, *Balanchine: A Biography* [New York: Times Books, 1984], 177–78). And later Anderson recalls that "such choreography as I put into the Circus was in turn directed by Lauretta Jefferson, Esther Junger, and Richard Barstow" (220). Anderson also omits Balanchine's name from his discussion of the *Ziegfeld Follies of 1936*, which the two worked on together; the dancers in it included Josephine Baker, the Nicholas Brothers, and Harriet Hoctor, and Fanny Brice and Bob Hope were featured comedians (see *Choreography by George Balanchine: A Catalogue of Works* [New York: Viking, 1984], 127–28).

8. Balanchine had already created several works to music by Stravinsky in Leningrad, but first collaborated with the composer in 1925 on *Le Chant du rossignol*, for Serge Diaghilev's Ballets Russes. There followed many other collaborations, including, by 1942, *Apollon Musagète* (1928), *The Card Party* (1937), and *Balustrade* (1941).

9. Taper, 177–78.

10. Gene Plowden, *Merle Evans: Maestro of the Circus* (Miami, Fla.: E. A. Seemann, 1971), 136–37.

11. Taper, 178.

12. Zorina, 259.

13. See Jennifer Donaghy, "An Exploration of Performative Roles for Animals in American Popular Culture" (Ph.D. diss., New York University, 1996) 175.

14. Brooks Atkinson, "Going to the Circus," *New York Times*, April 19, 1942, sec. 8, 1.

15. "Circus Opens Amid New Brilliance," *New York Times*, April 10, 1942, 14.

16. Hammarstrom, 87.

17. See Donald F. Lach, "Asian Elephants in Renaissance Europe," *Journal of Asian History* 1 (1967): 133–76.

18. *Zoological Recreations* (1849), qtd. in "The Elephant as Actor, Ballet and Rope Dancer," Dance Index, *Clowns, Elephants and Ballerinas* (New York: Dance Index-Ballet Caravan, Inc., 1946), 146.

19. See Barbara Barker, *Ballet or Ballyhoo: The American Careers of Maria Bonfanti, Rita Sangalli, and Giuseppina Morlacchi* (New York: Dance Horizons, 1984), for an account of ballet in the United States in the nineteenth century.

20. Atkinson, in "Going to the Circus," wrote: "George Balanchine and Igor Stravinsky have collaborated on the 'choreographic tour de force' of an elephant ballet by hanging some silly skirts on the noble beasts and writing some new dissonances for the brass band. But don't worry; it is still an act of performing elephants, and the skirts and the girls do not ruin it much."

21. "The Dance of the Hours" section is set to music from the opera *La Gioconda* by Amilcare Ponchielli.

22. Alastair Macaulay has noted this similarity ("Disney's Dances," *Dancing Times* 80, no. 951 [December 1989]: 264). Although the scene was a parody of the *Water Nymph Ballet*, Zorina herself did not serve as a live model for Hyacinth Hippo. The model for the animation was Hattie Noel, an actress; Irina Baronova, who danced with the Ballet Russe de Monte Carlo and had been one of Balanchine's "baby ballerinas" for that company in the early 1930s, was the animation model for the ostrich ballerina, Mlle. Upanova (John Culhane, *Walt Disney's* Fantasia [New York: Harry N. Abrams, 1983], 170).

23. See Hammarstrom, 94.

24. See Culhane, 167; and Robin Allan, *Walt Disney and Europe: European Influences on the Animated Feature Films of Walt Disney* (Bloomington: Indiana University Press, 1999), 155–58.

25. Although *Fantasia* became very popular in later years, at first it was not a successful release. Indeed, in 1942 *Variety* reported that the film "was admittedly the problem child of the RKO exploitation and distribution departments," because it had been marketed to children who did not at all appreciate it and often demanded a refund. Once an adult audience was targeted, the film's box office ratings improved ("Fantasia Bally Eyes Adult B.O., Foregoes Try for Youngsters," *Variety*, April 22, 1942, 15).

26. Moreover, when, during one of the breaks between sections, the musicians take time out to improvise a little jazz, *Fantasia* seems to say that high-art European symphonic music and American vernacular music are close relations and can comfortably coexist.

27. Balanchine wrote, "Nowadays at concerts of the greatest philharmonic orchestras in the world, the receptivity of the audience is so low that they have to be provided with little stories explaining the action. I have seen row upon row of listeners at a concert following the 'plot' in their programs while a symphony is being played—a note on the bassoon, the entrance of the villain; drums, a thunderstorm is coming" (George Balanchine, "Notes on Choreography," *Dance Index* IV [March–April 1945]: 20).

28. Robert Greskovic, *Ballet 101: A Complete Guide to Learning and Loving the Ballet* (New York: Hyperion, 1998), 195. See Greskovic's analyses of the pas de deux in the major ballets he discusses in that book, and also my analyses of the Grand Pas de Deux in *The Sleeping Beauty* and the Pas de Deux in *Agon*, in *Dancing Women: Female Bodies on Stage* (London: Routledge, 1998).

29. See Culhane, 162–79. The animators state clearly that they *were* satirizing ballet and ballerinas.

30. Janet M. Davis, "'Instruct the Minds of All Classes': The Circus and American Culture at the Turn of the Century" (Ph.D. diss., University of Wisconsin–Madison, 1998), 105–7.

31. Thomas Skillman, quoted in Davis, 106.

32. See Davis, 107–39.

33. Clausen, *I Love You, Honey, But the Season's Over.*

34. Thanks to Claude Conyers, Nancy Reynolds, Mary Lee, Martha Swope, Robert Greskovic, Lynn Garafola, Joan Acocella, Erin Foley, Circus World Museum, Michael Peterson, Alan Read, Shannon Steen, Stacy Wolf, Karen Dearborn, and Noël Carroll.

Contributors

JOAN ACOCELLA is a staff writer for the *New Yorker*, where she writes about dance and books. She is the author of the critical biography *Mark Morris* and the editor of the recent, unexpurgated *Diary of Vaslav Nijinsky*. With Lynn Garafola, she edited *André Levinson on Dance*. She has also written books on literature and psychology. She was a Guggenheim fellow in 1993–94 and is a fellow of the New York Institute for the Humanities.

SALLY BANES is past president of the Society of Dance History Scholars and the Dance Critics Association. Her books include *Terpsichore in Sneakers*, *Democracy's Body*, *Greenwich Village 1963*, *Subversive Expectations*, *Dancing Women*, and *Reinventing Dance in the 1960s*. Banes is also a former editor of *Dance Research Journal* and the producer/director of the video documentary *The Last Conversation: Eisenstein's* Carmen *Ballet*.

LYNN GARAFOLA is a dance critic and historian. She is the editor of *Rethinking the Sylph: New Perspectives on the Romantic Ballet* and the author of *Diaghilev's Ballets Russes*. She lives in New York City.

ANDREA HARRIS is assistant professor of dance at Texas Christian University. She holds a Ph.D. from the University of Wisconsin–Madison, under the mentorship of Sally Banes. Her performance credits include the Martha Graham Dance Company and Li Chiao-Ping Dance. She was also the assistant editor for Banes's 2003 book, *Reinventing Dance in the 1960s*.

Index

Before, Between, and Beyond